From Anarchism to Reformism

From Anarchism to Reformism

A study of the political activities of
Paul Brousse within the First International
and the French socialist movement 1870-90

DAVID STAFFORD

The London School of Economics and Political Science

Weidenfeld and Nicolson
5 Winsley Street London W1

SBN 297 00238 4

Printed in Great Britain by
Cox & Wyman, Ltd, London, Fakenham and Reading

To my family

Contents

Foreword

The history of the French socialist movement is rich and varied, and French social thought has contributed much to our ideas about reform and revolution, and about the nature of the just society. Moreover, in France, Marxism never became the dominant orthodoxy in the working-class movement as it did for so long in Germany, while the vitality of French parliamentary life provided a constant challenge to French socialists, and obliged them to think about the possibility of attaining their goals by constitutional and political action rather than by a direct revolutionary assault on the established order.

In the development of these ideas and in the process by which a unified socialist party emerged in France, the career of Paul Brousse is of considerable importance, and it is strange that no systematic study of Brousse has been attempted, even in France, before Dr David Stafford's interesting work. Brousse was an anarchist in his early years, an adherent of Bakunin and of the doctrine of direct action and of 'propaganda by the deed'. He ended up as President of the Paris Municipal Council and as an advocate of municipal reform whose ideas came close to the 'gas and water socialism' of the English Fabians. Dr Stafford's close analysis of the stages of Brousse's career shows that this development was not as inconsistent as might at first sight appear. Even if Brousse abandoned anarchist ideas of direct action, he retained many of his anarchist presuppositions and developed that aspect of the anarchist tradition which derives from Proudhon and which stresses the importance of local social groupings and of local communal organization. Brousse's 'possibilism' illustrates one direction in which anarchism could develop if anarchists were prepared to abandon the intransigent and utopian aspects which are characteristic of much anarchist thought.

Paul Brousse was an international figure, active in the anarchist and socialist movements in Switzerland and Spain, as well as in

France. Dr Stafford's researches have thrown new light, not only on
Brousse's own career and contacts, but also on the history of the
international socialist movement in the obscure years between the
end of the First International and the founding of the Second. Brousse
not only reflected the changing climate of ideas among socialists and
anarchists in the seventies and eighties; he also played an important,
and hitherto largely unknown, role in establishing the international
links which led to the Paris congresses of 1889 and thus to the founding of the Second International.

Many of the accepted views about the international socialist and
anarchist movements in this period have been coloured by the
Marxist emphasis of much of the source material and historical writing about the First and Second Internationals. It is only recently that
a number of scholars, especially in France, have questioned some of
the current beliefs about the international socialist movement in the
late nineteenth and early twentieth century and about the history of
socialism in France, and have undertaken the detailed research
needed to explode myths and to fill in the gaps in our knowledge. Dr
Stafford has made a valuable contribution to this process of detailed
reassessment by his use of the original sources and by his new evaluation of Brousse's importance. Paul Brousse has been unjustifiably
neglected; and this book will give English readers (and, indeed, it is
to be hoped, French readers also) knowledge of a figure who in the
standard histories of socialism remains a shadowy one, as well as
throwing much light on the development of socialist thought in
France and on the complicated origins of the French Socialist party.

James Joll

Preface

Paul Brousse (1844–1912) played an important and hitherto relatively neglected role in the First International and in the French socialist movement during its formative years. The domination of Marxist historiography, and Brousse's own evolution from extreme anarchism to reformist socialism – which made it difficult to place him firmly in any one tradition – were largely responsible for this neglect.

Brousse's first political activities were within the Republican opposition at the end of the Second Empire, but his real political apprenticeship was within the First International. He became an opponent of Marx and the General Council and was expelled from the Montpellier section of the International in September 1872, the same month as the Hague Congress. This experience deeply influenced him and had important consequences later.

During a brief period of exile in Spain Brousse came into contact with, and partially absorbed, Bakuninist ideas. In September 1873 he fled to Switzerland and took an active part in the affairs of the Jura Federation of the International, at that time the centre of the opposition to the General Council and the nucleus of the incipient European anarchist movement. He became a leading exponent of the theory of 'propaganda by the deed' (la propagande par le fait), as a result of which he came into conflict with the more moderate leading figure of the Jura movement, James Guillaume, whose leadership he seriously challenged. On the international level Brousse's espousal of propaganda by the deed matched the violent anarchism of the Russian and Italian socialist, and helped to widen the growing division between anarchism and the mainstream of the socialist movement. Brousse's activities on these two levels have not in the past been appreciated.

After 1877 Brousse was mainly concerned with the revival of the socialist movement in France. This revival, combined with the growing isolation and ineffectiveness of the anarchists, led Brousse to change his ideas on political tactics, and when he returned to France in 1880 he had abandoned the central tenet of anarchism, abstention from use of the vote, although he continued to believe in the ideal of an anarcho-Communist society and the importance of activity at the local, municipal level.

Brousse offered an alternative to the revolutionary Marxism of Guesde and Lafargue who had succeeded in foisting a Marxist Programme on the socialist party founded at the Marseilles Congress of 1879. He effectively mobilized and articulated resentments dating from the period of the First International against the supporters of Marx, and by 1882 had replaced the Marxist Programme with a reformist one and displaced Guesde and Lafargue in the leadership of the party.

The Fédération des Travailleurs Socialistes de France (otherwise known as the Possibilist Party) remained the strongest of the socialist parties in France in the 1880s. The alliance between Brousse, the theorist of possibilism, on the one hand, and the traditional leadership of the Parisian working class on the other, did not however survive the crisis presented by the joint challenge of Boulangism and of electoral success in Paris, the main stronghold of the Party. Brousse was an ardent exponent of the need to defend the Republic against Boulanger and of the need to exercise political power, positions many of whose implications the majority of the Party did not accept, and which consequently led to its disintegration after the Chatellerault Congress in 1890.

Before the Fédération disappeared however it had played an important role in the revival of the international socialist movement leading to the foundation of what later became known as the Second International in Paris in 1889. Brousse was instrumental in mobilizing support for this movement throughout the 1880s, and it was only at the last moment that he failed to prevent the Marxists establishing their predominant influence within the new organization, after a struggle which recalled – and was seen by its participants to recall – the conflicts which had split the First International twenty years before. The Party's domestic programme of reformist socialism was of importance too, as it anticipated and prepared the way for the later adoption of reformism by large sections of the socialist movement in France.

The position of the French Possibilist Party, both within the wider French socialist movement and at the international level, and

Brousse's role within it, have been neglected in the past, and it is the concern of this book to repair the omission. It does not however seek to be a comprehensive biography of Brousse, and the reader will find that often the focus shifts from Brousse himself to the movements with which he was involved. This is mainly because I have been primarily concerned with Brousse's political activities and not with details of his personal life, which are the quite legitimate concerns of a biographical study but not of one of this kind. It is doubtful whether at present sufficient material could be found for such a biographical study. Indeed the scattered and scarce nature of the source material has been one contributory reason for the relative neglect of Brousse in previous studies, and is of course a general problem with studies of this kind. Many valuable documents of the history of the European socialist movement in the nineteenth century were destroyed by their authors or recipients through fear of police action; those which remained were often scattered by political exile or, provided they were not destroyed in ignorance, dispersed by predatory archivists. It took the lifetime of a Nettlau to bring many of them together again.

In Brousse's case virtually no letters addressed to him during the period under examination survived. They were either destroyed or mislaid during his frequent involuntary changes of address. Unfortunately many of those which survived were apparently destroyed later by his family, and there is little of political significance in its possession. The letters which Brousse himself wrote are widely scattered. Some were retrieved by Nettlau and are to be found in the Nettlau Archives in Amsterdam; others found their way into James Guillaume's collection and are in the State Archives in Neuchâtel. In Neuchâtel also, but in a private collection, are several highly significant letters he wrote during the critical period of his evolution from anarchism to reformist socialism. Other letters are to be found in archives in Paris and in Italy.

Material about Brousse and the movements with which he was connected is to be found in police archives in Montpellier, Paris, Berne and Brussels. In addition to this is the often more valuable *militant* literature of pamphlets and newspapers in which the marrow of the movement was exposed. But this literature is equally scattered, and as long as the spirit of the times worked against any re-evaluation of Brousse, the difficulty of access to the relevant material was in itself an important obstacle to a reasonable and adequate interpretation of his contribution to the European and French socialist movements.

In my own attempts to bring this scattered material together and to present what will, I hope, be a useful contribution to the history of the European socialist movement, I have received help and encouragement for which I should like to express my gratitude. The research was financed by grants from the Department of Education and Science and the Central Research Fund of the University of London, and I am grateful for this help. In particular I should like to acknowledge the help I have received from many people: the staffs of the International Institute of Social History in Amsterdam and of other archive collections I consulted in Paris, Montpellier and Neuchâtel; Professor Carl Landauer, with whom I had a fruitful correspondence and discussion; M. Marc Vuilleumier of the University of Geneva, who put me in contact with M. Blaise Jeanneret, who holds many of Brousse's most interesting letters and to whom I am also grateful; M. J.-M. Guesde, the grandson of Jules Guesde, who allowed me generous facilities to consult material at his disposal; Mrs P. H. J. Scott-James, the granddaughter of Paul Brousse, who provided me with useful information about Brousse's personal life and character; Rodney Barker, whose criticism and advice on the final drafts were invaluable; Antonia Luccioni, who inspired me to undertake the study in the first place; Mr William Pickles, who supervised and encouraged my work throughout and without whom I would have fallen by the wayside long before its completion; Professor James Joll, who kindly advised me on certain aspects of the study; Mrs Marion Horn, who assisted me in proof reading and many others who at one time or another gave me assistance. The mistakes are all my own.

London, January 1970   David Stafford

Note: Full bibliographical details of books referred to in footnotes and an explanation of abbreviations are provided in the bibliography.

Introduction

Paul Brousse is one of the few among the founding members of the
French socialist movement about whom there exists little information, no biographical study and no adequate evaluation; one has
to search through the meagre information of biographical diction-
aries or in the footnotes of socialist historiography.[1] There are many
reasons for this neglect – some of which have been mentioned in the
Preface – not the least of which however was the nature of the commitment of the European socialist movement – and hence of its
historiography – in the last quarter of the nineteenth and the first
half of the twentieth centuries.

With the establishment of the Second International in 1889
Marxism became the dominant *credo* of the European socialist movement, in terms of which even dissenting groups tended to formulate
their views.[2] This remained very largely true until after 1945. The
historiography of the movement – the outlines of which were laid
down during the period of the Second International – reflected the
preoccupation with a particular (i.e. Marxist) theory of historical
development, a revolutionary terminology and commitment to centralized political action by the working class. Consciously or un-
consciously historians of the movement tended to be guided by these
preoccupations. Moreover as many of them were *militants* their
history made little attempt to be objective. In addition the nature of
Marxism as a teleological doctrine meant that other doctrines, antecedent or contemporary, were easily consigned to the
dustbin of history when viewed in the light of the inevitable victory of the proletariat. Ideas, men and movements tended to be considered only in their relationship to this end. The 'failures', the
'misfits' and the 'heretics' were discarded from the socialist lineage;
and in this context the reformists, the anarchists and the revolutionary syndicalists were the outcasts. If reformism and revolutionary syndicalism were at least rivals which could be argued with,

anarchism, on the other hand, tended to become a simple term of abuse.[3]

Since the collapse of the German Social Democratic Party in the 1930s and the changed total European situation after 1945, the evolution of socialist thought, combined with radically changed material conditions, has provided a new perspective from which the history of the socialist movement can be examined. The inevitable victory in Revolution of the proletariat becomes less and less of a reality – if it ever was one – as the economic predictions on which it is founded are not realized and as the structure of society changes. New formulae and tactics for socialism are implied. The major post-war change has perhaps been the growing commitment of the socialist movement to the democratic control of structural change – planning – which presents a very different face from the orthodox socialism of the previous decades, and it brings into highlight hitherto discredited features of its past. Thus, for one historian of the French socialist movement, totally new judgements are called for:

... si nos prédécesseurs ont souvent jugé le mouvement socialiste qu'ils avaient sous les yeux en fonction de l'évolution qu'ils escomptaient, nous réclamons le droit de l'analyser aujourd'hui en fonction de l'épreuve que l'événement ultérieur a imposée aux formules proposés et en fonction des problèmes actuellement posés.[4]

Thus new preoccupations in the present compel new preoccupations with the past; and in this case lead to a more sympathetic considera-tion of the French 'reformist' (for want of a better word) socialists. For if there is a direct line of descent through Blanqui–Marx–Guesde and the PCF (Parti Communiste Français), there is another through Proudhon–Marx–Brousse/Malon–Jaurès and Blum. The two have often coexisted in an uneasy synthesis, and each drew from Marx in some way or another. In so far as the second tradition is concerned, Proudhon, Jaurès and Blum have been well studied, while Brousse and Malon who imprinted their peculiar stamp on the nascent socialist movement have on the contrary been undeservedly neg-lected.[5]

The same phenomena have likewise contributed to a revival of interest in anarchism and anarchist movements. On the one hand, Soviet Communism and Western Social Democracy have between them, in their different ways, denied and opposed the revolutionary voluntarism which provided an important element in the origins of the organized socialist movement. It is alleged that both have become conservative and bureaucratized, and the new Left now looks back, in search of its socialist pedigree, not to Lenin or even to Trotsky but to the critique of Rosa Luxembourg, the opposition of the Kronstadt workers to the Bolsheviks and the anarchist movement of the Makhnovites. It was the black flag of the anarchists, not the red flag, which symbolized the days of May 1968 in Paris, and the chief spokesman of the 22 March movement, Daniel Cohn-Bendit, identified himself as an anarchist – albeit as a 'Marxist-anarchist'. The new Left throughout Europe extols the self-government and self-emancipation of the workers as against the innate authoritarianism of Leninism with its concept of the party as the sole bearer of socialist consciousness. Leninist ideology is seen as being in direct contradiction to the declaration of Marx's Inaugural Address of the First International that 'the emancipation of the workers must be brought about by the workers themselves'. This critique of Leninist socialism and the emphasis on the self-government of the workers is very closely related to, and derives a great deal from, the long-standing anarchist critique of the dominant socialist tradition.

On the other hand the anarchist critique of Marxist socialism, carried over into a critique of democratic socialism, where this merely confronts one bureaucracy with another within the accepted framework of the modern industrialized State, and its critique of the State itself, find sympathizers whose commitment to socialism is less certain. The anarchists are, by and large, anti-technological, anti-political and anti-economic. Unlike Marxism, anarchism challenges many of the assumptions on which twentieth-century industrial civilization is based. Its basic premises are opposed to the increasing omnipresence of the State and the Corporation, and its appeal is as much to the alienated professional man and intellectual as to the committed socialist. Hence there has been a spate of literature on anarchism and its movements in recent years.[6] One might also add that this revival of interest in anarchism has probably been aided by the fading from memory of Fascism, with which the anarchist movement shared certain corporatist features.

This background helps to explain why Brousse has been neglected, and why there is a need to re-examine his role in the history of the socialist movement. For Brousse was in turn (omitting the very first years of his political activity) both an anarchist *and* a 'reformist'. *Both* commitments made him unpalatable to the orthodox Marxist

socialists; and as a 'renegade' anarchist he incurred the hatred and
contempt of most of his former allies, leading to quite unjustifiable
slanders on his character. *Le Révolté,* for example, less than two
years after he had abandoned anarchism, talked of 'la souplesse
féline de Brousse, un fin mâtois, politicien par tempérament et conspirateur par goût, rompu à toutes les ficelles du métier et ayant
toujours trois ou quatre combinaisons de rechange en poche'.[7] In
fact it is difficult to imagine a less favourable evolution from this
point of view: son of a wealthy family, radical republican, member of
the First International and opponent of its General Council,
anarchist, 'possibilist', Paris Municipal Councillor, President of the
Municipal Council, host to the most-hated European monarch,
Alfonso XIII, in 1905, and Deputy. If anyone amongst the founders
of the French Socialist Party appeared to follow the traitor's path, it
was Paul Brousse.

There is more to it than that, however. The authoritative book on
the anti-authoritarian and anarchist traditions within the First International is that of James Guillaume, a book of immense value and
considerable documentation.[8] Even before he left the Jura in 1878
Guillaume was however on bad terms – at least politically speaking –
with Brousse, whose anarchism he considered to be extreme.
Brousse's political evolution after his return to France in 1880 was
such as further to alienate the two men. After 1905 when Brousse, as
President of the Paris Municipal Council, received the King of Spain,
Guillaume, who was then living in Paris and writing his history of the
International, severed all relations with him and refused even to
approach him for information. He wrote instead to Jean-Louis
Pindy, a former *militant* within the Jura Federation, for information
about Brousse.[9] It would be surprising if Guillaume's attitude – and
he was a notoriously dogmatic and intolerant person – was not
reflected in his treatment of Brousse's role in the anarchist movement.
Part of this study (particularly Chapter 3) is concerned with what is
considered an unbalanced view of Brousse as presented by Guillaume.
Privately Guillaume considered Brousse to have had more real influence in the Jura than Bakunin, but he minimized his importance
when writing *L'Internationale*.[10] In a high-minded endeavour to
conceal divisions within the Jura anarchist movement which had
sprung from Bakunin's involvement, this minimization of Brousse's
role was not solely explicable in personal terms. Guillaume was also
reluctant to reveal the nature and extent of Bakunin's conspiratorial

activities within the International. Yet Guillaume had differed on important points with Bakunin over theoretical and practical issues, and in later years, when he was involved in the French syndicalist movement, he was inclined to lay undue stress on those elements which had anticipated it. 'Qu'est-ce que la Confédération générale du Travail, sinon la continuation de l'Internationale?' he asked in the Introduction to his final volume. This approach in itself was not helpful to a balanced appreciation of Brousse's contribution, for Brousse revealed a consistent coolness towards syndicalist action throughout his career; and at the time Guillaume was writing his history of the International he was actively working in the SFIO (Section Française de l'Internationale Ouvrière) against revolutionary syndicalist tendencies within the socialist movement.[11]

Guillaume's syndicalist bias was not shared by Nettlau, who interpreted the anarchist movement in very different terms. This caused considerable friction between the two men when Nettlau began his biography of Bakunin.[12] Fortunately this friction did not last too long, and with Guillaume's (grudging) assistance Nettlau began his long history of the anarchist movement[13] in which the imbalance in the interpretation of Brousse's role created by Guillaume was offset. Even then however it was beyond Nettlau's purpose to discuss Brousse's activities with the French socialist movement, and his anarchist activities were never satisfactorily related to his activities as a reformist socialist.

Because he was a reformist socialist Brousse was neglected as a result of the deadweight of Marxist historiography. The Amsterdam Congress of the Second International in 1904 imposed unity on the French socialist movement and entrenched doctrinaire Marxism as its official ideology. Although in practice this was to be moderated by the leadership first of Jaurès and then of Blum, the result was an enhancement of Guesde's position as the defender of Marxist orthodoxy in France, which thereby lent strength to and encouraged the credibility and acceptability of those histories of the French socialist movement which laid stress on its Marxist origins. Most of the books which laid the foundation for the historiography of the movement were written at about this time, and they invariably stressed the role played by Guesde and his followers in the origins of the Party at the expense of the 'non-orthodox' groups.[14] The retrospective application of facts and judgements true for the movement in the 1890s or 1900s to the years of the origin of the Party had a lasting effect on this historiography.

It may well have been true that Guesde's Parti Ouvrier Français (POF) was 'l'épine dorsale' of the French socialist movement in the 1890s, as Kautsky claimed.[15] But this was when Guesde and his party had embraced *reformist* socialism, at least in practice if not in theory.[16] The mixture of Marxist ideology and reformist tactics proved highly successful: 'Independent Socialists and Broussists had always sought change through legal mechanisms; not until Marxists pursued reformism after 1890 did this tactic become a significant factor in socialist history.'[17] But even *before* 1890 reformist socialism had enjoyed far greater success than orthodox Marxist socialism represented by the POF. The latter was an extremely tender plant during the foundation years of the Party. The Marxist Minimum Programme adopted by the Party in 1880 was decisively rejected only two years later, and Guesde and Lafargue expelled. Of far greater significance than Marxism at that time were traditional strands of French socialism and the inheritance of the First International. The Party Programme as adopted at the St Etienne Congress in 1882 was in many important respects a reversion to the underlying beliefs of the First International. This was very largely the work of Paul Brousse and those associated with him.

Brousse's role in the anarchist movement has never satisfactorily been related to his role in the French socialist movement. It is hoped that this study will also show the logical line of development linking these two periods. The emphasis in anarchist doctrine on the need for action outside the framework of the State and within the framework of the local Commune provided the essential groundwork for Brousse's later reformist and municipal socialism.

However, the two periods interlock in another way. The political apprenticeship of all the founders of the French socialist movement was in the First International. This was true for Guesde, Lafargue and Malon as well as for Brousse. If the International as an organization died in 1876 or 1877, the issues fought out within it were to be fought out repeatedly within the national socialist parties created in the 1880s, and within the international movement such as it existed before 1889. The conflicts which marked the origins of the French Socialist Party are incomprehensible if not related to the history of the previous ten years and the bitter conflicts within the International. Paul Brousse's career in fact can largely be seen as a continuing statement of arguments first set out in the context of the struggle against the attempt of the General Council of the First International (IWMA) to impose a unity of theory and practice on the European working-class movement.

The First International[18] was the outcome of talks between leaders of the English and French working-class movement. It was founded for limited specific and practical purposes concerned with the day-to-day struggle for better living conditions. Composed initially of five national groupings, each with its peculiar view of the means and ends of working-class action, the Association and its organizational embodiment, the General Council sitting in London, was intended to act as a centre of communication and co-operation between them. Beyond a certain point their interests were, or were liable to become, divergent and irreconcilable. No common ideological standpoint bound them in any way.

Marx, who drafted the Inaugural Address and Provisional Rules of the Association, was well aware of the difficulties inherent in this situation. While his Address contained socialist conclusions, it laid heaviest stress on the condition of the working class and on those points on which common agreement could be established; and in the preamble to the Rules he asserted what, of all his pronouncements, was to permeate most widely and deeply into the consciousness of the European working-class movement – 'the emancipation of the working classes must be conquered by the working classes themselves'. At its inception the International was a *working-class,* not a *socialist* organization.[19] The General Council also recognized this in its report to the Brussels Congress of 1868:

Il n'y a que l'entente internationale des classes ouvrières qui puisse garantir leur triomphe définitif. Ce besoin a donné naissance à l'Association Internationale des Travailleurs. Elle n'est fille ni d'une secte, ni d'une théorie. Elle est le produit spontané du mouvement prolétaire, engendré lui-même par les tendances naturelles et irrepressibles de la société moderne.[20]

The impetus for the affiliation of the English trades unions had been the political issues of Italian and Polish independence and the American Civil War. It was made possible by the labour revival of the early 1860s, which in turn had resulted from the reaction of the skilled craftsmen to the economic crisis of 1857–9.[21] By about 1867 this impetus had weakened and the English trades unions began to play a lesser role. But by this time economic conditions on the Continent led to a wave of strikes in 1868 which considerably increased membership of the Association and led to the birth of a 'conscience syndicale' amongst the European working class.[22]

The result was an increasing militancy in the policies and ideology of the Association, reflected in the Congresses of 1868 (Brussels) and 1869 (Basle). Up to that point it had largely been accepted that improvements in the working-class condition could and should be sought for within the framework of capitalist society. The International was not revolutionary. But within the context of an increasingly militant struggle, in which the working class often found itself faced with an alliance of both the capitalist class and Governments (troops were frequently brought in to break strikes), the assumption gained ground that capitalism could no longer be expected to carry out the improvements demanded in working-class conditions.[23] A revolutionary and socialist solution found increasing support.

The Lausanne Congress of 1867 had called for the collective ownership of the banks and means of transport. The Brussels Congress (1868) passed a resolution calling for the collectivization of land as well as of mines, quarries, forests and means of communication. This decision was overwhelmingly endorsed at the Basle Congress, although there was wide disagreement over *how* such property was to be administered.[24] Two main results flowed from this commitment to socialism. First, the Association lost some of its early support, shedding those elements unable to accept the collectivization of land. These were two broad groups – the radical veterans of 1848 who had played a major role in the early years, and the intransigent Proudhonists.[25] Second, the Brussels and Basle decisions opened the way to discussion on the nature of this future society. This was from the very beginning a disputed question, and had in fact been left open after first being raised at the Lausanne Congress of 1867.

Here there had been a sharp expression of two conflicting positions on the attitude of the working class towards the State. In the debate on education, for example, whereas a large number of the delegates urged that the State should pay for and organize education, the French delegates expressed a deep hostility – based on their Proudhonist ideology – to State intervention; education was a matter for the individual and the State was an oppressive and dangerous apparatus. This anti-collectivist and anti-Statist posture also defeated an attempt by César de Paepe to introduce a motion on the collectiviza-tion of land. But this anti-collectivism was not an unconditional or absolute element in the Proudhonist faith, and the French delegates voted readily enough for the transfer of monopolies such as railways to 'social ownership'. On the other hand opposition to the State *was* virtually absolute. Hence in order to secure agreement on the transfer of monopolies the Congress agreed to postpone any decision on the *form* of ownership of transferred monopolies.

The Brussels Congress committed the International to the social ownership of land. Thus one element of 'pure' Proudhonism was defeated. But the argument over the form of ownership and control remained open and was made more acute by this decision. This issue was to be the cause of doctrinal dissensions within the International over the course of the next four years. If capitalist society was to be overthrown, the methods too still remained to be defined. The role of the working class and the relationship between economic and political emancipation became central issues for the International.

A majority of the delegates who voted for collective property at the Brussels Congress envisaged as their ultimate aim its decentralized control, under workers' co-operatives,[26] such as was advocated by César de Paepe, who had provided the initiative leading to the Brussels debate. A similar majority was apparent at the Basle Con-gress of the following year, although again no clear consensus emerged. If anything, however, it was syndicalism which dominated ideas on the subject.[27] Neither at Brussels nor at Basle was there any evidence that more than a small minority were consciously influenced by Marx's own ideas. There was far greater receptiveness for the anti-Statist theories of Bakunin.

Bakunin, who attended the Basle Congress, shared the view of Proudhon that the State was the greatest obstacle to the emancipa-tion of mankind. The State, in all societies, was the bastion of the ruling class, and in all its forms was to be condemned. A democratic State was not necessarily better than an absolutist monarchy. The society desired by Bakunin was 'a free grouping of individuals into communities, of communities into provinces, of provinces into nations, and, lastly, of nations into united states'. Unlike Proudhon, Bakunin was committed to collectivism and to revolution by violence, but this task, in theory at least, implied no tactical abandonment of the ideal. There was to be no separation of ends and means in the struggle for the destruction of the State. Centralized political action by the working class to conquer the State, as advocated by Marx, was anathema to Bakunin.

Bakunin's appearance on the scene annoyed and worried Marx, who was by now firmly entrenched on the General Council. He suspected – whether rightly or wrongly is outside the scope of this study – that Bakunin intended to challenge his own position within the International. In 1868 Bakunin had founded the International Alliance of Social Democracy, an organization which he intended to join to the Association. It formally applied for membership in December 1868, and the General Council rejected its application. Bakunin thereupon disbanded the Alliance and the General Council eventually agreed to accept membership of its Geneva section. Whether or not Bakunin ever 'really' disbanded the Alliance has proved a source of historical controversy ever since Marx and Engels, only four years later, published *L'Alliance de la Démocratie Socialiste et l'Association Internationale des Travailleurs*.

The doctrinal differences between Marx and Bakunin are not sufficient to explain the development of internal discord, leading to dissolution, which marked the International after 1869. It was a dispute over the organization of the International itself which led to this. To the extent to which these arguments derived from, re-fracted, and reflected conflicting attitudes towards the ends and means of the International's activities, the dispute was of course 'ideo-logical'. But it is not possible to draw any simple correlation between on the one hand 'anarchists' and opponents of the General Council, and on the other 'Marxists' and supporters of the Council. As will be seen the nomenclature for such labels did not even exist.

The implications for the International of the 'ends–means con-tinuum' of Proudhonism and Bakuninism were clearly set out in an article written by César de Paepe for the Brussels newspaper *L'Inter-nationale* in 1869: 'L'Internationale renferme en germe dans son sein toutes les institutions de l'avenir. Que dans chaque commune, il s'établisse une section de l'Internationale et la société nouvelle sera formée et l'ancienne s'écroulera d'un souffle.[28] That the International itself, as an organization, was the embryo of the society of the future, was a central tenet of what has loosely become known as the *anar-chiste* faction. But it was a view held equally by – and in fact it originated with – de Paepe, as by Bakunin and his disciples.[29] The Basle Congress saw many statements by representatives of the Belgian sections of the International similar to that of de Paepe's article in

L'Internationale.[30] The theory was crystallized in the succinct declaration of the Jura Federation, which had become a main centre of Bakunin's influence, in its famous Sonvilier Circular of November 1871:

La Société future ne doit être rien autre chose que l'universalisation de l'organisation que l'Internationale se sera donné. Nous devons donc avoir soin de rapprocher le plus possible cette organisation de notre idéal. Comment voudrait-on qu'une société égalitaire et libre sortit d'une organisation autoritaire? C'est impossible. L'Internationale, embryon de la future société humaine, est tenue d'être, dès maintenant, l'image fidèle de nos principes de liberté et de fédération, et de rejeter de son sein tout principe tendant à l'autorité, à la dictature.[31]

The Sonvilier Circular was a protest against the decisions reached by the London Conference of the International in September 1871, and against the alleged usurpation of powers by the General Council. The London Conference was a decisive stage in the internal development of the Association as it marked Marx's attempt to commit the International to his own political doctrine. This implied a changed role for the General Council. In 1864 Marx had accepted a mediatory role for the Council. With a variety of autonomous working-class organizations, each with its own ideas and organization, it was inconceivable that the General Council should have any directive role. But by 1871 circumstances had led Marx to change his mind about this. One important reason was the severe blow caused to the organization by the Paris Commune and the repression which followed. This gave the International a 'siege mentality' which led Marx to demand some tightening of the ranks. At a speech following the Hague Congress he was reported as having said that at a time when the Governments of Europe were planning a campaign of repression against the Association, 'il était sage et nécessaire d'augmenter les pouvoirs de son Conseil général et de centraliser, pour la lutte qui va s'engager, une action que l'isolement rendrait impuissante'.[32] It also led him to redefine the task of the International, which was now, he said, 'to organize and continue the forces of labour for the coming struggle'.[33] In addition there was the threat to Marx's own position from Bakunin, which led the former increasingly to use the Council as the instrument of his own direct control. [34] The result was the Conference of London which, under the firm control of Marx, committed the International to the doctrine of the need for the working class to capture political power. Resolution 9 of the Conference stated that 'dans l'état militant de la classe ouvrière son mouvement économique et son action politique sont indissolublement unis.'[35]

The increased assumption of power by the General Council at the Conference of London, and the commitment to a specific doctrine, was part of a miscalculation by Marx which cost the General Council the support of the majority of the national federations, many of which did not share the theoretical position of the Bakuninists. The opposition to the General Council sprang from other than ideological causes, although the hard core of resistance undoubtedly came from the sections and federations most influenced by Bakunin. These, at any rate, were the target of the General Council's pamphlet, *Les Prétendues Scissions de l'Internationale,* which appeared immediately prior to the Hague Congress of the Association in September 1872 and stated the General Council's case against Bakunin and Guillaume.[36]

The Hague Congress was, in Marx's eyes, decisive for the future of the International. He told Kugelmann that it was 'a matter of life or death for the International; and before I retire I want at least to protect it from disintegrating elements'.[37] As if to prove it, he appeared for the first time at one of the Association's Congresses. His aim was to increase the powers of the General Council and expel Bakunin and Guillaume. In these aims he was successful. The Congress voted for a motion giving the General Council the power to suspend sections and federations between Congresses, and voted narrowly for the Council itself to be moved to New York. It also voted for a resolution of the Committee of Enquiry into Bakunin's Alliance which called for both Bakunin's and Guillaume's expulsion. These decisions were reached only by narrow majorities which depended on the unrepresentative nature of the Congress. In terms of national federations, the General Council could rely for support only on the Germans and the German Swiss. Even the English Federation, for a long time a bastion of support for the Council, was no longer secure, and it disavowed the Hague Resolutions in January 1873. Within the following few months the resolutions had been repudiated by the French, Belgian, Spanish, American, English and Dutch Federations. The Jura Federation had immediately dissociated itself at the Congress of St Imier of September 1872.

The St Imier Congress was convened by the Jura Federation but it included, in addition to the Jurassians, representatives of the Italian and Spanish Federations. In its first resolution the Congress unanimously repudiated the decisions of the Hague Congress and refused to recognize the authority of the General Council. It affirmed the autonomy and independence of sections and denied the principle of majority decisions. The second resolution declared a Pact of Solidarity amongst the sections represented, and the third resolution, which has been called 'the essential statement of anarchist opposition to the Marxian tenet',[38] dealt with the nature of the proletariat's political action. It called for the destruction of political power, condemned the creation of any provisional revolutionary power, and rejected all compromise on the road to revolution. It read as follows:

Considérant:

Que vouloir imposer au prolétariat une ligne de conduite ou un programme politique uniforme, comme la voie unique qui puisse le conduire à son émancipation sociale, est une prétention aussi absurde que réactionnaire;

Que nul n'a le droit de priver les fédérations et sections autonomes du droit incontestable de déterminer elles-mêmes et suivre la ligne de conduite politique qu'elles croiront la meilleure, et que toute tentative semblable nous conduirait fatalement au plus révoltant dogmatisme;

Que les aspirations du prolétariat ne peuvent avoir d'autre objet que l'établissement d'une organisation et d'une fedération économiques absolument libres, fondées sur le travail et l'égalité de tous et absolument indépendantes de tout gouvernement politique, et que cette organisation et cette fédération ne peuvent être que le résultat de l'action spontanée du prolétariat lui-même, des corps de métier et des communes autonomes;

Considérant que toute organisation politique ne peut rien être que l'organisation de la domination au profit d'une classe et au détriment des masses, et que le prolétariat, s'il voulait s'emparer du pouvoir, deviendrait lui-même une classe dominante et exploitante;

Le Congres réuni à Saint-Imier déclare:

1º Que la destruction de tout pouvoir politique est le premier devoir du prolétariat;

2º Que toute organisation d'un pouvoir politique soi-disant provisoire et révolutionnaire pour amener cette destruction ne peut être qu'une tromperie de plus et serait aussi dangereuse pour le prolétariat que tous les gouvernements existant aujourd'hui:

3° Que, repoussant tout compromis pour arriver à l'accomplissement de la Révolution sociale, les prolétaires de tous les pays doivent établir, en dehors de toute politique bourgeoise, la solidarité de l'action révolutionnaire.[39]

The affirmation of the autonomy of national federations within the International permitted what became known as the St-Imier International to develop into an organization embracing non-anarchist dissident federations and sections, as well as the Bakuninists and other anarchists. Its *raison d'être* was not Bakuninist ideology but common opposition to the General Council. The issue was over organization and not ideology.[40] Within this anti-authoritarian International theoretical differences remained acute, as was to be seen at the 1873 Geneva Congress and at the Brussels Congress of 1874.[41] It is therefore misleading to see the history of the International simply and solely in terms of a conflict between Marxism and anarchism, and it is significant that these terms themselves did not begin to appear until after the critical phase in the history of the organization.[42]

The evolution of the vocabulary in terms of which the history of the International was often later to be described began in 1872 with the conflict between the General Council and its opponents. The process started with the publication of *Les Prétendues Scissions de l'Internationale,* written by Marx, in March 1872. This attacked Bakunin, the Alliance and the political philosophy underlying the Sonvilier Circular. Neither Bakunin nor any of his close followers, nor any of the opponents of the General Council, referred to themselves as anarchists, and it was not in fact until 1876 or later that the term was willingly adopted.[43] The *Prétendues Scissions* used the term in a pejorative sense; it referred to the Sonvilier Congress and the supposed dissolution of the old Fédération romande as *anarchiste,* and attacked the philosophy underlying the Sonvilier Circular:

L'anarchie, voilà le grand cheval de bataille de ... Bakounine, qui des systèmes socialistes n'a pris que des étiquettes. Tous les socialistes entendent par anarchie ceci ; le but du mouvement prolétaire ... l'Alliance prend la chose au rebours. Elle proclame l'anarchie dans les rangs prolétaires comme le moyen ... la police international ne demande rien de plus pour éterniser la république. ...[44]

The object of the attack was the Alliance, accused of threatening the International and the working-class movement with disorder or anarchy. The epithet *anarchiste* was used in its traditional sense[45] and indicated little more than opposition to the General Council. The converse of this was the development of the term *marxist*. Its first use was in the *Réponse de Quelques Internaux* published in the *Bulletin* of 15 June 1872 just over a month after, and in reply to, the *Prétendues Scissions*. It was also a rebuttal of charges made by Lafargue, Marx's son-in-law, in a letter the text of which accompanied the *Réponse*. This letter attacked the activities of the Alliance in Spain, which were of fundamental importance in the development of the General Council's campaign against Bakunin.[46] (Lafargue was sent to Spain by Marx to break the monolithic hold of Bakuninism, but he had only small and temporary success. The divisions within the Madrid Federation consequential on this caused bitter hatred of the General Council.)[47] The *Réponse* directed its attack firmly at Marx and his followers on the General Council, whose aim, it said, was to 'faire diriger toutes les fédérations par les hommes qui consentent à s'inféoder à Marx, et d'écraser sous la plus horrible calomnie tous ceux qui veulent garder leur indépendance et leur dignité'.

They were faced, the *Réponse* went on to say, with 'la réalité de la conspiration marxiste'. Lafargue it described as 'l'apôtre de la loi marxiste', the law being whatever Marx dictated (in this case his instructions to Lafargue *vis-à-vis* the Madrid Federation of the International), 'Marxist' was used to designate the group of men closely allied with Marx. The designation had little to do with theory *per se*. As the *Réponse* stated, many of the Jura Internationalists had read *Das Kapital*:

... ils l'ont lu, et ils ne sont pourtant pas devenus marxistes; cela doit paraître bien singulier à ce gendre naif. Combien y en a-t-il par contre, au Conseil général, qui sont marxistes sans avoir jamais ouvert le livre de Marx.[48]

This theme was enlarged on in the *Mémoire de la Fédération Jurassiene,* written by Guillaume in 1873, where there was frequent reference to 'la côterie marxiste', and 'les marxistes', in connection with the group surrounding Marx and the General Council.[49]

The evolution of this terminology throws light on the history of the International itself and provides an essential background to the development of the European socialist movement in the following decade. Neither the term 'anarchist' nor the term 'Marxist' was endowed with much theoretical content; both originated with the struggles within the International between the General Council and the national federations. This struggle, and the political vocabulary it produced, was to cast its shadow over much of the future history of the socialist movement, particularly that in France, and formed an indispensable part of the background to Brousse's activity.

Another important element in this background was the legacy left by the defeat of the Paris Commune and the effects this had on the French socialist and labour movements.

The dominating intellectual influence on the *militants* of the French labour movement in the decade preceding the Paris Commune was that of Proudhon. Although Proudhon was a contradictory and complex thinker certain of his ideas percolated through to the level of working-class leadership and exerted a strong influence on their outlook. These seminal ideas may be summarized briefly as: (a) a belief in peaceful social revolution aiming at the replacement of the State by economic functional groups, (b) the demand for the creation of free credit on a national basis which would enable small property owners to clear their debts and the workers to break free from the serfdom imposed on them by the wage system, (c) the belief that this development would lead to a society based on freedom, justice and equality, ruled by contract (what Proudhon called an-archia, or mutualist society). Towards the end of his life Proudhon reinforced the idea of the mutualist society with: (d) a theory of political feder-alism. These seminal political and economic ideas were underpinned by a substratum of moral and ethical ideas which together formed the Proudhonist syndrome: (e) belief in the patriarchal family unit and a concomitant idealization of womanhood, (f) belief in the moral worth of labour, (g) belief in education, both professional and intellectual, as the essential prerequisite of emancipation.

Proudhon's most influential work was *De la Capacité Politique de la Classe Ouvriére,* which became the handbook of the majority of the *militants* of the French labour movement and certainly of its most radical wing within the Commune: 'les délégués socialistes les plus notoires de la minorité doivent à cet ouvrage et au Principe Fédératif l'essential de leurs doctrines fédéralistes.'[50] This book was occasioned by the publication of the Manifesto of the Sixty by leaders of the Paris working class in 1864. The Manifesto, a landmark in the history of the French labour movement, called for the workers to seek direct and separate representation in the French Assembly. Proudhon hailed the Manifesto as an expression of the revival of socialism, although he simultaneously opposed participation in the elections on the grounds that within a bourgeois state the proletariat should concentrate on its own organization; a-politicism was a constant – but, it needs to be emphasized, by no means an essential – component of Proudhonist thought.

The Manifesto of the Sixty was a symptom of the development of the labour movement in the 1860s. After 1868 Chambres syndicales, or trades unions, began to be formed openly, and in 1869 several of the Paris Chambres united to form a federation which was, to all intents and purposes, identical with the International's organization in Paris.[51] Similar federations were established in provincial towns such as Marseille, Lyon and Rouen.[52] Towards the end of the Second Empire and in the climate of increasing labour and political unrest, this leadership was subject to constant Government repression which strengthened the influence of those elements within it demanding more militant policies. The numerous strikes which broke out at the end of the Second Empire crystallized the movement towards working-class organization. The anti- or non-political and peaceful emphasis was replaced by growing participation in the political struggle against the Empire of Napoleon III, so that by 1870 the leadership of the working class was both revolutionary and socialist and it had become possible to talk of a French socialist movement:[53] '. . . nous ne pouvons rien faire, comme réforme sociale, si le vieil Etat n'est pas anéanti,' said Varlin, the most outstanding leader of the working-class movement in Paris, and secretary of the Paris Federation.[54] The debates of the First International had been vital in converting many of these leaders to collectivism – a collectivism, moreover, which anticipated the revolutionary syndicalism of the 1890s; Varlin himself has been described as the direct precursor of the revolutionary syndicalists.[55]

In July 1870 the leaders of the International in France were sentenced to one year's imprisonment for membership of a 'secret society', and the capacity of the International for effective action in France was seriously damaged. In the same month too, the Franco-Prussian war broke out and by September Napoleon III had been forced to flee the country after the humiliating surrender of his army at Sedan. On 4 September the Republic was declared in Paris and a Government of National Defence formed. Despite the organization of an unexpectedly effective resistance to the Prussians by the Government the French were forced to accept armistice terms in January

1871. By this time Paris had been surrounded and besieged by the Prussian army for over three months, during which time the struggle against the Prussians had been partially transformed into a social struggle within France itself. Leadership in the extreme patriotic and republican movement passed to the Left, and several attempts at revolutionary uprisings both in Paris and the provinces were smothered by the Government. The propertied classes were generally anxious to make peace. After the armistice of January 1871 elections throughout France gave the monarchists and the Right an over-whelming victory and endorsed peace. Thiers, a conservative Repub-lican, was appointed Head of the Executive and promptly began to eliminate the danger from the Left. This meant, primarily, Paris, which had returned to the Assembly old-time Republicans such as Louis Blanc, Ledru-Rollin and Rochefort. Blanqui was sen-tenced to death for having led an uprising in Paris in October and the National Assembly, instead of sitting in Paris, was convoked at Versailles.

On 18 March 1871 Thiers ordered the army to remove the guns in the control of the Parisian National Guard. This was a signal for revolt by the population of Paris who had already been inflamed by the lifting of the moratorium on payments of rents and promissory notes imposed during the siege of the city. The legal authorities with-drew from Paris and on 26 March elections took place for a new Parisian municipal Government. This was called, in conscious evocation of the French Revolution, the Paris Commune.

The Commune was dominated by Blanquists and Jacobins. Its inspiration was patriotic, republican and working class. Its origins had little to do with the International or with socialism. It looked back to 1792, not forward to 1917. The members of the First Inter-national and the Proudhonists were in a minority,[56] and they pro-tested unsuccessfully on 28 April against the setting up, in imitation of 1792, of a Committee of Public Safety. The divisions within the Commune on this issue, between the *majoritaires* and the *minoritaires,* were to be continued in exile and were frequently seen as a parallel to the conflict within the International itself over the powers of the General Council.[57]

The Commune, during its brief life from 28 March to 28 May – when the Versailles troops massacred the last of its defenders in the cemetery of Père Lachaise at the climax of what became known as 'la semaine sanglante' – enacted social reforms which remained within the confines of the traditional radical programme. It decreed the separation of the Church and the State, confiscated the property of the religious orders, opened some secular schools, abolished night work in bakeries, the system of fines imposed on workers, and ordered the takeover of some of the workshops abandoned by their owners. None of these reforms was aimed at changing the relationship between capital and labour, and the Commune's legislation had nothing specifically socialist about it, although it is true to say that the impetus for its social and economic legislation came from the *militants* of the First International, such as Frankel of the Commission of Labour.[58]

This did not prevent the Commune from gaining the enthusiastic support of socialists all over Europe and from very quickly becoming, in their eyes, a socialist phenomenon. This process was best seen at work in Marx who, in his *Class Struggles in France,* saw the Commune as a working-class government, socialist in intent, and the model for future working-class governments:

It was essentially a working-class government, the product of the struggle of the producing against the appropriating class, the political form at last discovered under which to work out the economic emancipation of labour. . . . The Commune was therefore to serve as a lever for uprooting the economical foundations upon which rests the existence of classes, and therefore of class rule.[59]

The defence and praise of the Commune expressed in this pamphlet, which was issued as a document of the General Council of the International, played a major though not exclusive role in attributing to the Commune a socialist content. The Commune was soon to attain the status of myth in the eyes of the European socialist movement, especially within the later Marxist–Leninist tradition. Lenin described the Commune as 'the outstanding model of the great proletarian movement of the nineteenth century',[60] and he himself lies buried in his mausoleum in a Communard flag; while the cosmonauts of the Soviet spacecraft *Voshkod* took into space with them in 1964 a picture of Marx, a picture of Lenin and a ribbon from a Communard flag.

If Marx saw in the Commune the 'glorious harbinger of a new society',[61] so did the anti-authoritarians. Bakunin said that the Commune heralded revolutionary socialism and that Paris had inaugurated a new era.[62] The anti-authoritarians saw it as the

B

spontaneous expression of federalist, anti-statist and anarchist
ideas. James Guillaume said:

> La révolution est fédéraliste. . . .
> Le fédéralisme, dans le sens que lui donne la Commune de Paris, et
> que lui a donné il y a bien des années le grand socialiste Proudhon . . .
> est avant tout la négation de la Nation et de l'Etat. . . .
> Il n y a plus d'Etat, plus de pouvoir central supérieur aux groupes et
> leur imposant son autorité; il n y a que la force collective résultant de la
> fédération des groupes. . . . L'Etat centralisé et national n'existant plus,
> et les Communes jouissant de la plénitude de leur indépendance, il y a
> véritablement *an-archie*.[63]

The conclusion for the anti-authoritarians within the International
was twofold. First, the Commune carried lessons for the International
itself: ' . . . le peuple qui, dans les temps moderne a le premier formulé pratiquement le programme anarchiste du prolétariat, en
constituant la Commune libre de Paris, ne peut pas être pour l'autori-
tarisme.'[64] Second, the experience of the Commune greatly reinforced
the argument of the anti-authoritarians for the Communal structuring
of post-revolutionary society.[65] The main issue as it appeared to the
Federal Committee of the Jura Federation in 1872 was that of 'La
Commune libre' versus the 'Volkstaat', an issue of principle which,
it said, concerned both the theory and the practice of the socialist
movement.[66]

Thus the experiences of the Commune reinforced the theoretical
position of those who looked to it for lessons for the future.

The crushing of the Commune in May 1871 had several results
which it is useful to bear in mind in view of their influence on the
French working class and socialist scene in the 1870s.

So far as socialism was concerned, the failure of the Commune
discredited the Blanquist theory of the *coup de main* and led instead
to an emphasis on the need for *organization* and *propaganda*. At the
same time, and in a sense operating in an inverse direction in the
long term, it weakened that part of the Proudhonist *credo* which
placed faith in a gradual and peaceful evolution. The massacre of the
Communards and the savage punitive measures which followed (it
has been estimated that 30,000 people were killed or executed by the
Versailles forces) polarized class feelings and brutally emphasized
the antagonism of the workers and the bourgeoisie. This helped to
explain why, when the socialist movement revived in the late 1870s

after the period of repression, it looked with profound mistrust at any co-operation with the bourgeoisie. A premium was placed on the expression of extreme, revolutionary and even revengeful sentiments within the socialist ranks, and the presentation of straightforward reformist demands became to that degree more difficult.[67] The Commune ensured that a certain kind of rhetoric would become the indispensable tool of the socialist *militant*.

In the short term, the defeat of the Commune destroyed the labour movement and discredited socialist ideas (the thoroughness of the collapse of the labour movement, which had been developing along revolutionary syndicalist lines, has been seen as a contributory cause of the later separation of the syndicalist and socialist movements in France).[68] Largely because of its defence of the Commune the International became the scapegoat for it, and in March 1872 membership of the organization, or recruitment to it, became illegal in France through what became known as the Dufaure Law.

This reaction was not confined to France. In June 1871 Jules Favre, the French Foreign Minister, in a circular letter to the European Powers, denounced the International as a society founded on atheism and Communism, preaching war and hatred and a threat to civilized values. Although the joint European action which the circular called for was not forthcoming, Favre's denunciation found echoes throughout Europe where it was widely believed that the Commune had been planned and executed by the International. In July 1871 Bismarck proposed a conference of European powers to take common action against the society. The project foundered on the opposition of the British Government, but in November 1872 the German and Austro-Hungarian Governments made a joint declaration that the International was a direct threat to bourgeois society and therefore to be repressed. The declaration was followed by a more stringent interpretation of the existing laws which effectively put an end to the society's activities.[69] This reaction dominated the attitudes of European Governments over the following decade, hindering the development of an active socialist movement, which in any case in France had suffered a severe setback with the defeat of the Commune. The association between the Commune and socialism led the labour movement in France, which was seriously weakened by the death or deportation of its militant leaders, to concentrate after 1871 on moderate policies. Efforts were concentrated on forming Chambres Syndicales as a first step towards the creation of producers' co-operatives, which became the panacea of the movement. This moderation was also expressed in a rejection of strikes and, often, of all political action. There was too a widespread acceptance of the idea that nothing should be done to upset the institutions of the Republic.

It was only towards 1876 that this climate began to change and that an organized socialist movement began to emerge once again in France. Within this movement, control over which became contested between many of those who had been active within the International – such as Malon, Lafargue and Guesde as well as Brousse himself – the legacy of the Commune was, as has been suggested, a contradictory one. On the one hand, the repression of the Communards by the Versailles troops left deep and bitter memories of class conflict which were not easily forgotten and which became a central part of the ideology of the French socialist movement (the campaign for an amnesty of the Communards and the campaign for the creation of an organized socialist Party proceeded simultaneously). On the other hand, the memory and lessons of the Commune discredited the old Blanquist ideas of the *coup de main,* of the revolutionary uprising in the streets, and instead forced attention on the need for organization and discipline and the avoidance of premature action. Hence in the 1880s a party emerged which attempted to combine these two contradictory elements. In the Fédération des Travailleurs Socialistes de France revolutionary rhetoric was combined with a shrewd and realistic appraisal of the choice of strategies open to the Party. The activities of Brousse within this Party, which form the subject of the last two chapters of this study, were deeply influenced by his experience in the First International as an exile from France. It is to this that we now turn.

1

Brousse and the Midi, 1870-3

1. The end of the Second Empire, and the Paris Commune

Paul-Louis-Marie Brousse was born at Montpellier on 23 January 1844, the only son of 'une honnête famille . . . dans une position très aisée'.[1] His father, Victor-Léon Brousse, was the son of a grain merchant in Montpellier, and had married in 1842, at the age of twenty-eight, Clotilde Catherine Etienne Bonnet, seven years younger than himself, the younger daughter of Jacques-Louis Bonnet, a timber merchant, also of Montpellier. The young couple lived in the Bonnet family residence on the Boulevard du Jeu de Paume on the edge of the old city centre. It was here that Paul Brousse was born. His father had entered the University in 1833, obtaining in the year of his marriage his Diplôme de Docteur en Médecine; a year later he became an *agrégé* and in 1846 was appointed Head of the Chemistry Department in the Faculty of Medicine, a post which he retained until 1853, after which he continued to teach in the Faculty until ill-health forced him to submit his resignation in 1870. He died in 1881 at the age of 66.[2] About Clotilde Bonnet little is known. She was a devout Catholic, and one of her cousins was the liberal Archbishop of Lyons, Mgr Ginouilhac, who had at one time been Director of the Montpellier Seminary before going on to become Bishop of Grenoble. He was apparently a not infrequent visitor to the Brousse household, and in later years Brousse would joke with his anarchist friends about the days of his bourgeois childhood when the family table would be presided over by the family prelate.[3]

There was nothing in his family background to suggest the future revolutionary nature of Paul Brousse's political commitment; there was certainly no personal poverty to act as a driving force, and Montpellier itself was, as it remains, a prosperous oasis in the radical Hérault, which in turn was one of the few Departments in which real wages had increased during the years of the Second Empire.[4] Phylloxera was not to strike at this prosperity until a few years later. It would seem that Brousse's entrance into political activity was comparatively late and cautious, engendered by the political turbulence which marked the end of the Second Empire and in which, paradoxically, Montpellier, through Jules Guesde's activity on the radical Republican newspaper *Les Droits de l'Homme,* played a leading role. But this was not until 1869 when Brousse was twenty-five. Until then he followed the conventional path of the son of a respectable bourgeois family. The Medical Faculty of the University enjoyed a Europe-wide reputation, and Brousse entered it in 1865 after his father had bought him out of military service in March of that year at a cost of 2,300 francs. In 1867 a severe cholera epidemic swept the town and Brousse, then working as an intern at the St Eloi hospital, found his dedicated service during the epidemic rewarded by an Imperial decree granting him full exemption from all University fees. Later that year he left Montpellier and registered at the Law Faculty at Toulouse for two terms. However it seems that he stayed for only a short time for he took no examinations there, and it is likely that he was back in Montpellier by 1869.[5]

The Second Empire had little more than a year to live. Economic progress had slackened, there was a financial crisis and Napoleon III's confidence was being undermined by an increasingly vocal, if disunited, opposition. The press laws had been relaxed in 1868, and by 1869 Montpellier had become a provincial centre of Republican opposition with the publication of the newspaper *La Liberté,* edited by Arthur Ballue. One of its leading contributors was a little-known radical journalist from Paris, Jules Guesde. In November 1869 an attempt was made to channel widespread rural discontent in the region to the Republican cause with the foundation in Montpellier of the Caisse de l'Enseignement démocratique whose object was, according to Théodore Ferré, its founder, to 'éclairer les communes rurales sur les devoirs civiques des électeurs, afin de les amener à bien voter et à conformer leurs actes politiques à ceux de la démocratie urbaine'. Brousse was elected to its administrative committee at a meeting held on 14 November 1869 at the home of a lawyer, Brichon, adjacent to the Brousse residence on the Boulevard du Jeu de Paume, where the offices of *La Liberté* (to which he became a subscriber) were also situated. This is the first evidence of any political activity by Brousse, although on occasions later he himself dated this as having begun in 1868.[6]

Late in 1869, at about the same time as the establishment of the

Caisse, there was a schism within *La Liberté* between radical and conservative elements. Guesde and Ballue then attempted to gain support for a new and more radical paper. In February 1870 Brousse was elected, while still a medical student, to the administrative committee formed by Ballue in preparation for the paper's appearance. In May 1870 a society of which he also became a member was formed to provide capital for its publication, and the paper appeared shortly afterwards with Ballue as its chief editor and Guesde as its editorial secretary. *Les Droits de l'Homme,* as the newspaper was called, became a national focal point for radical opposition to the Empire and, following the Empire's collapse, to the conservative republicanism which made peace with Bismarck's Germany and crushed the Paris Commune. It was his activity on the journal which pushed Guesde to the extreme radicalism which culminated in his forced exile in the summer of 1871.[7]

Brousse's role on the paper was a minor one. So far as can be ascertained he published no articles for it, and his name did not appear in its columns. But there is evidence to suggest that he acted as an intermediary on its behalf in 1870 during a dispute with the conservative republicans over electoral tactics, and he was active in its administrative affairs.[8] It is possible too that in this period he spoke publicly on behalf of the radical cause. If his active role on the paper was limited, none the less the period of its publication was a critical and eventful one which could hardly have failed to influence him. The Empire collapsed in military defeat in September 1870, and this was followed by the period of political turmoil which ended with the trauma of the Commune, which *Les Droits de l'Homme* strongly defended at the cost of Government displeasure and heavy fines. On the outbreak of the Franco-Prussian War Brousse obtained permission to serve in the Army medical, rather than combatant, service. In November 1870 he was appointed as a staff-lieutenant in the National Guard (Hérault) and in February 1871, after the armistice, was appointed as a doctor to the 104th Battalion of the Garde Mobile at Rodez. He probably did not take up this post.

Most biographical sketches of Brousse mention his connection with Guesde and *Les Droits de l'Homme,* and in view of the later political enmity of the two men it is perhaps useful to establish their connection more precisely. It is unlikely that it was ever a close friendship. The two men, who were almost the same age, differed widely in background, experience and personality. In 1872, when

Guesde was in exile in Rome, he wrote one of the few letters known to have passed between the two to complain of Brousse's 'silence inexplicable et inexcusable' which only his (Guesde's) political commitment to common political ideas could allow him to ignore.[9] The evidence suggests that Guesde saw Brousse as a useful political ally in the Hérault after his own forced exile in 1871, and this usefulness coincided with a common opposition to the General Council of the International. In this same letter Guesde suggested ways in which the radical forces should be organized without provoking counter-action by the authorities; and in 1872 when Brousse was expelled from the Montpellier section of the International, Guesde came strongly to his defence. Later in the same year he proposed Brousse's membership of the Jura Federation and appears to have contributed at least one article to *La Solidarité Révolutionnaire,* the newspaper which Brousse, Alerini and Camet founded in Barcelona in 1873.[10] This political co-operation lasted only until about 1874, by which time Guesde was moving away from the anarchists, and although the two men maintained some correspondence[11] by 1876 they were, and remained, political rivals.

The events of March–April 1871 and the governmental reaction which followed helped to push many radicals leftwards to a point on the political spectrum where radicalism merged almost imperceptibly into socialism. Guesde had followed this path, and Brousse was to follow him. It was within the remnants of the radical movement following the defeat of the Commune that Brousse moved leftwards until, some time in 1872, he joined the International, an organization which was itself often regarded by its members as only one more element in the radical struggle against the conservative régime.

The period from May 1871 to March 1872 was an interim one. Although the Commune had been crushed and Thiers could exult over the dead corpse of socialism, the International Association was not yet an illegal organization in France, and radical organizations were relatively free to organize and spread propaganda. In the plebiscite of May 1870 about 40 per cent of the electorate in the Hérault had voted against Napoleon III, and in the municipal elections of April 1871 the provinces as a whole had voted almost solidly republican, with radicalism particularly strong in the South. With the threat of a Monarchist reaction in the autumn of 1871 Emile Digeon, leader of the abortive Narbonne Commune, who was acquitted at a trial held at Rodez in November 1871, toured the South establishing local radical committees and attempting to create a regional organization.[12] At a meeting held at Béziers – the seedbed of radicalism in the Hérault – on 17 December 1871, Digeon's initiative led to the establishment of a provisional committee for the creation of a radical newspaper as the first step to counter the Monarchist threat. Digeon was its President and Brousse, 'délégué de Montpellier', was nominated as its secretary.[13] A manifesto published by the committee, *Aux Républicains Radicaux du Midi de la France,* embodied radical Gambettist, rather than purely socialist demands. The attempt to found a newspaper appears to have been unsuccessful, for Digeon was back again in February 1872 with the idea of launching another paper, *La Fédération radicale.* Later in the same month, reporting on radical activities in the Department, a police official noted the strong organization of the Radicals, adding that: 'les agissements de l'Internationale trouvent dans beaucoup de ses membres des adeptes tout préparés'.

2. The International in the Hérault

There is considerable circumstantial evidence to confirm the police report quoted above, that the International established close links with the radical movement. Indeed, it would be surprising if it were otherwise. So far as Brousse was concerned his participation in Digeon's radical committee was the immediate prelude to his joining the International some time in 1872. But before going on to deal with this it is useful to look more closely at the context in which Brousse was to work, as it was to have an important influence upon his later political loyalties.

There is some sketchy evidence that the International took root in the Hérault prior to 1870. André Bastelica, the leading figure of the Marseilles section after 1868, who joined the Bakuninist Alliance in 1869, wrote to James Guillaume in April 1870 to say that he was contemplating travelling through the Hérault to establish sections of the Association, following a successful propaganda campaign in the Var, and a police report of a later date suggests that he had had some success. Noting the failure to establish a working-class organization by the radicals of Montpellier, the report continued:

Il n'a pas été de même de ceux de la ville de Cette [Sète] et même de

Béziers. Dans ces localités le sieur Bastelica a pu créer, sous le nom de comités fédératifs, de véritables sociétés secrètes d'ouvriers tonneliers, qui ont puissament contribué à entretenir une grande agitation dans le sein de la population et dont l'action se fait sentir plus particulièrement aux périodes électorales.[14]

It was above all Béziers which provided the stronghold of organized radical and socialist activity in the Hérault – as distinct from the anarchic *émeutisme* of the Sétois coopers. The spread of the 'démocratie viticole' (the vine-growing industry) had made it by 1848 a republican stronghold, and the 1851 *coup* of Napoleon III led to a widespread popular uprising in the area which was crushed with considerable brutality.[15] Many of the victims of the repression which followed (such as Emile Digeon) became prominent in the socialist movement of the 1870s and provided a link between the popular radicalism of the 1840s and the socialism of the International.

Early in April 1871 the Paris Commune delegated Jules Montels, a native of the Department, to Béziers, as one of several delegates sent by the Commune to provincial centres. Their aim was to: 'activer dans le province le mouvement communale, d'assurer la fédération de Gardes nationales, et l'établissement de la Republique démocratique et sociale,'[16] a mission in which Testut, the notorious French police spy, credited Montels with some success: 'l'agitation et la propagande socialiste avaient été nulles à Béziers . . . mais pendant le mouvement communaliste . . . un reveil considérable s'y produit – le résultat fut en partie l'œuvre de Montels.'[17]

Throughout the following decade Montels acted as an important, and the single most consistent, link between the socialists of the Hérault and those in exile. He was born at Gignac (Hérault) in 1842 or 1843, and as a young boy witnessed the 1851 insurrection against Louis Napoleon's *coup*, the repression of which left bitter memories which were to be resurrected in 1871, and which contributed in no small part to the regionalist and autonomist flavour of southern radicalism – as witnessed in a pamphlet published by Montels himself in 1881, a rehabilitation of a Biterrois martyr of the *coup*, entitled *La Justice de l'Ordre en 1851, La Vie et Mort d'André-Abel Cadelard*. Working variously as a clerk or commercial traveller he was in Paris when the Commune broke out, and it is possible too – although there is no evidence of this – that he was a member of the International at that time. Forced to flee from France by 'l'ouragan de l'année terrible', as he described it,[18] he went to Geneva where Guesde, with whom he had had close contact in the Hérault, gave him hospitality for a short time. He became a leading member of the French exile group within the International, the Section de Propagande et d'action révolutionnaire-socialiste, of which Guesde was a leading light. Unlike most of the exiles he took the function of the section – the spread of propaganda in France – seriously, maintaining correspondence with the socialists of Béziers and passing on to Guesde, who left for Rome in April 1872, details of the movement in the Midi and in Spain.[19] It was through Montels that the groups in the Hérault received copies of the reports of the International Congresses between 1873 and 1877, as well as various socialist newspapers and pamphlets.[20] He remained an active figure in the various Geneva socialist groups and in 1877 was, with Brousse, one of those who helped to found the French Federation of the International. He left for Russia in August 1877 where he obtained the post of tutor to Tolstoy's children. He returned to the Hérault in 1880 and some time later left for Tunis, where he died at Sfax in about 1913.[21] While in Switzerland he published a small pamphlet, *Lettre aux socialistes-révolutionnaires du Midi de la France,* urging abstention in the elections of 1876.

Whether or not Montels established a section of the International in Béziers is not clear. What is certain is that he laid the foundation for its establishment. With other sections in the Midi and the Hérault it provided the background to the beginning of Brousse's socialist activities, a background of particular importance when his activities became involved in the dispute between the General Council and dissident national federations.

Even prior to the Commune, the International had been considerably weakened in France by Government action. The defeat of the Commune forced into exile or eliminated many of its leading figures, and the conservative nature of the new régime seemed to have assured its extinction; 'on peut dire qu'en définitive l'Internationale était mort en France: le mouvement socialiste, brusquement intérrompu, ne devait reprendre son importance que beaucoup plus tard.'[22] A more recent observer notes that after 1871: '... l'Association n'a plus en France qu'une existence fictive, sinon précisément mythique.'[23] The statement however needs to be modified in so far as it applies to the Midi. What is noteworthy is the way in which the International continued to survive and even expand after May 1871. The London

Conference of September 1871 revealed the formation, or attempted
formation, of sections in various parts of France, often under the
stimulus of contact with refugees in Switzerland. This applied especially to the Savoy and Lyons areas. The Conference called on all
branches and federations of the Association to help in sending
socialist literature to France; authorized the Belgian, Swiss (Romande), and Spanish Federations to act as intermediaries between
local sections in France and the General Council; and called on the
Council to publish an address urging the French workers to struggle
openly against their Government.[24] It was generally agreed that action
would be most effective in the provinces as Paris was too closely
under Government surveillance.

To some extent these resolutions expressed hopes rather than
realities. But Seraillier,[25] corresponding secretary of the General
Council for France, followed them up by action aimed at building
up an organization in France on whose support the General Council
could rely in the internal conflicts within the International. On 5
November 1871 he wrote to a M. Calas, a clothworker and leading
radical at Pézénas in the Hérault: 'je vous prie de me donner le plus
d'adresses possible de citoyens socialistes auxquels je puisse me mettre
en rapport tout de suite pour continuer le propagande intérrompu par
les événements de Paris . . .' Calas was able to send Seraillier the name
of Louis Salvan, a cooper from Béziers who had been involved in,
and deported after, the 1851 uprising. Some short time after this
letter Salvan founded the Section Biterroise de l'Association Internationale des Travailleurs. At about the same time Larroque, the
leading Internationalist of Bordeaux, wrote a letter to Calas asking
for contacts in the area:

Veuillez me donner le nom d'un agent sûr à Lyon, Béziers, et dans la
plupart des villes du Midi. Le groups bordelais ne désire rien tant que
voir resserrer les liens de solidarité fraternelles qui doivent unir toutes les
sections méridionales. Un voyageur comme E.G. nous serait d'une
grande utilité dans le Midi pour donner plus de cohésion à nos
efforts. Liez-vous sitôt que vous le pourrez avec Toulouse, Montpellier,
Lyon.

Tâchons de nous organiser dans le Midi sans nous préoccuper de nos
discussions de famille. Vous m'aviez promis des lettres de Toulouse,
Lyon, Montpellier, rien n'est arrivé. . . . Veuillez donc donner mon
adresse au chacune des sections citées afin que nous puissions entrer en
correspondance. Organisons-nous en un mot dans tout le Midi. . . .[26]

Calas acted upon this letter, and within a short time regular correspondence was passing between Toulouse, Narbonne and the sections
in the Hérault. In January 1872 the organization was progressing
rapidly and Engels could write to Lafargue of the French groups
generally that: 'Seraillier is amazingly active. Naturally the results
achieved are not for publication, but they are good. The branches are
being reformed under new names, everywhere.'[27] In March 1872 the
Dufaure law made it an offence to be a member of, recruit for or
spread propaganda on behalf of the International. One of the effects
in the South was to weaken further the section at Toulouse, already
struggling with internal feuds between Blanquist and other elements.
On the recommendation of Calas, therefore, Seraillier sent to Toulouse in June 1872 a man called Dentraygues, a former railway
employee, whom Calas had introduced to the activities of the Association early in 1872. In Toulouse Dentraygues established contact with
Albert Masson, a railway guard employed by the Compagnie du
Midi, a member of the Association since 1866, the nature of whose
employment permitted him to carry correspondence between the
various southern sections of the International. Thus, despite Government action, contact between sections could be maintained.[28]

Dentraygues fulfilled his major role as the loyal delegate of the
southern sections for the General Council at the Hague Congress of
September 1872 where he voted for the 'marxists'. But on his return to
Toulouse he fell into disfavour and abandoned his activities. In
December 1872 the police caught up with him, he was arrested and
numerous letters from Seraillier, Masson, Larroque, Calas and the
Internationalists at Toulouse which were found at his home led to
the total collapse of the organization created by Seraillier. Widespread arrests followed, and a series of trials – at Béziers in February,
Toulouse in March and Montpellier in May 1873 – followed. Over
thirty leading members of the Association were imprisoned.

The collapse led to bitter recriminations between the supporters of
the General Council and the anti-authoritarians. Both Brousse and
Guesde were implicated, and it is necessary to go back to just before
the Hague Congress in order to follow the accusations and counter-
accusations.

Brousse joined the section of the International at Montpellier –
founded apparently by Calas – some time in 1872. Shortly before the
Hague Congress, when Dentraygues's nomination as delegate to the
Congress was being canvassed, Brousse urged the section to withhold

its subscription towards the cost of Dentraygues's journey to the Hague and to abstain from voting on the issue until the disputes within the International had been solved. This amounted to opposition to the General Council, and it is clear that Brousse was adopting a position similar to that of Guesde, although whether he was acting on his own initiative or that of Guesde is uncertain. Seraillier later insisted that Brousse was an agent of the Jura Federation, describing him as 'un misérable qui sur l'ordre parti de ses amis du Jura a jette [sic] le désorganisation dans cette section qui comptait alors près de 130 membres [sic]', and going on to add that Brousse's expulsion from the section was all the more justified as Brousse led 'une vie privée non sans reproches'[29] (a claim to be taken with the normal amount of scepticism due for such allegations in such a context).

Consequently, with the approval of Dentraygues, Calas had Brousse expelled from the Montpellier section at a meeting held on 19 September 1872. It led to a swift reaction from Guesde, then in Rome, who denounced the manœuvre in a letter sent to the Brussels Internationalist newspaper, *La Liberté*, published on 20 October. The letter made no mention of Brousse by name but it did mention Calas (although the name was misspelt as Colas). The Marxist version of what followed was given in the pamphlet written by Marx, Engels and Lafargue and published in September 1873, *L'Alliance de la Démocratie socialiste et l'Association Internationale des Travailleurs*:[30] 'la police, mise en éveil par la dénonciation de Guesde, surveilla Calas et immédiatement après saisit à la poste une lettre de Seraillier à Calas où on parlait de Dentraygues de Toulouse. Le 24 décembre Dentraygues était arrêté.' Guesde, in other words, was responsible for the destruction of the International in the South ('wer war nun der Denunziant Dentraygues oder Guesde?' Engels asked rhetorically).

Brousse and Guesde argued that far from Guesde being responsible, Dentraygues himself had probably given the game away; they argued that he was unreliable and – as was indeed indicated by his testimony to the police after his arrest – was probably a police informer. (In October 1872 Guesde had persuaded the Jura Federation to distribute a confidential circular to all the national Federal Councils of the International warning them of Dentraygues' activities.)[31] The allegation that Dentraygues was a dubious character seems to be justified. In October a member of the Toulouse section complained that he was acting like a dictator and was no more than

the 'homme de confiance de Karl Marx'. This in itself was no proof
of anything, except that it led the section to make further inquiries
about him, which revealed that: 'nous avons eu de tous les côtés des
plus mauvais renseignements sur son compte, de Cette, de Béziers, de
Perpignan on l'a rejeté [*sic*] et on en a instruit Larroque le délégue
de Bordeaux.' Furthermore, after his imprisonment Dentraygues
addressed a curious letter to McMahon which strongly suggested that
he had passed on information to the police prior to his arrest.[32]

The dispute has followed fairly predictable lines since – with historians sympathetic to the anti-authoritarians suggesting that Dentraygues was responsible, Marxist historians suggesting that it was
Guesde (who was then of course in the 'anarchist' camp). Willard,
the historian of Guesdism, seems to have discovered a nice solution
by suggesting Guesde was responsible, but only accidentally.[33]

Neither interpretation however does much justice to the French
police network. This had been aware for some time of Calas's activities. Not only was he a radical, and therefore in any case subject to
police surveillance, but he had in fact been denounced to the police
as a member of the International by an anonymous informer in
March 1872. The authorities had then placed him under especially
close supervision (which would almost certainly have involved interference with correspondence). As early as August Dentraygues had
been aware that the police were interested in his activities, and this
may well have resulted from the interception of mail.[34] But precisely
how the police discovered the ramifications of the organization in the
South is somewhat beside the point; the fact is that it was almost
certainly not the result of Guesde's letter.

This 'marxist' organization had however ceased to play the role
intended for it for some time prior to its collapse. Blanquists at
Toulouse and elsewhere and anti-authoritarians in the South and
East were steadily gaining influence. Marx had asked Seraillier to
speak to him frankly about the state of affairs of their organization,
and Seraillier transmitted the gist of this message to Sorge.[35] The
Hague Congress, Seraillier said, instead of giving a stimulus to the
movement, had had precisely the opposite effect, discouraging the
leading *militants,* who had fallen under the influence of more extensive and effective propaganda from the Jura. He had lost contact
with most of the southern groups even prior to the collapse of the
organization after December 1872.

This collapse affected the opponents of the General Council

equally. In January 1873 the *Bulletin de la Fédération Jurassienne,* which had been giving short notices of the progress of the Association in France, ceased to do so, and the groups which had come under its influence were broken up.

At Béziers on 22 February 1873 four members of the Association, including the founder of the Béziers section, Louis Salvan, were sentenced to periods of imprisonment of up to four months. In March the Toulouse trial saw the leading figures of the organization, Dentraygues, Calas and Masson, sentenced along with others to periods of up to two years' imprisonment,[36] and on 3 May Engels wrote to Sorge that: 'en France l'organisation est pour le moment fichue, et elle ne pourra se refaire que très lentement, puisque nous n'avons plus aucun rélation.'[37] The final blow in the series of arrests and trials came on 5 May when four members of the Montpellier section appeared before the Tribunal Correctionnel – or, rather, two appeared in person and two of them *in absentia* – Joseph Marmiès, a cooper from Sète, and 'Paul Brousse, etudiant en médécine'. The basis of the case against them rested on the evidence given to the police by Dentraygues (or found by them) and used at the preceding trials at Béziers and Toulouse. All were found guilty of having aided the International. Brousse was sentenced to four months' imprisonment, a fine of fifty francs and the suspension of civil rights for five years.[38]

Brousse had gone into hiding after the police laid their hands on Dentraygues, and early in 1873 he arrived in Barcelona. At the same time he allied himself firmly with the anti-authoritarians in Switzerland and had joined the Jura Federation, introduced by Guesde and seconded by James Guillaume, in September 1872. It seems apparent that his alignment was a consequence rather than a cause of his expulsion from the Montpellier section of the International.[39]

There seemed to be one obvious lesson to be drawn from the events of 1872–3; the International could not afford to risk in France a centralized organization such as Seraillier and the General Council had attempted to create. The collapse of the organization in the Midi provided the members of the International who were already disillusioned with Marx's activities on the General Council with further ammunition for their case. Guesde drew the lesson in a letter to the *Bulletin:*

Ce qui ressort du procès de Toulouse, ce n'est pas seulement le rôle inflame du fondé de pouvoirs de Marx et du Conseil général, mais la condamnation du système autoritaire dont Marx et le Conseil general sont les soutiens. Ce qui a permis, en effet, à Dentraygues de livrer à la police rurale les organisateurs de l'Internationale dans le Midi de la France, c'est la fonction d'initiateur attribué dans notre Association par le Congrès de la Haye à une autorité centrale. Laissez la classe ouvrière, dans chaque pays, s'organiser anarchiquement, au mieux de ses intérêts et les Dentraygues ne sont plus possibles:

1. Parce que les travailleurs de chaque localité se connaissent entre eux et ne seraient jamais exposé à s'en remettre à un homme qui puisse les trahir, les vendre;
2. Parce que en admettant même que la confiance qu'ils ont placée en l'un de leurs ait été trompée, le traître, limité à sa seule section, ne pourra jamais livrer qu'une section aux policiers de la bourgeoisie.

L'autonomie des sections, des fédérations, n'est pas seulement l'ésprit de l'Internationale, mais sa sécurité. Que nos compagnons français, éclairés par l'expérience, y songent![40]

This in fact was to be the pattern followed in France over the next few years. Even then there were disasters, such as the 'complot de Lyon' arrests of 1873.[41] As an organization the International was finally dead in France. But contact remained between groups of socialists within France and the exile communities in Switzerland and, for a short time, Spain; and the ideas of the International lived on to surface again in the socialist revival of the post-1876 era, often with the same *militant* leaders.

3. *Brousse and the Comité de Propagande Socialiste révolutionnaire de la France méridionale, Barcelona, 1873*

A small number of exiles from France fled to Spain following the defeat of the Commune. Spain was passing through a period of political turmoil, following the deposition of Isabella in 1868, which threatened to break into civil war at any moment. The situation seemed to offer, to many revolutionaries, the immediate possibility of a successful social Revolution. Spain was seen by many as their last hope; the Revolution, having been crushed in Paris, seemed to reappear in Spain. Bakunin for instance seems strongly to have thought it offered possibilities, and the failure of the International to accomplish anything there in 1873 played a great part in his crushing disillusionment. There was also a hope that Garibaldi might lead an

army to Spain.[42] The International was strongly established and its
sections were under Bakuninist influence. At a general Congress held
in Barcelona in June 1870 the Spanish Federation of the International
was founded. It became a centre of anarchist sentiment, thereby
acknowledging its debt to Bakunin's disciples who had first spread
the principles of the Association in Spain. The federation sided almost
unanimously with the anti-authoritarians in their struggles with the
General Council (thereby setting the scene for Lafargue's notorious
attempts to found a 'marxist' federation in Madrid), played a leading
part at the St Imier Congress, and in December 1872 at its Cordova
Congress accepted a decentralized structure which provided 'the
fundamental doctrine of Spanish anarchism'.[43]

Spain provided a convenient and natural refuge for Brousse. His
presence there was first noted in Barcelona in February 1873,
immediately prior to the abdication of Amadeus of Savoy and the
declaration of the Republic.[44] In Barcelona he met two other French
exiles, Camille Camet and Charles Alerini,[45] and it was through these
two who were strongly under Bakunin's influence, and as a result of
his participation in the activities of the International in Barcelona,
that Brousse became an anarchist. It was, at least, his first known
contact with anarchist ideas.

In April 1873 he founded, with Camet and Alerini, the Comité de
Propagande Socialiste révolutionnaire de la France méridionale (a
French-language section of the International at Barcelona
was already in existence), announced the projected publication
of a French-language newspaper, *La Solidarité Révolutionnaire,* and issued a Manifesto setting out the main aim of the Comité.
This made it clear that the main target of their propaganda was
France, although Spain was to provide the necessary revolutionary
base:

Unis pour la lutte économique, les travailleurs de tous les pays ont
déjà remporté sur ce terrain plus d'une victoire. C'est à la solidarité
ouvrière que sont dus tous ces succès. Aujourd'hui cette arme est appelé
à nous rendre de plus grands services encore. Il faut la transporter sur
un autre terrain que le terrain économique, sur an autre champ de bataille
que celui de la grève, sur celui de la révolution. Les circonstances sont
favorables, puisque en Espagne une période révolutionnaire vient de
s'ouvrir. Il faut dès aujourd'hui qu'une solidarité morale s'établisse
entre les prolétaires de ce pays et les travailleurs du Midi de la France ...
déjà les relations avec la France méridionale sont assurés: confié à des

mains amies, notre journal sera distribué surement à tous ceux à qui il
s'adresse. . . .

Nous nous placerons sur le terrain de l'anarchie . . . nous ne sommes
pas communistes, parce que ce système nécessite l'établissement d'un
grand pouvoir centrale; nous ne sommes pas non plus mutuellistes parce
que nous ne croyons pas à la constitution de la valeur . . . nous sommes
collectivistes. . . .[46]

Transparent in the Manifesto was the influence of Bakunin and the
optimism with which his supporters and many others regarded events
in Spain.[47] There was political chaos, a strongly-organized working-
class movement with a revolutionary (Bakuninist) ideology. The
formula seemed unbeatable. The *Solidarité Révolutionnaire,* which
first appeared in June, lambasted bourgeois society ('un cadavre
déjà en putréfaction') with the promise of instant destruction.[48] For
a time it seemed as though they might be right.

The inability of Pi y Margall – appointed as head of the Spanish
Executive in June 1873 – to implement a genuine cantonalist programme, and the resistance of the Carlist faction, led to a series of
local insurrections throughout Spain in the summer of 1873. The
Spanish Federal Committee of the International, while suggesting
that its members should partake 'as individuals' in the struggle
between the Carlists and the Republic, called for the dissociation of
the movement from the struggles of the bourgeoisie. The local insurrections were violent, some were temporarily successful (often in
fact with the active support of local Internationalists), but a total
lack of co-ordination and organization as well as insufficient popular
support led to their failure.

There was a brief moment however when, for the Barcelona Internationalists, the millennium seemed to have arrived. On 20 June a
group of Internationalists, with Brousse among them, seized the
Town Hall and resolved – as Brousse later told Kropotkin – 'faire la
Révolution ou mourir'.[49] The heroics were admirable, but like a
previous attempt by Bakunin at Lyons in 1870 they turned into
farce. Very simply, the revolutionaries were ignored and were denied
the opportunity of making contact with – let alone abolishing – the
representatives of Spain's 'putrefying corpse'. After some time, bored,
hungry and somewhat embarrassed, they evacuated the Town Hall
peacefully, and Brousse's first experience of insurrection was over.
It was followed a month later by an attempted General Strike, which

collapsed when the Government drafted large sections of the working class into the Army to fight the Carlists.

The Spanish experience was reflected in the columns of *La Solidarité Révolutionnaire*. On the one hand was the prognostication of the imminent collapse of the bourgeoisie, a class no longer fulfilling a useful function but maintaining itself in power through universal suffrage, capital and inheritance rights, embodied in the State. All means were therefore justified in the proletarian destruction of the State: 'Pour arriver à ce but, tous les moyens possibles doivent être les nôtres. Ils nous appellent la Barbarie et se disent la civilisation? Eh bien soit, c'est la guerre barbare qu'il nous faut.'[50] Once the Revolution broke out in Spain it would inspire France and Italy, and the Latin races would astonish the world. The language, the imagery, the impulse, were Bakuninist, reflecting at the same time *both* the violence of the Spanish situation *and* the lessons drawn from the failure of the Paris Commune. The Commune had provided a lesson for everyone; to Marx it was an inspiration and a legacy which could not be denied by the proletariat – yet at the same time a utopian venture which might have been avoided and whose defeat was the inevitable result of the backward nature of the French proletariat.[51] For Brousse and his exile compatriots, on the other hand, a different lesson was to be drawn; for in the Commune a previous tragedy had been repeated, but not as farce; the people, as in the June Days of 1848, had been sacrificed on the altar of the State, 'ce Dieu moderne dont une partie des socialistes attend encore aujourd'hui, après de si douleureuses expériences, son émancipation'.[52] The revolutionary experiences of 1848 and more especially of 1871 did not, as in the case of Marx, lead to doubts about the possibility of success for the French working class. They in fact reinforced a central dogma of anarchism – the argument against the State (i.e. in the French context, Versailles).[53] By a curious twist of logic the lessons which were drawn lent support to just such revolutionary ventures, rather in the Blanquist tradition – and, indeed, in the Bakuninist tradition – which Marx condemned. Yet this conclusion contained, and was encouraged by, a paradox implicit in the anarchism of the 1870s, a paradox provided for by the failure of 1871, but more especially by that of 1873 in Spain, which provided the other half of the background to *La Solidarité Révolutionnaire* and Brousse's political apprenticeship.

The anarchists held high hopes of Revolution in Spain. Its failure to break out resulted in a correspondingly deep depression which revealed itself most dramatically in Bakunin's disillusionment and eventual break with his followers – 'les événements de France et d'Espagne avaient porté à toutes nos espérances, nos attentes, un coup terrible'.[54] In October 1873 Bakunin issued his famous statement:

'. . . j'ai cette conviction, que le temps des grands discours théoriques est passé. Dans les neufs dernières années on a développé au sein de l'Internationale plus d'idées qu'il n'en faudrait pour sauver le monde, si les idées pouvaient le sauver. . . . Le temps n'est plus aux idées, il est aux faits et aux actes. . . .'[55]

This statement was far from a call to revolution, or even a condemnation of the internal disputes of the International, and far more a cry of despair and disillusionment. It continued, which is rarely noted: 'Ce qui importe avant tout aujourd'hui c'est l'organisation des forces du prolétariat, mais cette organisation doit etre l'œuvre du prolétariat lui-même.' For Bakunin and most other anarchists in the 1870s *the very hopelessness of the total European situation demanded exaggerated deeds,* which were in themselves inspired by the failures against which they were reacting. This is a common enough phenomenon of revolutionary movements,[56] but needs to be underlined if the doctrine of propaganda by the deed ('la propagande par le fait'), which played a central role in anarchist theory in the 1870s, is to be understood.

The phrase itself is normally attributed to Malatesta, who referred to it in a letter to Cafiero in 1876, or to other Italians, and is usually regarded as a reflection of the Italian experience at Bologna in 1874 when the anarchists attempted an unsuccessful insurrection.[57] But the theory was being propounded in the columns of *La Solidarité Révolutionnaire* during the Spanish insurrection of the summer of 1873:

La propagande révolutionnaire ne se fait pas seulement par la plume et par la parole, par des livres, par des brochures, par des réunions publiques, par de journaux; la propagande révolutionnaire se fait surtout sur la place publique, au milieu des pavées amoncelés en barricades, les jours où le peuple exaspéré livre bataille aux forces mercenaires de la réaction.

The first phase of revolutionary propaganda began, the article explained, with the diffusion of easily comprehended, and practical, ideas – such as those of Proudhon [! *sic*]. The second phase consisted in the formation of a small activist minority whose function it should be to inspire the people to overcome their indifference or powerlessness in the face of State oppression; this was to be accomplished by *action;*

Agir pour entrer résolument dans la troisième, la dernière période de propagande révolutionnaire. Une commotion sociale comme celle de la Commune de Paris ne laisse aucun ouvrier indifférent. Il faut courir après un livre . . . l'action révolutionnaire vient vous trouver jusque dans le foyer, au milieu de la famille, et vous force àl'attention. . . .

And, the article concluded: 'au point de vue socialiste nous sommes arrivés à l'action . . . agissons *ne serait-ce qu'au point de vue de la propagande.'*[58] Here, in essence, was the theory of propaganda by the deed, which amounted to what would be described now as 'direct action'. There was the implicit recognition that successful Revolution was for the moment impossible, which led to the conclusion that if it was to be maintained as even a faint hope a conscious élite had to encourage it by acts which were of value 'if only from the point of view of propaganda'. The doctrine was given additional and decisive encouragement by the events of 1870–3. If the masses were *potentially* revolutionary, *actually* they were indifferent, although the conclusion was never explicitly drawn and the anarchists continued to lace their medicine with strong additives of apocalyptic flavour. That was the underlying significance of the doctrine of propaganda by the deed, and it will come to the fore again when Brousse's activities in Switzerland are examined.

La Solidarité Révolutionnaire pointed unwittingly to another paradox inherent in the anarchism of the 1870s which is equally essential to a grasp of Brousse's evolution, both as a theorist and as an activist.

The critique of bourgeois society, and the outline sketch, of the desirable socialist society, derived much from Proudhon although, as with most of the socialist *militants* in the First International, his mutualism was rejected in favour of collectivism, and the lesson hammered home first by Proudhon in his *Capacité Politique,* then by Marx in the Provisional Rules of the Association, that 'the emancipation of the working classes must be conquered by the working classes themselves', had been thoroughly absorbed.[59] The corner-stone of this desirable future socialist society was to be *contract,* as Proudhon meant it – the source of obligation. The society was to be federal, structured around the autonomy of the individual, the autonomy of the Commune and the autonomy of the trade or industrial grouping ('la corporation'). These three units – the individual, the Commune, the corporation, represented *economic* realities; the worker, the unit of consumption, the unit of production, respectively. Thus a *practical* socialism, a socialism 'conforme aux principes de la sociologie', rejecting the abstract bourgeois concepts of the individual and majority will, would emerge.[60]

Having thus rejected the dogmas of liberal democracy in adopting what amounted to a syndicalist statement borrowed very evidently from Proudhon, the anarchists of *La Solidarité Révolutionnaire* rejected the one immediately apparent revolutionary weapon – the General Strike. This would seem surprising in view of the fact that the Spaniards often resorted to violent strike action, but is less so when viewed in the light of the failure of the General Strike in Barcelona in July 1873. This evidently had a profound effect on Brousse, for during the rest of his anarchist career he remained resolutely opposed to the General Strike as a political weapon. The explicit repudiation of the method came at the end of July in an article on the role of the Commune, in a series entitled *Le Socialisme Pratique,* and was linked to the underlying recognition of the futility of attempting Revolution. Accepting the three basic demands of the proletarian programme, the article said, it would seem logical to begin with the emancipation of the individual through the destruction of the régime of laws, i.e. the destruction of the State. This however was an impossibility, and there was no time to wait for the masses to grasp the idea. The corporation provided an arena of action in which the working class could understand their social condition, but it had no power – the struggle was always unequal, even if strikers co-operated amongst themselves in a general upheaval.[61] The sole effective means to Revolution lay *in the Commune,* 'le véhicule de la Révolution'.

The role of the Commune as a revolutionary agency was central to Brousse's theory of anarchism, and it is necessary thus to elaborate it more thoroughly. The Commune (the basic administrative unit of French administration, but primarily used as a generalized description of a basic political unit by the anarchists) was placed within anarchist theory on a quasi-sociological foundation, as a function of the industrial process, as has been seen. Brousse shifted the emphasis to the Commune as a locality where, in certain circumstances, the working class formed a self-conscious revolutionary majority and were thus in a position to seize power. He envisaged such Communes in terms of big cities such as Paris, London, Berlin, Lyons, Marseilles, Barcelona, Florence, Milan, etc. It is not clear what method he advocated for the seizure of power *within* the Commune (beyond the vague description of 'Révolution'), but what he did clearly stress was the need for there to be a majority of the working class: 'la propagande est toute faite où il y a plus d'ateliers que de salons et de manufactures que d'églises.' Once the Commune was seized appropriation would be carried out on anarchist principles: 'que tout ce qui est dans la commune, l'armée, la justice, les finances, les propriétés, deviennent les nôtres, nous appliquerons nos principes et l'expérience se chargera des détails.' However, it was added, this would not mark the end of the struggle: 'La Commune autonome, voilà le moyen, mais ce n'est pas le but . . .,' the end being total revolution.

This theory of Revolution contained within it a conclusion which carried major consequences both for anarchist theory in general and for Brousse in particular. If the working class could capture control of a Commune (in this case a big city), and apply within it the principles of a socialist society, then the Revolution was divisible. In a sense the conclusion was forced upon the anarchists by their insistence that – to put it one way – the means justified the end. While this would not apply to the final struggle with the bourgeoisie (where violent resistance would have to be met by violence) it would apply to the form of organization used to achieve the revolutionary goal. If future society was to be federal and non-authoritarian, so should be the instrument forging it. Indeed the new society was to be created inside the old, in the non-authoritarian structure of the International. This had been of course a central point of the anarchist attack on the General Council. The mandate given to Alerini, as delegate of the Section de Langue française de la Fédération barcelonnaise, to the Geneva Congress of 1873 read in part:

Considérant que son règlement particulier en se prononçant catégoriquement contre le principe d'autorité proteste par cela même contre l'existence d'un pouvoir central dans la société de l'avenir: que l'Association Internationale est appelée à être le germe et l'image de cette société, décide que son délégue votera l'abolition du pouvoir central.[62]

How then could successful Revolution be accomplished given that bourgeois society was highly authoritarian and centralized? Rhetoric could disguise some of the inconsistencies in the shaky answer most anarchists contented themselves with; and yet another was to accept the 'divisibility' of the Revolution, which led ultimately to reformism.

It has been argued[63] that the 'embryo' idea led to the abandonment of *any* idea of violent revolution by the French and Jura Internationalists:

> Il est évident que les branches françaises et jurassiennes de l'Internationale ne concevaient pas la destruction de l'Etat par un acte de violence, mais par une révolution pacifique; par une assimilation des masses prolétariennes dans la grande Association, celle-ci se substituerait finalement à l'Etat.

This claim seems extreme, if only because it was rarely believed that the bourgeoisie would peacefully surrender its power. But there is no doubt that the concept of substitution *could* easily lead to a belief in peaceful revolution and ultimately to reformism, and was responsible for creating the central dilemma which Brousse himself later had to face.

The dilemma faced by the anarchists on this issue was later made very clear, although not explicitly, in a report Kropotkin presented to the 1879 Congress of the Jura Federation, entitled *Idée anarchiste au point de vue de sa réalisation pratique.*[64] In this report Kropotkin accepted the possibility of the partial realization of collectivism but argued, as Brousse had done, that the disadvantages would be outweighed by the advantages, in that the collectivized areas would serve to convince the general population of their superiority. It was idle, he said, to discuss whether one should wait for the majority of the people in a country to be persuaded of its desirability before putting collectivization into practice, because it was inconceivable that, short of forming a government which would use force against the people, socialists would prevent collectivization taking place where the people were ready for it. He also argued that the inner force given to the Revolution by the simple fact of having collectivized property would be sufficient to resist attacks upon it. At the same time however he envisaged the revolutionary period as lasting several years, in order to enable the backward sections of society to 'absorb the new ideas' (that they might not wish to did not apparently occur to him). The conclusion that Kropotkin drew from this was that it was the duty of all socialists to *resist* the creation of a new revolutionary Government which could only stifle the free flow of ideas and immobilize the Revolution. This report simply resumed arguments which by that time had become familiar to the anarchist *militants,* and there was little original in it. But it provides a useful and succinct illustration of the failure of the anarchists to face satisfactorily the problem of power and authority in the Revolution and in post-revolutionary society, and highlights very clearly one flaw in the anarchist *credo* which provided the base for the emergence of an essentially reformist position. Brousse himself, once the revolutionary vision had faded came round to reformism. His possibilist tactics, which were essentially based on the premise that meaningful socialist measures could be achieved on the local level prior to Revolution at the centre, evolved in a logical way from his earlier anarchist position. Even at that early stage the emphasis placed by Brousse on the Commune as the revolutionary agency was essentially practical. Time and time again throughout the following few years he reiterated that it was in the working-class cities or towns that socialism could be achieved, and that to expect the whole of France to follow was absurd, dominated as it was by conservatism. Thus it is often difficult to see whether Brousse believed that society as a whole could be changed. Although he often stated that society would follow the socialist example set by the Communes – and thus by implication he adopted certain reformist tenets – he never provided any satisfactory answers and was probably not much concerned about doing so. He remained very much a man of action rather than of words, and never concerned himself over-much with the future. It was no mistake that he was later labelled by his enemies as a possibilist. As he said, he preferred it to being an impossibilist.

The primary object of *La Solidarité Révolutionnaire* was that spelled out in the Manifesto of April 1873 and repeated in its first issue on 10 June 1873 – to spread anarchist propaganda in the South of France:

de faire pénétrer quand même des nouvelles dans notre pays . . . de faire passer sous les yeux de nos frères la relation des efforts que l'on fait ici, afin qu'ils s'organisent, se préparent et que la révolution dont la péninsule va être le théâtre s'étende en France à leur profit.

Circumstantial evidence suggests that these efforts had some success, for copies of the paper found their way into France and some contact with groups or individuals in the South was maintained. A circular signed by Brousse, Camet and Alerini found its way to a secret Congress of members of the International held at Lyon in August 1873, and it is clear that copies of the newspaper were smuggled into France through Sète (at that time one of the most important ports in France).

It appears that these activities formed a bridge which linked former activists of the 1851 uprising with those who were to emerge later as leaders of the anarchist movement in the Midi in the early 1880s. (See Appendix 5A.)

Thus the French exile group in Barcelona helped to keep alive and spread the socialism of the International in the South of France, laying the groundwork for its anarchist commitment in the early years of the Socialist Party.

Following the removal of Pi y Margall from power in July 1873, and the beginning of a military reaction in Spain, Barcelona no longer offered a safe exile base. As early as 17 July Brousse and his fellow editors of *La Solidarité Révolutionnaire* were the subjects of police investigation, and may even have been arrested and imprisoned for a short while. This led them to decide to leave the country, and following more police moves in mid-August Brousse left Barcelona some time at the end of that month. He made his way to Lyons where he contacted members of the Croix-Rousse section of the International, and aided by one of its members, Boriasse, he crossed the border into Switzerland on 31 August, probably accompanied by Alerini, Camet and Garcia Vinas, a leading member of the Barcelona Federation.[65] His flight from Spain marked the beginning of a six-year involvement with the politics of the Jura Federation and the anti-authoritarian federations of the International, during which he emerged as a leading European anarchist and one of the most important of the French socialist exiles.

2

Brousse and the
Jura Federation,1873-7

1. Background

Switzerland was the main centre of resistance within the International
to the General Council, and the main centre for the French exiles of
the Commune. Many of the exiles took an active part in the work of
the International, and the conflicts within it between the General
Council and the national federations were consequently compounded
by issues which belonged in origin to the conflicts between the *majoritaires* and the *minoritaires* within the Commune.[1] Their presence in
Switzerland, and especially in Geneva, thus intensified the conflict
between the two factions within the International.[2] With the exiles
forming virtually separate communities of their own, riven by fruitless
recriminations over the past, their contribution was often restricted to propaganda of a dogmatic, inflammatory and largely unpro-
ductive nature. When Jules Montels left Switzerland for Russia in
1877 he described his weariness with the 'luttes stériles et écoeurantes
de l'exil' as a motive force in his departure.[3] But in the period immediately following the collapse of the Commune the exile groups
had fulfilled a useful function in organizing aid for other refugees and
organizing propaganda activities aimed at socialist groups within
France. In doing this they were continuing a task already begun by
the Swiss Internationalists.

From as early as the collapse of the Second Empire in September
1870, the Internationalists in Switzerland had given moral and
material help to the socialists in France. They were closely implicated
in an attempted uprising at Lyon in March 1871, and in May the
Paris Commune itself set up in Geneva a Comité d'action, 'chargé
d'éclairer le Midi de la France sur la situation de Paris et sur les sens
véritable de la révolution du 18 mars', a somewhat belated recognition of the need to obtain provincial support, which only a short time
before had prompted the dispatch of delegates, such as Montels,

to the provinces. Johann Philip Becker, the German revolutionary living in Geneva, revealed later that in April 1871 he had been asked to form a group of revolutionaries with the object of entering and provoking insurrection in the southern Departments of France, and that he had been given money for the purpose.[4]

Following the influx of French refugees into Geneva during the summer of 1871, a Section de Propagande et d'action révolutionnaire socialiste, a section of the International, was founded. Its two leading members were Jules Guesde[5] and Nicholas Zhukovsky (or Joukovsky), the latter a close follower of Bakunin. Zhukovsky had played a leading role in the spread of Bakuninism in Switzerland and his participation led to allegations by supporters of the General Council that the section was merely a continuation in a new guise of the Bakuninist Alliance, which had been formally disbanded in August. Zhukovsky and Guesde were later joined by Benoît Malon and Gustave Lefrançais, and the section became the centre of French exile activity, with lesser figures, such as Teulière, Claris and Montels, playing an active role. The section sent Guesde and Zhukovsky as its delegates to the Sonvilier Congress of November 1871, where the Jura Federation was formally established, and its connection with the anarchists was strengthened when Malon and Lefrançais (both Communard exiles), who had been trying to keep in both camps, were expelled from the 'authoritarian' Central Geneva section in December 1871.[6]

The main aim of the section was to provide an organizing centre for activities carried out within, or directed towards, France. In reply to a circular of the Jura Federation it defined its special task as propaganda within France of the principles of the International and the creation of propaganda groups dedicated to a general slogan – the creation of 'la Fédération des communes de France'. It noted that, in addition, its action was almost negligible in Geneva, but that it had had some success in maintaining organized activity in the South of France against the Versailles authorities.[7] To this end Guesde published for a short time a newspaper called *Le Réveil International,* printed in Geneva and distributed both in Switzerland and France, where copies were seized in Savoy and the Hérault at the beginning of October 1871.[8] Another paper, *La Révolution Sociale,* was published by the exile group, and the divisive reactions it provoked amongst socialist exiles caused the police to regret its disappearance early in 1872.[9]

The section became virtually ineffective in 1872 when many of its members left Geneva to look for work, and when Guesde went to Rome. Its task as co-ordinating centre for French groups was assumed by the Jura Federation.

The origin of the Jura Federation lay in the split within the Fédération romande, the French-speaking Swiss Federation of the International founded at the Congress of Geneva in January 1869, which took place at the Federation's Second Annual Congress at La Chaux-de-Fonds in April 1870. The origins of this split were various, but gradually crystallized, broadly speaking, into a division between the supporters and opponents of the General Council in London. The Council withheld its approval from the majority faction, which at the Congress of Sonvilier in November 1871 took the name Fédération Jurassienne and based its statutes on the anarchist principles of the Sonvilier Circular. (See p. 11.) Its leading personality was James Guillaume, a schoolmaster from Locle and a supporter of Bakunin. Guillaume was to dominate the activities of the Jura Federation for most of its existence, largely through the *Bulletin de la Fédération Jurassienne* which first appeared as the official organ of the Federation in February 1872.

The *Bulletin* carried reports throughout 1872 of renewed activities in France. In June it reported that several groups had joined the Federation, and at its Congress held at La Chaux-de-Fonds in August reports from French groups were presented.[10] At the Congress of St Imier in September 1872 Pindy and Camet represented 'plusieurs sections de France', and in November the *Bulletin* reported that a secret Congress of the French Internationalist groups had voted for the anarchist Programme.[11] These reports ceased following the arrest of Dentraygues, and the exiles reverted to using the Jura Federation as a centre of activity. In January 1873, when the International was being broken up in the South by police arrests, Bakunin wrote to Pindy: 'Tant que l'état de choses actuel existe vous devriez faire, il me semble, de la Fédération Jurassienne un centre provisoire de tout le mouvement internationale révolutionnaire de la France méridionale.'[12]

This role cast for the Federation was further enhanced later in 1873 with the collapse of the movement in Spain and the arrival in Switzerland of some of its leading activists. As a base for foreign exiles primarily concerned with the socialist movement in their own countries the Jura Federation was to be of considerable importance throughout the following decade to the French, Spanish and Italian revolutionaries.

2. *Congress of Geneva, September 1873*

The main role of the Jura Federation was however to provide a centre of resistance to the General Council, and it took the initiative in calling for a General Congress of the federations which were opposed to the Council. This met at Geneva in September 1873 and took the title of 'Sixth Congress of the International'. It opened on 1 September and was attended by twenty-four delegates representing seven national federations. Brousse, who had only just arrived in Geneva from Lyons, attended as a delegate of the Spanish Federation and of certain (unnamed) French sections. For the first time he came into contact with leading figures of the International, such as Hales and Eccarius from England, Andreas Costa from Italy, Garcia Vinas from Spain and Guillaume, Spichiger and Zhukovsky from Switzerland.

The main object of the Congress was to create a new anti-authoritarian structure for the International. It began by voting unanimously for the abolition of the General Council.[13] This was followed by discussions over what – if anything – should replace it. Immediately the divergences inherent in the organization, whose *raison d'être* was a common opposition to the Council and the 'marxist' clique, became apparent. The English delegates suggested the creation of a new central correspondence bureau, the Belgians and Jura delegates suggested the creation of three separate committees with different functions, while some of the Italians proposed that the functions of the bureau be rotated amongst the federations. Brousse revealed how deeply the anarchism learnt in Spain had influenced him when he came out against *any* kind of central organization. 'Had not the International survived the critical past three years without, or even in spite of, the interference of the General Council?' he asked. The answer was obvious, he said, and, having countered Authority by abolishing the Council, the Congress should not hesitate:

> Vous voulez abattre l'édifice autoritaire, l'anarchie est votre programme, et vous paraissez vouloir reculer devant les conséquences de votre oeuvre. N'hésitez pas – Vous avez donné un coup de hâche, une portion de l'édifice est tombé! Donnez-en un second, un troisième, et que l'édifice s'écroule.

His rigorous anarchist stance was shared by Andreas Costa of Italy and Victor Dave of Belgium. Guillaume adopted a more moderate position, suggesting that they should at least try *something;* it could always be abolished if found to be dangerous. The Congress finally voted for a solution similar to that proposed by the Italians, that a national federation should be nominated every year to fulfil the function of a Bureau international, charged with purely administrative functions. The Congress then drew up new statutes embodying the anti-authoritarian demands and retained, with minor modifications, the preamble to the statutes of the old organization.

If the new International was united only in its opposition to the General Council and was to break up itself very shortly over doctrinal issues, its member federations shared a common emphasis on the economic – as opposed to the political – structure of society as a means of emancipation and as a central feature of post-revolutionary society. The Congress agreed on the need for the creation in all countries of organizations of *corps de métier,* declared its solidarity with all workers struggling against capital, to whatever organization they belonged, and discussed at length a question which for the first time reached an International Socialist Congress – the General Strike.[14]

The General Strike had been recommended at the Brussels Congress of 1868, but only as one means in the 'war against war' and not as a means to social Revolution. At Geneva however it was put forward as an effective non-political means by which capitalist society could be overthrown, and it received strong support from the Belgians. The report presented to the Congress was however ambiguous, subordinating the question to the wider question of the international organization of the labour movement. It suggested that the Congress should not pronounce on the issue and thus reveal their tactics to the bourgeoisie. This was a useful device for shelving the issue,[15] and the Congress adopted a 'compromise' resolution which effectively did this:

Le Congrès, considérant que dans l'état actuel de l'organisation de l'Internationale il ne peut pas être donné une solution complète à la question de la grève générale, recommande d'une façon pressante aux travailleurs l'organisation internationale des unions de métier, ainsi qu'une active propagande socialiste.[16]

Brousse who, as has been seen, had been far from enthusiastic in

Spain for the strike method, made it clear that as far as ne was concerned there were better methods, although these very much depended on variable conditions in different countries:

... si la grève générale est un moyen pratique dans certains pays, ailleurs, en Italie et en France par exemple ce moyen ne pourrait pas être employé. Pourquoi, en France, où la grève générale est impossible, ne ferait-on pas la révolution sous forme d'un mouvement communaliste?[17]

Here he was committing himself openly to the tactic he had outlined in the columns of *La Solidarité Révolutionnaire* and to which he remained basically faithful. It was a reflection both of the backward state of the labour movement in France and of his belief that the Commune was the crucible of Revolution. To say that he was hostile to syndicalism would be to put it too strongly; but he constantly revealed a coolness towards it as a political *method* which marked him off from other anarchists such as Guillaume or César de Paepe, or indeed from two of his closest colleagues, Costa and Alerini, both of whom came out at the Congress in support of the strike as a revolutionary method.

In arguing against the General Strike, Brousse had pointed to the realities of the French situation where activity was limited to the creation or maintenance of small revolutionary groups. This argument touched on another issue which was discussed by the Congress – the relative weight to be given to exile and non-exile movements within the new organization. On this issue Brousse emerged as a firm defender of the right of the movement in France, however dispersed and fragmented, to have equal rights with those elsewhere.

During the preliminary discussions on the acceptance of credentials Guillaume had argued that delegates of the clandestine groups, provided that they were upheld as genuine by the federations with which they were in contact, should be admitted to Congresses of the International, but only with the right to a 'voix consultative', i.e. with no right to vote. While Claris of the Section de Propagande was opposed to admitting them at all – a curious position to adopt in view of the supposed policy of the section – Brousse attacked Guillaume's argument on the grounds that, by unfairly discriminating against the French groups who were merely responding to Government repression, it would throw them into the arms of the authoritarians (i.e. supporters of the General Council). Brousse won his

G

case, and these sections were finally accepted on equal terms with
regular sections to the Geneva Congress itself.

Discussion as to their position in future Congresses was postponed
until the new statutes of the organization were debated. In this debate
discussion revolved around the draft Article Eight, which stated that
illegal groups should have no right to vote. Brousse, who accepted the
need for thorough investigation of credentials, which was a primary
concern of the drafting committee, put forward with Montels a
motion to the effect that an illegal federation should have the same
rights as a legal federation, provided that its validity was established.[18]
Guillaume had slightly modified his previous position and now
argued that if the Committee's proposal were accepted an anomalous
position would arise where illegal sections were affiliated to a legal
federation but were denied the right to vote (some of the French
sections were affiliated to the Jura Federation). Such sections (where
affiliated to a legal federation) should have the right to vote
voix délibérative). This argument seemed to Brousse to carry the
dangerous implication that illegal sections should not have the
right to federate amongst themselves and thus form independent
national federations, and he opposed it. In the end, the Brousse–
Montels motion was carried, and Article Eight was dropped. The
issue was somewhat academic as votes in any case were not considered to have any binding effect, but it revealed Brousse's determination that the clandestine French groups should have equal
rights with others, and that a French Federation should one day be
formed.

Although comparatively minor, Brousse's contribution to the
Geneva Congress debates was important, for it pointed ahead to the
main themes of his contribution to the anarchist movement in the
following few years: his expressed preference for 'communalist',
rather than trade-union, action; his intransigent position *vis-à-vis*
the organization of the International, which ranged him alongside
Costa; and his concern with the clandestine French sections, their
position within the International and the state of the movement
within France.

His differences with Guillaume on these main issues were not
especially important in themselves. But in the light of later events
they were significant pointers to the future split between the two.

3. *Brousse and Bakunin*

Brousse had very quickly become absorbed in the affairs of the International. Having joined the organization only in 1872 he had been active within the French exile movement in Barcelona and had played a not insignificant role in the Geneva Congress. Having accomplished this he was not slow to make his own contribution to the controversies surrounding the internal affairs of the Association. This took the form of a pamphlet he published in 1873, shortly after the Geneva Congress, entitled *L'Etat à Versailles et dans l'Association Internationale des Travailleurs*. This was an attack on the principle of authority as embodied in the State – especially the Versailles State – and, within the International, in the General Council. It betrayed the strong influence of Bakunin, and in fact Brousse later told Kropotkin that 'Bakounine en à dit beaucoup de bien à l'epoque'.[19] Thus Brousse described the State in the following terms:

Ainsi donc, par *l'Education officielle* on prépare le corps électoral au respect de *l'autorité*; par l'exercice *du suffrage principe* il se donne un *pouvoir* faiseur des lois; une magistrature qui le juge, une *force publique* qui le frappe. C'est ce *Tout* qui l'écrase sous le prétèxte de le civiliser, ce *Tout* qui le tue, s'il se révolte, ce cortège d'institutions qu'on appelle *l'État*.[20]

The pamphlet gave a brief *résumé* of the major critiques of the State, emphasizing the importance of Saint-Simon's idea of administration replacing government. Predictably it laid great emphasis on Proudhon's formula of 'an-archie', the replacement of political functions by industrial functions, with the social order becoming merely one of contract and exchange. Brousse repeated the argument for the structuring of society around the three units of the worker, the trade union and the Commune, but increased the sociological gloss[21] and dissected with a plethora of medical anologies the major features of bourgeois industrial society. The 'corps social', he concluded, had certain functions to fulfil – production, consumption and exchange – each of which was fulfilled within the *corps de métier* (production) or the Commune (consumption and exchange); all the rest was superfluous, like the appendix. He then went on to quote with approval Bakunin's demand for the destruction of the State, 'la politique destructive',[22] and argued that a Bourbon restoration in France could well create divisions amongst the bourgeoisie which could advantageously be exploited by the workers for the destruction of the State. Turning to the International, Brousse went on to describe the creation of what he called a governmental apparatus at the 1871 London Conference, based on the domination of a sect which attempted to impose an official doctrine. And to the argument that the International should form a centralized and disciplined organization, he replied with the classical anarchist doctrine of revolution:

... on ne déclare pas une Révolution comme on déclare la guerre, et, lorsque par bonheur elle éclate, on ne le dirige pas de la même façon. Les mouvements sérieux ne naissent pas sur commande, en d'autres termes on ne *fait* pas une révolution. Nul Conseil général, nul comité révolutionnaire ne pourrait atteindre un but aussi déraisonnable ... Une révolution se prépare longuement dans l'intelligence collective des masses et le plus souvent son explosion est due à des circonstances secondaires. Elle est toujours d'ailleurs autonomiste par nature, empruntant au pays, aux idées, aux circonstances, un caractère spécial qui est le gage de son succès. On peut par la propagande socialiste unifier de longue main les aspirations des masses, donner aux efforts au moment de lutte une direction pratique et une forme aux résultants, mais là s'arrête l'action de l'activité humaine sur ces phénomenes collectifs de la vie sociale.[23]

It is clear therefore that Brousse was deeply influenced at this stage by Bakuninist ideology. But was he ever in any sense a 'lieutenant de Bakounine'?[24]

Bakunin's penchant for secret organizations is well-known and need hardly be elaborated on. Guillaume was reluctant to talk about it later, and in his history of the International merely mentioned the break of the intimité (the smaller inner group of Bakunin's disciples, founded in 1869 after the disbanding of the Fraternité Internationale) with Bakunin himself in September 1874.[25] On one occasion however he talked about it to Nettlau, who noted what Guillaume said as follows:

Ozerov n'était de l'intimité qu'au deuxième degré, pendant que Pindy se tenait encore plus loin et que Brousse en était tout à fait éloigné, au troisième degré, pourrait-on dire. On ne le considérait que comme un candidat à de futures relations amicales. ... Cafiero, Ross, Schwitzguébel, Guillaume formaient enfin le cercle le plus intime et ils exclurent, en septembre 1874, Bakounine de leur intimité, tandis qu'ils restaient ultérieurement liés. Entre-temps Brousse s'était rapproché du cercle, sans jamais tout à fait s'y agréger, de même que Pindy; ultérieurement P. Kropotkine s'y joignit en 1877.[26]

Further details can be found in a letter that Brousse wrote to Garcia
Vinas in 1880. (See Appendix 1.) This makes it clear that by 1877
Brousse was a leading member of the group, and Nettlau dated his
entry as having occurred some time late in 1873 after the Geneva
Congress.[27] It is also clear however that Brousse was never on very
close terms with Bakunin while the latter was active in the Jura. He
can only have met Bakunin in the period between September 1873 and
September 1874, probably immediately after the Geneva Congress
when with Alerini, Vinas and Farga Pellicer he visited the Russian at
Berne.[28] Shortly afterwards Brousse went to live in Lucerne,[29] and it
is unlikely that he saw Bakunin again. For some time he was deeply
influenced by him, but he was no man's disciple and like most of the
French *militants* of the socialist movement his mentor was Proudhon,
not Bakunin. His knowledge of Bakunin when he wrote his first
pamphlet was secondhand, and it is significant that Guillaume, who
had no particular reason to be charitable to Brousse, later stated in
his obituary of him that Bakunin had influenced Brousse only
slightly and said that he was essentially a 'jeune proudhonien français'. In this respect Guillaume's endorsement of Brupbacher's
assessment of the particular contribution Bakunin brought to the
Jura Internationalists – that he merely gave precision to attitudes
already adopted[30] – can be taken as a fair assessment of his influence
on Brousse. Zévaès's judgement of him as 'l'un des adeptes fervents
de Bakounine'[31] has consequently to be interpreted cautiously.

4. Berne: Natalie Landsberg

Having spent four months in Lucerne following the Geneva Congress,
Brousse finally settled in Berne, the federal capital. Through his
father's friendship with Professor Schwarzenbach, Director of the
Chemistry Faculty at the University, he obtained a post in the
University chemical laboratories where he was officially appointed
an Assistant in October 1875. He thus had one advantage not enjoyed
by many of the other French exiles, financial security, and this permitted him to play a far more active role in the life of the Jura Federation than that played by the majority of its *militants*.

He was thirty years old. Of medium height, with penetrating brown
eyes and a chaos of flowing black hair, and sporting the appropriate
revolutionary beard, he made a powerful impact on all those who
met him. Many years later one observer recorded that 'il a naturelle-

ment la mine d'un conspirateur; j'ai trouvé dans son pâle visage je
ne sais quoi de cette expression satanique qui faisait partie, vers 1830,
de l'idéal de beau ténébreux'.[32] He was impulsive and spontaneous
and had considerable charm – especially with women. He was something of a grandee, a born aristocrat, and he made no attempt to
hide his enjoyment of what life offered him. He was extravagant with
money and seems quickly to have exhausted the funds from which his
long-suffering mother supplied him (although the money was not
necessarily spent on himself). As early as 1888, when he was practis-
ing as a doctor in Paris, reference was made to his 'straitened circumstances' – and it appears that as early as 1883 at least he had
contracted large debts to cover expenses involved in his political
activities.[33] In his commitment to anarchism one senses that it was the
aristocratic ideal contained within it which attracted him, and it is
probably no mere coincidence that it was with Kropotkin, the aristocratic anarchist, that Brousse established his closest friendship in the
Jura. Guillaume, who came to know him well, placed his finger on the
quintessence of his personality:

... un méridional à l'intelligence déliée – comme l'a écrit Jaurès qui s'y
connait – ce qui veut dire, d'une part, un garçon très roublard, sceptique
à l'endroit des hommes, et sachant discerner ce qui est 'possible'; et
d'autre part, quelque contradiction que cela semble impliquer, un
théoricien quintessencié et batailleur, nourri de raisonnements abstraits
aimant à couper des cheveux en quatre. Avec cela, il avait l'amour de la
phrase, des mots sonores; il était éloquent et bruyant, uproarious,
comme l'a dit Kropotkine.[34]

Educated, energetic and eloquent, he was able to exert considerable
influence over other men; the discerning sceptic described by Guillaume could, in personal contact, achieve what few others working
with him were capable of. He was, in the words of another later
observer, gifted with 'une dexterité digne des prélats diplomates
d'autrefois',[35] or, from another point of view, 'un homme d'intrigue,
un politicien de couloirs'.[36] This judgement was reiterated in the
frequent acid comments of Engels during the conflicts surrounding
the formation and early years of the French Socialist Party. Engels,
like Marx, was apt – in a thoroughly non-Marxist way – to substitute
personal criticisms for more objective assessments of the motives and
effectiveness of his opponents. On one occasion, at the height of the
struggle between the possibilists and Guesdists for the control of the

French Socialist Party at the St Etienne Congress of September 1882, he told Bernstein that '. . . all the old Bakuninist tactics, which justify any means – lies, calumniation, secret intrigues – dominated the preparations for the Congress. That is the only trade in which Brousse is proficient.'[37] The striking impression one gains from all these descriptions of Brousse is that of a man with a keen political sense – a sense of what was possible or practical. Throughout his career he had little time – although he enjoyed indulging in splitting hairs – for theory as a guide to action; action was the guide to theory.

The Science Faculties of the University of Berne had greatly increased in size and prestige under Schwarzenbach's control. From fourteen students in 1862, the Chemistry Faculty had increased to 300 in 1871, the year in which Schwarzenbach held the Rectorship. The University was thus well placed when the Russian Government, in a successful attempt to break up the Zurich Russian anarchist colony, decreed that no Russian student at Zurich would be allowed back to teach in Russia. This was particularly serious for women students, as Zurich had been the first University to admit women on an equal footing with men and was still one of the very few which did so.[38] Such a move by the Russian Government seems to have been anticipated, for in the summer semester of 1872 a delegation of women students from Zurich had asked on what conditions they would be allowed to matriculate at Berne. In the following semester the names of two Russian women students appeared on the register of the Medical Faculty, and had increased to four by the next summer. The Russian decree against the Zurich colony was issued in May 1873, and in the first semester of the following academic year there were twenty Russian women students registered at Berne.[39]

Amongst them was a student from Kicinev in Bessarabia, Natalie Landsberg, who probably came from the Zurich colony. Some time in 1873 or 1874 she met Brousse and became his mistress. She bore him a child, Clotilde Léonie Jeanne, in 1880, after they had returned to France, and they were married in January 1886, only to separate about eight years later. She was good-looking, intelligent and a deeply politically committed woman, very much in the Russian populist tradition. Born in 1846 in Kicinev, she was the daughter of Zinovia Gregorievna and Joseph Mikhailovitch Landsberg. Her father was a Russian Government official – a Prefect of Police. Revolted by the persecution of the Jews in Bessarabia, reacting against her family aristocratic background, Natalie left Russia in

about 1866; to do this it appears she married a man from whom she
parted once across the border, which was a common enough device.[40]
She lived and dressed plainly and ascetically, believing in the 'socialist
life', the life to which the average populist was committed, and in this
she was the antithesis of Brousse. None the less she fully participated
in his political activities and devoted herself selflessly to them and to
him. It was she who provided most of the money for the newspaper
which Brousse founded in Berne in 1876, the *Arbeiter-Zeitung,* and
she was almost certainly responsible for bringing Brousse into contact with the Russian emigré groups in Switzerland and may well
have encouraged his adoption of extremist anarchist views.[41]

5. Brousse and the development of anarchist theory

The most important theoretical task facing the Jura *militants* following the Geneva Congress was to define a distinctive anarchist *credo.*
Beyond their belief in the need for collective property and the abolition of the State, together with a Bakuninist theory of Revolution,
the Jurassian anarchists had never clearly worked out details, except
on an individual basis. Guillaume wrote a fairly detailed scheme for
a 'commune sociale' in the 1871 *Almanach du Peuple,* and the term
appeared in the statutes of the Jura Federation. Similar ideas
appeared in some of the literature thrown up by the Paris Commune,[42]
and the fusion of Proudhonist federalism and collectivism had been
apparent within the First International, especially at its Basle Congress. However, these had been ideas put forward by individuals and
had not been considered by the Federation as an organization. This
consideration came only during the debates with César de Paepe and
his Belgian supporters over the theory of 'public services', when considerable time and energy were devoted to the theoretical ordering
of post-revolutionary society. Ultimately the dialogue led to the
formulation of anarcho-Communism.

The 'public service' theory was expounded by de Paepe at the
Brussels Congress of the International in September 1874.[43] It was in
effect an attack on the anti-Statism of the anarchists and a denial of
their theory of Revolution. Defining public services as those which
demanded public control to attain their proper ends – such as medical
services, communications, education and security – de Paepe said
they could be administered at two levels; that of the local Commune,
or that of the federation of Communes (society was to be organized

federally), which he called the State. He gave a detailed account of
how communal and State services should be administered, and while
insisting that services would be run by the State or local groups, such
as compagnies ouvrières, he said they should be *owned* by society.
He disagreed with those who argued for the abolition of the State –
those whom he called 'an-archistes' – for while they shared with him
the idea that economic groupings would take predominance over
political groupings (the shared Proudhonist basis), they failed to
account for the fact that in post-Revolutionary society there would
still be public services requiring to be run on a national scale by the
federative State. The State was an instrument to be used or abused
and it was up to the working class to see that it was used. Attacking
the anarchist theory of Revolution he said that, given the backward
state of trade-unionism in most countries, the structure he had outlined would have to be *imposed* following the capture of power. Thus
a 'dictature collective' would be called for. There were serious dangers,
he added, in the 'révolution anarchiste', mainly that of a lack of direction which would permit the diversion of the Revolution from its
true ends.[44]

The report challenged most of the implicit assumptions of the Jura
militants. In formulating their reply over the following months they
were led to define their position, and thus developed a specifically
anarchist consciousness. One of their basic objections to the 'public
service' theory was that by laying down a blueprint for the future the
way was opened once again to authoritarianism, whereas the Revolution itself would determine what future necessities were:

cette organisation devant être le résultat, non pas des spéculations
fantaisistes des penseurs, mais des expériences pratiques que fera naître
la révolution sociale. Cette révolution suscitant de nouvelles nécéssités
sociales immédiates produira elle-même un nouvel ordre social d'où
découlera l'organisation des services publics.[45]

None the less, having said this, the anarchists began to lay down the
outlines of the form in which they envisaged this society, and the
structure they produced was to become the common currency of
anarchist theory.

The objections voiced against de Paepe's report by Schwitzguébel,
the delegate of the Jura Federation to the Brussels Congress, were
that in the first place it took as its starting point human groups instead of individuals, and second, that it sought to *impose* an order

through laws dictated by authority. Against this the anarchists
believed first of all in the 'autonomy of the individual' who would,
freely and spontaneously, contract with the rest of society for specific
purposes, and second, in the free and spontaneous federation of
autonomous groups.[46]

The anarchists saw no contradiction between their concern for the
individual and the collectivist society they envisaged. The individual
could only be free when he had equal access to the fruits of man's
labour, and provided that authority was not permitted to re-establish
itself he would be free to develop his personality as he wished. Anarchism at this stage still shared many of its basic assumptions with
socialists of other schools and it was not until later, in the 1880s, that
individualist anarchism emerged as a distinctive element within the
anarchist movement.

In subsequent discussions within the Jura Federation, which the
Bulletin described as the most important debate since the discussions
on the collectivization of property, the nature of these free groupings
was further defined following the lines already indicated by Proudhon
and Bakunin. Prior to the Congress, in the mandate drawn up by the
Berne section, Brousse had said that the question as presented at
Brussels was wrongly conceived; the only real question to be decided
was how *all* branches of production would be organized, not merely
the public services.[47] This position became the accepted starting point
for discussion. At the Annual Congress of the Federation at Vevey
in August 1875, Schwitzguébel said that what was important was not
to determine what was and what was not public, but to realize that:
'l'action spontanée des masses populaires d'où [l'émancipation] peut
seule sortir, est, dès les premiers actes de la Revolution, l'affirmation
pratique du principe d'autonomie et de fédération, qui devient la base
de tout groupement sociale.'[48] The spontaneity of Revolution would
be matched by the spontaneity of the free federation of groups. The
workers within a community would contract together to form the
Commune, and the Communes would federate amongst themselves
to form a federation of Communes. Interlocking with, or parallel to,
this structure would be the local federation of trades unions, which
similarly would form regional and national federations. Society
would reflect the economic realities of the productive process, not the
political and hence 'artificial' structure of bourgeois society.[49] This
Programme had been described succinctly by Schwitzguébel two
years previously as 'l'idée de l'autonomie de l'individu dans le groupe,

du groupe dans la Commune, de la Commune dans la région, de la région dans l'internationalité'. It had, he said, received its practical sanction in the uprising of the people of Paris in March 1871.[50]

The contribution of Brousse to the process of defining more closely the anarchist image of future society was to give it a pseudo-scientific basis and to relate the non-authoritarianism of the anarchists to the structure of the International itself. He showed little interest in the detailed discussion of anarchist society which was done by Schwitz-guébel, and concentrated instead on the critique of bourgeois society and the examination of political method, which provided the basis for the anti-Marxist stance he adopted throughout his political career. Like the majority of his fellow socialists he was deeply imbued with the positivist spirit, which gave them the assurance that they *knew* society was moving in their direction – or rather that they were moving in its direction. Brousse summarized his analytical method in classic Comtist terms:

à réunir impartialement les faits, à en déduire ensuite une loi générale qui permette de prévoir l'avenir. Auguste Comte disait avec raison: *savoir* pour *prévoir*, prévoir pour *pouvoir*. Cette méthode est applicable aux choses sociales, car la société n'est pas, comme certains le croient, un être de convention, produit de la volonté humaine, mais bien une partie intégrante de la nature. A ce titre ces phénomènes relèvent de la science.[51]

Thus in his second pamphlet, *Le Suffrage Universel et le Problème de la Souveraineté du Peuple*,[52] published immediately prior to the Brussels Congress, he attacked universal suffrage as an unscientific way of reflecting the collective will of society: 'les sciences exactes, la sociologie comme les autres, procèdent par l'observation, l'ex-périence, le raisonnement, la déduction logiquement conduite; la brutalité du nombre n'a pas place en cette méthode.'[53] The 'brutality of mere numbers', the radical bourgeois panacea of universal suff-rage, reflected nothing of the organic structure of society. As an integral part of the natural process society was susceptible of a ruth-less scientific analysis. As a 'corps social', an organism, society should have the free and spontaneous use of its organs, reflecting its necessary functions. As in *L'État à Versailles,* Brousse concluded that the three-tiered structure of the worker, the *corps de métier* and the Commune corresponded to the basic functions of society – in-dividual work, collective work and its consumption. Post-revolu-

tionary society was merely the free reflection of the 'true' structure
of society, i.e. the *economic* structure.

Brousse did not however confine his critique of universal suffrage
to revealing its theoretical shortcomings, but attacked it on the basis
of French experience. Using Jules Guesde's trenchant attack on
universal suffrage as a reinforcement to his own[54] he illustrated how
universal suffrage had been used throughout the century as an instrument of the bourgeoisie, while posturing as the expression of the will
of the people. Suffrage could have meaning only when the working
class enjoyed economic equality with the bourgeoisie – a condition
dependent on Revolution, after which suffrage would be otiose.
Attacking the Blanquist concept of *political* revolution as a means to
social revolution as 'la plus irréalisable comme la plus dangereuse
des utopies',[55] he concluded that it would only be one more means of
confirming the bourgeoisie in power – for who would control such a
party if not they? Nor could this danger be avoided by the use of
working-class candidates in parliament, a tactic for which he, like
all anarchists, reserved his bitterest scorn. The very purity of the
working class lay in its attachment to, or communion with, the work-
process. Here Brousse revealed his debt to the spirit of Proudhonism:

le travail, oui le travail seul t'a donné ta force, ta morale, ta santé. Si tu
aimes la justice, c'est que tu as en à souffrir de l'injustice sociale: tu chéris
tes frères, les travailleurs, parce que tu es uni à eux par la solidarité de la
souffrance ... si tu veux renverser la civilisation bourgeoise, ne vis pas
de sa vie.[56]

This was an element in the French socialist tradition which obtained
particular significance within the anarchist movement, which placed
such emphasis on the creation of a new order within the framework
of the old. The argument gained force in the 1870s, with the Versailles
Government presenting a picture of political chicanery and uncon-
cern with any but the most class-prejudiced and short-sighted res-
ponses to events.[57] It led easily to an anti-intellectual *ouvrièrisme,*
which revealed itself in some of the debates at the 1873 Geneva Congress and later passed into the syndicalist tradition, although within
the anarchist movement in the Jura it never became a serious force,
blunted perhaps by the strong leavening of bourgeois intellectuals
and non-proletarian elements within its membership; the movement
here merely found in the Proudhonist argument a reinforcement for
its anti-parliamentarism.

In the second part of the pamphlet, and in a series of articles published in the *Bulletin*,[58] Brousse developed a critique of the International peculiarly his own. It was a development of that first expressed in *L'État à Versailles* and it laid the basis for his anti-Marxist stance within the international socialist movement.

The basic reason for the split within the International, he said, lay in the failure of the working class to break completely with bourgeois concepts. The working-class movement, untrammelled in the early years of the Association by old political formulae, had developed an organization based on the interests of labour in the form of groups and federations of groups – hence the local section of the International, and the local and national federations of sections. But it had failed to eliminate the bourgeois element, the parallel 'political' or 'governmental' structure of the Congresses and the General Council, with which in the early years it had coexisted in the struggle for collectivism. As the 'anarchic order' – the sections and federations of sections – increased in strength, so did the 'governmental' structure. The second period in the history of the International was therefore dominated by the question of whether the International was to become

... un Etat spécial organisé politiquement à l'intérieur et ayant des rélations politiques avec les Etats bourgeois, ou bien si elle sera franchement révolutionnaire, non pas révolutionnaire comme l'entendent les blanquistes, mais révolutionnaire dans le sens le plus large du mot.

The first blow against the tendency to turn the International into a State apparatus was at the Congress of the Fédération romande of 1870, when the anarchist majority had rejected the State and political action. This however had not prevented the General Council from establishing a State apparatus at the London Conference of 1871, and consecrating the deed at the Hague in 1872. The third and contemporary period in the history of the International was the overthrow of this political structure at Geneva in 1873 and the assertion of the spontaneous 'economic' structure – the sections and their federations. The State within the International had been destroyed and its Congresses now were merely the voluntary expressions of opinion, a form of propaganda.

Much of this was not new. It merely elaborated what Malon and Bakunin had already said.[59] What was new and significant was that in this pamphlet can be seen the beginnings of an interpretation of the history of the Association which was a reflection of the growing rigidity of sectarian differences within the socialist movement. There was an unreserved use of the epithet 'marxist' to describe the supporters of the General Council, a development which, as has been seen, began with the *Reponsé de Quelques Internationaux*. The tone of the pamphlet was unreconciliatory, and in placing the conflict squarely on the plane of principles it held out little hope of any *rapprochment* with the authoritarians.

It took some little time more for an openly anarchist consciousness to emerge. As has also been seen, 'anarchiste' was a term which had come into circulation very largely as a term of abuse, and it was avoided by those to whom it was applied. At the Brussels Congress Schwitzguébel rejected the term 'socialiste anarchiste' in favour of 'socialiste fédéraliste', while de Paepe gave the word its common connotation when he referred to 'la révolution anarchiste', meaning a disordered or chaotic Revolution. But throughout the period 1874–6 in the course of the dialogue with de Paepe and his Statist theory with its Jacobin concept of revolution, 'anarchiste' became an accepted term, reflecting a degree of self-consciousness which permitted the anarchists to distinguish themselves from other kinds of socialists and to denote a particular ideological position. This was something new.

One further step was needed before the process of definition was completed. This was the emergence of the theory of anarcho-Communism, which became an essential component of post-Bakuninist anarchism. Kropotkin became its leading theorist, although not its originator.

Anarcho-Communism was distinguished from the anarchism of Bakunin and his followers (generally referred to as anarchist collectivism) by its emphasis on *need* rather than *work* as the criterion of distribution. Not only the instruments but also the *products* of society would be collective property, at the free disposal of the members of society, organized (or organizing themselves) on the traditionally anarchist basis of the Commune, according to their individual needs. It was argued that within modern societies, where all industries were interdependent, it was impossible for payment to be proportionate to labour. To maintain this view, as the collectivists did, would simply re-establish a wage structure as authoritarian as that existing in capitalist society. The only way in which to achieve 'a society that recognizes the absolute liberty of the individual, that does not admit of any authority, and makes use of no compulsion to drive men to work'[60] was through anarcho-Communism. Traditional economics, which concentrated primarily on production and only secondarily on consumption, should be replaced by a new science which Kropotkin called the Physiology of Society, whose task would be to study 'the needs of humanity, and the means of satisfying them with the least possible waste of human energy'. The principle to be embodied in the Revolution was the principle of the Commune, the basis of the new social order. In this social order recognition would finally be given to the fundamental fact that in society accumulated wealth belonged to all: 'Everything belongs to all, all belongs to everyone! And provided each man and woman contributes his and her share of labour for the production of necessary objects, they have a right to share in all that is produced by everybody.'[61]

Anarcho-Communism, as its name suggests, implied an adoption of some elements from the utopian and Communist strand within the socialist tradition. Unfortunately, considering its importance in the history of socialism, its origins are somewhat obscure, although it is clear that it first appeared in the latter part of the 1870s amongst the anarchist groups connected with the International. The first mention of anarcho-Communism was made in 1876 by a French exile living in Geneva, François Dumartheray, who in a pamphlet entitled *Aux Travailleurs manuels partisans de l'action politique* announced the forthcoming publication of a pamphlet on the subject. This pamphlet has never been traced.[62] In May 1876 a letter signed 'P.R.' in the *Bulletin* called for the collectivization of the fruits of labour, but this letter seems to have passed unnoticed at the time. It was not until October of that year, when anarcho-Communism was adopted by the Italian Federation at its Florence Congress, that it became part of any anarchist programme. Even then it remained a largely un-noticed and uncontroversial theory, for despite mention in Brousse's *Arbeiter-Zeitung* and in the *Bulletin*, Kropotkin, the greatest exponent of the theory, later said that he remained ignorant of it until as late as 1879.[63]

It is clear that Kropotkin did not have much to do with the origins of the theory, and while the resolution at the Florence Congress certainly had some influence in the Jura it has been generally agreed by historians that the theory developed independently in the two countries.[64] In 1876, for instance, Guillaume had written his pamphlet *Idées sur l'organisation sociale*, which stated that after the Revolution there would be no need for consumption to be related strictly to work, and that there would be a general sharing-out of wealth.

Whatever the truth about the origins of the theory in the Jura, it had become sufficiently important to be discussed at the Verviers Congress of the International in 1877. Both Costa and Brousse came out as strong proponents of the theory in contrast to Vinas and Morago, the Spaniards, who remained strictly within the confines of traditional Bakuninist collectivism. Guillaume as usual played a moderating role, and his resolution stating that the anarcho-Communist solution was for each section to adopt or reject as it saw fit was passed. The resolution appears to have been passed with an amendment by Brousse to the effect that the adoption of anarcho-Communism should only be regarded as the second stage in the revolutionary process ('nous devons partager la question: immédiate et lointaine').[65] It was not in fact until 1880 that anarcho-Communism became written into the Programme of the Jura Federation as a result of Kropotkin's persistence. But by then it had become common currency among the *militants* of the movement.

6. The Berne section of the International

In April 1874 Brousse wrote to the Federal Committee of the Jura Federation to announce the formation of a section de propagande in Berne. This section was admitted to the Federation at its Annual Congress later in that month.[66] It is difficult to imagine a more stony ground for socialist activity. Not only was Berne the Swiss Federal capital, and predominantly German-speaking, but it lay to the east of the traditional centres of support for the Federation in the watch-making areas. Indeed the section grew only slowly to begin with. Brousse, in his correspondence with the Federal Committee as secretary of the section, complained continuously of financial difficulties and lack of support.[67]

The section's statutes defined its aims as: 'la propagande des principes socialistes, mais plus spécialement celle de l'organisation pratique de l'Internationale; sections, unions de métier; caisses de secours mutuels et de résistance, associations coopératives.'[68] The organization and structure of the International was a question which preoccupied Brousse a great deal. In November 1874 for example he wrote to the Neuchâtel section asking for copies of Malon's pamphlet *L'Internationale,* which was to form the basis of a study being undertaken by the section at its weekly meetings.[69] This study provided the basis for a pamphlet dealing with the organization of the Association with which Brousse was commissioned at the Annual Congress of the Federation at Vevey in 1875, after he had argued that such a work was the necessary complement to the statutes of the Federation, which provided the outline of principles. The outline of the projected pamphlet was presented to the 1876 Congress, but turned out to be – if a rough draft in the Archives of the Federation is the project as presented – an unoriginal and elementary description of the organizational structure, which the Congress quietly interred by distributing it amongst the sections for discussion.[70]

Brousse's energy and enthusiasm resulted, within a relatively short time, in the establishment of a solid nucleus of socialist support. It was usual for meetings of the leading members of the Jura Federation to be held at fairly frequent intervals to discuss matters of principle and common interest, and in October 1874 the Berne section was the venue for one such meeting. Presided over by Emmanuel Fournier, a former member with Brousse of the Section de langue française of Barcelona, the meeting discussed the public service issue, whose significance as a challenge to the anarchists was beginning to be realized. The participants left Berne with at least the impression that 'un solide noyau d'active propagande socialiste' had been established in Berne; and in the following March the *Bulletin* reported that a banquet held by the section in conjunction with the Fribourg section to commemorate the Paris Commune was the first time that public support had been shown in Berne for the Commune.[71]

Brousse was the inspiring force of the section, already revealing the impatience and fervour which was later to alienate him from Guillaume. His correspondence with the Federal Committee reveals him constantly prodding it to greater efficiency. In December 1874 he asked it to send him pamphlets to distribute, above all the account of the Brussels Congress and the *Almanach du Peuple de 1875*. A week later, when he had still heard nothing, he urged that at least the *Almanach* be sent – 'le fer est chaud, il faut le battre'. He continued to ask for the Brussels Congress debates for the following eighteen months, but without success.[72]

By the summer of 1875 the section was large enough to need re-organization. Following a public meeting held by the section in June, whose success led the *Bulletin* to remark that 'L'Internationale d'ailleurs fait dans la ville fédérale des progrès de plus en plus rapides', the section was divided into four groups, each group representing a district of the town and electing one member to each of the section's three committees. But the rearrangement proved unsatisfactory to Brousse. On 26 August a meeting of the section declared it dissolved and confided its possessions (finance, library) to the Federal Committee with the proviso that they should be returned if a new section were founded. On the following day several members of the dissolved section, including Brousse, founded the Section de Berne, adopted the statutes of the former section and applied for membership of the Jura Federation. The manœuvre was designed to get rid of the former treasurer of the section – a man named Castellon – and two of his friends, Lausraux, a Communard and Jarretout, who controlled the library of the section. This group alleged that the June reorganization had threatened Brousse's control of the section, and that whereas at first it had been content to permit him to dominate it, its members now wanted to act independently. Brousse in turn alleged that the minority group was worthless and hinted that it may have challenged his leadership: 'il y a parmi eux une véritable canaille et 9 idiots qui le suivent parce qu'il est frrrrançais parrrrisien [*sic*].'[73]

In any event, after this minor upheaval the new Berne section continued the work of its predecessor and from 1875 rapidly grew in strength. In the following winter the section organized a series of meetings between sections in the area – Sonvilier, Basle, Vevey, Geneva and Fribourg – with Guillaume, Schwitzguébel, Joukowsky and Lefrancais, as well as Brousse himself, as the leading speakers.[74] These meetings helped to increase membership, and in February 1876 the section lent its support to a strike of printers, aimed at gaining higher wages, which threatened to halt official publications of the Swiss Government. The event brought the activities of the section to the attention of the public, and at the beginning of March a Catholic newspaper, under the headline 'Le Socialisme à Berne', commented:

l'apparition du socialisme à Berne . . . est un fait qui ne doit pas passer inaperçu. L'audace avec laquelle se produisent ses doctrines inspire certains inquiétudes même dans le sein du libéralisme officiel . . . on ne croyait pas jusqu'à présent que le lèpre du socialisme put être facilement inoculée au peuple bernois, que des qualités solides semblerait devoir préserver plus facilement de ce poison du monde moderne . . . Le socialisme se prépare à faire une tentative sur l'ancien canton de Berne . . . il y a à Berne une section très active de l'Internationale. . . .[75]

Despite its alarmist overtones, the newspaper was hardly exaggerating the impression that the section under Brousse's leadership was making. Far from confining its activities to the French-speaking population of Berne, the International was gaining support amongst the German-speaking workers. The successful involvement of this section of Swiss society in the anarchist movement was another of Brousse's achievements.

At the 1874 Annual Congress at La Chaux-de-Fonds it was decided, largely on Brousse's insistence, that although the cost of printing the *Bulletin* in two languages was prohibitive, a flysheet in German should be printed and distributed amongst the German-speaking workers, who were very largely under the influence of the reformist Arbeiterbund and its leader, Hermann Greulich. Five hundred copies of the flysheet, the *Socialdemokratischer Bulletin,* about fifty copies of which went into Germany and were the first anarchist propaganda seen there since the 1840s, were printed in May 1874.[76] In Berne a small study group called the Socialdemokratischer Klub was founded in January 1875, changing its name a year later to Socialdemokratischer Verein. The Verein decided in March 1876 to commemorate by a public procession the declaration of the Paris Commune. The procession was broken up by a hostile crowd enraged at the sight of the red flag. Fortunately Brousse had decided to attend a similar meeting at Lausanne on that day, for much of the anger of the crowd was directed against his name and a German exile mistaken for him narrowly escaped being severely beaten up by the crowd.[77] Brousse blamed the personal campaign against him on the conservative newspaper of Berne, *Das Intelligenzblatt* (he referred to it as 'L'Intelligence plate'), which had already campaigned against his tenure of a University post which only Schwarzenbach's personal intervention had kept secure.

The occasion for this earlier attack on his position at Berne had been a meeting of Jura anarchists held at Bienne in the previous October. The *Feuille de Correspondance de Bienne* had reported the meeting in a rather lurid light, relating how a group of thirty socialists, 'drinking absinthe and vermouth round a huge table, had called for bloody Revolution and the guillotine', and (what seems to have shocked the paper most): 'quatre dames, une Français et trois Russes, fumant la cigarette et prenant aussi l'absinthe, prenaient part à la discussion.'[78] The foreign element in Swiss socialist agitation was one which provided a main theme for hostile press reaction, and

the *Intelligenzblatt,* following up on the report of the *Feuille,* had
pointed its accusing finger at Brousse, who was present at the meeting,
saying that only a few days previously the Berne Conseil d'Etat had
confirmed Brousse's position as an assistant to Schwarzenbach;
'Should such posts be given to foreigners who abused Swiss liberties?'
the paper asked, making it very clear its own views on the subject.
Fortunately for Brousse, Schwarzenbach came to his defence, and he
remained an assistant at the University until his resignation in the
early part of 1877.

The March demonstration had the immediate result of leading to a
rapprochement between the German-and French-speaking societies
in Berne, and on 21 April 1876 the Verein joined the Jura Federation.
At a meeting of the two sections on the following day Zhukovsky
urged the Verein to adopt the statutes of the French-speaking
section.[79] Brousse likewise urged their close co-operation, and when
the Verein did finally draw up its statutes, some time before August
1876, they carefully side-stepped the potentially divisive issue of
electoral tactics and went on to state that:

le mode d'action le plus important pour le Socialdemokratischer Verein,
parce que tous ses membres peuvent y prendre une part active, est la
propagande par la parole, par la presse, des principes du socialisme
révolutionnaire. En cas de révolution sociale dans un pays quelconque,
le Socialdemokratischer Verein déclare de son devoir à faire à l'organisation révolutionnaire de ce pays l'offre de son concours résolu.[80]

If Brousse's role in the establishment of the original Socialdemokratischer Klub is unknown, it is clear that he played an important
part in the Verein. His name headed the list of over sixty signatures
which followed the statutes, and Natalie Landsberg's name, as well
as those of half a dozen Russian students,[81] also appeared. If there
were any more doubt it would be dispelled by the appearance of *Die
Arbeiter-Zeitung,* a paper mainly edited by Brousse, on 15 July 1876.
It owed its appearance to Brousse's energy, Landsberg's financial
help[82] and the co-operation of three German exiles, Werner, Rinke
and Reinsdorf. It was, in Rocker's words:[83] 'The first organ in the
German language which represented explicit anarchist principles . . .'
As the newspaper explained in its first leading article:

The economic situation and the impending revolutionary crisis are more
important than the purely political agitation with which we are concern-
ing ourselves almost exclusively at present. It may be that tomorrow the

Revolution may burst upon us. Have we thought about the basic principles of the new society? In our opinion there remains much to be done in this respect. For this reason we wish to concern ourselves almost entirely with such matters of principle.[84]

The *Arbeiter-Zeitung* in fact appeared simultaneously with a new phase in the anarchist movement, characterized by a commitment to anarcho-Communism and propaganda by the deed. The paper published an account of the resolution on anarcho-Communism which was passed at the Florence Congress of the Italian Federation in August 1876,[85] and as early as December 1876 was recommending propaganda by the deed as an effective political method. Its extremism as compared with the *Bulletin* edited by Guillaume was very probably instrumental in preventing a *rapprochement* between the Jura Federation and the Arbeiterbund of Greulich, for which Guillaume may have been working at this time. Its appearance certainly led to a long polemic between the Jura anarchists and Greulich throughout 1876–7.[86] But the paper did not confine its attention to Switzerland. It also acted as a centre for anarchist activity in Germany in much the same way, although on a much smaller scale, as Becker's Geneva section of the International had served as the centre for the German sections of the Association. In August 1876 Reinsdorf visited Berlin, Leipzig and other German towns spreading anarchist propaganda. He met Johann Most, then still a member of the Social Democratic Party, on whom he made some impression, and in May 1877 there was an abortive plan to send him to the Gotha Congress of the German Party.[87] After the paper disappeared in August 1877 Reinsdorf and Werner became the leading exponents of anarchism in Germany, at least until Most emerged as the leader of German anarchism at the end of the decade. The paper even penetrated to Paris where Kropotkin found support for it amongst groups of Russian exiles.[88]

By the middle of 1876 Berne had become one of the main centres of the Swiss anarchist movement. The Socialdemokratischer Verein had about sixty workers and students amongst its membership, the Section de Berne about twenty, and in addition an Italian section was founded in June, following agitation amongst the Italian immigrant labourers who came for seasonal work. Meetings of the groups in Berne were sometimes attended by 200 people, no mean achievement at a time when support was falling off elsewhere in the Jura Federation.[89]

The prestige of the movement in Berne was enhanced by two events

in the autumn of 1876: Bakunin's death and burial there, and the
holding of the Eighth Congress of the International.

In June 1876 Bakunin had left Lugano in order to stay with his old
friend, Adolphe Vogt, in Berne. He arrived in failing health and died
in the Mattenhof clinic on 1 July. His presence had been unknown
to the Berne anarchists and Brousse was informed of it by a Russian
medical student only shortly before Bakunin died. The funeral on 3
July provided an occasion for a meeting of the leading Jura anarchists. Guillaume, Schwitzguébel, Zhukovsky, Elisée Reclus and
Brousse all delivered graveside speeches, Brousse speaking in the
name of 'la jeunesse révolutionnaire française'. The funeral was
followed by a meeting held at the Socialdemokratischer Verein where
a resolution was passed unanimously calling for the end of personal
and doctrinal divisions within the European socialist movement. It
was pointed out that the 1873 statutes of the International were
sufficiently broad to permit the entry of parties with political tactics
different from those of the anarchists.[90] This spirit of *rapprochement*
was reflected three months later at the Eighth Annual Congress of the
International, which was held at Berne – a considerable fillip for
Brousse's prestige within the movement. But ironically it was Brousse
who was to lead the opposition to such a *rapprochement*.

7. *The Berne Congress of the International, 1876*

The Berne Congress[91] was attended by the leading members of the
European socialist movement, amongst whom were de Paepe,
Guillaume, Vinas (under the pseudonym of Sanchez), Malatesta and
Brousse himself. The German Social Democratic Party sent one of its
deputies, Vahlteich, as an observer, while Greulich attended as an
observer of the Schweizerische Arbeiterbund. This representation
was a gesture towards reconciliation of the various socialist groupings
in Europe, a fact which was in itself a recognition of growing divergence and the hardening of doctrinal positions.

De Paepe had by this time come down more firmly on the side of
the Statists, defining the State as the representative of the general
interests of society. His commitment to the Jacobin concept of
Revolution was more explicit than at any previous Congress. He now
envisaged a transitory period after the Revolution in which the
workers would seize and use the powers of the State.[92]

In opposition to both de Paepe and Vahlteich the anarchists

reaffirmed their belief in future society as a free federation of autonomous Communes. Significantly, they revealed an increased emphasis
on the Commune rather than the local or regional federation of
trades unions as the nucleus of future society. Brousse went out of
his way to emphasize that the individual was not only a producer but
also a consumer; therefore, he said, there was need for a federation
of consumers represented by the Communes.[93] This emphasis foreshadowed the commitment of the anarchists to anarcho-Communism
which took place over the following two years. It can be seen both as
a reaction against the syndicalism of de Paepe, compounded by the
failure of the Jura Federation to gain much working-class support,
and possibly to the influence of the Italians who had adopted
anarcho-Communism at their Congress at Florence in the preceding
month.

The Congress revealed clearly that deep doctrinal divisions still
existed within the European socialist movement, and although a
resolution by de Paepe calling for the convening of a World Socialist
Congress to be held at Ghent in the following year was accepted, in
spite of Italian opposition and Spanish abstention, this indicated no
more than a wish to prolong the honeymoon and present a united
front to the outside world.[94] Disagreements developed as soon as
matters of substance were raised.

De Paepe's object in calling for the convening of the World Socialist
Congress was to consider a revival of the old International. While
both Guillaume and Brousse, for the Jura Federation, were adamant
that the Congress should not be convened to discuss the creation of
a new international organization – the St Imier International, they
argued was sufficient – they differed as to how the International
should be represented at the Congress. Guillaume suggested that each
federation of the Association should send a delegate, the ensemble
of delegates then forming in effect a collective delegation. Brousse
disagreed, saying that the International should be represented by
only one delegate or delegation, as should each of the other major
organizations such as the German Social Democratic Party and the
English trade-union movement. This of course was difficult to
reconcile with the theory on which the International was based – the
autonomy of groups and federations – but there was in Brousse's
mind the fear that, faced at the Congress with the question of political
participation in parliamentary activities, the federations would show
divergent viewpoints and the unity of the International would be

shattered (he was thinking especially of the Belgians). What this meant was that Brousse now saw the International as an *anarchist* organization (i.e. an organization committed specifically to anarchist doctrine). This contrasted with his previous position when he had seen it as an organization of autonomous movements committed to a variety of ends. This view differed from that of Guillaume who now – as before – was playing an intermediary role between extremes. Guillaume's view prevailed at the Congress, and Brousse took the issue sufficiently seriously to claim in a letter he wrote shortly afterwards to Jacques Gross, a co-*militant* within the Federation, that the Congress had challenged the whole basis of the International: 'il vient de changer à mes yeux le pivot même de notre action politique'. Since 1873, he continued, anarchism and abstention had been triumphant within the International, and at Berne itself he had even begun to win over the German workers to anarchism. The Congress had now put a question mark over anarchism. So far as he was concerned, he said, he would do his utmost through public meetings and propaganda on the subject of anarchism to force a firm direction on the movement before the World Congress at Ghent. He finished his letter by hinting at a split between himself and the *Bulletin* (i.e. Guillaume).[95]

This letter to Gross is important as it marks the beginning of the split with Guillaume and of Brousse's fervent advocacy of extremist anarchism over the next two years. It pointed forward to the effective opposition by Brousse to the conciliatory position of Guillaume, whose view of the Berne Congress was diametrically opposed to that of Brousse (he called it 'une affirmation énergique de vitalité).[96] This conflict between Brousse and Guillaume forms the main theme of the following chapter. Before examining that however it might be useful to summarize Brousse's position as it stood immediately following the Berne Congress.

In the period between his arrival in Switzerland in September 1873 and the Berne Congress of the International in September 1876, Brousse had built up a successful organization in Berne and had helped to spread anarchist propaganda amongst the German-speaking population, for whose benefit he had brought out the *Arbeiter-Zeitung*. He had published two pamphlets which set out in detail his views on anarchism of the movement in the Jura. His reaction to the conciliatory overtures towards other, non-anarchist components of the European socialist movement manifested at the Berne Congress indicated that the extremist views he had first expressed at the Geneva Congress had by no means moderated, and had indeed become intransigent. In the attempts to find some common ground between the rapidly diverging positions of the anarchists and the more orthodox socialists in the period 1876–7, Brousse's propagandist activities were, in conjunction with those of fellow anarchists such as Andreas Costa and Jules Montels, intransigent and unreconciliatory, and were instrumental in creating a deep and unbridgeable gulf between the two sides. They also led him into conflict with the doyen of the Jura anarchists, James Guillaume.

3

'A Universal Anarchist'

1. The conflict with Guillaume

(a) Propaganda by the deed

The defeat of the Paris Commune and the international climate of the following years deflated the revolutionary expectancies of the European socialists. At the same time the Commune gradually attained the status of a myth. This process was achieved by about 1875 or 1876[1] and carried particular force within the anarchist movement; the Paris Commune as an inspiration to action entered into its daily vocabulary. Prior to that, relative neglect of the Commune had been a noticeable and surprising feature of the movement.[2]

The *militants* of the Jura looked mainly to France for inspiration, believing that it was France which would eventually emancipate humanity.[3]

L'émancipation sera le résultat d'une révolution partie de Paris; au signal de cette révolution se leveront les peuples et *fragments de peuples* qui ont le feu révolutionnaire – la Suisse française, la Belgique française; quant aux flamands ils feront comme les Suisses allemands – ils nous regarderont tranquillement nous battre.

Their realization that nothing could be expected for some time from that quarter was compounded by the failure of the movement in the Jura to gain mass support, or even establish any fruitful contact with the working class. This latter failure was partly due to the crisis within the watch-making industry, the effects of which began to be felt in 1874. It had the result of concentrating the efforts of the Jura Federation on the need for effective propaganda.

The report of the Federal Committee of the Federation to the Annual Congress of 1874 called for the creation of small socialist libraries within each section so that members could learn elementary socialist principles, and it instigated moves towards frequent meetings between sections in order to discuss matters of common concern. The effort was directed mainly towards the education of the committed rather than to the conversion of the uncommitted. This inward-looking attitude was, by implication, criticized by Guillaume in the *Bulletin* in terms which suggested a pessimistic evaluation of the possibilities of popular support for the Federation. The people were not inaccessible, he argued, only

... pour se faire écouter d'eux, il faut leur parler un langage qu'ils comprennent, il faut savoir aller à eux fraternellement, ne pas se laisser rebuter par leurs préjugés, leur ignorance, souvent leur méfiance et leur grossiérté. La propagande chez nous ne se pratique pas avec assez de méthode et d'une manière assez soutenue; mieux conduite, et faite surtout sur un meilleur plan et avec plus d'entente de la situation, elle donnerait certainement des résultats, beaucoup plus considérables.

Propaganda was not enough, however. The economic crisis in the watch-making industry led, rather to the surprise of leading *militants,* to a diminution of support and activities, so that Schwitzguébel was led to declare at the Annual Congress of the following year that 'dans la période de réaction que nous subissons, le maintien des sections [est] déjà en lui-même un progrès'.[4] In fact the Federation had singularly failed to revolutionize the working-class organizations,[5] so that once again at the 1875 Congress a great deal of time was spent in discussing methods of socialist agitation and propaganda. On Schwitzguébel's recommendation it was agreed that sections should profit from every circumstance to organize propaganda meetings, should organize meetings among the working class, and should encourage the formation of trade and industrial sections. The Berne section (i.e. Brousse) urged in addition that members of the Federation should be encouraged to go and live in areas where there were no sections, and should if necessary be supported financially by the Federation in their efforts to build up support in such areas. In addition, he argued, the Jura *militants* should practise international solidarity and continue to help Communard refugees, on the grounds that 'la propagande des principes [doit] être appuyé par des faits'.[6]

One of the central difficulties was that the *militants* themselves had not yet received their education and had drawn no clear conclusions from the lesson of the Commune. It was probably no accident, therefore, that in February 1876 Brousse published, in the name of the Berne section, a Manifesto addressed to all the sections of the International

calling for a grand banquet to celebrate the anniversary of the
Commune, which would be followed by discussions on its implications for the socialist movement. The Manifesto read in part:

> Qu'est-ce que cette chose donc, la Commune? Cette chose qui reparaît
> invariablement à toute les grandes époques de l'histoire? Est-ce un
> principe, est-ce un instrument? Serait-ce à la fois l'un et l'autre?
>
> Si la Commune est un principe, il est urgent de savoir quel doit être
> son rôle organique dans une société scientifiquement constituée;
>
> Si la Commune est un instrument, quelque chose comme la véhicule
> de la révolution, la commune, compagnons, va revenir! Hâtons-nous
> alors d'étudier ces mouvements communalistes dans l'histoire et surtout
> celui de 71 afin que si ce dernier doit se reproduire, cette journée radieuse
> le 18 mars, n'aît pas pour lendemain cette journée funèbre, le 21 mai.
>
> Ces points d'interrogation méritent qu'on s'y arrête; cette énigme qui
> contient tout l'avenir, il faut en savoir le mot. Il faut en savoir le mot, car
> le sphinx révolutionnaire va repasser pour prendre sa proie ou sa réponse.
> La réponse? on l'a lui balbutiée au 18 mars, et il partit pour l'océan avec
> sa proie humaine. La réponse cette fois il faut l'articuler nettement, et
> nous pensons qu'il faut l'articuler nettement, et nous pensons qu'il faut
> que ce soit l'Internationale qui la lui donne. Pour cela il faut qu'il la
> connaisse. . . .[7]

The Manifesto indicated the considerable intellectual uncertainty
of the anarchists in defining the means and the ends of revolutionary
action in the period following the Paris Commune. Was the Commune
a revolutionary weapon? Was it to be a cornerstone of anarchist
society? Was it to be both, and if so what lessons were to be learned
from the experience of 1871? These questions reflected profound
uncertainty and came at a time when, as has been seen, the Jura
anarchists were groping towards self-definition and the formulation
of anarcho-Communism. Brousse's Manifesto was only one more
symptom of a situation in which doctrine was far from having been
replaced by dogma.

The meeting duly took place at Lausanne on 18 and 19 March.
Unfortunately no record of it was kept, but it was followed shortly
afterwards by an article of Guillaume in the *Bulletin*. In this article,
in an analysis of the reasons for the defeat of the Commune, Guillaume argued that the presence of the Prussian army and the failure
of the provinces to support Paris were only incidental factors; the
real fault lay with the revolutionaries themselves who had failed to
grasp what was needed. Hence the task now was to 'travailler sans

relâche à éclairer le peuple, à nous éclairer nous-mêmes, en étudiant et en discutant les divers points du programme de la Révolution . . .'[8]

Despite the fact that it was largely he who had initiated such a study it was not a project which, on its own, carried much attraction for Brousse, who in spite of unfavourable conditions had, by his own energy, succeeded in reversing the general trend of declining support for the Federation in Berne. Although he shared the basically pessimistic outlook on the chances of Revolution, he had begun his political career in the context of political turbulence and civil war and had developed his own idea of what propaganda should be in the columns of *La Solidarité Révolutionnaire*. At the Berne Congress he had heard Malatesta explain the background to the unsuccessful Bologna uprising of 1874 and the tactic adopted by the Italian socialists:

. . . la révolution consiste bien plus dans les faits que dans les mots, [etc.] . . . chaque fois qu'éclate un mouvement spontané du peuple . . . il est du devoir de toute socialiste révolutionnaire de se déclarer solidaire du mouvement qui se fait.

Moreoever, Maltesta had gone on to explain, the movement should seek to destroy existing institutions by force; a 'river of blood separated them from the future'.[9] Three months later Malatesta and Cafiero gave a more precise definition of their anarchist position on propaganda methods:

The Italian federation believes that the insurrectional fact, destined to affirm socialist principles by deeds, is the most effective means of propaganda and the only one which, without tricking and corrupting the masses, can penetrate the deepest social layers and draw the living forces of humanity into the struggle sustained by the International.[10]

The doctrine of propaganda by the deed expounded by Malatesta and Cafiero was a reversion to the 1873 formula of the Bakuninists in Spain, and it immediately drew Brousse's sympathetic attention. The *Arbeiter-Zeitung* became the first and foremost propagandist of the tactic within the Jura Federation, although it is doubtful if at first this was even noticed beyond the small circle of its immediate supporters. On 16 December 1876, two weeks after a brief mention of the tactic in the *Bulletin,* the *Arbeiter-Zeitung* recommended it as a method of action: 'We are primarily supporters of propaganda by the deed, of propaganda through action, always provided of course that this be treated seriously and not in an infantile fashion.'[11] The

doctrine, springing from the anarchist mystique of the intrinsic
revolutionary potential of the people, was to become a distinguishing
feature of the anarchist movement of the 1870s and 1880s, although
it very quickly became distorted into something very different from
that originally intended. The Benevento incident of April 1877 in
Italy was the most outstanding example of its application. This affair
involved a plan by Cafiero and Malatesta to provoke an insurrectionary uprising amongst the peasants in Southern Italy. In April
1877 small groups of anarchists occupied the village of Letino (near
Benevento), announced the deposition of Victor Emmanuel, and in a
symbolic gesture burned the land tax records. They had time to do the
same in the neighbouring village of Gallo before a battalion of infantry and two squadrons of cavalry forced them to disband and
disperse into the hills. Benevento, as an example of propaganda by
the deed, passed very quickly into the mythology of the anarchist
movement and was the first of a series of direct action activities by
anarchists which was to become a source of controversy and dissension within the socialist movement, and for many *militants* was the
touchstone by which socialist or anarchist orthodoxy was to be
judged. This kind of activity had however been anticipated (albeit on
a much less significant scale) in the Berne demonstration of 18 March
1877.

Guillaume later described this 'journée du 18 mars' as 'un incident
assez insignifiant'.[12] It certainly left no enduring mark on the European socialist movement. From another point of view however it was
of considerable significance, hinted at in Guillaume's further remark
that 'ce genre de propagande n'était pas celui qui convenait le mieux
au milieu où militait la Fédération Jurassienne'. Very briefly, it
signalized the growing divergence between Brousse and Guillaume,
the latter being opposed to Brousse's tactics and resenting his increasing predominance within the Jura movement. Brousse's effectiveness in rallying support for the International in Berne, and the
combination of events which led to attention being focused on it in
1876, had had the effect of making him an extremely influential
figure. Although Guillaume subsequently minimized this in his
history of the International it appears that he was seriously concerned
about it at the time. When Nettlau sent him a manuscript of his biography of Bakunin for comment, Guillaume noted at one point:
'Fâcheuse influence de Brousse à partir de 1876 environ: *il a eu
plus d'influence réelle que Bak* [unin].'[13] The 'journée du 18 mars'

crystallized the disagreement by emphasizing both Brousse's influence on the movement and the more intransigent attitude he was adopting on anarchist tactics.

The events of March 1876 in Berne, when the red flag carried by the procession had been attacked by a hostile crowd, led Brousse to a eulogy which marked the atmosphere in which a similar demonstration was planned to take place in the Federal capital on 18 March 1877, the anniversary of the Commune:

Le drapeau rouge a paru, le drapeau rouge a été déchiré, voilà la bourgeoisie dans l'ivresse . . . mais . . . comme l'ouvrier lui-même, le drapeau de l'ouvrier doit conquérir sa place au soleil, et pour cela nous savons qu'il faut qu'il soit déchiré et peut-être, hélas! troué de balles.[14]

When the idea for a repeat performance was put forward by several sections early in 1877, Brousse insisted that it be held once again in the federal capital. At a private meeting of the Jura anarchists held at La Chaux-de-Fonds in February 1877 he argued that such a demonstration would have enormous importance for the future of the International section in Berne. Guillaume disagreed, on the grounds that the Berne Internationalists were too preoccupied with what he termed 'une exhibition de parade' (i.e. a make-believe demonstration) and were neglecting the real purpose of the 18 March anniversary, which was propaganda for communalist and federalist ideas. Moreover, he added, it could have disastrous results, for either the procession would be attacked once again and the flag ripped to shreds or, if the Internationalists 'won', then their victory would run the risk of being achieved only at the cost of bloodshed or, at the worst, of loss of life (which, he hastened to add, was all very well in the Revolution, but not in a demonstration). But Brousse carried the day – 'il avait l'oreille des plus jeunes et des plus exaltés; sa verve mériodionale l'emporta'[15] – and the demonstration was agreed on.

It was clearly recognized from the very start that violence might break out. Kropotkin, the Russian anarchist who had arrived in exile in Switzerland only the previous month, wrote to Paul Robin, a French socialist who was then living in London, that: 'Quant à moi j'approuve entièrement de ce mode d'agir . . . ce sera de la propagande à coups de casse-têtes, et de revolvers s'il en faut',[16] while the circular of Brousse's section announcing the formation of a committee of organization and appealing for support gave an insight into the spirit in which the meeting was planned:

Nous ne devons pourtant pas vous cacher qu'une attaque de la bourgeoisie est possible. Il faut donc que dans la Jurassienne tous les socialistes qui n'ont pas le mot, Révolution, sur les lèvres mais qui l'ont aussi
au fond du coeur, ne reculent pour venir devant aucune sacrifice. Rien ne
doit les arrêter. Cet argument – la crise, ce prétexte – l'argent, existent
dans tous les mouvements populaires, et si on ne savait le surmonter une
fois il faudrait de propos délibéré se condamner à rester éternellement sur
le terrain de la théorie. Donc au 18 mars, tous au poste![17]

They were not disappointed. Brousse had written for the occasion a
militant song – which was sung to the tune of a popular Swiss
patriotic song – entitled Le Drapeau Rouge, whose refrain echoed
the remark he had made following the previous year's demonstration:

> Le voilà, le voilà, regardez!
> Il flotte, et fier il bouge,
> ses longs plis au combat préparés,
> osez le défier,
> notre superb drapeau rouge,
> rouge du sang de l'ouvrier![18]

The red flag had become the focus of the demonstration, which was
clearly conceived in a spirit of provocation, although there is no evidence to suggest that the anarchists did not believe they had every right
to organize a peaceful demonstration along these lines.

Members of the International, Communard refugees and sympathizers gathered in Berne from all parts of Switzerland for the
demonstration. In addition to Brousse and the members of the two
Berne sections, there were *militants* from many parts of Switzerland,
including Guillaume (who turned up with reluctance and, he claimed,
unprepared for violence), Schwitzguébel, Spichiger, Pindy and Kropotkin, as well as French and Russian refugees from Geneva.
Amongst these was Plekhanov, the leading light of the Kazan demonstration in St Petersburg of the previous December.[19] Several of the
participants were armed with sticks and truncheons.

The demonstrators – about 250 of them – gathered on the Place de
l'Ours early on the afternoon of 18 March, formed themselves into a
procession and moved off with Schwitzguébel at the head carrying
the red flag and preceded by a band. At the station they met demonstrators coming from Zurich and Basle. The procession then moved
off once again, but before it had gone more than a few yards the
Prefect of Berne, M. de Wattenwyl, accompanied by several

gendarmes, intervened to announce to Schwitzguébel that the carrying of the flag threatened public order, and it should be removed. Schwitzguébel refused. To reinforce the demand, several gendarmes – against Wattenwyl's orders – seized the flag Schwitzguébel was carrying, and immediately fighting broke out. Although fighting with drawn sabres, and reinforced by some soldiers, six of the police were seriously wounded. As the fighting was going on round Schwitzguébel, Brousse and several other demonstrators quickly hustled a second flag off to safety in the nearest café. After some time the demonstration continued to its original destination, the Langgasse, where it was greeted by a large and enthusiastic crowd which delegated four of its members to petition immediately for the release of those demonstrators who had been arrested. They marched off to the police headquarters and persuaded Wattenwyl to release the prisoners – there were only two of them – while the meeting continued at the Langgasse. When this meeting had finished it was followed by a *soirée familière* at which speeches, revolutionary songs and music alternated with the reading out of congratulatory telegrams and addresses from France (banquets commemorating the Commune were held at Sète and Béziers), Spain and other parts of Switzerland. On the following morning the *militants* paid a short visit to Bakunin's tomb and then dispersed to their various homes.[20]

The result of the demonstration was tremendous publicity for the activities of the International, a publicity which penetrated even to the columns of *The Times*.[21] Press reaction was almost unanimously hostile. The *Handels-Courrier* of Bienne characterized the Internationalists as 'excroissances de la société humaine', while the *Intelligenzblatt* reported (prematurely) that the Federal Government would bring in repressive measures against such demonstrations. A cause of particular bitterness amongst the anarchists was the attitude of the *Schweizerische Arbeiterbund* (Greulich's organization) in its organ *Die Tagwacht,* which called the demonstration a scandal – although *Vorwärts,* the organ of the German Social Democrats, was more sympathetic. An official inquiry was opened and investigations were carried out over a period of some months before twenty-nine of the participants were brought to trial – again amidst considerable publicity – in August.

Within the Federation the demonstration served to aggravate further the relations between Guillaume and Brousse. Although Guillaume slightly recanted some of his earlier scepticism, especially when the activities of the International were the subject of a mention in the opening debate of the following session of the Berne Grand Council in April, his tone in the *Bulletin* was restrained, his articles reflecting solidarity with the demonstrators rather than the exultant enthusiasm displayed by Brousse. He wrote to Kropotkin:

> Ici, l'impression produit par l'affaire de Berne me semble plutôt mauvaise que bonne; cela paraît avoir intimidé plusieurs de nos membres. . . .
>
> Théoriquement, je doute qu'avec une population comme le nôtre, des manifestations de ce genre aident à la propagande. A Neuchâtel, du moins, elles nous font plutôt reperdre le peu de terrain que nous avions gagné. Il est vrai que ce terrain était si peu sur, que ce n'est pas grand dommage.[22]

This final proviso was a pointer to the fact that Guillaume was losing influence over the main areas of support for the International, whose nucleus had moved from the old watch-making centres to Berne, Lausanne and Geneva.[23] Paul Robin wrote to Kropotkin from London expressing his own doubts on the value of such activities and, more significantly, his concern for the unity of action long displayed by the Federation:

> J'ai perdu petit à petit mes illusions sur notre nombre, et nos moyens matériels . . . votre lettre m'enlève la dernière sur l'accord qui règne entre les internationaux actifs sur les questions les plus essentielles. Je pensais qu'il existait un groupe compact en parfait accord, ayant tous les mêmes idées que Guillaume. De ce groupe j'étais. . . .[24]

Robin had hit the nail on the head: Guillaume's position was being challenged, and above all by Brousse. In letters both to Kropotkin and Guillaume, Brousse enthused over the results of the demonstration as seen both in Berne – where the section had doubled its membership – and in France, where it had produced a good effect amongst clandestine groups of the International.[25] The demonstration confirmed his belief in the need for direct action propaganda methods, i.e. *propagande par le fait*, of which he became the leading exponent outside Italy.[26]

It was above all however the example of the Italian anarchists and the Benevento affair which influenced the development of the theory of propaganda by the deed, although Brousse lent it a *nuance* which made his concept of the doctrine significantly different from that of Malatesta and Cafiero. What is of relevance so far as Brousse is concerned is that, at the same time as he was moving towards a similar tactic, the Italians threw the issue open to public debate within the European socialist movement – where it received a mixed reception – and gave him allies on the extremist wing of the anarchist movement. One of these allies was Andreas Costa, the organizing genius of the Italian socialist movement, with whom Brousse was to share over a number of years a strikingly similar political evolution.

Following the Benevento *débâcle* Costa fled to Switzerland. On 1 May Brousse wrote to Kropotkin that he expected Costa to arrive shortly, and on 10 May he wrote again mentioning that Costa had arrived, but with little more news of the affair than that already gleaned from other sources. On the following day Guillaume travelled to Berne to meet Costa face-to-face and obtain details of the affair, of which he privately disapproved very strongly, and publicly was noticeably cool about. So far as can be gathered Costa remained in Berne until August 1877, which was of considerable significance in the light of the fact that Brousse and Costa in that period emerged together as the undoubted leaders of the 'Left wing' of the anarchist movement within the International.[27] Whether or not there was direct personal influence of the one on the other cannot be proved, as there is no trace of correspondence between them – but it is more than likely; in any case they were already both moving towards a similar tactic, which brought them to the forefront of the international socialist movement.

In May 1877 the *Bulletin* announced that Costa would talk to a newly constituted section of the International at Geneva on 9 June on the subject of 'la propagande par le fait' – the first use of the phrase in print, at least in the *Bulletin*.[28] In July Guillaume was forced by illness to take a holiday for two or three weeks, and he left the editing of the paper in the hands of Kropotkin and Brousse. On 5 August an article written probably exclusively by Brousse but possibly in co-operation with Kropotkin, entitled 'La Propagande par le fait', appeared on the front page of the newspaper.[29] (For a similar article in *L'Avant-Garde* of 1878, see Appendix 3.)

In many ways this article merely repeated what Brousse had already written in *La Solidarité Révolutionnaire* four years previously on the role of popular agitation in bringing the working class into contact with the socialist movement. The basic message was: if the worker cannot read propaganda, or is too exhausted to do so, then action must show him the way. What, Brousse asked, had fixed in the minds of the people the principle of the autonomy of the Commune? The Paris Commune itself. The people could understand the principle only when

. . . l'idée eut été posée au grand soleil, en pleine capitale, sur les marches de l'hôtel de ville, qu'elle eut pris corps et vie, elle alla secouer le paysan dans sa chaumière, l'ouvrier à sa foyer, et paysans et ouvriers durent réfléchir devant ce point d'interrogation immense dressé sur la place publique.

But propaganda must not merely stimulate to action, it must teach. The Berne demonstration had revealed to the people the hollowness of the abstract liberties of the Swiss constitution, and at Benevento the socialists had burned the archives and revealed the superficiality of the State. The lesson was clear, and indicated the methods the anarchists should use in the revolutionary struggle – the conquest of the local Commune, whether leading to defeat or to victory:

Que l'on s'empare une fois d'une commune, que l'on y réalise la propriété collective, que l'on y organise le corps de métier et la production, les groupes de quartier, la consommation: que les instruments de travail soient dans les mains ouvrières, les ouvriers et leurs familles dans les logements salubres, les fainéants dans la rue; attaqué, que l'on lutte, que l'on se défende, que l'on soit vaincu, peu importe! L'idée sera jetée, non sur le papier, non sur un journal, non sur un tableau, elle ne sera plus sculpté en marbre, ni taillée en pierre, ni coulée en bronze: elle marchera en chair et en os, vivante, devant le peuple. Le peuple le saluera au passage.

This article is central to an understanding of Brousse's political outlook. Not only does it define the standpoint from which his possibilism was to evolve at the end of the decade (in this sense it marks no great evolution from his article of 1873, which similarly expressed the belief in the divisibility of the Revolution with the conquest – even if temporary – of local political power) but it also expresses his own deep and constant mistrust of theory as a guide to action. This is seen in the formulation of the tactic of propaganda by the deed as *example;* it did not matter if action was successful or not:

Les hommes qui ont pris part à ces mouvements [Kazan, Benevento, Berne] espéraient-ils faire une révolution? Avaient-ils assez d'illusions pour croire à la réussite? Non, évidemment. Dire que telle était leur pensée serait de les mal connaître, ou, les connaissant, calomnier. Les faits de Kazan, de Bénévant, de Bern, sont des actes de propaganda tout simplement.

The Manifesto of the French Federation of the International at the time of the affair also bore out the essentially propagandist nature of the tactic.

Pourquoi cette prise d'armes? Espérait-on le peuple mûr pour la révolution et croyait-on cette révolution possible? Loin de là ... la manifestation de Bénévant visait tout simplement un but de propagande.

La masse lit peu ... de quelle façon faire comprendre le socialisme à ces populations pourtant si misérables, si révolutionnaires d'instinct et arriérées? Les membres de la Fédération italienne ont voulu dans *un fait vivant* developper à leurs yeux notre programme; ils ont voulu par la *pratique* apprendre le socialisme aux opprimés que la théorie ne saurait pénétrer.[30]

So far as Brousse was concerned the tactic paid lip service to the anarchist mystique of the revolutionary nature of the people (propaganda was to 'remuer la conscience populaire'), while in fact expressing no faith in it in the particular historical context. His formulation of the doctrine provided the perfect intellectual safety net; if one tried the tactic and succeeded – then all well and good; if one tried and failed – then it was propaganda by the deed. The formula was foolproof, and as such is of considerable significance. It expressed the central point of dilemma of the anarchist movement in the years following the Paris Commune and the failure in Spain. It was more than an historical accident. It was the attempt of the anarchists to square the circle, to reconcile their rhetoric with their action.

It is unlikely that Brousse's concept of propaganda by the deed was shared in quite so negative a way by the Italians, Malatesta and Cafiero, who were more optimistic of the chances of Revolution and who probably believed Benevento could succeed. Brousse was more realistic and did not believe in the chances of successful action. This makes it all the more significant that it was with Costa, not Malatesta or Cafiero, that he articulated the doctrine, for Costa had played a somewhat ambiguous part in the Benevento affair and there was a subtle nuance between his position and that of either Malatesta or Cafiero.[31] The 'acts' which Brousse advocated were in no sense acts of popular revolt. They were propaganda tactics which took as their starting-point the acceptance that no revolutionary situation existed. The adoption of the doctrine of propaganda by the deed was thus a symptom of the critical moment reached by the anarchist movement, a crossroads from which its leading *militants* were shortly to diverge in varying directions. Brousse and Costa chose one way, Malatesta and Cafiero (the latter at least until he began to lose his sanity) the other, although for some time anarchist rhetoric disguised this growing divergence.[32]

On a different level the doctrine expressed Brousse's own personal need for action and his belief that theory played only a secondary role. This belief remained with him throughout his political career and was later illustrated clearly in his opposition to Guesde's intransigent and purist revolutionary stance. As late as 1897 he was still expressing this belief when he told Huret that he was not primarily concerned with the basic theories of socialism and that

> ... il ne suffit pas de faire au peuple de grandes théories, il n'y a que les *faits* qui l'impressionent: Fourmies a produit davantage que tous les bouquins de Lafargue, toutes les doctrines de Karl Marx, et tous les discours de Guesde.[33]

(b) *The Congresses of 1877*

The formulation of the doctrine of propaganda by the deed was accompanied by an increasingly intransigent attitude on the part of the anarchists towards other groups within the European socialist movement. This clashed with the conciliatory attitude of *militants* such as de Paepe in Belgium and Guillaume in Switzerland. It was a development within the framework of the International which Brousse was later to criticize:

> Les marxistes furent vaincus. ... Mais nous, anarchistes, qui nous trouvions parmi des vainqueurs, nous commîmes loyalement une faute analogue. Nous essayâmes de faire encasquer toute l'Internationale dans le cadre étroit de notre doctrine: nous vainquîmes, au Congrès de Genève, le gouvernementalisme de Eccarius, de John Hales: à celui de Berne, l'étatisme de de Paepe; nous restâmes maîtres dans l'Internationale, oui, maîtres, mais isolés, impuissants, en face des masses bourgeoises coalisées contre la classe ouvrière que l'esprit de sectes avait si malheureusement émietté. A dater de ce jour, l'Internationale, en réalité, était mort.[34]

What Brousse could well have added, but did not, was that he himself was one of those mainly responsible on this premise for the collapse of the International, for in the critical years 1876–7 he was one of the main architects in the design to turn the International into a purely anarchist organization. Within the Jura Federation, this was seen in the conflict with Guillaume which reached its height in 1877.

The differences revolved round several issues. First, there was the fact that Brousse was a challenge to Guillaume's leadership in the Jura movement – hence Guillaume's remark on the Nettlau manuscript, which has already been quoted (p. 80). The challenge was illustrated by the way in which Brousse had successfully persuaded the Jura *militants,* against the wishes of Guillaume, to support the March 1877 demonstration in Berne. This partly reflected a profound difference in temperament between the two men, which can best be illustrated by recalling what has already been said of Brousse and comparing Kropotkin's descriptions of the two men in his memoirs. On the one hand was Guillaume,

. . . small, thin, with the stiff appearance and resoluteness of Robespierre, and with a truly golden heart which opened only in the intimacy of friendship,

and on the other, Brousse,

. . . a young doctor, full of mental activity, uproarious, sharp, lively, ready to develop any idea with a geometric logic to its utmost consequences; powerful in his criticisms of the State and State organization; finding enough time to edit two papers, in French and in German, to write scores of voluminous letters, to be the soul of a workmen's evening party; constantly active in organizing men with the subtle mind of a true southerner.[35]

Second, on the theoretical level their opposition can be seen as an expression of the tension inherent within anarchist theory between the 'communalist' and 'syndicalist' strands, with Brousse, supported by Kropotkin, taking the communalist position, Guillaume the syndicalist one. These two separate perspectives, which to a large degree reflected a constant tension within anarchist theory, also implied two separate and distinct strategies for the anarchist movement. The communalist position coincided (historically) with the adoption of propaganda by the deed, while the syndicalist position placed the main emphasis on building up a solid base of organized support within the trade-union movement.[36] In fact this can be seen as the second round of a battle which had previously been fought out between Guillaume and the Italian followers of Bakunin, in 1872.

The occasion of this first conflict was the decision of the Rimini Congress of the Italian Federation of the International in 1872 not to attend the Hague Congress, but instead to call for a meeting of the opponents of the General Council at Neuchâtel. In contrast the Jura Federation decided to send delegates to the Hague. Here Guillaume came into conflict with Cafiero – who in the event went to the Congress – over the need to win over the Belgians and Flemings who, though differing from the anarchist viewpoint, were likewise opposed to the General Council. Guillaume considered that the need to gain the support of the Belgians and Flemings was of more importance than insisting on doctrinal purity, and he was prepared to moderate his views in order to achieve this end. The result was that the Declaration of the Minority, which was written by Guillaume, aroused Bakunin's criticism on the grounds that it was too moderate. Guillaume's continuing difference with the Italians at the St Imier Congress was later noted by Nettlau, who analysed the presence of two conflicting tendencies. On the one hand, he said, were Cafiero and Bakunin, relatively unconcerned with those who did not share their own ideas, and preoccupied above all with 'l'affirmation, action révolutionnaire'; and on the other Guillaume and the Jurassians, seeking 'la solidarité de toutes les fédérations de l'Internationale dans la lutte entre le capital et le patronat'. Guillaume's aim was to 'réunir et à maintenir ensemble, non les groupes anarchistes, mais tous les adhérents par une solidarité et une tolérance réciproques'.[37] Guillaume's viewpoint predominated at St Imier, and the anti-authoritarian International was established on the basis of the international solidarity of working-class organizations. (The dualism within anarchism between the syndicalist (broad-based) and communalist (narrow-based) traditions was later clearly revealed in the debates at the 1907 Amsterdam Congress of Anarchists. On the one hand was, e.g. Pierre Monatte and on the other hand the older anarchists such as Emma Goldmann and Enrico Malatesta.)[38]

Guillaume remained the foremost proponent of the establishment of a strong syndical basis for the Jura Federation – while still being strongly committed to an 'inner core' within it – and it was no accident that, having left the Jura and spent almost twenty years of self-imposed political abstention in Paris, he should re-emerge as a supporter of the revolutionary syndicalist movement. Indeed he prefaced the final section of his *Documents et Souvenirs* with the remark: 'Qu'est-ce que c'est La Confédération Générale du Travail sinon la continuation de l'Internationale?' Thus he did not consider, for instance, Kropotkin's ideas to be a 'true' expression of the ideas of the International. In a letter he wrote in 1912 to Fritz Brupbacher, who was in correspondence with him over the latter's projected biography of Bakunin, he dismissed the influence of Kropotkin (or Jean Grave, or Sebastian Faure, who were leading figures of the French anarchist movement from about 1880 onwards) on the rise of the French revolutionary syndicalist movement. He named instead Pelloutier and Pouget who had learned, he said, through Bakunin and others, 'les véritables idées de l'Internationale'.[39]

It was therefore quite consistent that Guillaume lent more weight than either Brousse or Kropotkin to the project for a Pact of Solidarity amongst the sections of the European socialist movement, which was one of the points put forward for discussion at the Ghent World Socialist Congress. Relying as he did on working class rather than doctrinal solidarity, Guillaume's position contrasted with that of Brousse, who was only secondarily concerned with syndicalist issues and was at this stage an anarchist purist who saw Guillaume's position at the Berne Congress as a threat to the basis of the (anarchist) International. In taking this position Brousse was supported by Kropotkin and Costa. Thus a further letter of Guillaume to Brupbacher is significant. In this letter Guillaume described his own position – and that of the Jura Federation – in the conflicts of the 1870s as reconciliatory, and went on to say that: 'l'attitude intransigeante était prise à l'occasion par des camarades étrangers accueuillis par nous dans la Fédération Jurassienne, comme Brousse, Kropotkin, Costa, etc.'[40]

In this statement Guillaume revealed more of the motive behind his decision to leave the movement (he left for Paris early in 1878) than he did in his *Documents et Souvenirs,* when he alleged personal reasons. Both Costa and Kropotkin became active in the Federation in 1877 and linked hands with Brousse in his own rivalry with the self-appointed 'moral guardian' of the Jura Federation. Guillaume's resentment against 'foreigners' in the Federation was justified from this viewpoint. While Costa remains something of an unknown quantity, Kropotkin was certainly closer to Brousse than to Guillaume and was influenced by Brousse's 'dynamism' which, in the view of his biographers, helped to turn Kropotkin away from Guillaume's parochialism.[41] It was certainly Brousse's influence for example which determined Kropotkin's cool attitude towards the Russian exile group in Geneva,[42] and the two conducted a fairly close correspondence throughout Kropotkin's stay in the Jura (February 1877–August

1877), creating together *L'Avant-Garde,* the organ of the French
Federation of the International. (See p. 106.)

The project for a World Socialist Congress and a Pact of Solidarity
had first been discussed at the Berne Congress. As has been seen, it
raised severe doubts in Brousse's mind. On 15 July, immediately
prior to the 1877 Annual Congress of the Jura Federation at St Imier,
he published an article on the subject of the projected Pact in *L'Avant-
Garde,* the newspaper which he had founded in June 1877. This was
strongly anti-conciliatory, and by implication anti-Guillaume. He
contested the conciliators' case on three grounds. First, those who
argued that the International as reconstituted in 1873 was sufficiently
broad-based to allow the entry of movements working towards a
common end, but with different tactics (which was the kernel of
Guillaume's position), overlooked the fact that in some countries the
International was illegal, and that therefore socialists would have to
accept illegality or association with it. Second, the Congress of
Geneva had been taken by the authoritarians as a defeat, and it was
unrealistic to expect them now to enter the existing organization.
Finally – and this was the most important factor – whereas the International in 1873 had responded to an actual situation, where each
national grouping *had* been autonomous and expressed the tactic
suitable and peculiar to its own country, this was no longer so. Here
Brousse referred to the creation of anarchist groups in Germany
following the propaganda work of *Die Arbeiter-Zeitung.* In such
circumstances, he asked, how was reconciliation possible? To expect
the German Social Democrats to be conciliators was equivalent to
asking them to commit suicide. Moreover, the experience of the last
year had revealed to the anarchists the absence of any conciliatory
spirit within, for instance, the *Arbeiterbund.* The only valid conclusion
was that the authoritarians were the enemies of the anarchists. If their
État ouvrier or their Volkstaat was ever accomplished it would be the
duty of anarchists to fight it – so why not start immediately? Brousse
ended his article by saying that he would welcome solidarity only on
condition that autonomy and freedom were written into the programme of each socialist group.

This Manifesto was issued to dissuade the Jurassians at their
Annual Congress at St Imier from supporting conciliation. Brousse
wrote to Kropotkin asking his opinion of it and suggested that, if he
approved, Kropotkin should draw up a circular to show to the
'intimes' before the Congress.[43]

The St Imier Congress of the Jura Federation met on 4 August. The main issue to be decided was the attitude of the Federation to the various issues to be discussed at the Ghent Congress. These were (a) the Pact of Solidarity, (b) the organization of *corps de métiers* (trades unions), (c) the attitude of the working class towards political parties, (d) the analysis of capitalist society and the trends of modern production. There was also the question of voting methods at the Congress, included on the agenda at the request of Brousse. On this latter question, the Congress decided that the Federation would be represented at the coming Congress of the International, to be held at Verviers immediately prior to the Ghent Congress, by several delegates of the Jura sections, each delegate having as many votes as sections he represented. On representation at Ghent the Congress left the matter open, but referrred the Federation to its decision on the Verviers Congress.

On the face of it this might seem to have represented a defeat for Brousse, who had argued at the Berne Congress in 1876 for a single delegation for the International at Ghent. But the position had now changed, and within the International the anarchists were in a much stronger position. Not only had Brousse's position within the Jura Federation itself been strengthened,[44] but the firm support of the Italians could now be relied on, and it is reasonable to assume that Brousse no longer feared the adverse influence of the Belgians as he had done in 1876.

The St Imier Congress reached no clear-cut decisions on the subjects to be discussed at Ghent. Having heard Brousse speak on the Pact, Montels on political action, Schwitzguébel on the role of the *corps de métier* and Costa on the tendencies of modern production, a committee composed of Guillaume, Brousse and Costa was formed to draw up a composite resolution. The Committee's report was a compromise between the positions of Brousse and Guillaume, with the balance tilting in favour of the former. Declining to draw up a precise mandate the report sought merely to lay down a general line of conduct. Having outlined and reaffirmed its anarchist *credo*[45] it continued by reserving the right to combat parliamentarism not only in Switzerland but in countries where it was liable to gain the support of the majority of the working class. This was a clear reference to Germany and Belgium, and thus a concession to Brousse. Moreover, the report continued, the anarchists should allow no attack on any organization which adopted anarchist tactics, and if a Pact of Solidarity was suggested at the Congress:

Ils ne devraient l'accepter que s'il laissait à chaque organisation, dans chaque pays, sa complète autonomie, et n'empêchait pas la propagande de nos principes même dans les pays où des principes et des moyens différents prévaudraient; ce ne devrait être qu'un pacte de solidarité économique. . . .

While this again reflected Brousse's position, the committee also stated that the delegates of the Federation should point out to the Congress that the International itself was an adequate organization for the co-operation of the European movements – an argument the validity of which Brousse had already questioned in *L'Avant-Garde* on 15 July. On the whole however the committee's report was favourable to the known views of Brousse and Costa, and Brousse certainly interpreted it himself in these terms.[46] The Congress had witnessed a spirit of militancy of which Guillaume must have disapproved. This was perhaps best expressed in the report of the Geneva Section de Propagande to the Congress. This report said that since the Berne Congress, when solidarity appeared possible, the events of Berne and Benevento had clarified the situation to reveal that the anarchists could not count on the solidarity of all sections of the socialist movement (a reference to, e.g. Guesde's attack on Benevento and Greulich's on the Berne Demonstration), singling out particularly 'les organes officiels du parti Marxiste . . . [qui] . . . nous ont prouvé que tout mouvement révolutionnaire leur est odieux'. Was solidarity possible when this group denied 'ce droit éternel inherent à l'homme, l'Insurrection'? It would be necessary to re-affirm at Ghent (a) the abolition of the State, (b) political abstention, (c) the inanity of working-class candidates, (d) the value of various means of propaganda and notably le propagande par le fait. The report continued:

les derniers événements de Berne et d'Italie ont été mal jugés, il serait très bon selon nous de profiter de l'occasion du Congrès pour les expliquer à nouveau et surtout pour démonstrer que la propagande par les actes est le plus efficace des moyens dont nous disposons.[47]

The St Imier Congress of the Federation was followed by the Ninth Congress of the International, which met at Verviers on 6 September, and was scheduled so that its closure should coincide with the opening of the Ghent Congress. Guillaume represented the main body of the Jura sections – twenty-two of them – while Costa was delegate

for several Italian sections, Brousse and Montels for sections of the
French Federation and Kropotkin for several Russian groups. In
addition Rinke and Werner represented sections in both Switzerland
and Germany, while there was a strong delegation from the Verviers
region, the last stronghold of anarchism in Belgium.

The central issue facing the Verviers Congress, as at the St Imier
Congress, was the position to be adopted at the forthcoming Ghent
Congress, and discussion on this was reserved till the final day of
debates. In the preceding debates however the quasi-unanimity displayed at St Imier between Guillaume, Costa and Brousse was
revealed as the uneasy compromise that it was. On the initiative of
one of the Spanish groups, the following proposition was put to the
Congress: 'Dans quelque pays que triomphe le prolétariat, nécessité
absolute d'étendre ce triomphe à tous les pays' – a 'permanent-
revolution' concept, consideration of which Guillaume attempted to
have put to one side by the Congress. Brousse and Costa however
presented a differently-worded but substantially identical resolution[48] which gained the approval of the Congress, with the exception
of Guillaume. Guillaume also appeared in a minority in a discussion
on propaganda by the deed, which the Spanish Federation insisted
should be dealt with by the Congress. Although Brousse, Montels and
Guillaume said they had no mandates on the question they agreed it
should be discussed. This revealed (predictably) Brousse and Costa,
supported by Rodriguez (Vinas) in favour (Costa: 'il est donc de
notre devoir de mettre cette solidarité en pratique et de le prouver
par les faits'), while Guillaume supported a simple declaration of
solidarity. The discussion however was ended with the decision to
pass to the next business – it was clearly too inflammable an issue to
be brought to a vote.[49] Guillaume later (1910) described the Congress
as the beginning of the split between the 'extreme Left' and the Jura
Federation. He added that it was largely Brousse's attitude which had
provoked the split. His statement gives a good indication of the clash
of personalities:

Brousse, depuis un certain temps, prenait de plus en plus, dans ses
allures, quelque chose de débraillé et de 'casseur d'assiettes' qui m'était
antipathique: son langage se faisait, à dessein semblait-il, vulgaire et
cynique. Après avoir rimé le chanson le Drapeau rouge, dont la valeur
poétique est médiocre, mais dont l'intention était excéllent ... après
avoir fait sur le préfet de Bern ... des couplets gouailleurs ... il avait
continué par un chanson qui me déplaisait fort, et dont le refrain était

'Pétrolons, pétrolons les bourgeois et leurs maisons'. A tout propos il entonnait cette scie, que je trouvais odieuse; et comme il me voyait hausser les épaules à chaque nouvelle audition de sa dernière oeuvre, il n'était pas éloigné de me traiter de réactionnaire.[50]

This was the first occasion on which Guillaume mentioned the growing divergence between himself and the 'extreme Left', although the division can, as has been shown, be dated earlier.

None the less, despite these disagreements general agreement was reached on the attitude to adopt at the Ghent Congress – a general agreement which once again reflected an acceptance of the views of the intransigent anarchists, but which Guillaume chose not to oppose either because he had been convinced by them – which is unlikely – or out of loyalty to the majority decision – which is most likely. The Congress reaffirmed in strong terms its rejection of political action, characterized all political parties as reactionary and passed a resolution which stated that syndicalist organizations varied in revolutionary significance according to their milieu, and that in no circumstances could they be effective unless committed to revolutionary ends.[51] And on the Pact of Solidarity the Congress stated flatly that:

... reconnaissant qu'un Pacte de Solidarité ne peut être conclu entre l'Internationale et des organisations dont les principes et les moyens d'action sont différents des siens sur des essentiels, passe à l'ordre du jour.

Similarly, on the possible creation of a central corresponding bureau for all the European socialist movements, the Congress declared that the Federal Bureau of the International was adequate for the purpose, and rejected in advance any proposal to create a new organization of any kind. The anarchist intransigents, represented by Brousse, Costa and Vinas, had triumphed.

From the Verviers Congress the main body of delegates went on to the World Socialist Congress at Ghent. Here there were represented in addition to the Internationalists the 'political' Belgians (especially the Flemish), with César de Paepe as their main spokesman; the German, Swiss and Hungarian Social Democrats, represented by Liebknecht, Greulich and Frankel: the Commonwealth Club and the Kommunistischer Arbeitverein of London, represented by Hales and Maltman Barry; and a miscellaneous collection of various groups including the French Communard group in London, represented by

Bazin, and the Italian reformist socialist groups, represented by Tito Zanardelli.

The brainchild of de Paepe, the Congress was from the outset a disappointment, as de Paepe himself admitted to Malon. If he no longer expected, in the face of the intransigent anarchists, the creation of a new international socialist organization, he *had* expected more delegates from Germany (Liebknecht was its sole representative, and he arrived late and left early) and, of greater importance, he had expected to obtain the support of the English and French trade-union movements,[52] neither of which was represented.

The first topic of discussion – the tendencies of modern production – had been originally designed, when the project for the Congress was first suggested by de Paepe in 1876, to promote a discussion on collective property. But as the Congress was more narrowly composed than originally intended, and included only delegates who were already committed to collectivization, the discussion turned on the modalities or organization of collective property. This led to a predictable conflict between the anarchists and the State socialists. De Paepe expressed the fear that the possession of property by groups would lead to corporate monopoly, while Brousse and Guillaume argued that this would be avoided through contract and mutual guarantees. A discussion on the value of political action led to a violent argument between Liebknecht and Guillaume. Then the Congress went on to discuss the Pact of Solidarity, having decided that discussion on the *corps de métier* be postponed till after the debate on the Pact. De Paepe was to be further disappointed in this discussion, in which he argued forcefully that a Pact would help to prevent the irrevocable division of the European socialist movement into two hostile camps. But, as he wrote to Malon, the intransigent attitudes of the anarchists, who held that the International itself provided the necessary basis for any reconciliation (which they believed in any case to be impossible), influenced a sufficient number of delegates to defeat his proposition; Greulich, the *bête noire* of the Jura anarchists, voted with them on Guillaume's motion rejecting the Pact, as did Frankel of the Hungarian Social Democrats, while Barry, Zanardelli, Liebknecht and six others abstained. The Pact had fallen through. Later at a private meeting the 'authoritarians' set up their own federal bureau and declared their mutual solidarity.

With the rejection of the Pact, a project for the creation of a correspondence bureau to centralize information such as statistics on working-class conditions – which had been included on the agenda of the Congress assumed some importance. Guillaume tried to salvage this last hope. He admitted that the bureau would probably not function, but argued that it would be 'aux yeux de la bourgeoisie hostile comme un signe extérieur de l'unité du socialisme, un signe comparable à notre drapeau rouge qui malgré nos divisions n'en reste pas moins notre emblème à tous'. It was possibly, in its reference to the red flag, a sop to Brousse. But Brousse remained as intransigent as ever, and with Costa and Montels he made up the minority of three which voted against the proposal – a minority which de Paepe described as 'trois anarchistes-ultras, trois enragés et illuminés'.[53]

The Congress in fact consecrated the division within the socialist movement. With the existence of two organizations, the Federal Bureau (Ghent) and the International, organizational form was given for the first time to the split between the anarchists and socialists which had assumed a distinctive ideological content in the course of the preceding two or three years. This, and not the Hague or Geneva Congresses, was the final stage in the logic of events leading from the divisions within the First International.

2. The International and France: Brousse's role

It has been seen how Brousse played a crucial role within both the affairs of the Jura Federation and the Congresses of the International. But these were not the only spheres of his interest or activity. Indeed after 1877 they increasingly took second place to Brousse's interest in the development of the socialist movement in France.

His concern for the future of the movement there had been seen at the Geneva Congress of 1873, when he had fought for the right of the French sections to be treated on an equal footing with those of other countries. With the cessation of reports from France in the *Bulletin* after January 1873 it becomes difficult however to establish the extent and nature of the contact between the socialist movement in Switzerland and that in France, virtually forced underground by the Dufaure law and the trials of 1873. It is difficult also to know on what scale a genuine socialist movement existed in France, although it is clear that contact of some kind continued between the French and Swiss – or French refugee – socialists. Trials at Lyons in 1874 revealed that many of the leading local *militants,* such as Camet, were in quite close contact with the Jura. Individual refugees, such as Montels, kept in contact with groups inside France. But, as Nettlau said, the 'still life' of the International in France contrasted sharply with the vigour of the Italian and Spanish organizations which were more active than they had ever been before the crisis years of 1870–1.[54]

None the less it is evident that Brousse attempted some kind of organization in France following the Lyons trial of April 1874, for in the following month he wrote to the Federal Committee of the Jura Federation:

Le mouvement socialiste est loin d'être mort en France. Abattu à Lyon part le dernier procès il se relèvera bientôt dans cette région. Quant au Midi proprement dit, il vient de s'y former une fédération. Je fais au Comité cette confidence sous le sceau du secret le plus absolu. L'Internationale française vivra si on ne fait pas la faute d'attirer sur elle par des publications ou des correspondances l'oeil de la police. . . . [P.S.] . . . la 'fédération' ne fait pas partie de la fédération jurassienne mais se fera probablement représenter à Bruxelles comme l'an passé à Genève par une délégation spéciale.[55]

This report however is only a very insubstantial straw in the wind, and it was not until 1876, when the socialist movement was beginning to revive independently in France, that the French connection assumed any great importance in Brousse's activities.

The energies of the French labour movement after the defeat of the Commune had deprived it of its leaders and broken its organization were largely channelled into non-militant activities. The leader of the movement in these years was Barbaret, under whose influence it rejected strike action and concentrated on the creation of Chambres syndicales as the prior condition for the creation of producers' co-operatives, which were claimed as the panacea for the workers' problems. Politically the movement tended to support the Republicans.

By 1876 however the position had begun to change. Workers' delegations had been sent to the Vienna and Philadelphia International Exhibitions in 1873 and 1876, and in 1876 the first Labour Congress was held in Paris. Although the resolutions passed by the Congress were moderate, and reflected the predominant belief in co-operation and education as the levers of social progress, the Congress also called for separate class representation in Parliament. Chabert[56] one of the outstanding members of the delegation to

Vienna, and later to be one of the leading *militants* of the Possibilist Party in Paris – was one of those who called most firmly for separate representation.

The anarchists in the Jura praised the Congress, if only because it had succeeded in taking place. The most fulsome praise however came from Jules Guesde, by this time a fully-fledged socialist, who had returned to Paris in 1876. Writing in *Les Droits de l'Homme,* a Paris radical newspaper (with no connection with its namesake of a few years previously), he claimed that in establishing its separate class identity the Congress had been an event of the first order, and a fact of great political consequence. This and other articles by Guesde brought him in touch with a group of students who met regularly in the Café Soufflet in the Latin Quarter to discuss socialism, and he soon became its most influential member. Shortly afterwards Guesde was introduced to Marxism by Karl Hirsch, a German journalist who had been associated with the German Internationalists, and in November 1877 the group founded *L'Egalité,* the first newspaper in France to propagate Marxist – or rather semi-Marxist – ideas.

These developments took place within the context of the steady improvement in the position of the Republicans in France from 1876 onwards. The general elections of January 1876 produced a Republican majority in the National Assembly, and talk began to be heard of an amnesty for the Communards. On 16 May 1877 however the French President MacMahon dismissed his Prime Minister, the conservative Republican Jules Simon, and a period of political crisis followed in which the Monarchists (the 'Right') attempted to stem the tide of increasing Republican strength. This was the '16 May crisis'. Throughout the summer of 1877, following the dismissal of the National Assembly and the preparations for new general elections, France was in a state of political upheaval which contributed in no small part to some of the more extreme invectives of the French anarchist exiles. The October elections – for which the anarchists urged abstention – confirmed the strength of the Republicans and the weakness of the Right; fears of a *coup* by the Right which had been expressed soon dissolved. The senatorial elections of January 1879 further confirmed the Monarchists' decline and MacMahon resigned shortly afterwards, to be succeeded by Jules Grévy, a Republican. Although none of this meant that socialists could expect any degree of power within the near future – Grévy indeed even refused to contemplate Gambetta, the radical leader, for the Premiership – it did mean that normal civil liberties were gradually to be restored, the Communards were to return to France and the socialists were to enjoy both the hope and the means of creating a popular movement. If the crisis of 16 May led to the expression of extremist solutions on the anarchist side, the steady improvement in the political situation after the end of 1877 contributed to a new emphasis on the building up of a legal and organized party, and was ultimately to remove some of the most effective arguments the anarchists had employed for their total rejection of political action. This however is to anticipate.

At least as early as the middle of 1876 Brousse was in contact with the Guesdist group in Paris. The occasion was a projected International Students' Congress, which had first been suggested at the time of Michelet's funeral in May 1876. The Congress was to be distinctly socialist. The members of the organizing committee called themselves 'atheists, revolutionaries and socialists',[57] and the corresponding secretary, Victor Marouck, and its main organizer, Emile Massard, were both members of the Paris socialist group, and later entered the *l'Egalité* circle. In June 1876 Brousse wrote to *Les Droits de l'Homme* offering to assist the committee in any organizing work it required,[58] and from June to August – when the Paris police finally stepped in to ban the Congress – he remained in correspondence with Massard in Paris, and even formed a committee of socialist students at Berne, apparently to choose a delegate to the Congress.[59]

His contacts with the Paris group of socialists appear therefore to have been amicable in these early stages. But this was of short duration and did not last beyond about the middle of 1877. By July 1877 Kropotkin was writing to his friend Paul Robin in London that he was planning to visit Paris with the purpose of contacting Brousse's friends and 'paralysing the influence of Guesde'.[60] Guesde had of course been in disfavour with the anarchists ever since his strong attack on the Benevento affair of the preceding April, and his increasingly 'marxist' orientation merely served to aggravate the hostility. There were indications of some kind of *rapprochement* between the French anarchist exiles in the Fédération française and the Paris group in the middle of 1878, when Guesde defied an official ban on the holding of an International Socialist Congress in Paris; but this was in the nature of an exception, and it seems clear that from 1877 onwards Brousse considered Guesde as a political rival on all major counts.

The committee formed for the Student Congress of 1876 seems to

have continued in unofficial existence for some time after the intervention of the authorities, for it was responsible – or alleged by the
police to be responsible – for the spread of an exile publication, the
Almanach de la Commune, which was smuggled into France from
Geneva and was reported to be in circulation amongst students in
Paris in December 1876.[61] It appears that the leading figure in Switzerland responsible for its distribution was Natalie Landsberg, to whom
French socialists were requested to address queries on this and other
exile publications. In order to facilitate its circulation in France it
appeared under the curious title of 'L'Exil de Monseigneur Mermillod,
évêque de Genève et le sieur Carteret', under the name of a Catholic
publishing company.[62] This pamphlet was one of the rare co-operative ventures between the Jura anarchists and the far from-homo-
geneous Genevan French–Russian exile group, and was primarily
designed for circulation in France where it is more than likely that
it was also bought and distributed by the Russian exile group there.[63]
It is clear that Brousse was connected with several leading members
of the Russian communities both in Switzerland and France, and in
February 1877 he paid a secret visit to Paris where he stayed with a
man called Schneider, the owner of the Russian bookshop and library
in Geneva and the financial backer and owner of Peter Tkachev's
'Jacobin' newspaper, *Nabat* (the Tocsin).[64] In the same month the
Almanach was reported by Kropotkin as ready for a second edition,
and basing himself on reports from Brousse, Kropotkin wrote enthusiastically of the revival of the French socialist movement which,
he said, was taking a 'purely anarchist' direction; the news, he said,
was 'réjouissant', and in the Jura Federation the refrain was everywhere 'La France, La France'. This enthusiasm was the direct result
of Brousse's journey, the object of which had been to visit sections
of the International (but which probably became limited to a visit to
Paris where Brousse had several contacts in addition to the Russian,
Schneider).[65]

Allowing for Brousse's natural enthusiasm it is evident that he
saw enough to convince him of the need to concentrate on the reviving socialist movement in France. The visit led him to cancel a plan
previously agreed upon to go to Verviers in order, as 'l'homme le
plus influent, éloquent et le plus énergique', to help to revive the
moribund Belgian anarchist movement by taking over control of its
newspaper *Le Mirabeau.*[66] From early 1877 onwards Brousse's main
interest in militant anarchist activity was instead directed towards

France where an organized socialist movement was starting to emerge from behind the crumbling façade of the MacMahon régime. This concern was one partly shared by the *militants* of the Jura who had, as has been mentioned previously, partially inherited from Bakunin an almost mystical faith in Paris and France as the vanguard of Revolution. But the main work (mainly of propaganda) was left to the French exiles in the Jura and at Geneva, aided by such outstanding figures as Kropotkin who occasionally himself would smuggle pamphlets across the border. One side effect of this changed orientation of interest by Brousse was to focus the attention of the French secret police network on his activities. Following a meeting on the French border addressed by Brousse in the summer of 1877, Oscar Testut described him in a report to the Paris Prefecture of Police in somewhat exaggerated terms, as

... secrétaire correspondant de la section de Berne (section de propagande). Cet individu, qui est l'un des agitateurs les plus dangereux de l'Internationale en Suisse, entretient des relations avec les anciens affiliés de Béziers, Cette, Lodève, Narbonne, Montpellier et même Toulouse.[67]

A review which had some success in penetrating into France was *Le Travailleur,* a monthly publication of the Geneva exile group.[68] But as with most of this group's efforts it gained the disapproval of the Jura purists as being too eclectic and as betraying Jacobin and 'public service' tendencies,[69] so that very shortly Brousse was to set up his own organization independent of the group. He did however work quite closely with one of the Geneva exiles. This was Jules Montels, who has been mentioned previously in connection with the activities of the International in Hérault. Since the break-up of the Geneva Section de Propagande and its exit from the Jura Federation in 1874, Montels had been active within the constantly changing groups of exiles, and was for some time a member of the Cercle d'Etudes Sociales, which was responsible for the publication early in 1876 of a series of abstentionist pamphlets aimed at the French working-class movement. He himself had written one of these, *Aux Socialistes Révolutionnaires de la France méridionale.* In May 1877 the old Section de Propagande was refounded with Montels as its secretary. It entered the Jura Federation, and it was the proceeds of a meeting at which Brousse spoke on 'L'Etat et l'Anarchie', on 26

May, which enabled the group to pay Costa's journey from Berne to talk on propaganda by the deed on 9 June.

But this contact with Montels was exceptional and served merely to emphasize the distance between Brousse and the Geneva exiles. He preferred to work relatively on his own, with the co-operation of Kropotkin and Pindy,[70] and in the early summer of 1877 he laid the foundations for the effective propaganda of the ideas of the International in France with the publication of the newspaper *L'Avant-Garde,* and the organization of a secret Congress of delegates of the French sections of the Association.

The skeleton of a French Federation of the International had existed since the Geneva Congress, when Brousse had insisted on its right to exist as an autonomous organization. Brousse and Pindy had represented the French Federation at the Berne Congress of 1876 at which Brousse had taken the opportunity to define its Programme as illegal and revolutionary. It contrasted markedly with the Programme adopted by the first French Labour Congress of the same year:

... les membres des sections secrètes de l'Internationale française ont un programme différent, et se placent sur un autre terrain; leur activité principale s'exerce en dehors de la légalité, elle a par but d'organiser les ouvriers pour la révolution. Cela ne les empêche pas d'ailleurs, à côté de cette action secrète, de se mêler publiquement aux organisations pacifiques tout en travaillant en secret à leur organisation propre, ils entrent dans tous les groupements publiques, et ils y apportent leur propagande socialiste révolutionnaire.[71]

In preparation for the creation on a firm basis of a federation of French sections of the International, Brousse began to arrange for the foundation of secret groups throughout France. He also organized a secret Congress, which was financed by Natalie Landsberg and was held on 19 and 20 August 1877, immediately after the St Imier Congress of the Jura Federation. It was attended by delegates representing twelve sections of the French International, a notable extension of strength since the Berne Congress, where only three sections had been represented. Ballivet, a leading *militant* of the socialist movement in Lyons, was present as well as the French *militants* within the Jura such as Montels, Brousse and Pindy.[72]

The Congress passed seven resolutions which were published shortly afterwards in *L'Avant-Garde* on 25 August 1877, of which three deserve quoting in full. They defined the attitude of the French Federation towards propaganda, popular movements of discontent and the strike.

The second resolution dealing with propaganda read as follows:

Le Congrès, considérant que les moyens de propagande varient avec les milieux dans lesquels s'agitent les sections, et respectant le principe d'autonomie proclamé dans le programme, laisse à chaque groupe le soin de choisir le moyen de propagande qui lui convient. Cependant il recommande à l'attention des sections les moyens suivant; pour les villes, une active propagande par le livre, le journal, la brochure; pour les campagnes l'entrée dans les métiers qui voyagent de socialistes dévoués; partout, dès que la force de l'organisation rendra la chose possible, la propagande par le fait.

The fifth resolution declared that:

La Fédération française décide qu'elle profitera de tous les mouvements populaires pour développer dans les limites du possible son programme collectiviste et anarchiste, mais elle invite les groupes qui la composent à ne pas compromettre leurs forces au profit de la victoire d'un parti bourgeois.

And the sixth resolution urged sections to exploit strikes:

Dans les cas où des grèves éclateraient dans les contrées où les sections françaises ont de l'influence, les sections de la fédération française devront profiter de la circonstance pour donner à la grève un caractère socialiste révolutionnaire, en engageant les grévistes à faire disparaître leur situation de salariés par la prise de possession de vive force des instruments de travail.

The second resolution revealed very clearly the limited possibility and effectiveness of propaganda by the deed as envisaged by Brousse and the Federation; it was only *one* means of propaganda amongst many, to be used only when a certain level of organization had been achieved. It also pointed forward to one of the main forms of propaganda adopted when the movement had, in the 1880s, become narrowed down to a purely anarchist sect uninterested in gaining popular support at the expense of doctrinal purity. This was the use of 'les métiers qui voyagent', in fact a traditional theme of socialist propaganda, which were to become the backbone of the anarchist movement in the 1880s with the widespread use of 'marchands ambulants' as anarchist propagandists.[73]

The sixth resolution provided a good example of what form such propaganda could take, and revealed a strong syndicalist orientation which reflected the revival of the labour movement in France.

The fifth resolution was ambiguous. On the one hand, it could be taken as a condemnation of collaboration in bourgeois politics, and in the context of the summer of 1877 this would seem most likely with the movement for Republican unity in the face of the MacMahon threat. On the other hand, it could be taken as a clear warning of the dangers of ill-considered insurrectionary action which would merely aid the general European bourgeois reaction – exactly what had been achieved by the Benevento affair. If this were the case it would certainly underline very effectively the actually cautious position of Brousse concealed behind his anarchist rhetoric. This once again leads to a comparison with Andreas Costa, whose own attitude to the Benevento affair – in which, significantly, he was the only leader of the Italian socialist movement (apart from the Malonist-inspired reformists in the North) not to take part – was noticeably cool. In appearance advocating an extremist policy, Brousse was in fact laying a great deal of emphasis on the need for organization and propaganda and, as has already been stressed, his doctrine of propaganda by the deed reflected a pessimistic assessment of the possibilities of a Revolution.

The Congress went on to discuss the approaching Congresses of Ghent and Verviers. It upheld the decisions of the St Imier Congress, adding however that it could only accept a Pact of Solidarity if such a Pact permitted anarchist propaganda in countries where parliamentary socialism was predominant – a specific endorsement of Brousse's position. The Congress elected Brousse and Montels as delegates to the Congresses and appointed a Federal Committee for the Federation. Brousse, as editor of the Federation's newspaper *L'Avant-Garde,* was not officially a member of the Committee, although he played an influential role in its work.

L'Avant-Garde had appeared on 2 June 1877, and it continued to appear fortnightly until seized by the Swiss police in December 1878. The idea of publishing such a newspaper had first been discussed during Brousse's enforced stay at La Chaux-de-Fonds in April. On 30 April he wrote to Kropotkin announcing that the journal would appear on 13 May under the title of *Bulletin de la Fédération française.* Brousse asked Kropotkin to take responsibility for the International news section. He ended his letter by defining the readership aimed at:

'tâchons de viser les deux catégories de nos lecteurs: l'étudiant parisien, qui veut de la théorie, et l'ouvrier du Midi qui erre entre les syndicats, Gambetta, et l'Internationale', a clear echo both of the Manifesto of the French group in Barcelona in 1873, with its emphasis on the workers of the South, and of Brousse's recent visit to Paris and his contact with Massard and the Paris student community. In a later letter, advising Kropotkin of what he should provide for the International news section, Brousse stressed the need for insistence on first principles, and said that in view of the ignorance of these amongst the French working class it was necessary even to *moderate* the attack:

Pour une feuille qui débute je suis absolument d'avis qu'il faut nous abstenir de tout attaque directe. Apprécions froidement les choses au point de vue de nos principes; nous aurons une touche d'autant plus fort quand une polémique s'engagea. Nous avons a faire *l'education complete* (ne l'oublions pas!) de nos lecteurs.[74]

On 28 May he wrote to Kropotkin again, announcing that the paper would appear with the title of *L'Avant-Garde*. It was finally with this title that it appeared on 2 June. Although officially the organ of the French Federation, the newspaper was far wider in scope than Guillaume's *Bulletin* (which was often parochial in outlook) and certainly more stimulating, reflecting the active personalities of both Brousse and Kropotkin. Kropotkin later admitted in fact that *L'Avant-Garde* had been founded by himself and Brousse (mainly Brousse) when they felt that the *Bulletin* was becoming too insipid,[75] another symptom of the rivalry between Brousse and Guillaume. In addition to its sale in Switzerland the paper was circulated clandestinely in France (where it had some effect as a medium of anarchist propaganda in the South) and circulated – how effectively cannot be established – in London (among the French exile groups), Belgium, Spain and Germany, while copies possibly even reached the United States. In April 1878 it merged with *Le Travailleur* of Geneva to replace the *Bulletin de la Fédération Jurassienne* which had collapsed on Guillaume's departure for Paris. Consequently it enlarged its format, widened its range of contents and ceased to act exclusively as the organ of the French Federation, although it retained its title.

From the very beginning its leading articles dealt with events of international and theoretical significance, as well as with French affairs. Its style was unmistakably that of Brousse, who wrote most of its articles. It was lively, provocative and written often in familiar idiom. Its duration coincided with the peak period of Brousse's activity when he was, as Kropotkin said, of incontestable value and in 'tout sa verve'.[76]

The Programme of the Federation was published in the first issue of the paper. It called for the collectivization of the land and the instruments of labour, thereby marking a development on the Programme of the International. This aim was to be achieved by the spontaneous uprising of the majority of the people whose first task would be to destroy the State by Revolution. The Revolution could not be merely national, but should be international. Thus the Federation belonged to the International, which was the realization of international working-class solidarity. Once the State was destroyed it would be replaced by a society based on contract and liberty:

... la formation libre des groupes humains autour de chaque besoin, de chaque intérêt, et la libre fédération de ces groupes ... le programme peut se résumer en ces termes: Collectivisme, Anarchie, Fédération libre.

The tactics the journal prescribed were, on the face of it, violent and extreme. The first issue called for violence in no uncertain terms:

L'expérience a parlé! Loin de nous la voie pacifique et légal! A nous la voie violente qui a fait ses preuves! Laissons les radicaux à leur radotage pacifique, allons aux fusils, suspendus aux murs de nos mansardes. Mais si nous les épaulons, ne les laissons refroidir et s'éteindre que lorsque nous pourrons faire resonner leur bruit non seulement sur le sol d'une république, mais encore un sol qui soit la propriété collective du paysan et de l'ouvrier.

In its third issue the paper called for 'La Commune par l'Insurrection'.[77] The appeal to violence drew heavily on the myth of the Commune, now rapidly becoming established, and on the atmosphere of the current political crisis in France. It became the rhetoric of those who were, simultaneously, aware of the need for organization and propaganda ('nous avons à faire l'éducation complète de nos lecteurs'). Even the article which called for insurrection laid down solid organization as its essential prerequisite:

... il faut déserter les urnes et peupler les barricades, et pour cela, il faut s'organiser. Donc que l'on ne perde pas un temps précieux, que l'on s'organise pour appliquer le premier point de notre programme, l'insurrection.

The principle which was to be embodied in, and give form to, insurrection was the principle of the autonomy of the Commune:

A travers l'histoire, la Commune a toujours été d'abord le moyen de réaliser dans la cité ce foyer intellectuel si favorable à l'éclosion de l'idée, la forme materielle de l'idée nouvelle: elle a été ensuite l'insurgé qui a lutté pour généraliser cette idée, pour le faire sortir des murs qui entourent son berceau, et pour la généraliser dans toute l'étendue du territoire.... Posée au grand soleil, sur la place publique, par ce que nous appellerions au aujourd'hui la propagande par le fait, l'idée devait se généraliser.

The logic of this fundamentally anarchist concept of Revolution now pushed Brousse further along the path which led eventually to his possibilism. Instead of holding up 'the society of the free federation of autonomous Communes' as an abstract ideal, the necessary result of anarchist Revolution or the result of inexorable historical necessity, he now firmly related it to the political geography of France. Noting that no party had an absolute majority at any time, and that the pattern of French politics was one of a series of coalition governments (except at times of authoritarian rule), Brousse pointed out that in certain areas certain parties were predominant; Left-wing radicals or socialists in the large cities, conservative Republicans in the smaller provincial towns and Monarchists in the rural areas. If France were to be organized on the basis of the federation of Communes which respected these divisions, the contrast between the happiness and welfare of the socialist cities and the clerical misery of the rural areas would be such that after two years no Monarchist would be able to pull the wool over the eyes of the working-class electorate again. Such a state of affairs would be of outstanding propaganda value for the socialist movement.

At this stage Brousse's formulation of the concept of propaganda began to appear absurd. He was now stretching it to accommodate the hypothesis of socialist control over a considerable period of time in a large city or town. His basically reformist conviction that socialism could be effectively achieved on the local municipal level was, to say the least, placing heavy strains on the credibility of his internationalist anarchist rhetoric, which kept him for the time being on the Left wing of the European socialist movement.

For the French elections of 14 October 1877 the French Federation circulated in several large towns in France a Manifesto, written by

Brousse, which the Monarchists and MacMahon supporters found useful to circulate themselves as an example and warning of the danger from the Left. In common with the entire French exile community the Manifesto denounced both the Monarchist and bourgeois republics, recalled the memories of 1848 and 1871 and called for complete dissociation from the politics of the bourgeoisie. Following the elections *L'Avant-Garde* continued its attack on the Republic. In November 1877 it published a second Manifesto reaffirming abstention, after it had been widely and incorrectly rumoured that Pindy, who signed the Manifesto as secretary of the Federation, had disavowed the October Manifesto. In December the newspaper called once again for insurrection in the shape of a Communard uprising.[78] In taking this line on the elections Brousse and his associates within the Fédération française were in sharp opposition to the policy being pursued by Guesde and the l'Egalité group in Paris. On 18 November 1877 the *Bulletin* strongly attacked Guesde for having recently urged the working class to vote for the Republicans in order to thwart the Monarchists, and quoted against Guesde his article in *L'Almanach du Peuple* of 1873 in which he had attacked universal suffrage. The *Bulletin's* attack marked the end of the limited *rapprochement* between the Jura anarchists and the Paris group which had been hinted at in Brousse's establishment of relations with the group in 1876. It was a reflection of the growing ideological separation between the anarchists and the socialists which had been symbolized by the Ghent Congress, and dated from at least as early as Guesde's strong criticism of the Benevento affair.

Probably the most significant contribution of the French anarchists grouped round *L'Avant-Garde* was however not its verbal polemics from across the frontier but the introduction of the collectivist motion at the Second Working-class Congress held at Lyons in 1878. The newspaper had put forward a detailed programme of discussion at the end of 1877, and in its replies to the various questions put forward for debate at the Congress had affirmed on each occasion the need for a revolutionary socialist solution. On female labour it considered the problem subordinate to that of the general emancipation of the working class; on the role of trades unions it urged them to overcome their concern with the immediate improvement of conditions and prepare the way for socialist Revolution. Industrial crises and unemployment, the third issue on the agenda, were described as capable of solution only through the destruction of capitalist society;

while education as a means of emancipation was dismissed on the grounds that its beneficent effects could find fertile ground only after the prior overthrow of bourgeois society, when 'integral poly-technical education' would replace the non-functional bourgeois system. It rejected absolutely the representation of the working class in Parliament, arguing that even if the bourgeoisie would consent to it (which the Federation doubted) it would be absurd for the socialist movement ever to expect the legality or legitimacy of any majority the working class might obtain to be admitted; no class would ever voluntarily abandon control. Moreover, it was pointed out, the dangers of the corruption of working-class candidates far outweighed any possible gains. On the sixth and eighth questions, the usefulness of a pension fund and the elimination of social problems such as vagrancy and prostitution, the Federation again stated that no satis-factory solution could be found outside the framework of a socialist society. On the seventh question the Federation called for a unity of effort between the rural and industrial workers.

Although the Lyons Congress which opened on 28 January 1878 refused to admit delegates of 'study' (i.e. socialist) groups – a reform of admission procedures for which socialists had been pressing – the Congress marked a definite stage forward in the development of working-class consciousness, and was far from the reactionary or conservative event it has sometimes been made out to be. Out of a total of over 150 delegates only about ten were committed to collec-tivism, but their arguments were listened to sympathetically. The delegates from southern departments, especially, revealed a growing radicalism on the issue of co-operation which had been widely, if not unanimously, accepted as a remedy for social problems at the Paris Congress of 1876. These delegates now saw it as a tac-tical means rather than as an end in itself. With the entire body of delegates there was a radical spirit, an acceptance of class antago-nism and of the need for independent working-class action, which marked a significant development from the spirit of the Paris Congress.

It was against this background that Ballivet, delegate of the mechanics' union of Lyons, presented the main theses of collectivism. With Dupire of Paris, whose resolutions had probably been drawn up by Guesde,[79] he presented a motion calling for the collectivization of the land and the instruments of labour. Ballivet was a member of a secret section of the International in France and had attended the

Congress of the French Federation in August 1877. According to Guillaume:

> ... la participation de Ballivet au Congrès ouvrier de Lyon eut lieu à la suite d'une entente avec la commission de la Fédération française de l'Internationale, et les rapports qu'il y présenta ne sont pas une oeuvre personelle, mais *une oeuvre collective* qui avait été rédigé en commun.

The resolutions presented by Ballivet were in fact drawn up by Brousse, Kropotkin, Montels and Dumartheray. Ballivet's main contribution to the debates was a report entitled *La Représentation du Prolétariat au Parlement,* a report which can reasonably be attributed to Brousse personally.[80] Much of it merely repeated phrases and sentences from the resolutions of the French Federation on the agenda of the Congress. It concluded with a four-point Programme outlining the tactics which should be adopted by the working class in France: the complete separation from all bourgeois politics; the organization of trades unions for revolutionary ends; the creation of propaganda and study groups; and the federation of these trades unions and study groups in order to exploit areas of popular agitation and direct them to revolutionary ends. The object of this Programme was described in the classic terms of the anti-authoritarian Internationalist tradition:

> ... en un mot, provoquer, dans le sein même de la société actuelle l'organisation de la société libre de l'avenir, de sorte que le jour amenera la mort de la société bourgeoise, la société nouvelle soit à côté toute prête pour la remplacer [sic].

The Congress thought otherwise however and voted for the principle of working-class candidates on the first ballot. It also rejected the joint motion on collectivism put forward by Ballivet and Dupire. This rejection provoked hostile comment on the Congress by Guesde in *L'Egalité* and Lefrançais in *Le Travailleur,*[81] but Brousse was more optimistic. While admitting the conservative character of the Congress, he pointed out that as merely the second stage in the revival of the socialist movement it was not to be derided, and contained the germ from which a truly socialist party would emerge in the near future. On this count, Brousse revealed a more pragmatic and realistic attitude than either Guesde or Lefrançais, at the same indicating that he was already beginning to modify his intransigent revolutionary posture.[82] This was not however to become clearer until later in that year.

(a) *The Fribourg Congress and the* L'Avant-Garde *affair: the evolution towards reformism*

Brousse's growing interest in the revival of the movement in France did not however preclude a continued concern with the affairs of the Jura Federation. Indeed, if the evolution towards socialism of an independent working-class organization in France influenced the development of Brousse's own political ideas towards reformist socialism at this time, the climate which made this change possible was provided by the collapse of the Jura anarchist movement following the Congress of the International at Verviers and the International Socialist Congress at Ghent in the summer of 1877. It is therefore necessary to examine this period more closely.

Brousse returned to Switzerland after the Ghent Congress. Of the seven delegates from the Jura he and Guillaume were the only two to return to a movement which was rapidly losing strength. One reason for this decline was the collapse of the movement at Berne following the 18 March demonstration. Thirty of the demonstrators had been brought on trial in August and had been sentenced to terms of imprisonment ranging from sixty days for two of the participants who had struck police officers and brandished swordsticks, to forty days for Guillaume, thirty days for Brousse himself and ten days for the others. In addition all prisoners were ordered to pay costs and damages, while all foreigners who had participated were banished from Berne Canton for three years. It was this last measure which practically finished the movement in Berne as its leading *militants* had been foreign socialists. It is likely that these results of the 18 March demonstration caused Brousse seriously to re-examine the usefulness of propaganda by the deed as a tactical concept. In one sense the demonstration had been a dramatic success, receiving widespread publicity and producing a distinctive impression. On the other hand, it had effectively destroyed the movement in Berne, cut the ground from under Brousse's own feet and further separated the anarchists from the mainstream of the socialist movement. Brousse was too much of a pragmatist not to see the dangers of indulging in, and ultimately taking refuge in, this kind of activity. His month in prison seems to have provided him with an opportunity for reflection, for it was at about this time that evidence began to appear of a more realistic approach by him towards the tactics to be followed.

Brousse began his sentence on 2 October 1877, immediately following his return to Switzerland, sharing a cell with two non-political prisoners in the Kafigthürm. Despite a cheerful and colourful account of daily prison routine which he sent to the *Bulletin* the imprisonment had a serious effect on his health. According to Pindy it was at Brousse's own insistence that he shared a cell with ordinary prisoners, and when he was released his health was considerably damaged. For six weeks he stayed at Pindy's home in La Chaux-de-Fonds where Landsberg nursed him back to health 'with the most absolute devotion'.[83]

The sentence of banishment from Berne on Brousse had led to the immediate collapse of the *Arbeiter-Zeitung*. But Brousse still had a means of communication through *L'Avant-Garde* and, occasionally, the *Bulletin,* as well as through public speeches. One such speech at Berne on 24 December 1877, a few weeks after his release from prison, on the subject of the Programme and tactics of the socialist parties, hinted at a possible change in his views. While reaffirming traditional parts of the anarchist Programme, such as electoral abstention and the uselessness of an International containing several groups committed to varying methods, Brousse went out of his way to stress the need for 'des conditions sérieuses' for propaganda by the deed. At the same time he called for the creation of socialist parties. By this he evidently did not mean parties committed to political action, but rather a greater degree of organization within the anarchist movement. In making such an appeal Brousse was conforming to a general desire already apparent in France *vis-à-vis* the labour movement. In fact the phrase 'le parti socialiste' seems to have come into general currency with the holding of the Lyons Congress.[84]

Brousse's interests were by this time increasingly directed towards France. The movement in the Jura had failed to establish itself amongst the working class, and partly as a result Guillaume himself was looking to France for inspiration. He spent a great deal of his time writing reviews and magazine articles and planning his departure for Paris, where he finally arrived in May 1878. He alleged primarily personal reasons for his departure, but it is clear that he also found his influence outdone by that of Brousse, whose contribution to the Jura movement he described in the following unflattering terms:

... l'influence de Brousse, non à Berne seulement, mais dans les montagnes jurassiennes, n'était pas toujours bonne: elle flattait, chez les plus jeunes le goût des manifestations de parade; elle s'exercait ... dans un sens bien différent de celle qu'avait possédé autrefois Bakounine: et si une part dans l'activité personelle de Brousse était faite à la propagande théorique, cette propagande s'attachaient plutôt à de vaines discussions de mots, à des subtilités quasi-métaphysiques, qu'aux questions d'organisation pratique et de lutte économique, qui dans notre esprit, à nous Jurassiens autochtones, avaient toujours tenu la première place.[85]

This would seem however to refer to the period prior to the return of Brousse and Guillaume to the Jura in September 1877, for Brousse himself became much less active in the latter part of 1877 and throughout 1878. With the departure of Kropotkin (who did not return after the Ghent Congress) he had to spend more time in writing articles for, and editing, *L'Avant-Garde,* while as resident in Zurich he was in any case to some extent out of the mainstream of the movement; and he seems to have been preoccupied with plans for publishing a popular work to spread the new notion of atomic numeration in France[86] (a work which never, apparently, saw the light of day). It was a symptom of the general decline of the movement that there was no general meeting in 1878 to celebrate the anniversary of the Commune as there had been in 1876 and 1877.[87]

The Jura anarchists, deprived after March 1878 of their own journal, suffering from the general and long-term crisis in the watchmaking industry and almost isolated within the European socialist movement, began to realize the hollowness of much of their rhetoric. This led to a re-examination of some of the fundamental tenets of their faith. At a meeting of the Federal Committee of the Jura Federation on 23 May 1878 the creation of an anarchist party was discussed, and although the project was dismissed on the grounds that the International was sufficient in itself, the Committee agreed to the holding of a general meeting of the anarchist sections at Neuchâtel on 9 June.[88] The initiative for the meeting came from leading French exiles connected with both *Le Travailleur* and *L'Avant-Garde,* and took place in order to discuss basic issues of anarchist tactics. The meeting discussed – and rejected – the formation of an anarchist party; decided that *L'Avant-Garde* would continue the work of *Le Travailleur;* held that the attitude of the anarchist movement towards the State socialists should be discussed at the forthcoming Fribourg Congress of the Federation; but gave its own opinion that while

E

upholding a conciliatory position on the economic struggle they should stay firm in maintaining anarchist principles. This indicated that these principles were beginning to be undermined somewhere. The meeting also discussed, apparently without providing any solution, the need to organize conferences in the Jura, which apparently had ceased after Guillaume's departure in May.[89] It went on to recommend that the federal committee should organize subscriptions to give financial help to *L'Avant-Garde,* and should also appeal for 'une direction au journal satisfaisant aux voeux des sections'. In addition it recommended that the Federation should set out its views in a memorandum on the questions to be discussed at the forthcoming International Socialist Congress being organized in Paris by Guesde. Finally, in discussing the agenda of the forthcoming Fribourg Congress of the Federation, the meeting suggested that the following question should be included for discussion: 'En présence de la crise actuelle y a-t-il lieu de travailler à une réorganisation des forces ouvrières ayant pour but la sauvegarde immédiate des intérêts du peuple?'[90]

The Neuchâtel meeting hinted that three basic tenets of the anarchist faith were being questioned: the traditional autonomous structure based on the independence of the local section; the unqualified hostility to the State socialists which, if reaffirmed, was clearly not so widely accepted as previously (and the decision to co-operate with the Paris Congress suggested this was not as intransigent as in the past); and, third, the belief that no meaningful reforms could be obtained within the frame-work of capitalist society. The challenge to this belief was clearly caused by the economic crisis and the material hardships being suffered by the workers in the watch trade. But these rumblings of discontent were minor compared with the radical break in tactics which Brousse was to suggest two months later at the Fribourg Congress.

If one article of faith had united individuals through the entire spectrum of the anarchist *credo* it was the abstention from all electoral activity. At the Fribourg Congress, held between 3 and 5 August 1878, Brousse questioned the validity of this traditional anarchist tenet.[91] The first question on the agenda of the Congress was the need for an *exposé* of anarchist principles. A document drawn up by Elisée Reclus, which summarized briefly the arguments he was to deploy in his book *Évolution et Révolution,* was read to the Congress. This was followed by a speech from Brousse in which he laid down the main points which should be presented in the *exposé*. There were three, he said: (a) the anarchist conception of the form of future society. As *practical* men, he insisted, realizing that society could not be totally changed immediately, they should then lay down (b) their 'desiderata immédiats', and (c) the methods to be adopted to attain these desiderata.

This introductory outline indicated the direction and the extent of Brousse's challenge to the traditional anarchist position. By posing an intermediate stage between the present and future society he was making his first major break from orthodox anarchism. He went on to deal with each of the three points in greater detail. On the first point he repeated his well-aired argument for the placing of society on a rational basis, conformable to the scientific laws of society. On the economic level this involved the freedom of the individual through the collectivization of property, and on the political level the destruction of the State and its replacement by the principle of autonomy – which could, he said, be first applied at the regional level.[92] On the second and third points, the question of immediate demands, he anticipated the possibilism of which he was to become the acknowledged leader three years later. The anarchists, he said, did not believe it was possible to establish in one stage the society he had just described. Thus it was necessary to ask which parts of the programme were 'immédiatement possible'. He suggested that communal autonomy should provide the main immediate demand:

. . . s'il est de localités que nos idées ne pénétrent que lentement, il est des communes, foyers intellectuels, où on les accepte plus vite. Si donc on obtenait l'autonomie des communes, on pourrait instaurer dans certains centres certain côtés de la société nouvelle et faire aux yeux de tous *la preuve par le fait* de l'excellence de nos principes et la possibilité de leur application.

If the anarchists were to gain control of the Commune, he went on to say, it would be foolish to expect immediate realization of the anarchist society. The sons of bourgeois society could not be expected to put into practice immediately the precepts laid down by the anarchist-Communist philosophy, and moreover it would be foolish, he said, to risk all by asking for all. Thus the anarchist-Communist programme should be relegated to the second stage of application of socialist principles. The necessary minimum was a society organized on the basis of the collectivization of land and the instruments of labour, with Communism being applied by those groups which desired it. It would ultimately become universally established. The immediate Programme of the anarchists should therefore be the autonomy of the Commune, the collectivization of land and the instruments of labour and the freedom of local groupings such as trades unions and political groups.

Brousse then went on to discuss the tactics of the anarchist movement. It was here that he suggested the need for a fundamental change of attitude. The anarchists, he said, devoted much of their time to propaganda, but it was necessary also to *act*. While history taught them that the conquest of power by the vote was an illusion, and while the necessary force for the ultimate revolutionary task was to be created by propaganda (propaganda by the deed), there were occasions when propaganda in all its forms became impossible. In such circumstances, he asked, was it expedient to abstain absolutely from all electoral action? The text of the debate gives his own answer:

L'Orateur pense que, même comme moyen de propagande, le vote est d'un usage pratique presque toujours dangereux. Mais, il ne le proscrit d'une façon absolue; il ne lui oppose pas le non possumus papal. Il est des cas, dit-il, où la destruction de l'Etat est encore impossible dans son ensemble, mais où un vote peut avoir par le vote un rouage enrayé [*sic*]; où il est possible d'opposer un rouage à un autre, *une commune par exemple au governement*; dans ces cas il regarde l'emploi du vote comme pouvant avoir son utilité [my italics].

Thus, as with violent methods, electoral activity was merely a form of *propaganda,* and thus not a committed tactic of the anarchists. As with violence and the adoption of the tactic of propaganda by the deed, Brousse's advocacy of the usefulness of electoral action was framed so as to provide a comfortable safety net. If the tactic was a failure it would merely be a failure of propaganda. This at least was the implicit reasoning behind the argument, which was a virtual recognition of the failure of propaganda by the deed and of the hostility of the contemporary political climate to the realization by other than peaceful means of socialist demands. It marked the beginning of a new stage in Brousse's political career, although not one he was able to pursue until his return to France in 1880. The intervening period was to be one in which he carried out a systematic re-examination of the tactics of the anarchist movement.

Kropotkin, who by this time had returned once again to the Jura from Paris, followed Brousse in speaking to the Congress. But he made no mention of the need for the adoption of electoral tactics and the Congress, while affirming the need for the collectivization of land and the instruments of labour and the destruction of the State, left the matter open for further discussion. This was in a sense a minor triumph for Brousse, for previously the anarchists had shown outright and uncompromising opposition to electoral action.

The second question before the Congress was the theoretical and practical value of demands for Communal autonomy. Schwitzguébel pointed out the failure of the anarchist movement to obtain popular support. This was largely, he said, because the people were afraid of the socialist solutions they were offered, and he suggested that Communal autonomy, as one of the points of the anarchist programme, could provide the starting-point for popular agitation and open the way for the eventual realization of anarchist principles. As with Brousse, Schwitzguébel was calling for a major re-examination of anarchist tactics (as with Brousse, he was very shortly to leave the anarchist movement),[93] and his speech won Brousse's approval; not so much however on the grounds of its implied moderation but on the grounds that the tradition of Communal autonomy would provide, as it did in 1871, the basis for a movement of mass support. Following Schwitzguébel and Brousse, Kropotkin outlined his argument for the autonomy of the Commune which he later developed at the following (1879) Congress of the Federation.[94] It became a central theme of Kropotkin's anarchist philosophy; society was moving towards the disintegration of large national States and their replacement by the free federation of autonomous Communes. Future Revolutions would be carried out under this flag, and it was within the Commune that the first sketches of future society would be made. Thus to work for 'la commune libre' was to work on the side of History, and on a more mundane level it was to work within the best framework for the stimulation of popular grievances and for the 'réalisation insurrectionalle de nos idées'.

In the general discussion which followed, Brousse's suggestions on the value of the vote were strongly attacked by Rudolf Kahn, who said that the anarchists had always insisted on the realization of their total Programme. He opposed the use of the vote in the Commune on these grounds, and at this point came close to illustrating the

far-reaching implications of what Brousse had said. Brousse replied
that he was not merely advocating political participation *per se,* but
was merely attempting to move closer to the 'details' which preoccupied the vast majority of the people. As a *principle,* i.e. as the
expression of popular sovereignty, he rejected the vote as he had
always done. As an instrument of action it was nearly always useless
and often dangerous, sapping the will of any revolutionary party –
and here he referred to the German Social Democrats.[95] None the
less there were occasions on which the vote could be usefully adopted,
and he gave two hypothetical examples. The first was in reference to
the amnesty campaign which by then was beginning to focus into a
powerful group the diverse socialist elements inside France. Instead
of indiscriminately presenting Blanqui's candidature, he said, it
would be far more effective to concentrate it on a centre where a
'natural' majority existed. When Blanqui was elected the virtually
certain invalidation of the ballot by the Chamber (which is what did
happen) would reveal the true reactionary nature of the French
State and thus enlighten the people as to the real issue which faced
them. It was, in other words, another form of Brousse's propaganda
by the deed. And as a second hypothetical example, he put the following case:

Supposons – le fait a existé – que dans une commune française la
majorité des électeurs se rencontre ouvrière et que la minorité soit bona-
partiste. Si les ouvriers s'abstiennent, les bonapartistes seront élus, ce
qui blessera le sentiment populaire. Pour entraver cette élection, ou bien
un parti ouvrier légal devra se former, ou la majorité anarchiste devra
présenter des candidats et ne pas s'abstenir. Dans ce cas, ne vaut-il pas
mieux que les anarchistes s'emparent par le vote de la commune, qu'ils se
mettent comme usufruit dans les mains des paysans le sol arable de la
commune, et dans celles des ouvriers les bâtiments communaux? S'ils
réalisent ainsi en partie la propriété collective dans la commune, il est
certain que la lutte commencera entre eux et le pouvoir central; c'est-à-
dire qu'une situation révolutionnaire sera crée.
    Quand on ne peut pas encore renverser dans son ensemble l'Etat, qu'il
est même impossible momentément d'essayer sa force contre lui, il vaut
mieux déranger, même par le vote, les rouages qui le composent, les
enrayer, que de rester les bras croisés à les regarder tourner tranquillement.
    Pas plus que le vote, la violence n'est un principe socialiste, cependant
contestera-t-on que l'emploi de la force révolutionnaire ne soit une
nécéssité? Eh bien! l'usage de vote peut aussi quelquefois être utile. Il ne

faudrait donc pas, par orthodoxie abstentionniste, proscrire ce moyen d'action d'une façon absolue.

In effect this was a total repudiation by Brousse of the anarchist *credo*. By saying that in a crisis, such as the threat of a Bonapartist victory in the elections, the anarchists should participate in the election, he was by implication reversing the attitude he had adopted at the time of the MacMahon 1877 crisis, when, by urging abstention, he had drawn a firm demarcation between the anarchists and the socialists. Had this merely been an expedient to prevent a reactionary seizure of power it could have been argued that it was not fundamentally contradictory with anarchist beliefs. But the argument amounted to more than that, for the second point to be noted in his speech was the argument that the anarchists, in voting, should *accept* their electoral mandate and exercise power. Furthermore, once in power they would realize in large part the socialist Programme of the collectivization of the land and the instruments of labour. This was a purely reformist concept which in the early years of the French socialist movement was to separate Brousse and the possibilists from the Guesdist socialists. Finally, in saying that abstentionism should have no place as orthodoxy, Brousse was defying what could be described as the central tenet of the anarchist faith, the touchstone which separated it from other schools of socialism. Like Costa,[96] Brousse disguised both to himself and others the implications of his statements by means of some of the formulae of anarchism – such as the firmly held belief in anarcho-Communism as the ideal society to be aimed for – and by use of revolutionary rhetoric. But the beginning of his possibilism, which is glimpsed throughout his career in the 1870s, can firmly be placed in his contribution to the Fribourg Congress of 1878.

The majority of the delegates to the Congress supported Brousse, but in view of Kahn's objections took no decision and put the question aside for further study. They then went on to discuss and accept Schwitzguébel's arguments for the reorganization of the working-class movement, if necessary (and probably) outside the framework of the International, with a view to defining 'un but immédiatement pratique' (the issue raised at the Neuchâtel meeting of May).[97] The Congress ended by expressing solidarity and sympathy with the banned International Socialist Congress of Paris.

The amnesty campaign, and the agitation for Blanqui's candidature from January 1878 onwards which ultimately culminated in the general amnesty of 1880, provided one motive for Brousse's change of attitude. It is clear that he was by this time anxious to return to France, and in fact he was dissuaded from doing so by Kropotkin early in August 1878. Later in the year both men were expressing disillusionment with the Jura movement and showing impatience to return to France. Kropotkin wrote to Paul Robin in November:

L'Avant-Garde vivote à peine et si . . . Brousse et moi partons au mois de février toute organisation va tomber ici . . . une section ne vit que lorsqu'il y a un homme plus au moins sérieux et intéressant. Car . . . l'Internationale jusqu'à present, et surtout à présent, n'est qu'une société d'études.[98]

Brousse was however to leave Switzerland in a manner which he could hardly have predicted.

If he was beginning to question basic tenets of the anarchist *credo,* his reluctance to draw the logical conclusions led to the curious paradox of *L'Avant-Garde* being suppressed for expressing extremist anarchist sympathies, thereby creating a misleading impression of Brousse's political views at that time.

The circumstances surrounding the suppression of the newspaper in December 1878 gave it the reputation of a regicide newspaper with Brousse as the arch-assassin, an opinion often endorsed by those who could and should have known better (such as Malon).[99] The accusations sprang from the attitude adopted by the newspaper to a wave of assassinations and attempted assassinations which threatened the crowned heads of Europe in the course of 1878. Vera Zasulitch shot the chief of the St Petersburg police on 5 February 1878. There were attempts on the life of the Kaiser by Hoedel and Nobiling in May and June 1878. General Metzenoff was stabbed at St Petersburg on 16 August 1878, and there were attempts by Moncasi on Alfonso of Spain on 25 October 1878 and by Passanante on the King of Italy on 17 November 1878. The attitude of *L'Avant-Garde* was supposedly (and the supposition was strengthened by the successful suppression of the paper and the trial of Brousse which followed) wholly favourable to these political murders or attempted murders. In fact on closer examination the attitude of the newspaper was, to say the very least, ambiguous – and certainly more finely nuanced than widely imagined. Its very ambiguity must in part have been a reflection of Brousse's personal dilemma when faced with the breakdown of his anarchist beliefs.

The attempts of Hoedel and Nobiling on the Kaiser occurred before the Fribourg Congress. *L'Avant-Garde* refused to join in the widespread press denunciations and was particularly incensed by Liebknecht's over-hasty and somewhat self-righteous dissociation of the German Social Democrats from the *attentats* (he called Hoedel a 'madman') The paper said that certain forms of murder were justified – such as regicide, or the killing of a factory owner by a worker in cases of great industrial oppression. These entered the ranks of murders which could be approved. However, the newspaper went on to say, this did *not* preclude judgements as to the validity or value of *particular* acts, and as far as Hoedel's attempt was concerned, it could be counted as of virtually no value:

... quant au parti anarchiste la mort de l'empéreur ne lui fournissait aucun avantage, elle ne lui apportait pas même un de ces actes de *propagande par le fait* qui, compris du peuple, entrent dans ses moyens d'action.[100]

In other words the Hoedel attempt was *not* an act of propaganda by the deed. The theme of the need for *collective* action which, contrary to a widespread impression, characterized the formulation of 'propaganda by the deed', was repeated on the occasion of Nobiling's attempt which followed shortly after that of Hoedel. Brousse wrote a front-page article entitled 'La Propagande par le Fait' (see Appendix 3), and made it clear once again that political murder was not a method to be adopted uncritically:

Les noms d'Orsini, de Feische, de Nobiling resteront toujours un peu obscurcis dans l'histoire ... tandis que dans les reflets sanglants de ces mots 'Commune de Paris' tout enfant qui sait lire, lira son avenir.

Brousse went on to insist that anarchists should choose the *best* means, and pointed out that the actions of Hoedel and Nobiling were of extremely limited value, reflected a 'Republican' rather than a socialist outlook and in addition risked misrepresentation which could destroy any value they may carry. They were not 'intentional actions' ('actions voulues'), such as the actions of the anarchists at Berne and Benevento. Had Hoedel and Nobiling been 'anarchistes conscients' they would have waited longer and done better (whatever this meant). There was no disavowal of either Hoedel or Nobiling. But the sense of the article clearly meant that such acts were not

regarded as suitable means of action and did not come in the category
of propaganda by the deed.

However, *L'Avante-Garde* came down far more firmly in favour of
Moncasi's attempt against King Alfonso of Spain. The author of the
article was never revealed. It began by stating that regicide was not
one of the aims of the International, nor was it one of its approved
methods, its object being to change *institutions,* not to kill tyrants.
But it then went on to say that in certain circumstances assassination
could provoke a revolutionary situation. Reviewing the Spanish
situation it came to the conclusion that: 'il est donc certain que, dans
ces conditions, si le coup de pistolet d'Oliva [Moncasi] eut atteint son
but, il aurait rendu un grand service à la révolution . . .'[101] This was
nothing if not an incentive to any Spaniards reading the article to
attempt again to assassinate Alfonso. There is no evidence that
Brousse disagreed with the contents of the article, and writing two
years later in the Paris newspaper *Le Citoyen* on the occasion of the
assassination of Alexander II he said that he had approved of it:

> . . . j'eusse voulu que Moncasi réussit, et j'applaudis de tout coeur au
> succès de nos frères, les nihilistes russes. Lorsque de l'exécution d'une
> seule homme on peut faire sortir une régime meilleur et faire l'économie
> d'une révolution sanglante, j'estime qu'il ne faut pas hésiter. C'était le
> cas de Moncasi. . . . Mais dans la France de notre époque le moment de
> l'attentat semble passé pour faire place à une action plus large, la levée de
> boucliers d'une classe toute entière.[102]

According to Kropotkin[103] it was this article and also an article
planned for publication on 2 December 1878 (No. 41 of the paper),
written by Schwitzguébel and entitled 'Les régicides', which provoked
Government action against the paper. As articles were unsigned it
was extremely difficult to attribute responsibility, a difficulty increased by the fact that the paper was edited collectively – an editorial
committee having been established, formed of five members of the
French Federation, after the paper succeeded the *Bulletin*. This
committee gave Brousse and Schwitzguébel leading responsibility as
chief editors. It was Brousse however who dominated the newspaper,
and in the words of the Swiss Procureur-Général:

> Paul Brousse était bien l'âme de l'Avant-Garde, il en soignait presque
> seul la rédaction, sans lui le journal ne se serait pas soutenu . . . il a pris à
> la publication du journal une part beaucoup plus grande que tous les
> autres.[104]

The committee never met regularly; Loetscher and Rossel, two of its members, took no part in its affairs; Jeanneret only occasionally helped Spichiger in circulating the paper, while Schwitzguébel, its joint editor, contributed only a few articles. It was Brousse who translated articles sent from abroad, arranged the format and paid money out of his pocket (or possibly that of Landsberg) when there were financial difficulties. None the less, for all Brousse's domination of the paper it was more than his personal mouthpiece, especially after March 1878 when it took over the previous function of the *Bulletin*. It appears in fact that there was some discontent at the line the newspaper adopted, and attempts were made to assert the control of the Jura *militants* over its editors. The resolution taken at the meeting of the Jura anarchist section on 12 June indicated that it did not meet with the approval of everyone (it was perhaps significant that this followed immediately after the articles devoted to Hoedel's attempt on the Kaiser); Pindy for example protested very strongly against the projected publication of Schwitzguébel's articles on 'Les Régicides', and to all intents and purposes he ceased to co-operate with the Jura Federation after the affair – largely because it involved him in the threat of expulsion from Switzerland. Brousse had to tread with considerable care the path between the 'extremists' (characterized by the author of the Moncasi article) and the 'moderates' (e.g. Pindy), as well as defining satisfactorily his own attitude.

It may well have been that the wave of assassinations provided the catalyst which led Brousse to the radical revision of his views which took place over the course of the next year. The Hoedel and Nobiling *attentats* took place before the Fribourg Congress, which was the first public occasion on which Brousse indicated the direction in which he was now moving. Nettlau, on the basis of observations made by Kropotkin, later suggested – and there is no reason to disagree with him – that:

The Avant-Garde now became the organ of the Federation ... the lively personality of Brousse increasingly annoyed Guillaume, but Kropotkin, who at that time knew Brousse more intimately, asserted that Brousse was also weary and was looking towards France, and that especially when the *attentats* began believed he saw the beginning of a struggle of which he did not wish to become the victim. His rhetoric continued, but his faith had gone. In addition, Brousse and Kropotkin were very much involved with the beginning of the French workers' movement and began to devote their propaganda activities to it ... for all genuine working-class movements Kropotkin had the warmest of interests, and Brousse, whose revolutionary will exhausted itself in words, was genuinely pleased to be able to participate in the working-class movement in a less exposed way.[105]

On 10 December 1878 the Swiss Federal Council decided on the suppression of *L'Avant-Garde*. As early as October the activities of foreign – mainly German – exile socialists had been brought to the attention of the Swiss Government following a speech in the Reichstag by Eulenberg, the Prussian Minister of the Interior, on the subject of foreign press reactions to the Hoedel and Nobiling attempts. This led to a discussion within the Federal Council on the need for a revision of the rights of political asylum. On 28 November *Der Bund*, a Berne newspaper, drew attention to *L'Avant-Garde* specifically, pointing out that it advocated 'assassination', and on the following day the Federal Council asked the Prefect of La Chaux-de-Fonds what measures the Neuchâtel authorities were planning against the paper, 'dont le langage et la tendance sont de nature à troubler les bons rapports qui existent entre la Suisse et les Etats étrangers'.[106] The decision of 10 December was communicated to the Neuchâtel authorities on 12 December. The Neuchâtel Department of Police and Justice, on failing to obtain an undertaking from the printers of *L'Avant-Garde* that they would both cease publication of the newspaper and give an undertaking not to publish again any such paper, placed seals on the printing presses. This prevented the printers from printing any newspaper at all – which led to a full-scale controversy which occupied more attention than the suppression of *L'Avant-Garde* as such. The Neuchâtel authorities had in fact blundered. In the first place the Swiss Penal Code specified that action in press offences had to be taken against the editor and not the printer. Second, the Neuchâtel cantonal government was in the control of the Radicals, and its action in blocking all publications by the printers resulted in temporary disappearance of the local Liberal (i.e. conservative) paper, *La Patriote Suisse*. Thus the affair immediately raised the question of freedom of the press and provided a useful stick with which the Liberals proceeded to beat the Neuchâtel and Federal Governments. *The Times* reported that:

> The suppression of L'Avant-Garde is causing considerable excitement and is much discussed by the Press. The suppression itself is applauded. ... But the way in which the decree of the Federal Council was carried out ... is seriously censured.[107]

The over-hasty action of the Government which had led to the clumsy suppression of the paper caused its action to be questioned by fourteen Liberal deputies on 17 December, when the measures were described as arbitrary and unjustified and were compared even unfavourably to measures against the press taken in Germany. Anderwerth, Head of the Federal Department of Police and Justice, justified the action against the printers on the grounds that there was no single editor of the paper and that it was impossible to discriminate against one of those involved in the short time available. He re-affirmed Switzerland's policy of giving asylum to political refugees provided they did not embark on action hostile to foreign Governments.[108]

Shortly afterwards the printers were allowed to start up their machines, and the federal authorities began to look for the guilty editor of L'Avant-Garde. Had the Government acted with more deliberation they would have been aware that on 11 December a report to the Conseil des Etats had already described Brousse as its leading figure, adding that he was 'un esprit ardent, exalté, ayant un besoin d'agitation et de domination que peuvent seules satisfaire les théories de nihilisme et de la révolution sociale'.[109] Consequently, on the request of Morel, the Procureur-général, who was put in control of the affair on 25 December following a Government decision two days earlier to continue with its action against the paper, the Vaud cantonal authorities arrested Brousse on 26 December at his home in Vevey, where he had been living for some weeks for health reasons. He had admitted full responsibility for the contents of the paper as soon as the judicial inquiry had begun at La Chaux-de-Fonds. He was held virtually incommunicado for over three weeks, allowed to see only Natalie Landsberg and Elisée Reclus (who lived at Vevey), and then on the condition that – in Kropotkin's words – they talked only about 'rain and snow'.[110] He was finally released on bail of 2,000 francs, which was in the main provided by his father, on 27 January 1879.

The report of the Procureur-général presented to the Federal Government in February stated that only against Brousse could charges be substantiated. This was regrettable, the report added, in view of the fact that it was evident that in Switzerland a movement seeking 'universal revolution, violence, theft, and assassination' was spreading its doctrines amongst the Swiss population, and (which was apparently infinitely worse) exploiting students

who 'se montrent d'autant plus ardents à vouloir régénérer la société par
les moyens violents qu'ils apportent moins de sérieux à leurs études'.[111]
(He did however have the good grace to add that this phenomenon
was 'rien de nouveau, et s'est vu de tout temps'.) The exaggerated
tone of his report similarly marked his speech against Brousse at the
trial which was held in the Great Council Chamber of the castle of
Neuchâtel on 15 and 16 April. It was to become the stereotype of
many such attacks on anarchists in the future. The association of
anarchism with assassination, theft and violence had been made, and
L'Avant-Garde made it stick even more firmly than before.

The trial took place before a large public composed in the main
of members and sympathizers of the International, as well as several
students from Berne. Brousse was charged with violating Article 41
of the Federal Penal Code in various articles published in *L'Avant-
Garde*. The Article read as follows: 'Quiconque viole un térritoire
étranger ou commet tout autre acte contraire aux droits des gens est
puni de l'emprisonnement ou de l'amende.' The offending newspaper
articles were classified into two groups, the first dealing with the Mac-
Mahon crisis of 1877, the second dealing with the assassination
attempts of 1878.[112]

Morel based his case on an attempt to label the doctrines of
L'Avant-Garde as corrupt and subversive, and in fact placed little
emphasis – it is doubtful if this would have been possible – on the
threat it had posed to international peace and stability. He concentrated on arousing the just indignation of the jury, describing the
doctrines of *L'Avant-Garde* as attacking:

... tout ce que nous avons appris à respecter; il attaque l'ordre, la loi,
l'autorité, la vie des particuliers, celle des magistrats, celle des souverains;
il respecte ni la famille, ni la réligion, ni la propriété, ni la patrie.

Propaganda by the deed, he continued, was nothing less than assassination. The Federal Government had the right to safeguard the
independence of Switzerland whose existence depended on the good-
will of her neighbours. He dealt hardly at all with the strictly *legal*
case, on which Fauquiez, Brousse's defence counsel, concentrated.
The defence case rested on an attempt to prove that the 'acts' referred to in Article 41 could not refer to articles in the press, and
Fauquiez brought forward several precedents to reinforce his case.
He ended his defence speech by saying that the trial was merely a
'procès de tendance' (a tendentious trial) and that the convenience

of foreign governments had been placed above the freedom of the press.

Brousse then spoke in his own defence. As traditional he took advantage of the platform presented him by giving an *exposé* of anarchist ideas and countering the allegations of Morel. Correcting the common misinterpretation of what anarchism stood for – anarchic disorder and bloody chaos – he defined its aim as the spontaneous, natural and scientific order in which the rule of the majority would be replaced by each making his own law through the reign of contract. Even if a small minority disregarded such contracts:

... le régime des contrats est encore possible puisqu'il suffirait de l'existence d'un Etat qui en soit le gardien comme l'entendait Proudhon, pour assurer l'ordre. Certes, la présence de cet Etat ne serait que transitoire: dépouillé de la plus grande partie de sa besogne législative, il ne serait qu'un Etat diminué, un Etat en décadence, en dégénérescence, une sorte de premier pas vers l'élimination sociale, complète et définitive de l'Etat.

This was the first occasion on which Brousse had accepted any form of the State at all, as either a temporary or a permanent feature of post-revolutionary society. It was another indication of his changing views, and as if to compensate for it he devoted an extremely powerful and effective part of his speech to attacking the liberal conception of individual property and to demonstrating the desirability and necessity of the collective ownership of the means of production. In this he used arguments derived from both Herbert Spencer and John Stuart Mill, thereby tailoring support for his arguments to the possible sympathies of the jury. In the middle of the argument however he was cut short by the President of the Court.[113]

Passing on to discuss *means,* Brousse said there were two apparent ways to achieve the society they were seeking; evolution or Revolution. If he had the freedom to choose, he said, there would be no doubt as to where he stood,:

... pour ne parler que de moi ... je n'ai ni la soif des persécutions ni le goût du martyre ... je n'aime pas l'éxil pour l'éxil, la prison pour la prison, les suffrances pour les charmes qu'elles procurent. Qu'on me donne le plus petit espoir qu'une évolution normale est possible, qu'on lui permettra de modifier au fur et à mesure tous les organes sociaux qui doivent l'être, et de révolutionnaire déterminé je deviens à l'instant un enragé évolutionniste.

But he said he saw no immediate hope that the bourgeoisie would yield. Everything pointed to violent Revolution in the relatively near future. He spoke with the voice of the disappointed bourgeois himself. There was no mention of hostile class interests or an historical dialectic which demanded Revolution; what created a revolutionary situation was the resistance of the bourgeoisie in a situation in which it could, if it so desired, act otherwise. The resistance of the bourgeoisie to socialist demands was contrasted with its own claims from 1789 onwards, and its hostility to and fear of anarchist violence with the great moments of the struggles for individual liberty. Was it for the sons of those who had fought in 1848 to reproach socialism with preaching the need for insurrection? Was it for the nation of William Tell to deny the value of political assassination? Had not Orsini lived in Zurich, and had he not been praised by the press for his noble republican character? Yet when Hoedel and Moncasi and Passanante had acted, they were execrated and their defenders persecuted. So far as this last point was concerned, Brousse sought to set the record straight:

... nous n'avons *conseillé* le régicide à aucun de nos lecteurs; nous nous sommes *étonnés* qu'il ne soit pas produit dans telle ou telle éventualité; nous l'avons discuté; nous avon *regretté* que puisqu'il avait été essayé contre le roi Alphonse il n'ait pas abouti; nous avons *approuvé* toutes les exécutions russes; enfin nous avons toujours *sympathisé* avec les jeunes hommes qui se sont sacrifiés et toujours maudit les rois, les princes les empéreurs. Voilà, en effet, notre crime.

This was a fair summary of the attitude of *L'Avant-Garde*.

Turning to the legal case against him Brousse argued, as Fauquiez had done, that Article 41 of the Penal Code could not be used to include press offences – which were *encouragements* to the prescribed acts but not acts themselves; as such they did in fact find special mention in various other articles of the Penal Code. (That his prosecution under Article 41 was of doubtful validity was suggested later by a Report of 1885[114] which discussed the Article and dismissed it as of no value in the prosecution of such offences.) He ended his speech by seeking to discredit the Swiss federal authorities who, he said, had clearly acted under duress; otherwise why had they not acted eighteen months previously in 1877 when the first group of articles for which he was being tried had been published?

It was an extremely effective speech. The *Neue Zürcher Zeitung* commented on it in these terms:

The defence of Brousse, delivered with a typically southern vigour, fluency, and rare lucidity, must arouse a certain sympathy. The young fanatic of 35 speaks with the energy and power of an apostle certain of the holiness of his mission.[115]

It would have been surprising if the attractive personality of Brousse and the effectiveness of his speech, in contrast with the weakness of the prosecution case, had not created an atmosphere favourable to him. This was reflected in the Court's sentence. He was found guilty on only one of the charges against him – concerned with the group of articles on assassinations – and the Court rejected the heavy sentences demanded by the Procureur-général (Morel had demanded a year's imprisonment, twelve years' banishment from Switzerland, and a 500 franc fine). Instead it sentenced him to two months' imprisonment, ten years' banishment, and a 200 franc fine and costs.[116] Accordingly Brousse was imprisoned in the prison tower, formerly forming part of the old town defences, overlooking Lake Neuchâtel.

The trial and the publicity surrounding it helped to establish for Brousse the reputation of an extremist anarchist, ironically at the very moment when he was evolving towards a more moderate socialism. Under the title 'A Universal Anarchist' the Geneva correspondent of *The Times* described Brousse as 'one of the most remarkable and highly cultured of the leaders of the new sect of universal anarchists'. Outlining Brousse's professional career (the article referred to him throughout as Dr Brousse) the correspondent continued:

. . . it is no new thing to find philanthropic sentiments associated with the profession of a ferocious political creed, and the late editor of the Avant-Garde advocated regicide and even promiscuous murder with a cynical coolness that Marat in the columns of the Ami du Peuple could scarcely have rivalled.[117]

It is doubtful if Brousse would have been flattered had he been aware of the comparison with Marat, but whether he liked it or not the *L'Avant-Garde* case was the beginning of a new stereotype of the anarchist and of anarchism which had, in the words of *The Times,* 'revolution for its starting point, murder for its means, and anarchy for its ideals'. The *Journal de Genève* described anarchism in an even more lurid light:

. . . un culte nouveau qui commence, une greffe buddhiste que les mains Mongoles nous ont apporté du fond de l'Asie et qu'elles s'efforcent de

faire prospérer sur le tronc vermoulu des civilizations occidentales . . .
on est ici en présence d'un phénomene de l'ordre réligieux, d'un fanatisme d'une espêce particulière, aveugle et contagieux, malheureusement,
comme tous les fanatismes. . . .[118]

During the period between the suppression of *L'Avant-Garde* in
December and his trial at Neuchâtel in April, Brousse had helped to
found a new anarchist paper. This was one of the outstanding
anarchist papers of the century, *Le Révolté,* and like *L'Avant-
Garde* its main target was France. While Brousse was under arrest
in December and January, Kropotkin made arrangements which he
had already discussed with Brousse for publication of the newspaper
which was to replace *L'Avant-Garde.* He found greater support in
Geneva than in the Jura, where Brousse's arrest had caused
demoralization and a reluctance to risk prosecution. On 17 January,
while Brousse was still in prison, Kropotkin wrote to Paul Robin
that one of two projects for a newspaper would be implemented;
either a clandestine *L'Avant-Garde* or a non-clandestine paper
dealing with economic and social matters, and 'laissant tranquille
les rois'. He added that general opinion was in favour of obtaining
Brousse's opinion. When Brousse was released he and Kropotkin
agreed that the paper should place greater emphasis on economic
questions than *L'Avant-Garde* had done, and it was decided that
Kropotkin would be chief editor with Brousse and Schwitzguébel as
sub-editors.[119] This newspaper finally appeared under the title of *Le
Révolté* on 22 February 1879, with a capital of only 25 francs and an
initial publication of 2,000 copies.

It was a gamble which paid off. *Le Révolté* soon attained a circulation far greater than that ever enjoyed by *L'Avant-Garde.* Its first
leading article was entitled 'Nous sommes des Révoltés' and was
written by Brousse.[120] It reflected the new emphasis of the anarchists
on economic and social issues, but had lost none of the vigour of
L'Avant-Garde. Brousse lambasted capitalist society in violent terms.
He described a vivid picture of its corruption:

En bas, le producteur en guenilles, simple roue, appendice vivant de la
machine, noir, suant, secoué comme elle, moins bien entretenu qu'elle,
libre! . . . oui, libre comme elle de mêler au grand vacarme son grince-
ment de dents.

En haut, le fainéant, l'aristocrate, le maître! Il trône, ce Jupiter patron,
dans le luxe splendide, les pieds mous dans les riches tapis; bijoux,

chaînes, montres, breloques luisent sur le gilet moderne, au lieu et place qui tâchait le blason sur l'antique pourpoint.

Even worse off, he continued, than the men who slaved in the factories were the women, forced to supplement their meagre wages with the wages of sin – and he evoked the image of the honest and virtuous working girl victim to the advances of the idle sons of the capitalist class. It was this society, he concluded, which led socialists to 'laisser monter du coeur l'indignation amère, et sortir de nos lèvres le cri de protestation du Révolté'.[121] It was a fitting finale to his career in Switzerland, although the violence of his language gave no indication of the reformist tactics of the socialist movement he was very soon openly to advocate.

He was due to be released from Neuchâtel prison on 16 June. On 30 May the Neuchâtel authorities asked the Federal Council to grant Brousse a safe conduct on release, which it refused. The Council similarly refused a request that Brousse be given 14 days' grace in which to clear up his personal affairs before leaving the country and refused a second request for a 48-hour period of grace. Consequently he left Switzerland immediately on his release and was accompanied by a gendarme to Porrentruy where 'un homme influent de la localité et connaissant Brousse' led him across the frontier into France. Here he made for Montbeliard with the apparent intention of making for Calais, which suggested that he intended to go to London. That he was undecided where to go is apparent from a letter he wrote to Paul Robin on the day before his release.[122] In the event he seems to have changed his plans, and went instead to Brussels.

4

From Anarchism to Reformism: exile in Brussels and London, 1879–80

The end of his exile in Switzerland marked a definitive stage in the development of Brousse's political career. The beginning of anarchist terrorism, the decline of the Jura movement with its failure to establish any popular basis, the growing isolation and sectarianism of the anarchists within the European socialist movement – which Brousse himself had largely helped to create – and the development of the socialist movement in France itself, were factors which led him to examine some of the tenets of the anarchist faith. It has been seen how already at the Fribourg Congress of the Jura Federation he had started this process. The suppression of *L'Avant-Garde* was followed by Brousse's trial, imprisonment and expulsion from Switzerland, and it was to be in exile in Brussels and London that he followed through the consequences of this re-examination and laid down the broad strategy which he was to pursue within the French socialist movement.

Brousse had arrived in Brussels by 21 June. Thanks to papers provided by a close friend in the Jura, Gustave Jeanneret, a *militant* of the Federation who was soon to make his name as a painter, he had encountered no difficulty in crossing through France into Belgium. By 27 June he had been joined by Natalie who had stayed with the Jeanneret family at their home a short distance from Neuchâtel during Brousse's imprisonment. It is from their correspondence with Gustave Jeanneret that details of Brousse's activities and changing political views can be established.[1]

Brousse had no illusions about the precariousness of his position – Natalie Landsberg described them as having 'un pied à Bruxelles l'autre prèt â prendre le train pour Londres'[2] – but believed that if he avoided political meetings the risk of expulsion could be minimized. In fact it was only seven weeks before he was expelled, seven weeks of almost unrelieved gloom and depression. He was, for one thing, in bad health. This had been a reason for moving from Zurich to Vevey in 1878. His imprisonment at Neuchâtel had done nothing to improve it and it was aggravated by the Brussels climate. For another he was short of money, at least to begin with. Although his father had helped to bail him out of prison in January, and still apparently sent occasional sums to him, the costs of the Neuchâtel trial had fallen solely on his shoulders.[3] He had thus to practise as a doctor, an activity which at least compensated for the far more trying intellectual isolation and inactivity forced on him by the threat of police action. This and Landsberg's company helped to make life tolerable.[4] The city itself he found unattractive, without even the virtues of a modern industrial structure. The revolutionary Brussels of 1830 had disappeared to make way for 'bankers, traders, the idle and the rich'. The cost of living was high, the weather terrible, and his meridional soul found no comfort anywhere: 'Point de couleurs à la plume, pas de chaleur au coeur; je deviens abstrait comme un problème de géométrie analytique.' Moreover the state of the Belgian socialist movement thoroughly discouraged him. Most of the socialists were 'en plein 1830 français', divided between those who spent their time in personal slanders on the one hand and those who sacrificed, or concealed, their socialism in the hope of obtaining a Republic on the other.[5] The old unity of the International had broken up, and he found only one anarchist, Egidius of the *Cri du Peuple*, of interest – 'jeune, sans études, sans goût du travail, bon garçon, mais fou. Triste! très triste!' – while the other anarchists connected with the *Cri* – for which Paul Robin was vainly attempting to obtain financial support from Kropotkin and the Jura anarchists, such as Bastin and Piette – pleased him in no way at all. It led him to the following conclusion:

Plus je voyage, plus j'observe, plus je réfléchis, plus je me convainque que le parti anarchiste doit se transformer sous peine de mort; que s'il se transforme, s'il s'adapte au milieu nouveau crée par des circonstances nouvelles il peut être un magnifique et très puissant parti d'opposition, pacifique ou révolutionnaire, à son choix.[6]

On 10 August he wrote to Jeanneret telling him that he had plans to found a newspaper under the name of a Belgian – a project requiring great caution as the police were keeping a close eye on him. Indeed they were, for on the following day he received notice to quit the country within twenty-four hours on the grounds that he had attended a meeting held at Verviers on 17 July. Brousse denied this,

although a police report of 25 July had mentioned his presence at the
meeting where he was alleged to have given an account of his trial,
imprisonment and collaboration on *Le Révolté*.[7] This report had been
followed up by reports received from the Montpellier and Neuchâtel
authorities, and a royal decree of expulsion was drawn up on 5
August. The timing of its application may well have been delayed so
as to coincide almost exactly with the expulsion from Belgium of
Johann Most, the renegade and anarchist member of the German
Social Democratic Party.[8]

Expelled from Belgium, Brousse and Landsberg made for London
where they remained for practically a year. Although Brousse clearly
wanted to return to France he seems to have feared arrest. Despite the
fact that his sentence had expired and that the partial amnesty had
been implemented he did not leave London until after a full amnesty
had been proclaimed. It was during this year in London that he
finally determined the position he was to adopt when he returned to
French socialist politics in 1880. The break with his anarchist past
was a difficult one in that it involved breaking with many personal
friends. It was also an incomplete one, in that he never abandoned
his belief in an anarcho-Communist ideal. Consequently he sought to
disguise the transition, as did Costa, both for his own and other
people's comfort. But this did not alter the fact that a critical and
qualitative change occurred during this period.

Like most foreign exiles in London in the nineteenth century he
was appalled and horrified at its poverty. He wrote to Jeanneret, the
young artist, on 3 September:

> Je ne croyais pas avoir autant de motifs de vous dire que votre place
> était dans un centre comme Londres! Vous dites que les sujets sont
> partout, mais qui a vu la misère de Londres de près vous dira comme moi
> que nulle part comme ici on ne trouvera des sujets de réalisme socialiste.

He enlarged on his impressions in a letter written in November:[9]

> Je voudrais vous voir ici. Certes, les modèles ne vous manqueraient
> pas; un penny . . . ou 2 vous trouveriez des modèles de viande humaine,
> tout que vous voudriez. Et quels modèles! quel réalisme! quelle misère!
> Je ne chercherai pas à vous les dépeindre, je n'y réussirais pas. . . .

But he did his best and described a scene he had just witnessed:

> Un homme, aveugle et saoûl, tenu au poignet par sa fille, enfant de 17
> ans à l'oeil gris d'acier, mais vague de whisky et de gin. Plus de chair

aperçue que de chiffon. Ce groupe s'arrête, le père s'embarrasse dans les pas de sa fille, roule, tombe, sa fille le suit, ventre en l'air. Chacun passe, regard, détourne les yeux, poursuit son chemin. Je m'arrête stupéfait. Le Policeman s'approche, commande deux voyous, fait charger sur une charette et conduit au poste cette famille en tas.

Ce spéctacle est chose ordinaire à Londres. Si je me fâche, on rit! Vous n'avez rien vu me dit-on! Nous irons au quartier des pauvres. Je tremble d'y aller!!!

London in fact provided him with his first experience of working-class urban misery, an experience which struck him deeply. It can only have had the effect of leading him further along the path towards demanding that the socialist movement concentrate on immediate improvements in working-class conditions.[10]

Unlike his stay in Brussels, that in London provided no threat of expulsion and he was able to carry on unhindered his political activities. He quickly made contact with the large exile community, and as early as September mentioned plans drawn up with several friends for the creation of a newspaper (which did not finally appear until March 1880). He was extremely critical of the resolutions drawn up at a meeting held at La Chaux-de-Fonds on 12 October in place of the Annual Congress of the Jura Federation. These resolutions had affirmed anarcho-Communism as the aim of the Federation and collectivism as the necessary transitory stage, but had suggested no further solution to the problem of practical ways of achieving it than those maintained in previous years. Brousse wrote to Jeanneret, who had been present at the meeting:

... on n'y a pris aucun décision d'avenir. Je vous dirais d'ailleurs que je suis fort affecté de ce qui se passe. Costa et moi – avec raison à mon sens naturellement – nous allons d'un côté; nos amis suisses me semblent se cristalliser dans une orthodoxie anarchiste hors de saison. Les événements marchent et les laissent à côté.[11]

The parallel he drew with Costa's evolution is an interesting one and merits further examination.

The most important anarchist propagandist and organizer in Italy following the 1872 St Imier Congress, Costa had as early as the beginning of 1877 shown signs of awareness that the Italian anarchist Programme of insurrectionism was open to criticism. In his notorious open letter to Nicotera, the Minister of the Interior, of January 1877 he said:

By means of conspiracy a change in the form of government can be obtained; a principle can be dispossessed or punctured and another put in its place, but it cannot achieve social revolution. . . . To do this is a matter of widely diffusing the new principles in the masses, or better, to awaken them in them, since they already have them instinctively, and to organize the workers of the whole world, so that the revolution occurs by itself, from the bottom to the top and not vice-versa, either by means of laws and decrees or by force.[12]

The 1877 insurrection at Benevento was the work of Cafiero and Malatesta, not of Costa, who maintained an ambiguous attitude towards it; having written the letter to Nicotera he then wrote another agreeing with Malatesta and Cafiero, which suggests a certain degree of confusion in his own mind – as does the fact that he took no part in the fiasco and later denied that the Italian Federation as an organization had had anything to do with it. Yet at the 1877 St Imier, Verviers and Ghent Congresses he adopted an extreme position alongside Brousse. Shortly afterwards, in Paris, he wrote to Anna Kulisciov, his mistress, that:

. . . de notre côté, il y a peu a espérer . . . ceux qui pensent comme nous ne sont pas nombreux. . . . Il faut commencer par le commencement; nous avons besoin d'une propagande immense. Un gouvernement qui nous permettait de nous réunir, de nous associer et de publier quelque chose, voilà ce qu'il nous faudrait. . . .[13]

Costa continued to associate with anarchist circles, but there were differences between him and the Parisian group, caused possibly by his association with Guesde and with Tito Zanardelli, one of the leading Italian reformist socialists. Imprisoned in May 1878 for membership of the International in Paris, he was amnestied on 5 June 1879 – ten days prior to Brousse's release from Neuchâtel. Two weeks previously he had written that the socialists should exploit the demands for a Republic (in Italy) which were certain to follow the period of reaction. The anarchist movement, he said, should occupy itself with the problems of the working class, rid itself of sectarian isolationism and concentrate on practical action. On 27 July – when Brousse was in Brussels – he wrote his open letter 'To my friends in the Romagna' which, while trying to keep a foot in both camps at once, strongly criticized the anarchist Programme:

. . . since the failure of revolutionary attempts deprived us of liberty for entire years, or condemned us to exile, we unfortunately lost touch with the daily struggles and practice of real life; we closed ourselves up too much and worried more about the logic of our ideas and the composition of a revolutionary programme that we tried to actuate without delay, instead of studying the economic and moral conditions of the people and their sensed and immediate needs. . . . Let us profit from the lesson of experience. Let us complete what was interrupted. Let us throw ourselves once more among the people and strengthen ourselves in them.

And he went on to propose collectivism and the federation of autonomous Communes as the immediate Programme of the Socialist Party, with anarcho-Communism retained as its ideal.[14]

This Programme compared almost identically with the Programme put forward by Brousse at the Fribourg Congress, and his critique of the traditional anarchist Programme compared with that made in Brousse's letters to Jeanneret. It is tempting (and especially so in view of Brousse's own acknowledgement of the parallel between their evolution) to posit a direct influence of one on the other, as in the case of their mutual 'extremism' in 1877. But as in the case of 1877 it is impossible to prove any direct contact. Indeed the contrary is suggested by Brousse's reaction to Costa's activities in Paris in 1878 and from his letter to Vinas of February 1880.[15] It therefore seems probable that their evolution from anarchism to socialism was accomplished separately, a response to changed circumstances which led them – and many others – to modify their tactics. In a sense both of them had begun to penetrate the anarchist myth of the instinctive revolutionism of the people as early as 1877, by the very fact of realizing its contingent non-revolutionary nature. Hence both insisted heavily on propaganda to educate the people, though at that stage the purpose of education, in their minds, was merely to awaken an instinctive revolutionary potential. But in the following two years, with the destruction of the International in Italy, its moribund display in France and its non-existence in Germany (where the socialists had to fight against the anti-socialist laws of 1878) both were brought to realize the dilemma which faced them. As Brousse had often said, propaganda by the deed was *not* attempted revolution but propaganda to educate the people. This none the less demanded the same justification, i.e. a reasonable chance of success, and good organization. After two years of inaction forced upon the anarchist movement by Government repression in most European countries the credibility of the *militants* of the movement in this tactic was impossible to maintain. Brousse and Costa themselves simply ceased to believe in it. Costa expressed the dilemma perfectly: '... insurrectionism, if practised, leads to nothing if not the triumph of reaction and, if not practised, it leads to the disesteem of him who preaches it and remains purely verbal.'[16] It was because neither of them was prepared either to sustain a 'verbal insurrectionism', which led to what Brousse described as 'une orthodoxie anarchiste hors de saison', or to accept the continued triumph of reaction which consigned them to prison or the roles of mere spectators, that Brousse and Costa dropped their outright rejection of the State and came to accept the value of electoral activity. This conclusion was reached independently by each, on the basis of parallel but separate experience.

Nor is there need to resort to the *dei ex machina* which Guillaume provided to explain their evolution. Writing to Fritz Brupbacher in 1912, in a letter additionally interesting as an insight into Guillaume's own position, he said:

... votre jugement sur Brousse et Costa est erroné! S'ils ont changé, ce n'est pas du tout parce qu'ils auraient 'der Massenbewegung alles geopfert'. Quand Brousse et Costa se disaient 'anarchistes', quand à Verviers et à Gand ils se séparaient des autres délégués de l'Internationale en refusant tout rapprochement avec les ouvriers des pays où dominaient la Social-Demokratie (tandis que de Paepe et moi nous voulions ce rapprochement) c'est simplement qu'ils étaient des *exaltés*, s'enivrant de *mots creux*, et qu'ils ne comprenaient pas la question; ils n'avaient rien là, ils ne connaissaient pas encore Marx et le marxisme. Ils le découvrirent un peu plus tard, et alors ce fut une véritable *révélation*: ce fut leur chemin de Damas et ils tombèrent à genoux en criant 'Seigneur, pardonne-moi de t'avoir persecuté!' Il faut ajouter que l'influence de femmes contribua beaucoup à leur conversion – Mlle Landsberg pour Brousse, Mme Makarievitch [Kulichoff] pour Costa. ...[17]

To deal with the second of Guillaume's points first. While Kulisciov (as she was better known) may have influenced Costa, as Hostetter seems to suggest[18] it is extremely doubtful if Landsberg influenced Brousse in this direction. Indeed in the absence of any kind of definite proof it could be argued that she influenced him in the other direction – towards anarchist extremism – as she appeared on the scene in about 1875 and took some part in the organization of the Berne demonstration of 1877. But she was not of the stature or significance of Kulisciov and from what is known of her it is more probable that Brousse influenced her than *vice versa*.

The first of Guillaume's explanations of the change in the loyalties

of Brousse and Costa – the influence of Marx and Marxism – was
equally mistaken. In Costa's case it is clear that Marxism had virtually no influence on his change of loyalties, which was the result of
experience and represented a reform of, not a complete renunciation
of, the anarchist Programme (however much this led him into all
kinds of contradictions). Marx and Marxism played no part in
Costa's change, although *afterwards* it was rationalized by Costa in
Marxist terms.

Much the same happened with Brousse. As his letter to Vinas (see
Appendix 1) shows he saw his own evolution as a development,
through experience, of his anarchist beliefs. There is no evidence at
all to suggest that Marx in any way influenced Brousse,[19] and his later
position as an anti-Marxist and as the leader of the non-Marxist or
even anti-Marxist socialist party in France shows clearly that the last
thing Brousse did was 'to fall at Marx's knee and beg forgiveness'. It
is true that Brousse recognized Marx's status as a masterful econo-
mist and critic of capitalism, but he refused in any sense to accept as
final what Marx said and completely rejected the political content of
Marxism. Suspicions that his visit to Marx when he was in London
led him to Marxism were voiced by Kropotkin in 1901, when he told
Nettlau that:

> Marx gave him a couple of polite words, said he was a good economist,
> and then Brousse wrote the terrible series 'La crise, sa cause, son
> remède' ... which began reasonably and ended in Marxism; the long
> article almost brought *Le Révolté* to an end.[20]

Kropotkin's explanation, admittedly several years after the event, was
wrong certainly on one and possibly on two counts. In the first place,
it is not even clear that he had his facts correct. The series was begun in
Le Révolté on 4 August 1879 (when Brousse was still in Brussels) and
ended on 20 September 1879 (only shortly after his arrival in London). According to one source Marx was visited by Brousse in March
1880.[21] In the second place, the series of articles to which Kropotkin
referred, which was published anonymously as a pamphlet in 1879,[22]
dealt with the long-term crisis in the Jura watch-making industry
caused by the closing of American markets, and was certainly not
Marxist – although Brousse on one occasion quoted from Marx on
the internationalization of the market. It attacked the inadequacy of
various relief schemes put forward in the Jura and said that the basic
fault lay with 'le défaut d'harmonie entre les intérêts capitalistes et

les intérêts travailleurs'. This was hardly the language of Marxism, although the argument led to the conclusion that only the collectivization of property could remedy the situation – but this in itself was not a conclusion peculiar to Marxism. There was no evidence in the pamphlet of any absorption of the theory of class struggle or of the proletarian mission. Such a conversion would in fact have required a very considerable change of outlook, if only for the very simple reason that a mere change of tactics by an anarchist – an acceptance of the need for political action – did not thereby make him a Marxist; the *anticlassista* postulate of anarchism reflected very different premises about human society and behaviour from those assumed by Marxism.[23] In one sense Marxists were correct in describing anarchism as 'reactionary', for anarchism referred to 'the people', or to 'the working class' rather than to 'the proletariat', as the vanguard of Revolution. (One of the clearest exponents of this *anticlassista* view was Malatesta.) Once Brousse – or any anarchist – accepted the need to choose between unpalatable alternatives and accepted political action, his standpoint was invariably affected by this component of anarchist thought. Thus it was less extraordinary that Brousse eventually allied with the Republicans to defend the Third Republic against the Boulangists than it would have been had he adopted the rigorous class position of Guesde and adopted a neutral position in what the French Marxists considered to be a conflict between factions of the bourgeoisie.

It *is* true that later, during his exile in London, Brousse began to refer to 'la lutte des classes modernes',[24] a token of Marxist influence, and by 1882 had openly acknowledged the error of the anarchists in believing the State to be the prime cause of social evil. He wrote:

> ... les anarchistes ne comprirent pas que, pour atteindre à une société an-archique, sans gouvernement, il faut d'abord égaliser réellement les citoyens et faire, pour cela, usage transitoire des pouvoirs politiques et administratifs dans la Commune, le département l'Etat; nous n'avions pas observé encore que le gouvernement n'est pas la cause du mal social existant, mais seulement son résultat inévitable, que le gouvernmentalisme est un des produits de l'inégalité et que l'anarchie exige, pour s'établir, l'avènement préalable de l'égalité entre tous les citoyens.[25]

To some extent this was a concession to the Marxist thesis that the State was the political expression of an economic reality – although even this argument could be quarrelled with on the grounds that

Brousse hinted at the old Bakuninist heresy of 'l'égalisation des classes'. But that Brousse was far from uncritically adopting Marxism is apparent from several sources in which he often attacked its narrowness to a degree which amounted to its denial. He said for instance that Marx's historical materialism was too 'simpliste'; economic environment was merely one factor in the determination of man's development. He also scorned any intellectual subservience to Marx: 'Marx [n'est pas] un pape infaillible et . . . il n'[est] pas Dieu'.[26] If he occasionally adopted Marxist terminology this was no more than a concession to what increasingly became the vocabulary of the European socialist movement in its attempt to provide itself with an irrefutable scientific basis.[27] Moreover this limited adherence to Marxism, if it can even be called that, came *after* he had abandoned anarchism. It was the failure of anarchism, not the strength of Marxism, which caused Brousse (and Costa) to change their tactics. This is seen if we return now to his exile in London.

The friends referred to in his letter of 3 September were members of a study group founded by Zanardelli when he arrived in London in 1878, the Circolo di Studi Sociali, which included amongst its members French, Russian and German exiles such as Leo Hartmann and Gustave Brocher, the latter of whom became a close friend of Brousse. The milieu in which Brousse found himself was conducive to the re-examination of political attitudes, for the exile community in London provided a melting-pot for socialist theory in which individuals of mixed origin and outlook pontificated, argued and discussed the entire spectrum of socialist opinion, often with results of considerable confusion.[28] Zanardelli for instance had been a leading representative of the reformist wing of the Italian socialist movement which, under the influence of Malon, had been growing in importance since the mid-1870s. At the 1877 Ghent Congress he had voted for the pact of mutual assistance between the 'State socialists' – and had at the same time supported insurrection as a tactic of the socialist movement. In London in 1878 he published a small bilingual newspaper, *La Guerre Social* (*La Guerra Sociale*), of ephemeral existence and of extreme revolutionary invective, which expressed sympathy for the assassins of 1878 and was denounced for doing so by the English politician Bradlaugh.[29] His reformism was, to say the least, unstable. Costa, it is worth noting, in his attempt to keep a foot in both the anarchist and socialist camps, pursued what often seemed like a similar policy to that of Zanardelli and saddled the Italian Socialist

movement with 'maximalism'. This London exile community, a
microcosm of the wider confusion within the European socialist
movement, provided the background of intellectual ferment in which
Brousse clarified, formulated and expounded his new tactics.

He too oscillated somewhat uneasily in his loyalties. On the one
hand he became closely associated with Gustave Brocher whom,
according to Nettlau,[30] he won over to anarchism and with whom he
was apparently quite friendly. (Brocher went on to take a leading role
in the organization of the 1881 International Anarchist Congress in
London.) Similarly he tried to keep up his friendships in the Jura and
often insisted that he remained loyal to the ideals of the anarchist
movement. On the other hand, as can be seen from his correspondence with Gustave Jeanneret, his criticism of anarchism continued
and matured. But even then he referred to his new outlook as a
development of anarchism, as in his letter of 3 September when he
mentioned that he was corresponding actively on the 'programme
anarchiste interrompue par mon expulsion', adding that he did not
yet regard it as time to discuss it publicly. Clearly what he had to say
was critical. In October he drew the parallel between his own and
Costa's evolution, and in a letter of December (1879) he indicated the
trend of his evolution in outlining a newspaper project and asking
Jeanneret if he could rely on support for it in the Jura. This letter
said in part:

> Je trouve l'occasion de rédiger à Londres une feuille socialiste, heb-
> domadaire, du format des grands journaux parisiens. Voici comment se
> ferait la chose:
>   Tribune ouverte à toutes les écoles socialistes;
>   Accueil joyeux à toute polémique de principes;
>   Mise au panier impitoyable de toute dispute personelle;
>   Amas de renseignements.

He was slightly more frank in a letter he wrote on the same day to
Jules Guesde asking for his collaboration. In this he mentioned that
he would be joint editor with Zanardelli – a useful name to mention
to Guesde but anathema to the Jura anarchists after Zanardelli's
faux pas at the Ghent Congress in denouncing the Benevento affair.
He gave a list of the collaborators he hoped to obtain; in addition to
Guesde there were Malon, Costa, Xavier de Ricard, Elisée Reclus
and Kropotkin. The paper was planned to appear on 1 February, and
Brousse calculated it had a good chance of survival as it was starting

with an initial capital of £100. In fact this plan fell through and the paper did not appear until April. The financial backer, an unnamed individual with whom Brousse had professional connections, offered only £50 at the last minute, and rather than rely on the financial support of those whom he called the 'étatistes' Brousse temporarily abandoned the project.[31] In a letter to Jeanneret of January 1880 he further outlined the kind of newspaper he had in mind:

... je comprends aujourd'hui le journal autrement que *L'Avant-Garde* et *Le Révolté*. Il est bon certainement que chaque groupe distinct ait son organe, mais cela ne suffit pas, et il est une chose plus utile. Là voici:

Il faut un grand journal où par la confrontation amicale de nos diverses doctrines, il sorte une série de points communs pouvant former le programme de revendications immédiates *de tout le parti*.

And he went on to criticize the anarchists:

... nos amis font des sottises orthodoxes. Avant un an vous n'aurez plus en Suisse aucune organisation debout. Je désire ardemment me tromper, mais je crains d'y voir très clair. Un parti dont les vieux membres s'écartent peu à peu, et *nécessairement*, les uns par fatigue comme Guillaume hier, et comme Schwitzguébel demain; les autres par tactique nouvelle comme Costa et moi; dont les membres comme Levaschoff [Kropotkin] partiront un jour, *et qui ne fait plus de jeunes*, parce qu'il ne sait pas sentir son milieu, est un parti condamné à sort à courte échéance. . . .

A month later on 17 February he wrote his letter to Garcia Vinas announcing his departure from the 'intimité jurassienne' and discussing whether he should quit the 'intimité internationale' created at La Chaux-de-Fonds (see Appendix 1). He acknowledged his previous sectarianism and outlined the need for a Programme suited to the realization of practical ends acting as a unifying force for the various socialist sects. This was necessary, he said, if the united forces of the bourgeoisie were not to crush them. He explained what his own policy was:

Rester ce que je suis, anarchiste communiste, révolutionnaire; mais prendre une pièce importante de ce programme, l'appropriation collective du sol et de l'instrument de travail et en faire une revendication immédiate en m'unissant pour l'obtenir à tous les socialistes qui le revendiquent comme moi. Ceci obtenu, je demanderai autre chose.

In these two letters he had not only made the harshest yet of his criticisms of the anarchists, but had also laid down the general

strategy he planned to adopt in France – the union of various groups
for specific and well-defined purposes, with a full acknowledgement
of the differences between them. These differences would be sub-
ordinated to the primary specific demands. According to the letter to
Vinas the point of common accord amongst the French socialists was
the collectivization of the land and the instruments of labour,
although Brousse said he personally would have preferred communal
autonomy. Yet in a letter to Jacques Gross of 12 May 1880[32] he
indicated that, as the conquest of the Communes was agreed upon
from *Le Révolté* through to *L'Egalité, this* formed the basis of unity.'
'. . . quand nous serons maîtres des municipalités, que les bourgeois
seront vaincus, nous nous diviserons encore en anarchistes, étatistes. . . .' It would seem that Brousse was treading carefully so as to
conciliate the anarchists (he was especially anxious to gain circulation
for his paper in the Jura), and thus put forward communal autonomy
as the point of unity. It was the policy he eventually came to adopt,
and it is possible that the supposed agreement among the French
socialists on collectivization as the area of agreement was a fantasy.
Whatever the case it is evident that at this stage Brousse placed great
emphasis on gaining anarchist support, referring Vinas (for example)
to the Fribourg Congress in justification of his acceptance of the
electoral tactic, saying that agreement with the Jurassians would not
be impossible on this issue.

The projected newspaper finally appeared in April 1879. In a letter
of 27 March Brousse announced the formation of a Club International des Études Sociales which would publish its own monthly
paper of which he was editor. Gustave Brocher, on the other hand,
later denied that Brousse played more than a co-operative role on the
venture, the idea of which, he said, had originated with Zanardelli
even before Brousse arrived in London; it certainly did not 'belong
to Brousse'.[33] It is evident that Brousse played up his own role in
Le Travail, doubtless to sweeten the pill for his anarchist friends. That
it needed sweetening considerably is shown in another letter he wrote
to Jeanneret at about that time:[34]

Le plan d'élaboration des programmes sectaires est fini, bien fini. Aux
prix de longues luttes intestines, tout ce qui était programme prévisible
est fait. Mais pendant que nous livrions à ce travail de quintessence, que
nous plongeons dans les abstractions de la métaphysique sociale, les
masses ne nous comprenaient plus ou nous quittaient . . . les groupes
qui, maintenant, ont resté sectaires sont condamnés à mort par la force

même des choses. Ils mourront nécessairement; c'est une affaire de temps ... du point de vue de la presse – le seul point de vue dont je veuille m'occuper aujourd'hui – ils seront réduits à un rédacteur (Kropotkine) ... mais pour attaquer *tous* les métiers ainsi[35] il faut être plusieurs, et pour être plusieurs, il faut se placer sur le terrain des concessions mutuelles.

The newspaper, he continued, had obtained the collaboration of many socialists:

... une douzaine de spécialistes, vidant douze sacs au lieu d'un; pouvant se partager le travail et faire *en détail* du socialisme, non plus abstrait, mais concret ... nous sommes là, tous, des anarchistes de nuances diverses, mais au lieu de chercher ce qui nous divise nous cherchons ce qui nous rapproche, et nous le trouvons.

These ideas Brousse formulated in the leading article of *Le Travail* which appeared in April, entitled 'Le Parti Socialiste'. This is worth reproducing in entirety, as it is the clearest summary of Brousse's new strategy:

La lutte des classes modernes, depuis longtemps commencée, poursuivie à travers ces épisodes, les journées de juin et les batailles de la Commune, semble près d'aboutir. Nous avons à prendre garde.

La classe bourgeoise est solidement organisée; nul n'en doute. Le monopole de tous les moyens de production – source de toutes ses jouissances – lui assure une puissance énorme: encore entoure-t-elle cette 'forteresse du Capital' de tous les 'ouvrages avancés' de la politique, de l'économie, de la jurisprudence, de l'administration, de l'Etat. Lois, juges, bourreaux, militaires, grands services publics, et mouchards, toutes ces pièces s'harmonisent à son profit en une forte armure, forment un tout placé sous la main de son gouvernement – dans les pays où la classe est le plus menacée, sous le couvert de la forme politique qui 'la divise le moins', sous le bonnet de cette pauvre et grelottante République, conquise pourtant par le peuple, pour lui, et au prix du meilleur sang ouvrier répandu.

A cette armée solide, résistante, petite par le nombre et le courage, mais admirablement outilée, qu'oppose le Prolétariat? qu'opposons-nous?

L'audace. Le *nombre.*

Mais quel nombre? est-ce le nombre organisé? non, hélas! Mais, heureusement, *c'est le nombre qui s'organise.*

Jusqu'à ce jour, les socialistes, sous l'influence de milieux économiques inégalement développés, s'étaient parqués, logiquement en somme, en groupes, en sectes, différents, Mais, oublieux des points communs de

F

leurs programmes, par cela même les plus prochainement réalisables et
les plus scientifiquement établis, préoccupés surtout de divergences
d'ordre théorique, ces groupes, ces sectes, entrèrent en lutte, au lieu de
s'unir. Lutte intestine! très vive, menée avec talent de part et d'autre,
nécessaire peut-être à la nette formation des doctrines, mais fatale,
puisque, en fin de compte, elle n'a laissé dans le monde international que
des vaincus.

Incapable, chacun, d'asseoir son hégémonie sur les autres, il ne restait
plus, si l'on voulait former contre l'ensemble bourgeois la somme des
forces ouvrières, qu'à finir la lutte et qu'à chercher l'union sur les points
communs.

Cette nécessité a été comprise par beaucoup. Sauf quelques points
où la lutte fratricide se continue en vertu de la force acquise, un vaste
mouvement de décomposition et de recomposition se fait dans le
socialisme. Chaque groupe retournant à son point de vue primitif, paraît
se préoccuper d'avantage de la pratique que de la théorie, du réalisable
que du désirable. Tout en conservant l'intégralité de son programme, de
ses espérances et de ses souvenirs, jusqu'à la nuance particulière du
rouge de son drapeau, chacun peut entrer, sans forfaire, dans un parti
plus général, plus capable d'action immédiate puisqu'il serait plus puissant par le nombre, formé autour de quelque grande revendication
poursuivie par tous et par toutes, comme la conquête des Communes et
l'appropriation collective des grands moyens de la production. Ensuite
le triomphe obtenu, la classe ennemie domptée, chaque fraction, devenue
plus forte de sa part de victoire, évoluant dans un milieu plus progressif,
reprendrait sa route et sa liberté.

C'est à ce mouvement de reconstitution des troupes prolétariennes
que nous voulons aider de toutes nos forces. Nous trouverons bientôt la
récompense de cette sagesse dans le spectacle de la grande majorité du
prolétariat unie, marchant en rangs serrés sous des couleurs communes,
à l'encontre de la petite armée bourgeoise avec l'élan que donne la
certitude mathématique de la rompre au premier choc, de la vaincre et de
l'écraser.

The publication of this article drew the sympathetic attention of
Benoît Malon, editor of *La Revue Socialiste*, who was urging the
same general strategy for the socialist movement in France, and he
published part of it in the *Revue* in May 1880.[36] A similar argument
was repeated in *Le Travail* by Hartmann in an article entitled 'Le
Mouvement socialiste révolutionnaire russe', which contrasted
the divisions within the Western European socialist movement
with the relative unity of the Russian movement, and propounded
the autonomy of the Commune (*obhschina*) as the focus of the

movement, 'le but pratique que nous poursuivons, l'objet de nos tendances'.

As he emphasized to Jeanneret, Brousse placed great emphasis on the newspaper. In his eyes it was a publication to transcend all national publications such as *Le Révolté* and *L'Egalité*. *Le Travail*, a monthly publication, would not threaten their existence but it would counter their tendency to national isolation. This national isolation, Brousse said, was the hallmark of the present tendency within the socialist movement, and he was concerned to reverse it.[37] That *Le Travail* should not seem to be threatening *Le Révolté* was a major concern (his personal view was that the latter newspaper was its own greatest enemy), and in fact he persuaded the Jura Federation to recommend the paper in a circular to its sections, where it was received with reservations.[38]

After June 1880 however the fate of *Le Travail* ceased to interest Brousse personally. Precisely what his position in the editorship was is not clear, but he was a member of the committee of the Club International des Études sociales which dealt with the newspaper. He resigned from this committee in June 1880, either in anticipation of his impending return to France or as the result of a dispute with Zanardelli which occurred at about that time.[39] The full amnesty of July 1880, which applied to all political crimes and misdemeanours committed before that date, removed any doubt about his safety in returning to France. The Italian Embassy in London reported his departure to their Embassy in Paris – it was rumoured he was heading for Italy – which passed the information on to the Prefecture of Police in Paris, who in turn informed the Montpellier authorities. The police there reported that he had arrived on 25 July and was staying with his family.[40] On 18 August he presented his thesis to the Medical Faculty of the University[41] and then spent about another month attempting to moderate some of the extreme anarchism of socialist groups in the area.[42] He then returned to Paris and joined the Cercle d'Etudes of the 18th arrondissement, where he took up residence in October.[43] He now threw his energies into the creation of a unified Socialist Party.

To all intents and purposes Brousse had abandoned his anarchist past, although he tried to maintain contact with former co-*militants* on a personal and even political level, continually suggesting that his evolution was a reform, not abandonment, of anarchism. In one of his last letters to Jeanneret he reiterated his criticism of the anarchist movement:

Plus je vois les choses de près, plus j'y réfléchis, plus j'y songe, plus je suis convaincu que – sous peine de mort – il nous faut modifier notre tactique. Nous nous mettons par l'abstention en dehors du mouvement de l'histoire. . . . A mon sens, le travail sera long. Il faut nous placer sur le terrain de l'autonomie des programmes et des groupes, et sur celui de l'entente sur les points communs. Et, pour que les anarchistes puissent entrer dans ce concert il faut qu'ils fassent quelques concessions de tactique et qu'ils votent dans certains cas.[44]

That he was willing to accept the vote as a tactic he had made clear often enough. He had laid out the general strategy he believed should be adopted by the socialist movement in his article in *Le Travail* on the need for unity on the basis of certain agreed, limited and practical objectives; and he had made it clear also that as an *ideal* he remained faithful to anarcho-Communism and still held to certain of the tenets of anarchism, such as the belief in autonomy both as a means and as an end. These were the policies for which he worked thenceforward within the French socialist movement.

5

Brousse and the Foundation of the French Socialist Party, 1880–2

The historiography of the foundation of the French Socialist Party has largely developed along the lines spelled out in a pamphlet published by Jules Guesde and Paul Lafargue in Paris in 1883, *Le Programme du Parti Ouvrier*.[1] With minor modifications this argument may be summarized as follows: Socialism was virtually destroyed in France following the defeat of the Paris Commune, and only began to revive with the establishment in Paris in 1876–7 of the collectivist group whose central figure was Guesde. This group – and its newspaper *L'Egalité* – spread Marxist doctrine and thereby revived socialism. While the working-class Congresses of Paris and Lyons in 1876 and 1878 had rejected collectivism, the conversion of the working-class movement to Marxism was achieved by Guesde at the Marseilles Congress of 1879. Guesde then drew up in collaboration with Marx, Engels and Lafargue a Party Programme which committed the Party to Marxist socialism. Having further rid the Party of co-operatist and anarchist elements the Guesdists then found themselves faced with a breakaway movement headed by Paul Brousse and Benoît Malon, a movement whose aim was to overthrow Guesde[2] and replace his Programme with one which amounted to radical opportunism. At the St Etienne Congress of the Party in 1882 Malon and Brousse succeeded by their underhand intrigues in ousting the Guesdists, who then picked up the 'real' thread of the Party at their Roanne Congress and conserved its socialist Programme. The Guesdists were in the mainstream of the French socialist movement and indeed, were the true founders of it.

This very roughly is the orthodox interpretation. Recent works have done something to modify it, notably by pointing out Guesde's limitations as an interpreter of Marxist doctrine.[3] On the whole however these interpretations have remained within the limits of the general framework and have concentrated on the internal nature of Guesdism rather than on Guesdism's wider role within the socialist

movement. Yet the evidence suggests that this role was of less significance than has generally been accepted.

The first group openly to advocate collectivist ideas in France after
the repression of the Commune was the Cercle d'études philo-
sophiques et sociales, founded in Paris in 1875, which published a
review entitled *Philosophie de l'Avenir*. It propounded the socialism
of Colins[4] which, if it confined itself to the collectivization of land
and rejected Revolution, provided a theoretical framework for *militants* who later became more radical. Four of the members of this
group were later to play a leading role in the working-class newspaper
Le Prolétaire.[5]

In many parts of France the connection between working-class
militants and the International had never entirely been broken, and
both in membership and organization the working-class movement
continued to build on the framework laid down at the end of the
Second Empire. The Commune was a less traumatic break than often
believed.[6] Exile literature filtered in from abroad, apparently with
some success,[7] and as has been seen it was from the anarchists in
Switzerland that the first collectivist motion was placed before the
working-class Congress at Lyons in 1878.

The L'Egalité group was, as the 'orthodox' interpretation holds,
undoubtedly the most effective single source of collectivist ideas
which embraced all forms of property. It operated freely in Paris
after 1877 and included amongst its members Labusquière, Marouck
and Calvinhac, future possibilists; Gautier and Crié, future anarchists; and Massard and Deville as well as Guesde himself, future
Marxists. This nucleus had been introduced to Marxism by Karl
Hirsch, a German exile, but the doctrine spread by *L'Egalité* (the
name of the group was taken from the group's newspaper) was a
hybrid revolutionary collectivism which quoted more from Blanqui
than from Marx and which came to rely heavily on Lassalle's iron
law of wages.[8] It was also equivocal towards and partially influenced
by anarchism. When Guesde and other members of the group defied
a Government ban on the projected International Congress due to be
held in Paris in 1878, and were arrested and tried, *L'Avant-Garde*
called their action an example of 'propagande par le fait' and stated
that Guesde, Massard and Deville were anarchists, quoting from
Guesde's *Catéchisme Socialiste* to prove it; this was not difficult as
the *Catéchisme* demanded the destruction of the State in virtually
anarchist terms.[9] It is of course true that this particular assessment

reflected a temporary move towards *rapprochement* between the anarchists and socialists; but it is also true that the L'Egalité group included anarchists amongst its members and, as Fournière said later, the distinction between anarchists and socialists was more often than not purely verbal.[10] The 1878 trial of Guesde and the publication of his pamphlet, *Le Collectivisme devant le 10ème Chambre*, which gave a résumé of the collective defence of the accused – a Manifesto of socialism – had enormous propaganda value and contributed significantly to the growing strength of the socialist movement. The value lay, essentially, in its underlining of the idea that the working class had nothing to expect from the Governments of the Third Republic so long as they depended on others than themselves to fight for them. In aggravating class divisions the Government placed a strong weapon in the hands of the working-class *militants*, '... une chose fut demontrée; la classe ouvrière n'avait plus à attendre son salut que d'elle-même, et formuler au sein de ses Congrès son programme de classe...'.[11]

The conclusion was endorsed by the experiences of the amnesty campaign, which more than any other single factor created a class consciousness amongst the French working class and prepared the ground for the formation of an independent political party. The campaign for an amnesty for the Communards imprisoned by the Versailles Government began in 1876, with amnesty as the central point of the electoral platform on which Emile Acollas stood as a socialist candidate. By that time the myth of the Commune was well established, and it served as a rallying point for the diverse socialist groups, whose unity of action on the issue reached its peak in 1879. Having focused on Blanqui's candidacy in 1878 the campaign took a slightly different turn after March 1879 when a partial amnesty was declared. By distinguishing between a criminal hard-core element and a misled (but none the less culpable) majority in the ranks of the Communards the partial amnesty actually intensified feelings of class hatred, further separating the socialists from the Radicals. Rival organizations to help the returning exiles were created under socialist control. A new Blanqui candidature was put forward, and he was elected at Bordeaux in April 1879 only to have his election annulled. These campaigns laid the essential organizational framework for the creation of a working-class party:

From the movement to help the repatriated Communards had come the first really enduring coherent organization the socialists had had in France . . . the functional base, therefore, for a vigorous socialist movement was already in existence before the Congress of Marseille . . . and had come into existence through the movement to aid the amnestied.[12]

The campaign was centred in Paris, and the leading role was played by a group of working-class *militants* associated with *Le Prolétaire*.

Le Prolétaire, which was the long-awaited consummation of resolutions passed at the Paris and Lyons Working-class Congresses for the creation of a working-class paper, appeared in November 1878. Although it was published by a co-operative society, L'Union des Travailleurs, the journal was not as has sometimes been stated 'co-opératiste'.[13] It was, after the disappearance of the first *L'Egalité* in July 1878, the spearhead of the amnesty campaign, and until the publication of the second series of *L'Egalité* in January 1880 it was virtually the sole either working-class or socialist newspaper in Paris. Owned and administered by working-class *militants* the paper lacked any of the sophistication of *L'Egalité* and reflected, rather than directed, the aspirations of the radical working class. One of the points held against it by committed socialists was that before the Marseilles Congress it was uncommitted on the collectivist issue. This was true, but did not mean that it was anti-collectivist; it was in fact non-sectarian, and articles both advocating and opposing collectivism could commonly be found in the same issue. *After* the Marseilles Congress it became wholly committed to collectivism, albeit a collectivism which derived from many different and contradictory sources. In *Le Prolétaire* Marx rubbed shoulders with Colins, and de Paepe and Proudhon with Lassalle.[14] If to begin with *Le Prolétaire* gave prominence to the traditional Proudhonist outlook of the Parisian working class, this did not preclude a developed class-consciousness nor demands for the formation of an independent political party. From the beginning the paper published articles committed to collectivism by Prudent Dervillers who as early as December 1878 was arguing for the need to overthrow bourgeois society on the basis of Lassalle's iron law; as time passed his articles became more revolutionary in tone.[15] He became a convert to the collectivism popularized by Guesde's pamphlets and later became an anti-Marxist and supporter of the possibilists.

Le Prolétaire, as stated above, made no commitment on the eve of the Marseilles Congress on the need for collectivism. But a declara-

tion of views by the candidates for its new editorial board immediately prior to the Congress revealed that almost all favoured
working-class candidates, at least as a means of propaganda.[16] There
was in fact a national campaign by this time for the creation of a
'parti ouvrier'. The climate was provided by the lessons drawn from
the amnesty issue. Early in 1879, after the publication of his *Programme et Adresse des Socialistes révolutionnaires français* in April –
which called for the collectivization of the land and the instruments of
labour and became one of the seminal documents of the socialist
movement – Guesde toured the provinces urging the creation of a
socialist party.[17] An excellent speaker and propagandist, Guesde concentrated his energy into winning over the trades unions in preparation for the Congress, and through Lombard, the secretary of its
organizing committee,[18] he was able to exert considerable influence.
But he was not the only one. *Le Révolté*, on which Brousse was still
co-operating, defined the necessary aim of the Congress as the
creation of 'un programme . . . d'un nouveau parti distinct, un parti
purement ouvrier',[19] and thus swung behind Guesde the strong
anarchist support in the South and East. In fact Lombard, the supposed mouthpiece of Guesde at the Marseilles Congress,[20] was not
only in regular correspondence about the formation of a socialist
party with Benoît Malon, then editing the review *Le Socialisme
Progressif* in Switzerland,[21] but was deeply influenced by anarchism
and was ultimately to break with Guesde to edit a possibilist newspaper, *L'Autonomie Communale*. Indeed, after the break with
Guesde Lombard later hinted that the L'Egalité group was afraid of
its *lack* of control over the Congress. In reply to a series of articles by
Lafargue in *L'Egalité* (3rd series, 1882), which attacked autonomist
ideas within the Party, Lombard wrote:

. . . nous voudrions qu'on revint aux décisions prises par ce Congrès de
Marseilles qu'on qualifie de *mémorable*, et qui, à cette époque, quelques
jours avant sa tenue était en suspicion par ceux-la même qui s'appuient
sur ses décisions. Il y aurait même un curieux travail à faire sur ce
sujet.[22]

Lombard's own ideas at the time reflected far more the influence of
the anarchists and the federalists than any ideas of Guesde. Thus at
a meeting of the Marseilles Cercle d'Études sociales on 5 February
1879 Lombard said that the basic theme of the modern socialist movement was 'les libertés communales et l'association des

travailleurs'. At the same meeting he attacked centralizing and authoritarian ideas within the socialist movement and called for a Programme based on federalism and collectivism.[23] In the South (and it is notable that its delegates dominated the Congress) the newspaper edited by Xavier de Ricard at Montpellier, *La Commune Libre* (which had Guesde as one of its contributors), was responsible for spreading a federalist collectivism which gained the support of *Le Révolté*.[24] This newspaper played a considerable role in gaining support for the Congress.[25]

The sources of collectivism within the French socialist movement immediately prior to the Marseilles Congress were therefore extremely diverse. It is misleading to attribute its spread solely to Guesde and his group which, even where it made a major contribution, spread a doctrine which could only tenuously be described as Marxism, since it contained strong Lassallian, French 'utopian' and anarchist elements. In the South anarchist influence was extremely strong and set its imprint on the party created at the Marseilles Congress.

1. *The Marseilles Congress, 1879*

Two major decisions were made by the French working-class movement meeting at Marseilles with delegates from socialist groups at its Third Annual Congress. First, the creation of a working-class political party, and second, the commitment to the collectivization of the land and the instruments of labour as the means of social emancipation. The two decisions need to be kept separate, for the one – the creation of an independent party – did not necessarily imply the other. As Blum later pointed out[26] the Lyons Congress of 1878 had already gone a considerable way towards the creation of an independent working-class political party, while at the same time confirming, in a modified form, its belief in co-operation.

None the less the Marseilles Congress marked a decisive change in that it committed the movement to the abolition of the wage-earning class, to the rejection of co-operation, to the collectivization of the land and the instruments of labour and to the constitution of a separate, organized, working-class party. But the precise nature of this commitment was not clear. Lombard, strongly under the influence of the anarchists, played a vital role both on the organizing committee of the Congress and in its debates.[27] He was aided by

Fauché and Fournière of the Paris L'Egalité group. Their speeches revealed an enormous diversity of intellectual influences. Fauché for example based his whole argument for the abolition of the wage-earning class on Lasalle's iron law.[28] Lombard in an extremely long and detailed speech outlined the ideal that the working class should oppose to that of the bourgeoisie as being:

... la socialisation ou collectivisation du sol et des instruments de travail, l'instruction intégrale et professionelle, la fédération et l'autonomie des communes, et la constitution d'un quatrième Etat, remplacant logiquement le troisième Etat.[29]

Marxist, Lassallian or anarchist? Malon was probably correct in claiming[30] that Lombard's speech reflected his own influence – seen in the references to 'le quatrième Etat', a Lassallian concept which he had popularized, but clearly this was only part of the truth. The anarchist influence was widely apparent too, and could be seen both in the resolution on collectivism and in the resolution calling for the creation of the party. The former stated that property and machinery should be in the hands of the Communes and producers' groups,[31] while the latter was conceived in terms which echoed Lombard's speech early in the debates of the Congress when he had said that it was for each group, Commune or region to define the appropriate method of expropriation.[32] The Party was named the Fédération du Parti des Travailleurs socialistes de France and was to be composed of six largely autonomous regional organizations. No Party Programme was drawn up (although agreement was reached on the need for political action).

The concessions to anarchism were made necessary by its strength in the South, the anarchist background and sympathies of many of the delegates, and the thin dividing line which, in any case, often separated anarchism from other strands of socialism. There was, in addition, a strong anarchist pressure group at the Congress.[33] It was interesting that *Le Révolté* gave the decisions of the Congress its almost unqualified approval – 'le prolétariat français se déclare ainsi pour le vrai socialisme' – only regretting it had decided on electoral action, a decision forced by the linking of this resolution with that calling for the creation of a party.[34]

Given the diversity of influences it was difficult to find any basis for a common Programme. Bestetti, the delegate of the Paris shoe-makers, was probably expressing the majority view of what issue faced the working-class movement at the Congress when he appealed to the delegates in these terms: 'constituons le parti ouvrier, sachons faire nos efforts nous-mêmes, et mettons en pratique cette devise qui a déjà remué tout le monde, l'émancipation des travailleurs par les travailleurs eux-mêmes', and followed the appeal with a list of reformist demands. The address of the Communard refugees in London, likewise calling for the creation of an independent party, defined the drafting of a Programme as 'la plus épineuse de celles que vous aurez à résoudre', warned that no Programme should be the *credo* or exclusive catechism of a sect, and demanded one of immediately applicable social reforms.[35] The Congress had created a party of the working class; it had also decided that the emancipation of the working class could be accomplished only in socialism. But the connection between the two decisions (which were linked together in the same resolution) was unclear. Was the Party's Programme to include collectivization, was it to be revolutionary or was it to be reformist? The leading proponents of collectivism were revolutionary, but the majority of the trade unionists present were probably of Bestetti's opinion. Even the collectivist *avant-garde* was merely a 'coalition hétéroclite groupant les marxistes, les anarchistes, et les futurs possibilistes',[36] with fundamental disagreements over the ends and means of working-class action. In some way or other this *avant-garde* had to find unity and at the same time keep in touch with the aspirations of the working-class movement.

2. *The Minimum Programme*

The Marseilles Congress decisions were followed by various suggestions for the Programme of the Party. In Paris the Union fédérative du Centre was formed as the regional organization provided for at Marseilles, with Fauché as its first secretary. In April 1880, six months after the Congress, the Union discussed – but dismissed in face of the opposition of the L'Egalité group – a Programme drafted or inspired by Deynaud of the XVIII (Montmartre) group, which called *inter alia* for the collectivization of the land and the instruments of labour, the abolition of inheritance, the abolition of the Senate and Presidency, the autonomy of the Commune and the civil and political equality of women.[32] The Fédération du Nord began to outline reforms which it considered should be included in the Programme, such as freedom of the press, the reduction of the working day, a single tax on incomes and free education. Achille le Roy – a *militant*

associated with *Le Prolétaire*, who had been exiled in Switzerland and
who was to end his days in the USSR – had already, prior to the
Marseilles Congress, laid down a list of nineteen transitory measures
for the improvement of working-class conditions in a small pamphlet
entitled *Les Réformes Sociales Urgentes*,[38] a compendium of social
and political demands which he claimed would give the working class
the indispensable conditions of emancipation. They included the
abolition of the laws on the press and association, the reduction of
working hours, free obligatory secular education, the equality of
women, the suppression of the standing army, direct taxation and the
separation of the Church and State. These were presented as practicable reforms.

The reformist spirit was predominant within the labour movement,
and Benoît Malon attempted to canalize it into a coherent Party
Programme. Acting as the spokesman of the movement – although he
was still living in Zurich – he began to co-operate with Guesde and
Lafargue.[39] In view of the enormous significance that the Programme
which Guesde finally drafted for the Party was to have in the disputes
between the Havre and St Etienne Congresses of the Party, it is
worth examining in detail the circumstances in which it was drafted.

There was from the very beginning a conflict over what the Programme should attempt to achieve, a conflict reflecting the differences
between the *revolutionary* posture of Guesde and the reformist aspirations of the working-class movement. The correspondence between
Malon and Guesde in the period immediately prior to the formulation of the Programme reveals some of this tension.[40]

Malon had been closely associated with the anarchists in the First
International, and although he kept his doctrinal distance he had
sided with them in their fight against the General Council. In 1876 he
finally broke with them over the issue of whether one should support
the Republic against the Monarchist threat, and since then his name
had been anathema to the anarchist purists. In the period between
1876 and 1880 he had gradually formulated a reformist strategy for
the French socialist movement. Guesde's strategy, on the other hand,
was frankly revolutionary, aimed at the construction of a small and
doctrinally élitist Party:

Si je suis révolutionnaire, si je crois comme vous à la necessité de la
force pour trancher dans le sens collectiviste ou communiste la question
sociale, je suis comme vous l'adversaire acharné des mouvements à la
Cafiero qui – utiles peut-être en Russie – ne correspondent ni en France

ni en Allemagne, ni en Italie, à aucune exigence de la situation . . .
Comme vous, je suis persuadé qu'avant de songer à l'action il faut avoir
constitué un parti, une armée consciente, au moyen d'une propaganda
aussi active que continue. Comme vous enfin je nie que la simple destruction de ce qui existe suffise à l'édification de ce que nous voulons, et je
pense que, pendant plus au moins longtemps l'impulsion, la direction
devront venir d'en haut, de ceux qui 'savent davantage'. C'est dans ces
conditions que depuis ma rentrée je me suis occupé de former ce 'parti
ouvrier indépendant et militant' que vous déclarez si justement 'de la
plus haute importance' en vue des événements qui se préparent.[41]

Having entered into correspondence with Guesde over the formulation of a Party Programme, Malon, who envisaged a three-point
Programme with a philosophico-historical introduction written by
himself, an industrial and commercial section written by Guesde and
an agricultural section written by Lafargue, very quickly revealed the
existence of a fundamental difference of opinion between himself on
the one hand and Lafargue and Guesde on the other. Early in April
1880 he wrote to Guesde warning him of the dangers of creating a
revolutionary *avant-garde* out of touch with the working-class.

. . . je crois qu'il vaut mieux faire l'inventaire de la science sociale,
propager l'idée social, agiter et organiser la classe ouvrière en vue
d'abord de luttes immédiates sur le terrain politique et économique, et
secondairement seulement pour la lutte révolutionnaire que nous ne
pourrons ni ferons [accomplir], car la révolution ne sera victorieuse que
lorsque les 100,000 socialistes qui la tenteront ne seront qu'une avant-
garde [ayant] derrière eux le peuple soulevé . . . il est certain que la classe
ouvrière en masse ne viendra aux socialistes militants que si ceux-ci lui
fournissent un aliment immédiat de luttes et des réformes à obtenir:
Dura lex sed lex . . . le Congrès de Bordeaux est un avertissement dont il
faut tenir compte. De plus j'ai reçu pas mal de lettres de province où la
même crainte est exprimée. . . . Nous pouvons prévenir le danger par le
moyen que vous indique [*sic*]. Nous avons de grandes forces entre les
mains et si vous voulez nous pourrons faire quelque chose de décisif avec
le concours de Lafargue (reflet de Marx). Si vous acceptez nous nous
mettrons de suite à l'oeuvre et nous nous partagerons la rédaction.
Nous imprimerons sur nos journaux et la *Revue Socialiste* ferait
tirer en brochures. Reste les détails à discuter si vous acceptez le
principe.[42]

In a letter to Lombard of 11 April 1880 Malon made the same
point, criticizing a Manifesto of the Marseilles socialists for its

omission of this central point of immediate demands. He mentioned the discussions with Guesde, and his own view that the Programme should contain demands for the conquest of the municipalities, working-class candidates in Parliament, the abolition of the 'budget des cultes', etc. He stressed the need to prepare for the 1881 legislative elections if the working class was not to follow the Radicals: '[le *peuple*] *veut agir*, et jamais il n'acceptera d'attendre la justice ou la Révolution des *décades du siècle* comme le lui proposent les anarchistes.' He criticized what he called the outright revolutionism of the anarchists, saying that the situation at the moment was clearly evolutionary:

. . . si par le vote on pouvait trouver la place et éviter les horreurs de la guerre civile, ne serait-ce pas mieux? . . . Ne dédaignons pas les réformes qui en outre soulagent momentanément d'innombrables souffrances. N'oublions non plus que plus la condition du peuple est améliorée, plus les idées s'élevent, et plus la révolution sociale a des partisans. . . .

This argument applied equally of course to Guesde's rigid Marxism.[43]

Guesde apparently did accept the principles laid down in Malon's letter, but Malon felt it necessary to ask for a clarification of his position on the question of *immediate* demands:

Pensez vous que jusqu'au jour de la Révolution il faille se borner à se préparer à la lutte et l'organisation de demain. Les masses ouvrières veulent de l'action au jour le jour. Elles veulent par exemple voter, devons nous les laisser sans motive suivre les radicaux? Ne pourrions nous pas après avoir affirmé nos principes révolutionnaires et collectivistes, faire un programme de revendications immédiates en quelque sorte électorale et sur lequel nous nous compterons au jour du vote?

He went on to say that he believed this Programme, presented in such a way as not to scare off the Chambres syndicales ('dont plusiers chancellent de nouveau, vous le savez aussi'), could have enormous success.[44] But Guesde remained hard to convince and seems to have suspected Malon of flirting with the Radicals, for three weeks later Malon wrote, apparently reassuring Guesde: 'Il est bien entendu qu'il ne s'agit pas de faire un programme radical, mais d'affirmer le socialisme dans son intégralité.' The Programme would however, he continued, be concerned with immediate demands such as the abolition of the 'budget des cultes' and of standing armies, the take-over of railways and mines and the development of public works. These demands would probably gain them the support of most groups. He ended by saying: 'Lafargue à qui j'avais demandé des notes m'écrit que Marx fera le projet (ceci entre nous). Je n'ai rien contre quant à moi et j'ai écrit à Laf . . . que je signerai d'avance ce que vous deux vous auriez décidé.'[45] Malon was apparently confident that everything was under his control, despite the fact that he had agreed to Marx's involvement; for a week after this he wrote to César de Paepe saying that the Programme of immediate demands had been sketched out and agreed by the two Parisian newspapers (*L'Egalité* and *Le Prolétaire*) and certain working-class groups. He himself was playing an intermediary role between the revolutionaries and the 'évolutionnistes' and was profiting from the situation in his organization of the Party.[46]

But Malon's role as the honest broker of the movement misfired, as he later recalled.[47] Some time within the three weeks following his letter to de Paepe he received a letter from Brousse in London, with whom he had recently made contact and whose article in *Le Travail* he had warmly welcomed in the *Revue Socialiste*. This letter told Malon that Guesde had arrived suddenly in London, and after several days of discussions with Lafargue, Engels and Marx at the latter's home had drawn up a political Programme to be adopted by the French Party. Brousse did not favour the Programme and warned Malon against it. Brousse's view of the tasks of the French Socialist Party was, at this stage, practically the same as that of Malon. In the *Revue Socialiste* of 5 May 1880 Malon had argued, in an article entitled 'Les Partis ouvriers en France', that the Party should seek to obtain 'le plus de réformes de détail possible' and should unite *all* socialists for a 'programme d'action'. This was identical to the argument in Brousse's article in *Le Travail* of April. It appears that Brousse had been approached by Lafargue with a view to helping in drafting a Programme for the Party, but had refused on the grounds that he suspected 'une intrigue Marxiste'.[48] Brousse's information was confirmed two days later in letters to Malon from Guesde and Lafargue who, having dispensed with him for the drafting of the Programme, none the less thought it best for its chances of adoption by the movement that it should be presented in his name.[49] Malon considered the Programme too short – clearly it did not satisfy his demands for a Programme of immediately obtainable reforms – but counting on it being supplemented by the Party groups he agreed to lend it his support, having first gained the approval of *militants* such as Lombard, Prudent Dervillers, Achille le Roy and J.-B. Dumay.

Less than a month later the Programme was published in the socialist press.[50]

Details of the meeting in London given by Engels to Bernstein throw more light on the attitude of Guesde and Lafargue to Malon and Brousse. Describing how Marx dictated the preamble to the Programme, while Guesde formulated the actual points, and noting Guesde's insistence on the minimum wage demand ('theoretical nonsense'), Engels stated that Brousse knew of the meeting and wanted to be present but Guesde, who expected Brousse 'to get involved in long-winded discussions about misunderstood phrases', insisted that he be excluded. Engels gave his own opinion of Brousse, which coincided with that of Guesde – 'the greatest muddlehead I have ever encountered, removing the anarchy from anarchism but retaining all other phrases and especially tactics'. As for Malon – who, as has been seen from the correspondence with Guesde, knew of Lafargue's plan to involve Marx, despite his later omission of the fact – Engels said he had expected to be invited to London by Lafargue but the Marxist group had decided otherwise – he could come if he wanted, but why invite him?[51]

Bernstein was never totally in agreement with Marx's or Engels's evaluation of the differences within the French socialist movement, and in 1925 when his correspondence with Engels was published he was very critical of it. He blamed them *and* Guesde for creating an atmosphere of mistrust amongst the leaders of the movement on the eve of its unification behind a single Programme. 'It was an act of unparalleled clumsiness' for Guesde to insist that Brousse, the trusted person of a considerable wing of the Party, should be excluded – even the more so as he was living in London at the time – while Malon, who had been abruptly discouraged from corresponding with Marx in 1877, needed the assurance that he would be welcome in London if he made the journey from Zurich.[52]

Bernstein had spotlighted one very basic cause of the conflicts which shortly broke out in the Party. This was the almost total mistrust displayed by Brousse and Malon – but especially by Brousse – towards what he called the 'côterie marxiste'. He was given every reason to believe that there was another Marxist 'conspiracy' afoot, similar to that within the International, and it was significant that according to his own account (which may or may not have been true) he had turned down an offer from Lafargue to co-operate in the drafting of the Programme. Such was the degree of mistrust existing

from the previous decade. Writing to Herman Jung in 1882 he
recalled how, when in London, he had told Jung that Marx and
Lafargue would not confine themselves to giving the French socialists
advice but would seek to have 'la haute main sur les hommes et les
choses du parti'.[53] In 1882 he felt his suspicions to have been fully
justified. As will be seen later in this chapter the history of the International was profoundly to affect the judgements *both* of Lafargue
and Guesde *and* of Malon and Brousse on events within the French
Socialist Party, and acted as a constant barrier to co-operation or
conciliation.

But there were other reasons why the Minimum Programme, as it
became known, failed to create a united movement. It was interpreted very differently by *L'Egalité* on the one hand and *La Revue
Socialiste* and *Le Prolétaire* on the other. The preamble laid down the
creation of a distinctive working-class political party as the indispensable condition of emancipation, and stated that as one of the
means to this end universal suffrage would cease to be an instrument
of exploitation and become one of emancipation. As a means of
organization and struggle, it was stated, the elections would be fought
on the accompanying Programme of minimum reforms. This Programme, divided into a political and economic section, included
amongst its demands the abolition of the press laws and of the law
against the International, the abolition of the religious budget, the
creation of a popular militia and the administrative freedom of the
Commune; it also called for the establishment of a legal minimum
wage, the establishment of the eight-hour working day, and the
abolition of all indirect taxation. (See Appendix 7 for full text.)

By its very minimum nature the Programme lent itself to differing
interpretations. *L'Egalité* presented it as a Programme embodying
reforms which were limited, specific and theoretically possible within
the framework of bourgeois society, but which the bourgeoisie would
reject and thereby prove the necessity of Revolution. *La Revue
Socialiste* (Malon) picked on two of its demands, the reduction in the
working day and the administrative autonomy of the Commune
(Part A, Article 4) as the most significant, besides which the others
were secondary; the latter point would help to prepare the socialist
order:

... nous permettra de nous exercer dans les choses administratives ...
chemin faisant, nous pourrions encore jetter les bases de la propriété

communale et préparer la grande fédération socialiste des communes par la fédération administrative économique, intellectuelle des premières communes acquises.[54]

Apart from its federalism this conclusion suggested that significant *socialist* gains could be achieved within the framework of the capitalist order with the expropriation of property within the Commune, and it interpreted the Programme as the first step in the socialists' winning of political power. It thus contradicted the revolutionary conclusions drawn by the Guesdists.[55] It also laid stress on the Programme as a force of unity amongst various socialist groups. *Le Prolétaire* likewise regarded some of the articles as capable of realization, but criticized the omission of certain reforms such as laws on hygiene, which could immediately improve working-class conditions. Prudent Dervillers backed Malon's position on the conquest of municipal power.[56] These differences merely reflected once again the conflict between a predominantly reformist working-class movement and the extreme revolutionism of Guesde, who appears to have lived in practically daily expectancy of the Revolution, and for whom the working-class movement was something of an antipathetic reality.[57]

While the Minimum Programme was generally well-received in the socialist press, in fact it gained far less support within the labour movement than has generally been acknowledged. The Congress of the Western region of the Party held at Bordeaux in June 1880 rejected the title of Congrès socialiste révolutionnaire. The Congress of the Fédération du Nord at Lille failed even to support collectivism,[58] while at the Congress of the South held at Marseilles and the Congress of the East held at Lyons – both in August 1880 – anarchist resolutions opposing the electoral tactic adopted by the Programme were passed and the whole Programme criticized as not revolutionary enough, and even retrograde.[59] *Le Révolté* had strongly attacked the Programme, not only on the grounds that its commitment to electoral action inevitably meant a commitment to parliamentarism, but also on the grounds that *all* Programmes are minimum, and if this one was intended to be practicable the minimum wage demanded was an absurdity. It described the Programme as a 'méli-mélo de fragments des programmes intransigeants, assaisonnés de projets de réformes concernant le travail ... et de certaines veillêtes socialistes', and remarked on the striking discord between the preamble and the actual points of the Programme which it considered 'misérable', a mixture of expedients taken from the bourgeois radicals – the Programme of the International had been better.[60] Jean Grave, the leading spokesman of the French anarchists, described the Programme as 'de la confiture pour faire avaler la pilule électoral', and the anarchists left the Party in the following year.[61] Therefore both the reformists *and* the ultra-revolutionary elements found grounds on which to criticize the Programme. The reformists wanted more practicable points while the anarchists wanted everything.

If the comments of *Le Révolté* were not enough to move the anarchists to reject the Programme, then Lafargue stepped in very quickly to repair the omission with a violent attack on them in an article entitled 'Le Parti Ouvrier et L'Etat Capitaliste' published in *L'Egalité* in August.[62] As the 'gardien vigilant de la doctrine'[63] Lafargue castigated the anarchists – although he merely named his victims as 'abstentionists' – as 'des émasculés qui ne savent que jougler scolastiquement avec des mots', as 'des révolutionnaires en pantoufles' whose theories were mere 'parlotages de la métaphysique révolutionnaires qui font pâmer d'aise des déclassés bourgeois, qui s'imaginent être des Marat, des Ferré . . .'. The anarchists, he concluded, were reactionaries hawking around their plagiarisms of laisser-faire economists: 'être anarchiste, c'est être bourgeois'.

The article had a disastrous effect and Lafargue proved, not for the first or last time, that his arrogant polemics were capable of triggering off discord within the Party.[64] Not only did it arouse the hostility of those who were anarchists, who would probably in any case have rejected the Programme and left the Party (which is what most of them did); it also deeply offended those who had been anarchists and yet remained to be convinced of the value of political action, or those who *had* accepted it and in some way squared this with their anarchist past. On the day following the appearance of the article Jules Montels told Guesde that it betrayed German influence and that, just as Marx had maligned the defeated French in 1871, so Lafargue was maligning those who, if misguided, remained loyal to the working class and socialist cause. He continued by saying:

Décidément, je reste *anti-allemand*, c'est-à-dire *anti-marxiste* et j'attendrai pour me prononcer sur l'Etat collectiviste ouvrier que l'Allemagne nous ait contraint un de toute pièce [*sic*]. Qu'ils ne parlent pas tous de révolution, mais qu'ils en fassent une. Voilà 30 ans que les allemands nous l'annoncent. Hélas, je ne vois jamais rien venir. . . .[65]

Montels was not alone in his reaction. Collectivists throughout the South protested against the Marxist attitude, and Malon urged Guesde (upon whom the counter-attack descended) to postpone a series of meetings he was to give in the region. Thus he wrote to Guesde some time in August that if he gave the meetings, 'vous ne feriez qu'exciter les anarchistes qui ont pour vous une espèce de haine très vive', and followed it up with a later letter by saying that 'les sarcasmes sanglants de Lafargue ont révolté au point que des cercles *collectivistes* se sont déclarés *anarchistes* et ont écrit au Prolétaire contre les articles en question.' A few days later he told Guesde not to go either to Sète or Béziers, where he had not even been requested as a speaker, and in a following letter said that after consulting with the Marseilles group he advised the postponement of the visit:

... vous ne sauriez croire combien les dernières attaques de Lafargue ont surexcité même les non-anarchistes. Il faut bien que je vous le dise. Je n'ai pas trouvé un seul homme ... pour le défendre ... au fond tous les méridionaux sont un peu anarchiste.

For this reason Malon urged Guesde to co-operate with him on *L'Emancipation*, the daily paper he was planning to publish in Lyons which would be open to all sections of the socialist movement: 'Une trève est indispensable, consentez à le faire avec moi dans l'Emancipation. C'est plus important que vous ne croyez.'[66]

These events usefully illustrate three factors, each of considerable importance in the critical years of the foundation of the French Socialist Party: first, the association of Marxism with Germany and German interests which, more especially in the later 1880s, could act as a catalyst for anti-Marxist or anti-Guesdist feeling;[67] second, the strong and decisive influence of anarchism in the South which made it the backbone of resistance – apart from Paris itself – to Guesdist socialism; and third, the parallel frequently drawn between Marx's attitude in the 1870s, both towards the 1870–1 War and within the International, and the attitude of the Marxists in 1880. The 'Marxist conspiracy' thesis established for the history of the First International was carried over into the foundation of the French Socialist Party.

If the Minimum Programme gained little support in the provinces it at first, apparently, enjoyed considerable success in Paris where it was adopted at the Congress of the Centre region (the Union fédérative du Centre) in July 1880.[68] The adoption of the Programme at this Congress, and its subsequent adoption by the National Congress of Le Havre in November 1880, laid the basis for future Guesdist claims that the French Socialist Party had adopted Marxism. Yet this was far from being the case. Despite the July Congress Paris never became a Guesdist stronghold and in fact provided the backbone of support for the reformist socialists, while the Havre Congress, in adopting the Programme, did so with conditions and amendments which made it virtually meaningless.

It was noticeable that of the list of groups and societies having approved the Programme appearing in *L'Egalité*, only two were from Paris. In the three weeks which elapsed between the Programme's publication in *L'Egalité* (30 June 1880) and the opening of the Centre Congress it appeared to have made little headway even amongst the section of the Parisian working-class movement committed to collectivism. Jules Joffrin for instance (who was to become one of the stalwarts of the Possibilist Party) said that the Programme had 'nothing socialist' about it and that:

> Le programme du Parti socialiste doit être composé de manière que nos exploiteurs ne puissent l'accepter et qu'il ne puisse y avoir aucune confusion ... la suppression de l'armée permanente n'est qu'une tartine qui ne peut figurer à aucun titre dans une programme socialiste.[69]

In other words the Programme was not revolutionary enough. Yet it was perhaps this factor which ultimately led to its adoption, for it represented the middle ground between, on the one hand, the Clemenceau Radicals[70] and the Alliance Républicaine Socialiste (the ex-Communard group),[71] and on the other the intransigent anarchists and 'pétroleurs' who renounced political action, who vigorously opposed the adoption of the Programme at the Congress,[72] and who ultimately left the Party in 1881. In the absence of any suitable alternative, presented as the Programme of the leading *militants* of the movement, such as Malon and Lombard, and with the pressing need to agree on a Programme for the 1881 elections, the Programme was adopted. But this scarcely amounted to any ideological commitment and in any case could only be taken as binding on the Centre region. Not only was the Programme amended in certain ways which suggested a concern for immediate practical reforms, but on the fourth and fifth questions on the agenda before it the Congress voted for the possibility of immediate practical reforms which was in some contrast to the overwhelmingly revolutionary tone of its debates.[73] Above all however it was not clear as to what precisely the Programme had committed the Party, not only in the sense that there was no fundamental agreement as to its implications – as witnessed in the differing interpretations by *La Revue Socialiste* and *L'Egalité* at the time of its publication – but also in that when the Parisian municipal elections of January 1881 began to be debated within the Party, no one quite knew whether the Programme applied to that particular situation. At a meeting of the Union Fédérative on 2 September the question was discussed but no agreement reached, except that research should be conducted into which arrondissements would be likely to field successful candidates should the Programme be adopted. Guesde pointed out however that the purpose of the Programme was not to win elections but to organize for revolution ('une révolution de fusil'), and therefore to that extent the decision of the Union was anti-Guesdist by implication (in that its decision was clearly motivated by electoral considerations).[74] This was borne out in December when it created a Comité Central ouvrier socialiste which on 1 January 1881 published in *Le Prolétaire* a 'Programme électorale municipale'. This Municipal Programme was, in fact, the work of Brousse.

3. *The reaction against the Minimum Programme*

Brousse had returned to Paris from the Midi in the late summer of 1880 and settled in the 18th arrondissement where he soon became the leading member of one of its small socialist study groups. He had opposed the Minimum Programme since its inception and he continued to do so. At a meeting organized by the groups of the 1st and 2nd arrondissements on 24 October 1880 he was reported as having spoken against the Minimum Programme, saying that his own group was drawing up a Municipal Programme 'd'application possible immédiat, un commencement de revendication, de l'autonomie communale'.[75] He enlarged on this theme in Malon's *L'Emancipation* on 5 November:

> Quand donc les ouvriers conscients de leur intérêts de classe consentiront-ils à prendre directement et eux-mêmes la défense de ces intérêts? Dans l'impuissance où ils sont de saisir l'Etat ... pourquoi ... ne s'emparent-ils des municipalités agricoles et industrielles où ils sont en majorité?

He protested against the Minimum Programme being presented by the official organ of the Party as its exclusive Programme (it was published in *L'Emancipation* on 4 November 1880), and obtained from Malon the declaration that it was merely a *minimum* one which could be enlarged upon. Malon himself seems to have been nearer to Brousse than to Guesde on this issue. In *L'Emancipation* of 6 November 1880 Malon wrote an article entitled 'La Conquête des Municipalités' in which he said that one of the most important tasks of the proletariat 'dans l'ordre réformiste' was the capture of municipal power:

... comme la bourgeoisie des derniers siècles, le prolétariat et ses alliés socialistes ne sont pas encore en mesure de transformer par une action révolutionnaire d'ensemble la vieille societé, ils doivent commencer par s'emparer des positions immédiatement prenables: les municipalités des centres les plus démocratiques.

None the less Brousse withdrew his collaboration on the paper.[76] Later in the same month he outlined his Municipal Programme to a meeting of the '18th' group, at which leading Parisian *militants* were present, and urged the need for working-class candidates in the elections of January.[77] Presented by Brousse in co-operation with the Montmartre group the Municipal Programme was published in *L'Emancipation* on 20 November 1880, with a sympathetic welcome by Malon (see Appendix 4). It became accepted as a basis for discussion by the majority of the Parisian socialist groups,[78] and when published in a somewhat amended form in *Le Prolétaire* was accompanied by a Manifesto of the Central Electoral Committee which called the conquest of the Communes the 'premier pas dans la voie de l'affranchissement définitif et complet du prolétariat'. The Programme was adopted by at least four of the arrondissement groups in the January elections, when the Party won 15,000 votes.

Brousse's argument against the Minimum Programme had been strongly reinforced by the resolutions passed at the Fourth National Congress of the Party held at Le Havre in November. A preliminary serious split took place when the organizing committee, which had come under the control of the co-operatists, attempted to exclude the collectivist groups which thereupon withdrew and held their own Congress. This Congress then went on, in effect, to undo the work of the Centre Congress of July. On the fifth question on the agenda (De la représentation du Prolétariat aux corps élu) it adopted a resolution which stated:

> Le Congrès national socialiste-ouvrier du Havre déclare tenter une dernière expérience aux élections municipales et législatives de 1881, et pour le cas où elle n'aboutirait pas, ne retiendrait purement et simplement que l'action révolutionnaire.
>
> Le Congrès prend pour base aux élections de 1881 le programme minimum ci-dessous; mais invite toutes les circonscriptions en mesure d'avoir une programme plus accentué à agir dans ce sens. Il est entendu que ce programme n'établit qu'une des formes de groupement et que le but constant du prolétariat est d'activer la Révolution par tous les moyens possibles.[79]

This was largely a concession to the anarchist fringe which was very much in evidence at the Congress,[80] but it had the effect in the long term of sanctioning the activities of the reformist wing of the Party. The reformist position was immeasurably strengthened in addition by the inclusion of two new articles to the Programme. These made municipal socialism an essential part of the socialist Programme. Article 11 (the original Programme had ten Articles) demanded the cessation of the alienation of property owned by the Communes and the State, while Article 12 called for:

> L'affectation par les municipalités des fonds disponibles à la construction, dans tous les terrains appartenant aux communes, de bâtiments de natures diverses, tels que maisons d'habitation, bazaars de dépôts, pour louer sans bénéfice aux habitants.[81]

Municipal action of this kind was to become the central issue between the Guesdist and possibilist groups within the Party in Paris. The adoption of the resolution was a severe blow to Guesde, and *he never accepted the validity of the decisions of this Congress.*[82] Municipal socialism, which emphasized the possibility of effective action on the local level, was in complete contradiction to the central tenets of Guesdist doctrine.

In the month following the Paris municipal elections Brousse and Malon founded, in co-operation with the small group connected with *Le Prolétaire*, a study group called Le Travail. Its statutes were framed in Marxist and revolutionary terms but referred (significantly in the light of later developments within the Party) to the need for greater organizational unity without the establishment of a 'governmental' apparatus.[83] The formation of the group was of some significance. The differences of opinion within the Party could to some extent be accommodated within the feeble organizational structure created at Marseilles, but by 1881 the need to give the Party a central direction had become apparent to both Guesde and Brousse. This inevitably helped to crystallize the doctrinal differences between them. The rest of 1881 was to be occupied, in so far as internal Party developments were concerned, largely with arguments over new organizational forms the party was to adopt.

4. Conflict within the Party: the defeat of the Guesdists, 1881

Brousse strengthened his position within the Party, notably in Paris, during this period. In addition to being the corresponding secretary for the Le Travail group, Brousse was the prime mover behind the creation of a new Comité central électoral du Parti Ouvrier, and he strengthened his grip on the Union fédérative with the replacement of Fauché by Frenot as secretary of its Federal Committee.[84] The Guesdist Egalité group, hitherto the single most articulate and organized group with the Union fédérative found itself steadily and effectively opposed by the Broussist groups.

The first major conflict occurred over the 1881 national elections for which the Party had, in the first place, adopted the Minimum Programme. The conflict was compounded by personal rivalries. In October 1880 the founding members of *L'Emancipation* – Malon, Brousse, Guesde, Deville and Brugnot – had renounced any intention of standing as candidates in the forthcoming municipal and national elections. This move was taken not because they were opposed to electoral action but so that no imputations as to the unfair use of influence to gain election could be made. Immediately prior to the August 1881 legislative elections the question was raised whether these engagements were still valid in view of the fact that *L'Emancipation* had long since ceased publication. The answer given by the majority of the Party organizations was that they were not.[85] The opportunity offered for dissociation from the Minimum Programme was too great for Brousse and Malon, however, and both refused to stand for election (in contrast to Guesde who stood at Roubaix). Criticized in *Le Citoyen* on the ground that no one should scruple to hold himself back in a revolutionary situation, Malon replied that they still felt themselves bound by their previous engagement not to stand, and that anyway they were not in a revolutionary situation.

(This reply would alone have been sufficient to arouse the ire of the Guesdists.) It was backed up by a joint letter from Brousse, Deynaud, Paulard and Malon on 13 August denying that the Party as a whole had released them from any engagement. The motive behind the scrupulous stand of Brousse and Malon was undoubtedly the wish to avoid association with a Programme which they were certain would prove electorally unpopular.[86]

On this they were proved correct. The socialist gain nationally over the figures for the January municipal elections was a mere 20,000, and the Guesdists were hard pressed to find a convincing explanation of why this did not represent a check to their progress. The elections highlighted the basic controversy over the Programme and led to considerable ill-feeling amongst the leading *militants*. It provoked a personal polemic between Massard (Guesdist) and Fournière. Malon resigned from *Le Citoyen* shortly afterwards, and he and Brousse made derogatory remarks about Guesde's candidature at Roubaix; Guesde reciprocated by alleging that Brousse had attempted to stand on an Allianciste Programme at Montpellier. Brousse's name was in fact put forward at Montpellier and he received a number of votes at the election; but he had dissociated himself from this. Attitudes towards Guesde's candidature were summed up at a meeting of the Federal Committee of the Union fédérative on 9 August 1881, which saw Guesde called an 'ambitieux' and terminated in disorder: 'il y a, on le voit, une sérieuse division, et les discussions ont lieu sur un tel diapaison que, plusieurs fois, le propriétaire a menacé de donner congé'.[87] The dispute also emphasized the need for a greater centralization of the Party, and marked a second important stage in the dispute between the reformist and revolutionary wings.

Before the end of August Fournière had called for the creation of a National Committee of the Party. The call was taken up by Malon: and in September Brousse devoted a series of articles in *Le Prolétaire* to the subject. He referred to the dangers of a monopoly of power accruing to powerful minority groups within the Party – a scarcely disguised reference to the Guesdists – and argued that the individual group should submit to the overall will of the Party which should be embodied in a national Federal Committee, to be elected by the Party Congress. The Committee's functions should be to administer and organize, not to govern. All decisions of policy should be made by the annual National Congress, and within the organized structure there should be a free flow of ideas:

... le parti doit constituer un grand service public qui soit pour chacun de ses membres ce que sont dans la société les postes, les routes, les télgraphes, dont tout citoyen peut se servir ordinairement sans faire abandon de ses idées, sans être contraint de déserter sa manière de voir.

Its role was more precisely formulated in a resolution of the group of the 12th arrondissement submitted to the Federal Committee of the Union fédérative on 27 September; correspondence with and between groups, publicity and propaganda, and the collection of statistics on the labour movement.[88]

The Guesdists were not in disagreement over the need for the creation of a National Committee, but came into conflict with Brousse over how it should be constituted and what its functions should be. The Broussist groups wanted it to be composed of five delegates from each of the five regional federations ('an instrument of federalism'), and in addition hoped to have *Le Prolétaire* declared as the official organ of the Party.[89] The Guesdists saw this as a device of Brousse to gain control of the Party, and argued that as only two of the regional federations were properly organized they could not all be fairly represented in the National Committee.

The dispute over the National Committee dragged on over the summer of 1881 within the Union fédérative. The Guesdists were defeated on practically every point; representation on the National Committee, representation at the Coire (Chur) International Congress,[90] representation at the forthcoming Fifth National Congress at Reims, the mandate of the delegate of the Union to the Congress, and the creation of an official party organ. (*Le Prolétaire* was adopted as the official organ of the Union fédérative in October.)[91]

When the Fifth National Congress of the Party opened at Reims in November 1881 the Guesdist faction, which eighteen months previously had carried the Congress of the Centre for the Minimum Programme, was in a minority and on the defensive. It had lost control of the Union fédérative and had little influence over the regional federations. Consequently resolutions by Brousse calling for the creation of a National Committee on the basis of regional representation, and the adoption of *Le Prolétaire* as the official Party organ, were accepted by large majorities. Following their adoption the Congress went on to debate the crucial issue of the Party's Programme. In a speech urging the Party to reconsider its commitment, Brousse attacked the Minimum Programme as narrow and dogmatic. It was, he said, alienating the *militants* of the movement, and a new Programme was needed – one which allowed for local demands and situations. Brousse and his supporters carried the Congress, which voted for the formulation of a new Programme:

> Considérant que le programme *minimum* ne répond qu'imparfaitement aux différents aspirations des travailleurs;
> Qu'il a éloigné du Parti ouvrier, et surtout du candidat ouvrier, plus de travailleurs qu'il n'en a rallié;
> Que les travailleurs d'un département ou d'un arrondissement ont des aspirations différentes;
> Le Congrès demande aux fédérations de décider que le comité ouvrier socialiste d'une circonscription ait le droit de rédiger son programme électoral, en s'en tenant, bien entendu, aux considérants communistes et aux constatations historiques et économiques du nouveau programme ouvrier qui sortira du vote des fédérations.

At the same time, presumably as a gesture of compromise, Brousse successfully put forward another resolution to the effect that the Minimum Programme should, however inadequate, remain in force for the time being.[92]

The Congress of Reims marked the end of effective Guesdist influence within the Party, and only within the Fédération du Nord did Guesde retain a foothold. Within the newly elected National Committee the Broussists, largely because of the practice of delegating national figures of the Party to represent the federations, had a permanent majority of about fifteen. Furthermore, Guesde's own brainchild, the Minimum Programme, had been officially condemned, and Brousse now called for the abandonment of all attempts to impose doctrinal Programmes on the Party. The strategy he sought to lay down for the Party remained as he had defined it in *Le Travail* in 1880, and he enlarged on this theme in an article entitled 'Encore l'Union socialiste' which he wrote at this time for *Le Prolétaire*.[93] He began by pointing out that doctrinal groups invariably lacked popular support. He himself had heard many fine revolutionary words in his lifetime, but what was needed at the present juncture was 'qu'on rend des actes possibles'. It was no use, he said, in affirming that in theory 'scientific Communism' (with which he identified himself)[94] was superior to other forms of socialism if, in fact, it merely presented a Programme which gained no one's support. He continued:

Certes, je suis de ceux qui veulent être communistes, anti-gouverne-mentalistes, révolutionnaires, mais surtout je suis de ceux qui veulent l'être pour de bon. Je préfère abandonner 'le tout à la fois' pratiqué jusqu'ici et qui généralement aboutit au'rien du tout', fractionner le but idéal en plusieurs étapes sérieuses, immédiatiser en quelque sorte quelques-unes de nos revendications pour les rendre enfin possibles, au lieu de me fatiguer sur place marquer le pas, ou, comme dans le conte de Barbe-Bleue, de rester perché sur toutes les tours de l'utopie et ne jamais rien voir venir de concret et de palpable.

One had, he went on, to take what could be taken from each situation. He and the group which supported him were advocating a new kind of politics,

... une politique nouvelle faite de science, c'est-à-dire fondée sur l'histoire et l'observation. Cette politique ... s'appelle, quand elle reste pure de tout calcul personnel, de son nom matérialiste et scientifique, la politique des possibilités.

This article was a definitive statement of Brousse's commitment to reformist socialism, of which an increasingly important part became the belief in municipal socialism as the effective means to a socialist society. (The Manifesto of the National Committee published in December called for 'la conquête des municipalités qui permettrait de tenter d'une manière sérieuse les applications socialistes'.[95])

The decisions of the Reims Congress, the abandonment of revolutionary socialism and the commitment to municipal action now provoked an open schism within the Party, and the arguments moved more openly on to an ideological level.

5. *Intra-Party polemics, 1882*

The content of the Guesdist counter-attack was indicated in several articles written by Guesde in *Le Citoyen* in November, shortly after the end of the Reims Congress. These attacked 'autonomie communale' as a utopian fantasy of the progressive bourgeoisie:

... parler d'autonomie communale ... c'est vouloir faire rétrograder l'humanité, c'est vouloir réintégrer l'homme fait dans l'uterus qui a pu et dû le renfermer à l'état embryonnique. ... Du jour où la fumée d'une locomotive a apparu sur l'horizon la commune était morte comme groupement humain autonome ... communalistes, mes amis, vous êtes les hommes du passé ... pulverisé qu'il est chaque jour par la machine à vapeur qui 'fait loi'.[96]

The remarks were ostensibly directed against the Clemenceau Radicals and their newspaper *La Justice*, which advocated a degree of municipal autonomy. They also served as condemnation of Brousse's reformist Programme. This became clearer with the appearance of a third series of *L'Egalité* in December 1881, the first leading article of which set the tone for the open ideological split with the reformists. Guesde wrote:

Ce sont ces idées ennemies qui sous leur ancien nom de 'fédéralisme' ou sous les noms nouveaux de 'communalisme' et d'autonomie' hantent encore un certain nombre de cerveaux ouvriers et rendraient impossible – en l'émiettant – l'action révolutionnaire prolétairienne, que l'Egalité, franchement et scientifiquement centralisatrice, s'attachera à démolir. . . . Quant aux autres, aux conservateurs à un titre quelconque, dont la myopie ou l'indécision recule devant la violence ou 'l'impossible', comme ils disent, qu'ils restent où ils sont. Il n'y a place, dans nos rangs, pour aucun genre d'opportunisme.[97]

Furthermore, he went on to say, *L'Egalité* would work for the recasting of the National Committee and for the maintenance of the Minimum Programme.

The appearance of *L'Egalité* coincided with the decision of the Montmartre socialist group to adopt Joffrin as its candidate at a forthcoming parliamentary by-election, on a Programme which replaced the preamble of the Minimum Programme (drafted by Marx in London in 1880) with that of the statutes of the First International (drafted by Marx in London in 1864), and which replaced the points of Guesde's Programme (of June 1880) with that of Brousse's Municipal Programme (of November 1880, as amended and as published in *Le Prolétaire* in January 1881). Joffrin's opponent in this radical arrondissement was Lafont, a Clemenceau Radical.

The decision was discussed within the National Committee on 9 December. Guesde argued that as no new Programme for the Party had been adopted, Joffrin's abandonment of the Minimum Programme contravened the decision of the Reims Congress. At the Committee's next meeting on 12 December Brousse strongly defended Joffrin's Programme, arguing that nothing decided at the Reims Congress had suggested that the Minimum Programme could not be enlarged upon. He was supported by Labusquière who said that while he had originally supported the adoption of the Minimum Programme this had been *faute de mieux*, and he had never considered that it could not be improved upon:

Oui, je l'avoue, j'ai avalé ce programme jusqu'à la garde, quand il a été présenté, mais par discipline, pour ne pas fermer le parti aux timides, et bien convaincu qu'on pourrait non se tenir en deça, mais le dépasser.

Deville retorted that, on the contrary, the Montmartre Programme was a retrograde step and represented a dilution of the revolutionary commitment of the Minimum Programme. In fact both he and Guesde regarded the preamble to the International's statutes of 1864 as non-revolutionary, and this was consistent with their view of the International as a bridge between the progressive bourgeoisie and the socialists rather than as a purely proletarian organization.[98]

The derogatory references to the International provoked an angry reply from Joffrin himself in an open letter to Guesde published in *Le Prolétaire* on 7 January 1882. He recalled that he had defended Guesde at the time of the latter's dispute with the General Council over the Dentraygues affair in 1872, and he virtually accused Guesde of disloyalty to the socialist movement. Guesde, he said, was placing the interests of his own small sect against the interest of the Party, and had imposed upon it the Minimum Programme, 'ce programme [auquel] vous êtes allé donner naissance dans les brouillards de la Tamise et que vous vous êtes vanté ensuite d'avoir fait avalé *jusqu'à la garde* à votre parti'. Fanatical devotion to this Programme, he went on to say, had led Guesde and his supporters to withhold support for Party candidates of whom they disapproved.[99] Moreover Guesde had refused to accept the decision of the National Committee on 12 December which had declared that the Montmartre Programme was compatible with the decisions of the Reims Congress. Joffrin concluded by claiming that on specific points the Montmartre Programme was more revolutionary than Guesde's own; for instance, it had dropped the inheritance clause (and here he referred to the Marx–Bakunin quarrel over inheritance at the Bâle Congress of 1869); it had also dropped the demand for the minimum wage, which Marx himself considered an absurdity, and had incorporated the formula of the old French Communists, 'to each according to his need, from each according to his ability'.[100]

The debate over the Joffrin Programme was not the beginning of the split between Guesde and Brousse, but it introduced a new and important element into the Party controversy. The highly emotive issue of the First International reopened the sores of the Marx–Bakunin dispute, and *L'Egalité* with Lafargue as its leading contributor, lost little time in connecting with the past. In its third issue Lafargue began a short series entitled 'L'Autonomie', which commenced with a personal and virulent attack on Brousse, whom he referred to as a 'certain personnage, régicide en chambre et docteur en ignorance', incapable of seeing that autonomy was an historically-conditioned means of action, not an immutable principle of working-class action. Certain elements within the modern socialist movement too, Lafargue went on to say in a later article, were not aware of this either – such as the Jura anarchists who had 'tant potiné dans l'Internationale et qui avait la prétention d'imposer aux ouvriers leur théorie abstentionniste de tout action politique et leur chacun dans son trou.'[101]

The same issue of *L'Egalité* saw the theme taken up by Guesde. In a passionate defence against the allegations of authoritarianism by *Le Prolétaire* Guesde said that he recalled how, under the pretext of fighting authoritarianism:

... les anarchistes du Jura avaient organisé une aristocratie secrète composée de 100 frères internationaux dirigés par un comité secret résidant en Suisse. Pendant qu'ils accusaient ceux qu'ils appelaient les marxistes de vouloir la dictature, ces jésuites l'établissaient dans l'ombre. Les frères internationaux d'un pays organisaient une sous-aristocratie composée de frères nationaux qui cependant devaient ignorer toujours l'existence de l'aristocratie supérieure. Les ordres du Comité supérieur étaient transmis par les frères internationaux aux frères nationaux qui se mettaient en branle, intriguant, mentant, calomniant. La tactique était d'empêcher les sections et les fédéralistes de *l'Internationale* de constituer des comités représentatifs connus, responsables et controlables, et de ne permettre, pour amuser les naifs, que des boîtes à correspondance sans pouvoir et sans moyen d'action afin que les sections et les fédérations autonomes pussent être dominés par l'aristocratie secrète irresponsable et incontrolable.[102]

This was by way of introduction to his main point; that Brousse had been a member of this 'secret society', and no repetition of such practices could be allowed within the French Socialist Party.

Thus the basis of the Guesdist counter-attack was laid out in the early issues of *L'Egalité*. The long-apparent conflict of principle became apparent to the *militants* of the movement. But this conflict was made more irreconcilable, and was complicated by, the deliberate revival of hatreds and rivalries dating from the years of the First International. These rivalries sometimes cut across the simple antithesis of 'reformist' and 'revolutionary', or 'centralist' and 'autonomist'. The issues became personalized to a degree which placed potential allies on different sides of the fence, and which obscured many of the theoretical issues at stake. Derogatory references to the Communards or the Parisian Internationalists were not likely to win for the Guesdists the popular support of the Parisian working class, and indeed they merely served to embitter it. Defensible or not the Guesdists had worked themselves into a position where they enjoyed the support of only a tiny fraction of the socialist movement, and where they were seen to be attempting the disruption of the Party. Malon expressed a widely held view when in December 1881 he wrote to Fournière:

... il y a deux agents de Marx, Guesde et Lafargue, qui, per fas et nefas, veulent commander dictatorialement le parti, et si impossible, le briser (un comparse me l'a presque avoué).

Ceux qui voulaient cet été l'alliance radical ne sont pas plus révolu-tionnaires que nous. Ceux qui subordonnent d'une façon absolue la socialisation des forces productrices à leur préalable grande-industrialisa-tion ne sont pas plus communistes que nous.

Ce n'est même pas la guerre entre centralistes et autonomistes ... il y un parti que ne veut pas être mené par deux ou trois intrigants ... six mois encore de ces luttes intestines et le parti sera frappé mortellement.[103]

Early in 1882 the Party, as Malon predicted, began to disintegrate. Having failed to win the National Committee over to the Guesdist viewpoint, the delegates of the Fédération du Nord withdrew in January. This left the reformists in full control, and at a meeting on 5 February Brousse was appointed as the Party's secretary for in-ternal affairs.

Within the Union fédérative, the withdrawal of the Fédération du Nord from the National Committee was discussed at a meeting on 17 January. Attacked by both Brousse and Allemane for opposing Party policy, Bazin, the Guesdist delegate, dissociated himself from any decision the Union might take. This moved Paulard to demand the expulsion of L'Egalité group, and the matter was referred to the next meeting of the Committee of the Union. To precipitate the inevitable conclusion the group withdrew. Subsequently it was formally ex-pelled by the Committee,[104] and *L'Egalité* drew up a detailed justifica-tion of its own, and an indictment of Brousse's position. In an article entitled 'Une Exclusion nécessaire' on 22 January 1882 the paper referred the roots of the dispute back to the very origins of the Party

in 1880, when Guesde had fought within *L'Emancipation* to prevent
Malon from co-operating with the Radicals. It then went on to
denounce Brousse whom it accused of being responsible for the split
within the Party. Significantly it cleared him of any personal motive
for leading the Party along its present path, and said that Brousse had
only to be consistent with his anarchist past:

Ayant anarchisé dix ans après avoir proudhonisé plus ou moins longtemps, pour travailler à *décollectiviser* le parti ouvrier français, dans
lequel il entrait comme un ancien ennemi, il n'avait qu'à se croire à Gand
en 1877, alors que, contre Liebknecht et de Paepe, il 'tombait' la propriété collective.

The article conceded at least two things to Brousse; he played with
his cards on the table and he was consistent. He had always opposed
the Minimum Programme, and his Municipal Programme had been
conceived from his Proudhonist credo. His aim had always been to:

... démolir *L'Egalité* ... comme le plus solide boulevard de collectivisme
révolutionnaire, et, sous couvert d'*Union Socialiste*, créer un opportunisme (moins le mot) ouvrier faisant plus que s'accommoder de toutes
les réactions individualistes contre nos Congrès du Havre et de Marseille,
les provoquer ouvertement.

On the one hand, the article concluded, was the revolutionary
working class, which since 1876 had fought for socialism; on the other
hand were the politicians, tired of receiving 'pommes frites' for the
Party, and now in process of 'embourgeoisifying' it. And as a final
blow in this Guesdist counter-attack Lafargue, in an article entitled
'Le Possibilisme' castigated it as the abandonment of collectivism,
the espousal of petit-bourgeois idealism, and a reversion to federalism
which in 1871 had led to the bloody massacre of the Commune which
they (the true collectivists) would never have declared without
evidence of national solidarity.[105]

What in fact was possibilism? The Guesde–Lafargue interpretation, with its major indictment of 'radicalism' and 'opportunism',
eventually triumphed in socialist historiography. For Zévaès,
possibilism was:

... du capitalisme d'Etat, ou, si l'on veut, du socialisms d'Etat. Mais nul
ampleur de vues, nul aperçu sur l'évolution générale des sociétés. Une
conception de politicien. Les possibilistes ne sont que des politiciens
aspirant à prendre la place des radicaux comme ceux-ci ont aspiré à la
place des opportunistes.

Lafargue told Engels that: 'We do not regard the possibilists as socialists, but as *carpet-baggers* who use socialism to obtain political positions and municipal grants.'[106]

To dismiss it in this way is to misinterpret and underrate possibilism. By 1882 the possibilists enjoyed far more support amongst the working class committed to socialism than the Guesdists, and throughout that decade this continued to be true. It was also true that the possibilists, at least until the time of the Boulanger crisis and the formation of the Société des Droits de l'Homme in 1888, regarded the Radicals as their worst enemies. It was only after 1890, when the Guesdists themselves adopted a largely reformist Programme, that Guesdism took serious hold within the working class.

An essential component of possibilism was its avowed anti-Marxism. This was made explicit by Brousse in his pamphlet *Le Marxisme dans l'Internationale* which was published immediately prior to the St Etienne Congress of the Party in 1882. Brousse defined Marxism in the following terms:

> Le *Marxisme* ne consiste donc pas à être partisan des idées de Marx. A ce titre, et dans une très large mesure, beaucoup de ses adversaires actuels, et particulièrement celui qui écrit ces lignes, seraient marxistes.
> Le *Marxisme* consiste surtout dans le système qui tend non à répandre la doctrine marxiste mais à l'imposer, et dans tous ses détails.

The articulated opposition to Marxism was therefore less on a theoretical than on a political level. Marxism tended almost to become identifiable with *authoritarianism*, which in the French context meant Jacobinism or Blanquism, and with the strong Blanquist element in Guesde's interpretation of Marxism this was hardly surprising. Thus to Brousse Marx had attempted to become more than the great critic he was, and had fostered pretensions to the

> ... gouvernement absolu de tout le mouvement socialiste de son temps, et très sérieusement il croit avoir la pouce assez large pour que cette grande évolution sociologique garde sa seule empreinte. Je n'ai pas besoin de démontrer qu'en cela il se trompe: le socialisme de notre époque est *internationale*, mais il ne sera pas plus *pangermanique* qu'exclusivement *français*.

As for Guesde and Lafargue, whom Brousse saw as the agents of Marx, they were continuing a struggle which had begun in the International. Lafargue particularly became the object of this charge, for as a result of his activities in Spain in 1872 he was particularly associated with Marxism.

In another sense also possibilism was a reversion to the First International. In a re-examination of the history of the International Brousse saw it as a *working-class* movement first and foremost, based on the simple truth (which, of course, Proudhon had similarly stated), that 'l'Emancipation des travailleurs doit être l'oeuvre des travailleurs aux-mêmes'. This formula had been undermined by the attempts of various doctrinaire groups – amongst whom Brousse now placed the anarchists – to impose their own particular formula upon the movement. This, he said, had been to destroy the effectiveness of the organization, which had lost its concrete basis. This basis could only be

> ... un fait très simple, courant les rues, que chaque travailleur comprend, par cela seul qu'il travaille, l'opposition, l'antagonisme des intérêts entre le capitaliste et le travailleur, *le fait matériel*, en un mot, de la distinction des classes.[107]

He expressed a similar view in a letter to Jung in 1882:

> Quant au principe d'action du parti ouvrier; le voici, non pas d'après les votes du Congrès, qui dépendent toujours un peu des théoriciens, mais d'après l'examen sur place. Le grand mouvement qui nous emporte en ce moment a pour base la séparation de classes; tous les hommes qui sont actifs sont certainement des communistes-révolutionnaires, mais la masse de notre parti est surtout préoccupé de lutter comme classe contre la bourgeoisie; de là, demander des réformes. . . .[108]

The replacement of the 1880 preamble to the Minimum Programme by the preamble of the Inaugural Address of 1864 was related *not* to a wish to rid the Socialist Party of its collectivism and to become opportunist, but to find a rhetoric and a Programme capable of inspiring the working class to *immediate* action. In other words, to shift the emphasis from a socialist party to that of a labour party. This might well involve the Party in placing collectivism lower down on the scale of values, but this was not an end in itself. In this sense possibilism, as its name indicates, *was* a politician's concept in that it showed a concern to gain power, and it presented a challenge to Marxism very different from Bernstein's reformist socialism which was postulated on certain fundamental criticisms of Marx's analysis of capitalist economics. With Brousse the tactics of the movement were primary. His possibilism was linked closely with his original

Bakuninist belief in the dynamics of working-class action. To will the end was to will the *means*:

... nous avons fini par nous apercevoir-nous avons mis longtemps pour cela-qu'on ne réussissait pas une révolution sans avoir au préalable une armée. Tel est le motif qui a fait sortir le parti de la période des affirmations pures pour entrer dans la phase de l'agitation, de l'organisation, du recrutement. Or, qui veut la fin, veut les moyens. Aussi sommes-nous entrés résolument dans l'action électorale ... plaçons-nous résolument dans le monde réel, dans cette société où nous vivons. [Cf. his letter to Gross, 3 April 1883 (*Gross-Fulpius, IISG*, Appendix 2).]

This meant in effect that the Party was limited by what the majority of its supporters would tolerate. It was to be the very opposite of an élitist Party, such as that preached by Guesde, which remained as always an anathema to Brousse. In 1884 he devoted a small pamphlet entitled *Dictature et Liberté* to a refutation of the authoritarian and élitist concept of the Party. He took as his basic text the Programme of Tkachev's newspaper *Le Tocsin*, which claimed the right to leadership by 'des gens intellectuellement et moralement développés, c'est-à-dire par la minorité. Cette minorité, en vertu de son développement intellectuel et moral, a toujours eu et doit avoir le dessus sur la majorité.' This élitist view was attacked by Brousse, both on the explicitly Bakuninist grounds that a political party which cut itself off from the masses and considered itself superior to them could only be faced with intellectual and political sclerosis, and on the grounds that the dictatorship of 'those who know' could logically only produce a permanent state of revolt against itself. Moreover, the pretension to have found the key to history was profoundly antipathetic to Brousse. Both in *Le Marxisme dans l'Internationale* and in *Dictature et Liberté* he argued that the development of a Marxist doctrine was in fundamental contradiction with developments in contemporary social science. With their emphasis on empirical evidence, the social sciences had rendered obsolete any doctrinaire political Programme. For this reason, Brousse argued, Marxism should be classified with the old utopian and authoritarian socialist *credos* such as Blanquism and Jacobinism:

... le temps est passé des hommes qui se découragent quand ils ne peuvent faire accepter par le peuple leur petite système ou leur gros dada ... la politique moderne s'enquiert par l'observation, par les votes et les autres manifestations de l'opinion des volontés, des forces, des tendances des éléments humains: il trouvera des formules, il dégagera des résultats. Il ne tente plus de furieuses envolés vers l'idéal, il emploie ses connaissances de spécialistes à faire entrer dans le domaine des faits, non pas l'idée qu'il choie, lui plaît le mieux, mais celle qu'il a reconnu générale, commune, et qui, à ce titre, peut être réalisé. Il laisse l'impossible pour le possible.[109]

It was only in this way, he argued, that freedom could be maintained within and by the Party. The nature of this Party he had described in greater detail two years previously in 1882, in the first issue of *La Bataille*.

In this article he argued that the primary constitutive basis of the Party was the economic and political class division. This was the one factor subjectively experienced and therefore of practical value as a basis for action: other bases, which attempted to enlarge on or refine this primary fact, could only succeed in creating a divisive minority. This broad concept of the Party meant, and Brousse recognized it, inevitable differences of opinion over ends and means. But these differences he saw rather as divisions of labour; those who advocated syndicalist action were advocating one necessary means of action, and the same could be said of those advocating co-operation or reformism. None of these groups, he argued, could in itself form a Party powerful enough credibly to advocate victory for the working class. The penalty for any such attempt would be to throw half the labour movement into the arms of the bourgeoisie. Only by the recognition of *differences within* the Party could it claim a popular and working-class base. Only then could it claim to be a Parti Ouvrier and establish a solid link with the working-class movement.[110]

Behind this concept of the Party there was the belief that tactical unity could be achieved in the claim for immediate reforms, and – despite the rhetoric which laid stress on reformist tactics as presenting merely a challenge to lay bare the basic hypocrisy of the bourgeoisie[111] – Brousse formulated a reformist Programme composed of two main planks. The first was the 'public service theory'; the second was his theory of Municipal Socialism.

Brousse published his *Propriété Collective et les Services Publics* in 1883. It provided the theoretical underpinning to his reformism and was based, consciously, on a reversion to the collectivist theories expounded at the 1874 Brussels and 1876 Berne Congresses of the International by César de Paepe. The essence of these theories was, Brousse argued, the observation that within capitalist society itself

forms of collective property and social control were developing. This
observation was however to be distinguished from that of Marxism,
which remained essentially within the old utopian (non-scientific)
mould through its belief in a moral imperative for socialism which
presumed to lay down a logical and necessary order for its achievement. Thus Guesde's statement that expropriation should start with
industrial, pass through commercial and finish with agricultural
property was scientifically unsound because it ignored the actual
observable process by which collectivism was being achieved.[112]

For Brousse it was a general – though tendential and not absolute –
rule that all branches of production passed through the phases of
individual *métier*, competition and monopoly, ending in State intervention. This intervention created the Public Services:

> Le service public est le dernier terme du développement de chaque
> spécialité du labeur humain. Sa formation résulte de la nature même des
> choses, et il se constitue sous quelque gouvernement de classe que ce
> soit. On peut dire: les gouvernements changent avec les classes diverses
> qui font la conquête du pouvoir, mais l'Etat reste et continue son
> développement normal en transformant peu à peu chaque catégorie du
> travail humain ... l'Etat est l'ensemble des services publices déjà
> constitués: les gouvernements en sont les directeurs autoritaires.

In other words exclusive control of the State by one class, however
desirable, was not the *sole* condition on which it became an instrument of good. It was not necessary to destroy the bourgeois State
before such reforms could be achieved. Within contemporary capitalist society public services were developing of their own accord – for
example, railways and postal services.[113] While in certain circumstances their extension might involve retrograde developments, it was
the function of the Socialist Party to accelerate the general trend and
to control it, especially in those areas where the bourgeoisie showed
little concern directing it towards socially beneficial results.[114]
Eventually society would become one in which the public services
satisfied the needs of all on a Communist basis – the old anarcho-
Communist ideal of a free society with 'from each according to his
ability, to each according to his need' as its cornerstone:

> L'Etat socialiste serait donc dans l'avenir, autant que nos connais-
> sances actuelles nous permettent de le prévoir, un ensemble de services
> publics administrés non plus sous le commandement d'un gouvernement
> de classe mais sous l'impulsion de la volonté véritablement populaire, se

formant et se formulant en passant par les groupes de régimes et de métiers et leurs fédérations.[115]

When in 1897 Brousse was asked what possibilism was, he replied that its whole aim was to achieve as soon as possible the organization of public services for the immediate needs of the working class. One of the ways in which this end could be achieved was through municipal action.[116] Belief in Municipal Socialism was the second main plank of the possibilist Programme, and very clearly was an extension to a new set of circumstances of Brousse's anarchist belief in the Commune as the agency of social change. In a pamphlet he wrote in 1882 entitled *La Commune et le Parti ouvrier* Brousse argued that if his theory of the development of public services were true then the crucial question for socialism was no longer 'should one destroy or manipulate the powers of the State?', but rather 'on which of these powers is it easiest to lay hands?' The answer was simple and predictable – municipal power:

Encore en minorité dans l'ensemble du pays, sa défaite législative est assuré; en majorité dans les foyers ou l'on travaille, la victoire dans l'ordre administratif est certain. Le *pouvoir*, dont la conquête s'impose au prolétariat du fait même de la situation, c'est le pouvoir municipal, c'est la Municipalité, c'est la Commune ... la conquête des municipalités, voilà la premiere forme que prend pour notre jeune Parti ouvrier la tradition communale française.[117]

He did not claim Municipal Socialism as the final answer but at least, he argued, it would present the working class with the realities of power and give it valuable administrative experience. It would also help to break down the paralysing grip of the belief that the contemporary situation was immutable, and while Municipal Socialism was not in itself an end it would at least provide a stepping stone from theoretical to practical action. A Revolution, even a peaceful Revolution, could be disastrous both in general and for the working class in particular if they were not experienced in practical action.[118]

In May 1882 the Union fédérative du Centre, firmly under the control of the possibilists, held its Third Annual Congress.[119] Its opening Manifesto evoked the possibilist spirit: 'plus consciente dans l'action, elle veut aujourd'hui immédiatiser la lutte, la faire descendre des intentions et des phrases dans les faits.' Having first expelled the Marxist dissidents it went on to discuss three major questions of socialist action; the conquest of power in the Commune and the

State and the action of socialist municipalities; the value of strike action as a political weapon; and the usefulness of Congrès corporatifs (trade-union congresses).

On strike action the overwhelming opinion of the Congress was that it could only be useful as a means of working-class organization, not as a means of emancipation. This in fact was contrary to Brousse's own opinion. He not only held that the strike was an area of action which directly involved the ordinary working man who was concerned with higher wages, but also that as a weapon it was becoming stronger through the action of economic forces which rendered employers more vulnerable to machine stoppages. And, he argued, the English example proved that strikes could always improve working conditions.[120] However the issue was not forced to a vote.

The Congress then went on to state that Congrès corporatifs, so long as they existed, provided a useful field of socialist action. It completed its debates by giving overwhelming endorsement to what one delegate called the 'solution possibiliste', i.e. the conquest of municipal and central political power. The final resolution on political action did however reflect the considerable residue of revolutionary sentiment existing in Paris. It stated that the conquest of State powers was merely a preparatory means to Revolution, and that the conquest of political power in the municipalities was, while providing the circumstances for effective action, basically a means for provoking a 'mise en demeure' (challenge) to the bourgeoisie.[121] In spite of these reservations on the ultimate value of municipal action, following the Congress the Party launched into a campaign for the betterment of working-class conditions. This was directed primarily at the severe housing crisis in Paris.

Article 12 of the Programme voted at Le Havre had specifically singled out this problem as one in which the Party could seek immediate improvement. Since September 1881 the subject had occupied several public meetings organized by the Party,[122] and on 8 April 1882 Allemane, a prominent Communard who had returned from exile in 1880,[123] had written on the problem in *Le Prolétaire*. His article was followed by a brief editorial note, almost certainly written by Brousse, which said that:

Quand le parti ouvrier aura réalisé la conquête des municipalités, la première mise en demeure à faire à la bourgeoisie doit être celle-ci;

l'habitation, service public de la commune et le logement fourni au moins à prix de revient.

After Joffrin's election to the Paris Municipal Council on 7 May 1882 – the first successful Socialist candidate – the Federal Committee of the Union fédérative worked in close liaison with him on issues before the Council. The Committee was in fact by this time an adjunct of the National Committee of the Party, which itself set up in June 1882 a committee of five members (Brousse, Malon, Labusquière, Deynaud and Joffrin) to discuss ways of helping municipal councillors who were members of the Party and to discuss issues before the Parisian municipality.[124]

In the newspaper recently founded by Lissagaray, *La Bataille,* Brousse urged the construction of municipal housing for the working class. Whereas the Guesdists merely called for a tax on unoccupied property to relieve the acute housing shortage, Brousse rejected this solution as leaving unresolved the provision of cheap housing and, perhaps more important, the problem of the gross disparity in conditions between the badly- and the richly-housed (in the 2nd arrondissement the death rate was 1 in 65: in the 12th, 1 in 15). The only solution was new construction, and he quoted the Peabody Trust buildings in London as an example of the feasibility of providing housing at low rents. Moreover, he argued, such a programme would prepare the ground for the eventual expropriation of bourgeois property.

Much of the attack was directed against the big financial companies which were extending their control over the French economy. This control was not limited to housing. It affected for instance the supply of gas, and Brousse bitterly attacked the newly drawn-up agreement between the Paris Municipality and the Compagnie parisienne d'éclairage et du chauffage par le Gaz which gave the latter a monopoly. He applied the same critical gaze to the railways where he saw the gradual extension of the power of finance capitalism which, he said, found its spokesman in Léon Say, whose budgets were entirely the instrument of their control.[125]

It was on the question of the underground railway for Paris that Brousse really revealed himself as a supporter of the improvement of the working-class environment. A project was put forward by the Métropolitain and discussed in the Council in May and June. Brousse opposed it on the basis of two main principles which he laid down as essential for any system of public transport. These were (a) the provision of cheap and quick transport for the city's labour forces, and (b) the easing of congestion in central Paris. The idea he sketched out was for a system based on East–West and North–South axes, with Les Halles as the central point and the working-class quarters as its termini. Cheap public transport should then be provided from there to the outer boulevards, and the system should provide a twenty-hour-a-day service. In fact, Brousse said, of the five lines envisaged in the plan of the Métropolitain, only two fulfilled the conditions he laid down. The only satisfactory solution for the city would be for the municipality itself to take responsibility for the scheme.[126]

The overwhelming emphasis within the Socialist Party on Municipal Socialism after the May Congress exacerbated the hostility of the Guesdists. Referring to Brousse's pamphlet on *La Commune et le Parti ouvrier*, Guesde caustically remarked that 'il faut tomber de la lune – ou révenir du Jura bernois – pour s'arrêter seulement à l'hypothèse d'un collectivisme communale'.[127] While in *Le Citoyen* immediately prior to the Congress he said that if it rejected Municipal Socialism it 'aura sauvé le navire qui porte le Parti ouvrier et sa fortune d'un des plus dangereux écueils contre lesquels il puisse encore échouer'.[128] Municipal Socialism, it was argued, was worse than a petit-bourgeois illusion; it could not even fulfil the tasks laid down for it by the possibilists, as the municipalities were dominated by and in debt to the State. It could only conceivably be seen as a means of recruiting support for the 'army of the revolution'.[129] Lafargue, particularly, launched into a bitter broadside attack on Municipal Socialism and referred scathingly to Brousse as the 'doctissime docteur possibiliste'.[130]

Guesdist confidence was however shaken by the very evident support that the possibilist campaign on housing gained for Brousse and his allies. This success led Guesde, if only temporarily, to modify his revolutionary posture and concede something to the demand for realism. In an article in *L'Egalité* Guesde made the somewhat surprising admission that 'il n'ensuit pas que les diverses réclamations de l'humanité doivent être renvoyé *a priori* après la dépossession indispensable de la classe bourgeoise'; and he went on to say that in order to prepare the working class for Revolution the Party had to take up its complaints. On the housing issue it had no choice but to enter the struggle on the ground available to it which was why, he said, the (Guesdist) Fédération du Centre had decided to launch a campaign for lower rents.[131] Even within the framework of this argument however he held to his revolutionism by saying that the campaign would inevitably fail and its value could only be in the creation of 'une véritable fabrique de socialistes et de révolutionnaires'. Only two weeks later Lafargue was again propounding the intransigent revolutionary line.

6. The final break: the St Etienne Congress

The final stage of the split within the Party was opened by the resignation of Brousse and his supporters from Lissagaray's newspaper, *La Bataille*, in August, on the grounds that Lissagaray's dependence on advertising revenue from large financial companies had led him to influence editorial policy. Specifically, it was said, he had obstructed the completion of the series by Brousse on the Métropolitain and the Compagnie de Gaz and had undermined the role of the paper's editorial secretary, Labusquière. The affair developed into a contest between Brousse and Lissagaray which culminated in a personal confrontation of the two men at a meeting at the Salle Rivoli in the rue Saint-Antoine. The meeting gave overwhelming support to Brousse and upheld his claim that Lissagaray had given only lukewarm support to the Party and was therefore politically unreliable.[132] (The core of this charge was that Lissagaray had withheld support for a strike by the Parisian tanners, and Lissagaray's defence was that Brousse had failed to communicate to him their official request for assistance.)

The importance of this affair lay in the opportunity it provided for Brousse's opponents within the Party to start, or resume, their own campaign of personal vilification against him. In *L'Egalité* Lafargue seized on Lissagaray's allegation as support for an accusation he now brought forward against Brousse, namely that he had attempted to discredit Guesde's reputation at a time when Lafargue was still in London by spreading the rumour that he had received from the latter a suggestion that Guesde should be made leader of the Party. He (Brousse) had never produced the letter; nor had a letter from Lafargue to the Union fédérative enclosing a letter from Brousse in which it was suggested that the Party leader be chosen by a vote (a device, Lafargue said, to ensure Brousse's own election) ever reached its destination. It had been intercepted by Brousse whose strategy throughout the history of the Party had been to:

... établir la présidence dans le Parti, de s'en emparer, de possibiliser le
mouvement ouvrier, d'émasculer le programme par la suppression des
considérants collectivistes, de noyer ses revendications ouvrières avec les
blagues politiques du radicalisme sur la présidence, le sénat, etc.,
d'endormir le Parti avec des machines municipales. . . .[133]

This article provoked the strongest and most bitter letter to date
from Brousse, who had shown considerable restraint in the face of
frequent provocative statements by both Lafargue and Guesde. In
Le Prolétaire on 7 October 1882 Brousse, for the first time, gave
Lafargue a taste of his own medicine:

A Monsieur le docteur Paul Lafargue,
   Comme beaucoup d'autres socialistes, comme au temps de l'Internationale, M. Jules Guesde lui-même, je suis en butte à mon tour aux
calomnies et aux attaques de la côterie marxiste.
   Je ne m'en effraie pas outre mesure; mais il y a cependant des limites
que je ne laisserai pas dépasser.
   Que M. le docteur Paul Lafargue, qui vient de troquer, au grand profit
de ses clients, son métier de médecin pour une place d'employé dans une
compagnie d'assurances sur la vie, me traite de doctissime docteur, et
que dans chaque article il y revienne, je ne vois à cela d'inconvénient
aucun. Il montre par là qu'il n'a pas d'esprit et cela regarde ses lecteurs.
   Qu'il me traite si cela lui plaît de'régicide en chambre's'ans ajouter que
cette chambre au lieu d'être les salons de Londres où M. Lafargue
balançait son [?] fut pour trois fois la prison dans l'exil, cela importe peu
pour moi; pour lui c'est affaire de conscience.
   Mais que M. Lafargue parle à mon sujet de *falsification et de détourne-
ment de lettres* je trouve *la plaisanterie* un peu forte. Et comme, pour
être bonnes, les plaisanteries doivent être courtes, j'ai résolu que celle-ci
prendrait fin.
   Pour y mettre un terme, je propose à M. Paul Lafargue de régler
définitivement cette question de notre correspondance par la formation
d'un jury de constatation. Si M. Paul Lafargue refuse l'établissement de
ce jury, ou s'il s'ergote, il descendra à un niveau où l'on ne relève plus,
comme les calomniateurs de citoyen Chabert, que des tribunaux de police
de la bourgeoisie.
   Restera la question de savoir si je daignerai me servir de cette arme.
                                                                Paul Brousse.

Lafargue had gone too far. Brousse was able to capitalize on the
situation, and at a meeting of the Union fédérative on 22 August he
offered to resign. As he must clearly have expected the resignation

was rejected. Instead the meeting passed a resolution calling for the immediate cessation of all personal attacks within the Party.

The effect of this exchange was to crystallize sentiment within the Party against the Marxists. Brousse's personal standing was strengthened, and for the first time suggestions began to appear that Guesde and his allies should be expelled from the Party.[134] Shortly before the Sixth National Congress of the Party, due to be held at St Etienne in September, Brousse produced his swingeing indictment of the Marxist intrigues within the Party in his masterful political invective, *Le Marxisme dans l'Internationale et dans le Parti Ouvrier*.

The central point of this pamphlet was to draw a direct parallel between the actions of the Marxists within the International and their actions within the Parti Ouvrier. Brousse's argument was that just as Marx had sought to control the direction of the International and had altered its statutes at the London Conference of 1871, so Guesde had sought to enforce his own interpretation of the resolutions of the Parti Ouvrier, and had gone so far as to 'mislay' the records of the Le Havre Congress. But it was Lafargue who presented the real target. In 1871 he had acted as Marx's agent in disrupting the Madrid Federation. Now he was disrupting the French working-class movement. The conclusion was that such intrigues could not be tolerated within the Party and that their perpetrators should be expelled.

This set the tone for the Congress. The first question on the agenda was the question of Party discipline. While nominally this was concerned with the dispute between the rival Centre Federations, it was clear even before the Congress opened that it would turn into a public condemnation of the entire Marxist group. In fact the latter decided before the Congress met to break away from the Party, and made preparations for the holding of a counter-Congress at Roanne.[135]

When the Party Congress met on 25 September at St Etienne, a possibilist stronghold, the Guesdists were in a minority of 24 out of 102 delegates. They were slightly disconcerted when, contrary to expectations, the possibilist majority failed to adopt a contrary position to that of the Guesdists on the procedural question of voting. This would have presented them with an excuse for a walk-out. But in the second session the majority voted against a resolution which sought to place the Fédération du Centre (the breakaway Centre Federation set up by the Guesdists) and the Union fédérative on an equal basis and bar them both from voting on the disciplinary issue before the Congress. This provided the Marxists with a suitable occasion to

walk out of the Congress. On the following day they set up their rival
Congress at Roanne.

The Marxist walk-out was followed immediately by the Report of
the National Committee which was read by Deynaud. This began
with a preliminary justification of the need for discipline within the
Party, qualifying this by drawing a firm distinction between what it
called 'democratic' and 'authoritarian' discipline. It then went on to
examine at length the disputes between the two factions of the Party,
detailing the polemics between *L'Egalité* and *Le Prolétaire*, the disagreement over the elections of August 1881 and the subsequent
polemic between Massard and Fournière, the quarrel over the Joffrin
campaign in Montmartre, the creation of rival federations in Paris
and the attack on the municipal projects of the Party. The Report
laid the blame entirely on the shoulders of the Guesdists, and it concluded by saying that the Congress should consider their expulsion.[136]

Brousse followed Deynaud. He set the tone of his speech by saying
that his purpose in addressing the Congress would be to show that
within the Socialist Party certain members had attempted to follow
the same manœuvres as they had within the International, that is to
place themselves outside of and above the Party with the purpose of
imposing upon it their own particular doctrine. The solution, he said,
was simple; the dissidents should leave the Party, and time and
experience would prove who was right. No party based on an autonomist structure could tolerate a group such as the Guesdists which
refused the Party the right to adopt a position contrary to their own.
Brousse was able to season his indictment with quotations from
several letters of Lafargue to both himself and Malon, and these, in
conjunction with the clear historical evidence that the Guesdist
group had refused to follow the decisions of successive Congresses of
the Party, proved, he said, that:

> ... le petit groupe marxiste est en état permanent de rébellion contre la
> volonté du Parti, en état permanent de conspiration pour arriver à le
> gouverner. Une seule question, solution mise à part, reste à traiter: celle
> de savoir si cette conspiration, cette rébellion, sont impuissants ou
> redoubtables; en un mot, si l'existence du Parti court quelque danger.
> A cette dernière question je n'hésite pas à reponddre: Oui.
> L'autoratisme marxiste a en effet des moyens d'action sur la puissance
> desquels on ne réflechit pas assez.

What were these powers? Brousse meant the willingness of the

Marxists to use the powers of capitalist society, which led them inevitably into dubious ethical positions. In particular it had led Guesde to break his pledge over non-participation in the 1881 elections, and to collaborate on *Le Citoyen* without ensuring it was controlled in any way by the socialist movement. For one group to act in this way, harnessing these forces against groups *within* the Party, was, he said, a clear danger to which there were only two possible solutions; conciliation or separation. He continued:

La conciliation est impossible. On ne concilie pas l'eau avec le feu. L'entente, la fédération, peuvent être entre groupes autonomes decidées à respecter leur mutuelle independance. Elles se dissolvent par l'introduction d'un groupe autoritaire et dominateur. Or, par tradition historique, par tempérament, par programme, je puis dire: le group marxiste doit, jusqu'à sa victoire, si elle était possible, travailler, conspirer, pour conquérir la direction du Parti.

Ils ne peuvent pas, le voudraient-ils, se soumettre jamais aux décisions du Parti. Autoritaires, ils sont obéissants. Mais comment pourraient-ils obéir à la fois au vote de vos Congrès et à la volonté d'un homme extérieur au Parti, placé lui-même à Londres en dehors de votre contrôle?

Ils sont les ultramontains du socialisme: les ultramarins, on pourrait dire. Les ultramontains ne peuvent pas obéir à la loi de leur pays, parce que leur chef est à Rome. Les marxistes ne peuvent pas obéir aux decisions de leur parti, parce que leur chef est à Londres. On ne concilie pas le Parti ouvrier avec le fanatisme marxiste, pas plus que dans le monde bourgeois on peut reconcilier le cléricalisme avec l'Etat. Il n'y qu'une solution nécessaire; c'est la séparation de l'etat avec l'Eglise, c'est la sortie raisonnable ou forcée des capucins marxistes de l'Etat socialiste ouvrier.

Brousse's indictment of Marxism was probably the strongest ever to have been delivered by any of its opponents since Marx drafted the Inaugural Address. His argument contained all the elements to be found in later, twentieth-century, anti-Marxist polemic; historically, temperamentally and inevitably the Marxists were forced to conspire against the true interests of the socialist movement, and moreover in doing so they were the mere agents of a foreign presence. As if the Pope were not bad enough, they now had Karl Marx. The argument was concise and readily digestible. The notable thing was however the enormous appeal the argument carried. It spoke volumes for the mismanagement of the situation by Guesde and Lafargue in the mere two years which had lapsed since the foundation of the Party (and also, of course, of the damage done by Marx and Engels in the 1870s). Marx and Engels may well have put a brave face on things and argued that the division was inevitable, but the question then raised was why in that case bother to form a united Party in the first place? The pseudo-historical answer of Engels to the St Etienne split was no answer at all.[137] The split could be described in ideological terms (and in fact, polemics aside, Engels was capable of giving a reasonable explanation on this level). But this did not explain why the split took place *when* it did, and in such a short time after the creation of the Party. The answer to this was largely to be found in the clumsiness of Guesde and Lafargue and in the traditional commitments of the French socialist movement. The conspiracy thesis used to explain Brousse's victory, largely developed because neither Engels, Guesde nor Lafargue cared to see beyond the International, was facile.[138] On the other hand the 'Marxist conspiracy' thesis deployed by Brousse was more plausible. It was certainly more widely believed.

Brousse's speech was followed by similar calls for the expulsion of the Guesdists from the Party by Allemane, Paulard, Joffrin, Clément, Boyer and others. Paulard formally presented a resolution in this sense which called for the expulsion of Guesde, Lafargue, Bazin, Massard, Deville and Fréjac, and the automatic exclusion of any group which accepted them as members or delegates. This resolution was supported by 66 of the 82 delegates present.

With the Guesdists expelled the Congress then went on to vote for the abolition of the Minimum Programme. Each constituency was to have the right to draw up its own Programme, but there was to be only one preamble. This was to be a slightly revised version of Marx's 1864 preamble to the statutes of the International. (It embodied the demand for the eventual creation of a Communist society, achieved by means of the conquest of power in the municipality, Department and State.) The Congress then drew up a new set of rules embodying the main elements of the autonomist and federalist structure created at Marseilles, placing the seat of the National Committee permanently in Paris, and nominating *Le Prolétaire* as the official Party organ. The functions of the National Committee were to carry out the decisions of the National Congresses, act as a central correspondence bureau, arbitrate between disputing groups or federations when requested to do so, initiate discussions within the Party and organize propaganda campaigns. It had no power to enforce policy on the Party, which now took upon itself the name of Parti Ouvrier Socialiste Révolutionnaire Français.

The St Etienne Congress marked the apogee of Brousse's influence within the French socialist movement. The Marxist group formed only a small minority. The majority of the *militants* of the movement, Malon, Chabert, Rouzade, Clément, Joffrin, Allemane, Paulard, Prudent-Dervillers and many others, had followed Brousse. The possibilists had a virtual monopoly in Paris and had for a long time enjoyed strong support in the South and East, although here it was regional separatism, rather than positive identification with possibilism, which placed them amongst the opponents of Guesdist centralism. With the St Etienne Congress the possibilists had firmly placed themselves in control of the organized French socialist movement. This victory was to a very large extent the work of Brousse.

For him the wheel had now turned full circle. It was exactly ten years to the very week since he himself had been expelled by the Marxists from the Montpellier section of the International, and it was also ten years to the month since the Hague split. Since then Brousse had fought consistently against the Marxists; in Spain, where he came into contact with Bakuninism; in Switzerland, where he emerged eventually as a leading anarchist activist and one of the most important of the French socialist exiles; in Brussels and London where he formulated a non-Marxist political strategy for the socialist movement; and finally in France where, in addition to formulating an alternative socialist theory and tactic to that of Guesde, he united behind him all those socialists who were, for various reasons, opposed to Guesde's leadership. This unity was created in opposition to 'Marxism', a concept whose origins lay in the conflicts of the International, and which Brousse himself fostered and crystallized into a political weapon. As such the unity of forces grouped around Brousse in 1882 was in part a tactical alliance which, once the Guesdists had been expelled, began to break into its component parts. Indeed it was an ominous sign that the southern socialists, or at least its articulate minority, largely dissociated themselves from the St Etienne decisions. (See Appendix 5b.) And as early as 1884 one or two of Brousse's more distinguished allies in the anti-Guesdist struggle, such as Fournière and Gustave Rouanet as well as Malon himself, had broken away from the party.[139]

But if the Possibilist Party contained within itself at least some of the seeds of its own decay, these did not come finally to fruition until

1890 and the split with Allemane. Throughout the 1880s the Party
played a predominant role within the French socialist movement
which at this time was composed of several elements – the Guesdists,
the Blanquists and the independents. It also played an important part
in the revival of the international socialist movement and in the events
leading up to the foundation of the Second International in 1889. In
both these spheres of activity themes which had characterized
Brousse's previous political activities shaped in a familiar way events
in a context which in many respects was quite different from that
which had preceded. First, the Possibilist Party was an organized
Party, the building up of whose strength required different qualities
of leadership from those appropriate to a small revolutionary exile
movement or a group torn by internal rivalries where there was a
premium on political manœuvring and not-too-fastidious propaganda. The new environment, it could be argued, was not favourable
to Brousse's particular temperament. The slow and patient building
up of a Party organization was alien to him. It is certainly true to say
that within the collective leadership of the Possibilist Party – which
included working-class *militants* such as Joffrin, Allemane, Lavy and
Chabert – Brousse's role was somewhat eclipsed in the 1880s. The
narrative of possibilism in the 1880s is less a personal narrative of
Brousse's activities than in the preceding period. But it is not easy to
make any exact judgements as to the relative significance of each of
the leading Party *militants*, and it remained true that after 1882, as
before, Brousse was one of the most important Party propagandists.
Within the 'collective leadership' of the National Committee he
became one of the inner 'triumvirate' with Joffrin and Lavy; and as
one of the Party's municipal councillors after 1887 and Vice-President
of the Municipal Council in 1888, he carried considerable weight.
This however is more properly the subject of the next chapter.

6
The Possibilist Party, 1882-90

The guidelines establishing the main features of the Party's strategy had already been laid down before the St Etienne Congress. Underpinned by a belief that partial reforms within the structure of capitalist society were both possible and desirable, the Party moved towards the definitive formulation of a comprehensive reformist Programme. This was achieved in 1885. But prior to that, at the Seventh and Eighth National Congresses held in Paris and Rennes in 1883 and 1884 respectively, the Party consolidated its position in the aftermath of the St Etienne split. The resolutions of these Congresses indicated the general nature of the Party's future constitution and development.

The Paris Congress[1] established the seat of the National Committee of the Party in Paris, and on Brousse's suggestion specifically permitted elected members of the Party (i.e. those elected either as municipal councillors or as deputies) to be members of it. The Congress also decided that its members should join local syndicates or corporative groups, and it levied a membership subscription of one franc per month per group. Membership of the Party was conditional on 'une adhésion formelle au principe de la lutte des classes et aux règlements du Parti'. This latter regulation was of some symbolic significance. The Party's title had been changed at the St Etienne Congress from that of Fédération du Parti des Travailleurs Socialistes de France (adopted at Marseilles in 1879) to that of Parti Ouvrier Socialiste Révolutionnaire. Brousse sought at the Paris Congress to have this changed to the general title of Parti de Travail (i.e. Labour Party), with optional titles for local federations. This, he argued, would permit the formation of a broad-based class party.[2] As has been seen this was a familiar concept of Brousse's. In the event however the Congress accepted the title proposed by Joffrin, Fédération des Travailleurs Socialistes Français (FTSF), which it retained for the rest of its existence, while local (i.e. departmental) federations

were left free to choose their own titles. But although Brousse's proposal was rejected (as was a similar proposal he made the following
year at the Rennes Congress of the Party) it remained none the less
true that the sole theoretical requirement for Party members was
acceptance of the principle of the class struggle. The requirement on
the one hand drew a clear demarcation line between socialists and
radicals, and on the other hand permitted the formation of an 'open'
and broadly based Party, which distinguished it clearly from the
rival socialist groups such as the Blanquists, the Guesdists and the
anarchists.

The dropping of the explicitly revolutionary title adopted only the
year previously at St Etienne was also significant when taken in conjunction with a resolution of the Congress on Party tactics which,
while stating that contemporary capitalist society was heading towards Revolution more catastrophic than those of 1789, 1793, 1848
or 1871, confidently announced that there was no need to organize
the revolutionary forces of the proletariat by any public measures,
and simply gave the National Committee of the Party a mandate to
watch developments and make any necessary recommendations.[3]
The Possibilist Party did not live in daily expectation of the Revolution, unlike the rival Parti Ouvrier Français of Guesde, although it
maintained its revolutionary rhetoric.

Resolutions passed at the 1883 Congress pointed to some of the
issues which were to remain of central concern to the Party throughout the decade. Primary amongst these was the demand for both
national and international labour legislation. The influence of cheap
foreign labour (especially Italian) was becoming an issue within the
French labour movement at this time, and the Congress displayed its
concern with the problem by passing a resolution which rejected
anti-immigrant labour legislation as a solution and called instead for
legislative measures to compel employers to comply with labour
conditions demanded by the unions. The labour conditions demanded
by the Congress included the eight-hour working day with one day's
rest per week, the abolition of piece work, double rates for overtime,
and the establishment of Conseils de Surveillance nominated by corporations and trade-union groups. The Congress also called for the
repeal of laws impeding the free development of international contacts amongst the working class (i.e. the Dufaure Law), and mandated the National Congress to organize an international conference
later in that year. In the following year at Rennes the Party Congress

added to its demands for labour legislation those of equal pay for women, the abolition of child labour and regular pay for prison labour. It also condemned the trade-union law of March 1884 which had authorized the free formation of trades unions provided that their aims were strictly economic and that their rules and the names of their administrative personnel were deposited with the authorities.[4] In rejecting this law because of the legal obligations imposed on the unions, and in particular through fear that lists of officials could be used by Governments for repressive purposes, the Party was doing no more than the other socialist groups or the constitutive Congress of the Fédération Nationale des Chambres Syndicales held at Lyons two years later.

No National Congress of the Party was held in 1885, and its functions were assumed instead by the Annual Regional Congress of the Union fédérative du Centre. At this Congress the diverse resolutions of the preceding congresses were welded together with the existing Programmes of the Party to form the definitive possibilist Programme. This consisted of a national and a municipal section, each of which was sub-divided into a political and economic part. The preamble was taken from Joffrin's Municipal Programme of 1881 with the important addition of a reference to the conquest of power in the municipality. It reaffirmed the need for collectivization leading to a Communist society and for a separate class party of the working class. The Programme called *inter alia* for State intervention in several branches of private industry, with the ultimate aim of transforming them progressively into socialist public services in which the workers themselves would regulate their conditions of work, as well as for several demands which had featured in the Party's Programmes since 1881. In the section dealing with municipal action the Programme called for the creation of municipal public services such as gas and transport (Article 1), the establishment of municipal industries (Article 2) and the construction of municipal granaries, flour mills, bakers' and butchers' shops. (See Appendix 7.)

The 1885 Programme of the Fédération des Travailleurs was the culmination of a development which had begun in 1881 with the formulation of Joffrin's Programme. No significant changes were to be made to it, and it remained the quintessential statement of the possibilists' political aims, from which the main characteristics of the Party's activities in this decade can be derived. The specific and practical nature of the Party's Programme, successfully combined with a revolutionary rhetoric, helped to ensure that throughout this decade it was the Fédération, and not the rump Parti Ouvrier Français (POF) created by Guesde and Lafargue at Roanne, or the doctrinaire Comité Révolutionnaire Central (CRC) of the Blanquists set up in 1881, which enjoyed the strongest popular support. There was every indication at this time that the Fédération would form the nucleus of a future united French socialist movement, and in spite of the Party's weaknesses and the divisions within it which led to the disastrous split of 1890, the possibilists indeed were the largest and most politically significant of the French socialist parties throughout the 1880s.[5]

The main characteristics of the Possibilist Party in the period between the St Etienne Congress of 1882 and the Chatellerault Congress of 1890 can for convenience be summarized under the following four headings: (a) the emphasis on the need to build up popular support and to consolidate Party organization and, conversely, the avoidance of provocative tactics which might lead to Governmental repression; closely accompanying this outlook was the belief in the possibility of achieving practical reform, i.e. reformism; (b) the refusal to compromise with other socialist groups; (c) the emphasis on class-consciousness and the concomitant enmity with the radicals; (d) internationalism.

Each of these characteristics will be examined separately, and there follows an account of the events leading up to the split within the Party at the Chatellerault Congress of 1890.

1. Consolidation, organization and reformism

Memories of the Commune bred a highly developed class-consciousness both amongst the *militants* and within the leadership of the Possibilist Party, which contributed to the maintenance of a revolutionary socialist rhetoric. The black-edged editions of newspapers each May and the annual pilgrimages to the Mur des Fédérés at Père Lachaise bore witness to that. But these memories contributed too to a recognition of the harsh reality of the Party's essential strategic weakness and the inevitability of defeat in any conflict with authority. In Paris, the strongest principal base, the Party enjoyed the support of approximately 130 Chambres Syndicales (i.e. small local unions each confined to one trade) and could rely on 15,000 to 20,000 supporters at elections. Although this was infinitely larger than the support upon which either the POF or the CRC could rely it was on any count small enough to ensure that, except possibly in moments of extreme crisis in which the régime of the Third Republic itself was threatened by other forces, any revolutionary venture would be certain to fail. It was recognized that such a failure could be disastrous for the Party which even at the best of times was not fully assured of the tolerance of the authorities. This calculation on the part of the possibilist leaders meant that throughout the decade the Party studiously avoided any involvement in actions which could jeopardize its position by leading to repression by the régime.

The main issue on which this passive tactic was tested was that of demonstrations of the unemployed. Unemployment in Paris reached an extremely high rate of possibly between 200,000–300,000 in the period 1884–7 as a result of a slump in the building trade.[6] Unemployment thus became a major issue, and there were several demonstrations in Paris during this period organized by an *ad hoc* Commission des Ouvriers Sans Travail. The attitude of the possibilists was characterized by Jean Allemane on the occasion of one such demonstration late in 1883. In a leading article in *Le Prolétaire*, entitled 'La France Ouvrière', Allemane took the opportunity to stress where the real interests of the Party lay. In view of its importance for an understanding of the Party's tactics in this decade, the article is worth quoting at some length. Having agreed that since progress came only through the application of long effort, Allemane went on to say that:

... du manque de savoir, de l'absence d'organisation forte et consciente nous viennent les sanglantes défaites qui, en larges tâches de sang, marquent l'histoire du Prolétariat lequel, tumultueusement assemblé, croyait vaincre d'une seule poussée et par la seule puissance de son courage, les forces ordonnés de ses maîtres politiques et économiques. Cette confiance, au premier choc, l'a constamment trahi ... la classe ouvrière demeurera éternellement rivée à sa chaîne de misère si, malgré les sanglantes et cruelles expériences, elle ne se décide à faire litière de cette fausse théorie du coup d'épaule sans préparation préalable: cela fait les écrasements mais ne peut constituer un mieux être social. Que ceux qui s'illusionnent réfléchissent que malgré toute la propagande faite par les événements et les hommes, il est encore, dans notre pays, quatre millions d'ouvriers qu'aucun lien ne rattache à leurs frères de labeur et qu'à ce chiffre déjà considérable, il faut ajouter huit millions de femmes et d'enfants livrées en pature à la rapacité capitaliste.

Telle est, sans voile et sans périphrase, la situation vraie de cette France ouvrière, dont la situation économique et le manque d'organisation lui interdisent toute ingérance sérieuse dans la marche de notre politique actuelle.[7]

In strict accordance with this realistically pessimistic analysis of its position the Party refused to become involved with street demonstrations of the unemployed, and left the issue to be exploited by the Guesdists, the Blanquists and the anarchists who fought amongst themselves for control of the Commission des ouvriers sans travail, which in December 1884 came under joint Guesdist and Blanquist control.[8]

The emphasis of the possibilists was placed instead on electoral action. In the Paris municipal elections of May 1884 the Party's vote increased threefold over that of 1881 – from 11,000 to 33,000 – contrasting favourably with the mere 800 collected by the Guesdists and the 3,000 for the Blanquists; and although Joffrin lost the seat on the Municipal Council he had won in 1882, Chabert's candidature was successful. Throughout 1884 however the dominant theme of Party propaganda was on the relative apathy of the working class (an attempt to turn *Le Prolétaire* into a daily newspaper had failed in 1883, and in early 1884 the newspaper was succeeded by *Le Prolétariat* following the collapse of the Union des Travailleurs, the co-operative society which financed it). Early in 1885, in response to allegations that the Party had neglected the interests of the unemployed (it had in fact presented weighty evidence to a Parliamentary Committee on the subject), and on the basis that the working class refused to support their Chambres Syndicales, an official Party Manifesto urged that the working class should prove its strength in returning as many socialist deputies as possible to the Chamber of Deputies in the general elections of that year 'afin que nos mises en demeure ne se formulent plus timidement, mais qu'elles partent hardiment du haut de la tribune par la bouche de nos élus.'[9]

The General Election of 4 October 1885 produced an unexpected lurch to the Right with a considerable increase in the strength of the royalists and Bonapartists. None of the socialists' candidates was elected, and the possibilists in particular were struck by the blow as they had been optimistic that Joffrin, at least, would be elected.[10] A general mood of doubt in the future stability of the Republic began to appear, from which the possibilist leadership, and Brousse in particular, drew two important conclusions.

The first of these was spelled out by Brousse in a leading article in

Le Prolétariat following the election results, entitled 'Vive La République'. This article explicitly committed the Party to the support of the 'republican form' of government. The Republic was, Brousse argued: 'L'instrument nécessaire pour résoudre les différents problèmes sociaux', and he went on to say that: 'La République n'est pas le but, non, mais elle est la route qui y conduit, et moi, qui n'ai plus dans le dos les ailes de l'illusion, je n'espère pas franchir l'espace et je connais un seul moyen d'atteindre un but, c'est de passer par le chemin qui y mène. . . .'[11] And if, he argued in a later article, the Republic continued to remain under the control of those who cared nothing for its social and economic problems, it would perish. The solution therefore was to ensure that these problems were dealt with quickly.[12] The defence of the republican structure, if not of its Governments, was to become the primary concern of the possibilists in the following four years during which the Boulangist movement threatened to overthrow it.

The second conclusion was that nothing was to be gained by a refusal to recognize the extremely limited freedom of manœuvre open to the Party. In an article entitled 'Reflexions'[13] Brousse argued that as the Party was only one amongst many, and not a strong one at that, it was open to question whether it should continue to remain in grandiose isolation. Without providing any answers to his question, which he said was for the Party to decide (see section 2 of this chapter, p. 207), Brousse went on to say that given the Party's weakness – and the general weakness of the Left as revealed in the elections – its only justifiable course was that of seeking immediate satisfaction of the needs of the working class. The ultimate solution to the social problem remained the overthrow of the capitalist structure, and there existed intermediate objectives such as the minimum wage and international labour legislation. But neither of these was immediately relevant, Brousse argued. The Party should work with whatever means presented themselves and on any issues which touched upon its central objective, which he defined as 'la défense des intérêts ouvriers par tous les moyens appropriés et utiles'. He totally rejected what he described as the 'Suffer and the Kingdom of God will come' approach, and in a further article entitled 'Révolution et Emeutes'[14] Brousse launched a strong attack on those whom he described as 'revolutionaries by taste' the 'nevrosés, fanatiques, romantiques de l'insurrection' (which may well have been a reference to Guesde). Revolutionaries who did nothing but call meeting after meeting in preparation for the Revolution were totally irresponsible, he argued. He concluded caustically: '. . . il faut admettre avec Marx que la force est l'accoucheuse des sociétés, mais nous n'avons pas encore entendu dire qu'elle ait la puissance de leur faire des enfants.' One example of this rejection of insurrectionism was seen two months later in May 1886, when the Union Fédérative rejected a proposal that it should lend official support to a demonstration at which the red flag would be flown during the annual pilgrimage to Père Lachaise on 23 May. The Party's dissociation from the demonstration was sanctified by Allemane, whom no one could have accused of disloyalty to the Communards:

La classe ouvrière n'est pas prête pour la révolution, la ferions-nous même triomphante demain elle serait prématuréé. Nous ne cherchons pas de journée, nous n'avons pas le droit de faire courir le moindre risque inutilement à un camarade quelconque . . . le Parti ouvrier ira, lui, comme tous les ans, accomplir son devenir silencieusement et dignement.[15]

It was Allemane too who, early in 1887, urged the necessity of concentrating the efforts of the Party towards victory in the forthcoming Paris municipal elections of May 1887. This was because, he argued, the Party had passed the phase of needing to build up support, and propaganda was now the most important task.[16] The election of a party candidate, Faillet, in a municipal by-election in the 10th arrondissement in November, had been greeted enthusiastically; and for the May elections the Party's electoral efforts were co-ordinated by a central electoral committee set up by the Union Fédérative. The results were highly satisfactory. The Party increased its votes from 33,000 in May 1884 to 36,000, and saw nine of its candidates returned to the Municipal Council – the three sitting members, Joffrin, Chabert and Faillet; and as new members Brousse himself, from the 17th arrondissement, J. B. Dumay, A. Lavy, Simon-Soens, Paulard and Rétiès. The possibilists made up nine-tenths of the socialist representation on the municipal council – Vaillant, the leader of the Blanquists, being the only other socialist municipal councillor. This electoral victory followed only shortly after another significant triumph of the possibilists, establishment of control over the Paris Bourse du Travail.[17] This marked the high point of possibilist achievement, and there was no doubt that by 1887 the possibilists were the strongest of the socialist groups. The petulant comments of

Paul and Laura Lafargue on the strength and popularity of the possibilists in Paris at this time were a witness to their success *vis-à-vis* the Guesdists, a fact which even Engels was forced to acknowledge;[18] and early in 1888 Brousse wrote optimistically of becoming a deputy in the Chamber of Deputies within four years.[19]

2. *Refusal to compromise with other socialist groups*

One of the central claims of the possibilist leaders was that the Fédération was the sole legitimate socialist Party in France (just as the Guesdists argued that the POF was). It will be seen below (section 4) how this claim was significant in the context of the international socialist movement. Here it is sufficient to note that this attitude led the possibilists to respond negatively to prospects of socialist union which were broached in the mid-1880s.

Representative of the possibilist position on this issue were the arguments by Brousse and Allemane at a general assembly of the Union Fédérative in June 1884, shortly after the municipal elections, where Guesdist candidates had stood against possibilist candidates and split the socialist vote. Allemane virtually dismissed a plan for socialist union out of hand, saying that those who wanted it had only to join the Fédération, and he implied that a group gathered round Fournière (who had been expelled from the Party in the previous year, and who was now close to Malon)[20] was responsible for the campaign. Brousse said that any kind of fusion amongst the socialist groups was impossible, although he did not rule out the possibility of *ad hoc* alliances. These views were embodied in a resolution of the Assembly which virtually unanimously rejected the union proposals.[21] The issue was later discussed and rejected in May 1885 at the Centre Union's regional congress.

The setback of the 1885 parliamentary elections created the climate for a revival of unity proposals, and the Decazeville strike, which lasted nearly five months from January to June 1886 and gained much popular sympathy, seems to have acted as the necessary catalyst.[22] Union was discussed at a meeting in June 1886 of the Centre d'études Sociales, a study group composed of possibilist *militants*, of which Brousse was secretary. The idea was once again decisively rejected. If union was rejected, however, the same debate showed that the party was not united on electoral tactics and that a division of opinion existed between certain of the Party's leaders and the rank and file. Both Brousse and Dalle (the Party's secretary for that year) argued in favour of electoral alliances, Brousse on the grounds that refusal to countenance such alliances could only lead in the provinces to victory for the conservatives. This argument was supported by Adrian Meyer, a frequent contributor to *Le Prolétariat*, at a general meeting of the Union Fédérative on 10 August 1886. Meyer argued that a change in Party tactics was now necessary on the grounds that its aim should be to obtain the implementation of the articles of its Programme, and no longer merely revolutionary propaganda which had characterized the early stages of its activity. Thus, he argued, if the Party had not rejected electoral alliances during the general elections of 1885, it could have had four deputies in the Chamber. This argument was however decisively repudiated by the meeting, which passed a resolution stating categorically that alliances could be made only with candidates accepting the principles of the class struggle, the socialization of the means of production, and the Party label laid down by the 1885 Centre Regional Party Congress.[23]

The stand against any alteration in the electoral tactics of the Party was endorsed both by the Eighth Annual Congress of the Union Fédérative in August 1887, and by the Ninth Annual Congress of the Party at Charleville in October 1887. At the Charleville Congress one or two delegates from the provinces argued as Brousse had done at the meeting of the Cercle d'études sociales in the previous year. Their proposal was opposed by Simon-Soens, a delegate of the National Committee of the Party, and the first resolution of the Congress, drafted by Allemane, reaffirmed the principle of class struggle. Indeed the resolution went out of its way to emphasize the need to maintain the struggle 'without compromise or weakness against all factions of the bourgeoisie'.[24]

It would be a mistake however to see the significance of this difference of opinion within the Party in terms of the later split and antagonism between Brousse and Allemane. It would certainly appear that on this issue they found themselves on different sides, and it was quite logical that Allemane, the working-class victim of the Commune, should take a position which ranged him firmly against the slightest hint of collaboration with the radicals. On the other hand Brousse and Allemane were closely in agreement on several other important issues (the avoidance of violence and disorder, the need for the Party to concentrate on electoral activities and the reformist content of the Programme), and Allemane himself was to become the initiator and leading proponent of an alliance with the radicals in the Boulanger crisis of the following year. There is no evidence that this issue of electoral alliances was a cause of discord between Brousse and Allemane at this time, or that it caused a deep rift within the Party which demarcated the battle lines of the later division within the Party.

The discussion of electoral alliances – with the clear implication that this meant alliances with the radicals – brings us to consideration of the third characteristic feature of possibilism.

3. *Class-conscious and* ouvriériste *content*

Partly because of the discussions of 1886 over the desirability of electoral alliances with the Radicals, but mainly because of the formal alliance with the radicals in 1888 during the Boulanger crisis and the reformist content of its political Programme, the nature of possibilism has been frequently misunderstood. Contrary to a widespread misconception the Fédération was extremely class-conscious, and there was deep enmity between it and the radicals. If the memory of the Commune and its massacres served to make its leaders cautious of extremist tactics, it also served as a constant reminder of the basic and fundamental hostility of the bourgeoisie to the interests of the working class. Class-consciousness and the demand for the rigorous application of a socialist Programme were not the same thing. So that if the Fédération substituted the Joffrin Programme of 1881 for that of 1880 (the Marx–Guesde Programme) this was *not* – the point needs to be stressed – indicative of any *rapprochement* with the Radicals. The possibilists fought the radicals for the working-class vote, as did everyone else. By the same token, and as the most successful of the socialist groups in winning over working-class support, the possibilists were detested by the radicals, and until the exceptional crisis caused by the Boulanger affair there was no question of any alliance between them. This was seen clearly in the period following the municipal elections of 1887 when the radical group within the municipal council began to disintegrate as certain of its members began to move as a group towards the Left. This 'autonomous socialist' group, as it was known, far from seeking to ally with the possibilists, in fact treated the possibilists as its main enemy and tended to favour the other socialist groups – the Blanquists and the Guesdists – who were attempting to oust the possibilists[25] from control of the leadership of the Union Fédérative du Centre.

The traditional hostility between the possibilists and the radicals was dramatically challenged by the tactics of the Fédération in the Boulanger crisis. The reactions of the Party *militants* to the posture adopted by the Fédération signify the extent to which some of the fundamental premises of militant ideology had been challenged and disturbed. For this reason alone it is necessary to look at the possibilist reaction to the Boulanger crisis in more detail.

Boulanger first became a real political challenge to the stability of the Third Republic after the election of Carnot to the Presidency in December 1887 and Boulanger's forced resignation from the army in March 1888. Disillusionment with the Republicans was widespread, and demands were increasingly made for a fundamental revision of the Constitution. The possibilists shared many of these attitudes (and revisions of the Constitution were built into their Programme) but they were resolutely opposed to any alliance or association with Boulanger. The plebiscitary and nationalist content of Boulangism was seen by the Fédération as too dangerous an element with which to become associated, however justified much of Boulanger's support might be, and however much the bourgeois Republic might have failed to meet the demands of the working class. It was at the moment when the possibilists calculated that Boulanger threatened to overthrow the Republican structure of France that they came out not simply *against* Boulanger but also *for* a temporary alliance with other defenders of the Republican order. The possibilists judged that this moment had come after Boulanger's resignation from the Army in March 1888; previous to that, although they had openly attacked him[26] they had opposed any 'emergency' tactics largely on the traditional possibilist grounds that calm organization and the avoidance of any insurrectionary action was in their best interests;[27] or that Boulanger was not a significant threat.[28]

The new tactic was announced in a Party Manifesto of 24 March 1888. This stated that in the face of a dictatorship threat:

Nous sommes prêts, avec notre Parti, à oublier pour un instant les seize années pendant lesquelles la bourgeoisie a trahi les espérances du peuple; nous sommes prêts à défendre et à conserver, par tous les moyens, le chétif germe de nos institutions républicains contre tout sabre qui viendrait le menacer.

This Manifesto followed a public meeting organized by the possibilists at which, doubtless in order to forestall and counter criticism by *militants* of the Party's *volte face*, Boulanger had once again been attacked and his role in the Commune (as a colonel in the Versailles army) emphasized. Allemane was especially virulent in his attack on Boulanger on these grounds,[29] and on 8 April 1888 he brought out the first issue of *Le Parti Ouvrier*, a daily newspaper founded specifically to counter the Boulangist threat. It was only in May however that the possibilist leadership openly and specifically called for an alliance with the republicans against Boulanger. In a leading article in *Le Prolétariat* entitled 'Mobilisation Républicaine' Brousse argued on 12 May for a tactical alliance with Ranc and Clemenceau to dispose of Boulanger, after which the Fédération would once again assume its own direction. Allemane spoke in the same sense at a meeting at Rouen, and in *Le Parti Ouvrier* on 23 May he called for the creation of Ligue des Républicains for the defence of the Republic.

The Société des Droits de l'Homme was formed two days later on 25 May. It consisted of leading radicals such as Ranc, Clemenceau, Pelletan and Révillon, as well as the leading possibilists – Brousse, Allemane, Joffrin and Paulard. According to Joffrin, Allemane had been the main figure in conversations with the radicals about such an alliance[30] (and he became General Secretary of the Society). The signatories of the inaugural Manifesto who declared themselves 'Fils de la Révolution Française' stated that in order to safeguard their ultimate aim – 'the progressive realization of the constitutional, political and social reforms embodied in the Republic' – it was necessary to safeguard freedom of the press, of speech and of associations which it (the Republic) guaranteed. The objective of the society was 'the defence of the Republic for the unremitting fight against reactionary or dictatorial ventures'. The Manifesto of the Society was published in *Le Prolétariat* on 26 May, in its anniversary edition of the 'Semaine sanglante' – a useful and perhaps more than coincidental excuse for the newspaper once again to remind its readers of Boulanger's nefarious role in the suppression of the Commune; and asked by a correspondent of *Le Matin* if the decision risked splitting the Party, Joffrin replied that it did not, because: 'Le parti ouvrier est avant tout anti-Boulangiste; il se rappelle la conduit infâme du colonel Boulanger contre la Commune.'

The optimism expressed by Joffrin was misplaced. Dislike of the

H

radicals amongst the *militants* of the Party was stronger than their supposed dislike of Boulanger. It is clear that the decision to form the Société des Droits de l'Homme almost immediately created dissension within the Party, especially within the Union fédérative where meetings expressed concern at the alliance and accusations of non-consultation were made (not to mention accusations of treason from the other socialist groups such as the Guesdists and Blanquists). At a general meeting of the Party on 6 July it was agreed under pressure to put the issue to groups for a vote, and on 31 July the Union fédérative voted for withdrawal from the Société des Droits de l'Homme. Accordingly the possibilists regretfully but loyally withdrew in August 1888.[31]

This forced withdrawal from an explicit alliance with the radicals placed the possibilist leaders in a difficult position, as their long-standing rejection of militant action deprived them of a credible alternative policy. *Le Prolétariat* and *Le Parti Ouvrier* supported the candidature of Jacques, the republican candidate, in the Paris by-election of January 1889 at which Boulanger was overwhelmingly elected (in this they differed from the Guesdists and Blanquists, who put forward their own candidate). This meant that in fact possibilist tactics had not changed, and that they were still prepared to vote for the Republic in a straight conflict with Boulanger. But it was a policy which could no longer be pursued wholeheartedly and unreservedly because of the critical attitude of many of the Party's rank and file members. At the same time the Party once again, as in the unemployed agitation of 1884 and 1885, found itself in the position of opposing or attempting to play down militant action on its Left. Thus the leadership opposed any attempt to generalize a strike of navvies in Paris in August 1888, and Brousse (not without justification) accused the Blanquists, who became closely involved with it, of flirting with the Boulangists in its support.[32] Likewise in February 1889 the possibilists refused to join in nationwide demonstrations which had been voted for at the Bordeaux Congress of the Fédération Nationale des Chambres syndicales in 1888 for the eight-hour working day and a minimum wage. Joffrin justified their abstention in the Paris municipal council on the grounds that demonstrations of this kind could begin with slogans for the Republic of social reforms and end with demands for Boulanger.[33]

Thus the possibilists found it hard to present a really clear-cut and identifiable stand on the Boulanger issue after their withdrawal from the Société des Droits de l'Homme. Their initial courageous decision to oppose Boulanger (which contrasted with the equivocal position of the POF – especially Lafargue – and the Blanquists) had led logically to a tactical alliance with the Radicals in defence of the Republic. This was a clear and unmistakable commitment. But forced to renounce the alliance, the Party could only have compensated for it by a greater and more militant involvement on a non-political or extra-political basis; and this ran counter both to all their instincts and to their rational assessment of the situation, which warned them that to encourage popular demonstrations could only play into the hands of the Boulangists. (It was for this reason that early on in the Boulanger crisis the leadership had opposed the setting up of local anti-Boulangist action committees.) They were thus left in the politically unenviable position of having to give a circumspect support to the republican forces so long as the Boulangist danger to the Republic remained. Allemane made this clear in *Le Parti Ouvrier* on the eve of the parliamentary elections in September 1889 (in which he personally was an unsuccessful candidate). But as soon as it became clear that the elections had exorcized the Boulangist menace, Allemane called for the Party to return to its aim of bringing about the advent of socialism and defined the Party's immediate task as that of reuniting its forces and giving a sharper definition to its policies. This meant re-emphasizing its class character. The need was:

à se remettre à la besogne comme aux premiers jours de la création du Parti ouvrier afin de regagner le terrain perdu et d'empêcher le 'modératisme' multicolore de nous rejeter dans un péril peut-être plus grand que celui auquel nous venons d'échapper. . . . Après la lutte pour la République, la lutte pour la Sociale.[34]

It was over the policies of the Party in this post-Boulangist period that basic disagreement was to arise. The development of these conflicts is traced in section 5 below.

4. *Internationalism*

If the Fédération was the socialist party which most successfully sought the working-class vote in this decade, it was also the party which most effectively worked for and established international contacts and which most consistently campaigned for the re-establishment of a new International. Although the fruits of this campaign were snatched from it at the last moment, the Fédération des Travailleurs socialistes français and in particular the personal activities of Brousse, must be counted as one of the most important influences leading to the establishment in 1889 of the Second International.

The international activities of the Party are significant from two points of view: first, that of the struggle for recognition as the sole legitimate socialist party in France; and second, that of the 'internationalization' of demands for social reform and the attempt to forge an alliance with the English trade-union movement. These two aspects will be examined together and an account given of the process which culminated in the holding of two rival international Congresses in Paris in 1889 to coincide with the centenary of the outbreak of the French Revolution.

The Ghent Congress of 1877 had effectively consecrated the division of the socialist movement into two hostile camps, and ended the era of the First International. No more international Congresses were held until 1881, when two Congresses were held, one at Coire (Chur) in Switzerland, and one in London. The latter was a purely anarchist affair which set up a new, anarchist International, which was to become known as the 'Black International'. The former was summoned by the Ghent Bureau (created in 1877) and was attended by, amongst others, Wilhelm Liebknecht for the German Social Democrats and Benoît Malon for the French Socialist Party. The Congress decided that the time was not yet ripe for the reconstitution of a new international socialist body, on the grounds that the majority of the national socialist parties were still in the stage of formation and that the parties in Germany, Italy and Austria were under legal threats *vis-à-vis* international action from their own Governments.[35] None the less the Congress entrusted to the French Socialist Party the convening of a further Congress, and at the St Etienne Congress of that Party in 1882 it was decided that this international Congress should be held in the following year.[36]

This resolution made some impact in London where the leaders of the possibilists, such as Brousse, Joffrin, and J.-B. Clément, had been in exile and had established contacts with leaders of the English working-class movement. In November 1882 a preliminary meeting took place in Paris between twelve representatives of the English trade-union movement, including Shipton of the London Trades Council, and leading possibilists. This meeting laid the groundwork for a larger Congress and, following the approval of the T U C Con-

gress at Nottingham in 1883, an international meeting was held in
Paris between 29 October and 3 November 1883. This Congress,
presided over by Broadhurst, secretary of the Parliamentary Committee of the TUC – and attended by eight British delegates who included Coulson, Shipton and Smith,[37] as well as by Costa for the
Italian Socialist Party, three Spanish delegates, and by the possibilist
leaders – was the first in a series of international congresses which
were held throughout the decade. It discussed three main questions:
first, international labour legislation; second, cheap immigrant
labour; and third, the abolition of the laws against the International.
As has been seen cheap immigrant labour was an issue within the
French socialist movement at this time, and it was Brousse who
argued at the Congress that international labour legislation was the
only effective way in the long run of solving the problem; once
international labour standards had been agreed and implemented
there would be no such thing as cheap labour. The *immediate* solution to the problem, expressed in the Congress's second resolution,
was seen in the enforcement of domestic wage rates for all foreign
workers. The first resolution of the Congress attempted to bridge the
inevitable gulf between the English trades unions and the Continental
socialists. The inevitability of the gulf lay in the fact that in England
there existed a strong trade-union movement which was non-socialist;
whereas on the Continent trades unions were weak and disorganized
and the leadership of the working class was assumed by the socialist
parties. The trades unions were reluctant to commit themselves to
any recognition of the need for State interference at the expense of
normal trade bargaining process, while the French and other socialists saw this as the only effective means of obtaining the agreed
desiderata, i.e. a reduction in the hours of labour. Consequently the
resolution passed by the Congress envisaged two means to this end:
(a) through organization; and (b) by the removal of obstacles in the
way of national and international legislation to that end. On the third
question, that of international association, the Congress voted
unanimously for the abolition of all discriminatory legislation.[38]

The Congress inevitably came under attack from the Guesdists, to
whom co-operation with the liberal English trades unions was
anathema, but both Allemane and Brousse defended the Congress on
the grounds that despite the somewhat anodyne resolutions (which
were inevitable) it was sufficient in itself that the Congress had even
taken place. According to Allemane the 'successful handling of the

touchiness of foreign parties' (i.e. the English trades unions) was one of the two major achievements of the Congress (the other was the fact that the authorities had not attempted to intervene). Brousse argued that such a Congress was at least a positive action, consistent with the basic premise of possibilism – the accomplishment of what was possible at any given moment. A year previously he had laid down in characteristically pragmatic terms the nature of the Fédération's policy towards foreign parties: '. . . la politique extérieure de chaque parti doit donc se borner à se bien renseigner sur la réalité des autres partis et sans préoccupation doctrinale, à leur tendre par-dessus les frontières fraternellement la main.'[39]

This pragmatic point of view characterized the international action of the possibilists throughout the decade, echoing the old inter-nationalism of the St Imier International. But if the Fédération was prepared to enter into fraternal international relations with other parties regardless of doctrinal considerations, this was not an un-conditional commitment, for it demanded reciprocity. *Le Prolétariat* made this clear in an article published at the time of the Paris Con-gress in which protestations of friendship with the German Social Democrats were made. The price of this friendship was however that:

. . . le parti allemand au lieu de traiter avec aigreur le parti français pour couvrir d'éloges la demi-douzaine de marxistes sectaires que compte encore le socialisme parisien . . . reconnaisse le parti ouvrier français qui existe et non le parti ouvrier français qui n'existe pas, qui n'a pas de voix aux élections, qui n'a pas d'organe lui appartenent, qui ne tient jamais régulièrement ni congrès régionaux ni congrès nationaux.[40]

Brousse enlarged on this theme in a letter to de Paepe of 1884 in which he stated quite specifically that the Fédération would not enter an International Congress which recognized the Guesdists.[41]

This criterion for co-operation, the demand that the Fédération des Travailleurs socialistes français be recognized as the sole legitimate French party, underlay the Party's international policy in this decade. This factor alone was sufficient to give significance to the 1883 Congress, because here already were foreshadowed the splits which were to mark the setting up of the Second International. It meant that progress towards the creation of a new International would not only involve the new element of a growing and separate trade-union consciousness, but would also be marked by some of the old conflicts which had previously split the international socialist movement. In particular this meant the conflict between, on the one hand the Marxists, represented by the Parti Ouvrier Français together with the German Social Democrats, and on the other, the upholders of a broader, less rigid and more 'autonomist' conception of what the International should be. A study of the process by which the Second International came into being reveals very clearly that the conflicts of the First International threw a long and distorting shadow, and that to a large extent the process was an end rather than a beginning and, moreover, a process which continued until the mid-1890s, up to the Congress of London in 1896, when the anarchists were specifically excluded from future International Socialist Congresses. Throughout this period 'c'est encore le vieux ton, le vocabulaire traditionnel, les prolongement d'anciennes querelles; l'esprit de la lre Internationale y prédomine toujours et les caractérise'.[42]

Certainly, so far as Brousse was concerned, his perception was very clearly shaped by his previous experience within the First International and had an important influence on his actions. In December 1883, shortly after the Paris Congress, he described in detail to César de Paepe how he envisaged the nature of future international endeavour.[43]

The first major point, he said, was the very elementary position that the possibilists could take part in future international Congresses only if they were recognized as the sole legitimate French Socialist Party; but on the other hand, he said, the German Social Democrats would never attend Congresses from which the Guesdists were excluded. For this reason alone Brousse thought it inevitable that in future there would be both Marxist *and* independent international conferences. This indeed was a central problem; and the problem of the existence of two rival French parties was to dominate and obstruct efforts to establish a new International over the following decade.

Brousse then went on to discuss the divergent views of the European socialist and labour parties. On the one hand, he said, was the English element, which believed exclusively in what he termed 'an economic' party (i.e. a labour or trade-union party); on the other hand were the Germans and the Guesdists who believed almost totally in a *political* Party; and in the middle were the possibilists, the Belgians, the Italians and the Spaniards, who wanted 'un parti économique doublé d'un parti politique'. Whereas the English trades unions had no doctrine, and the Germans made adherence to their doctrine a *sine qua non* of membership of their Party, the possibilists were flexible on this point and permitted a divergence of views within the Party. This had its analogue in the Party's conception of the future International. This, Brousse said, should be a federation of national parties without regard to differences of doctrine or tactics, and he contrasted this with the 'panmarxism' of the Germans and of Guesde. This led him to the conclusion that there could be agreement only between the English, the Belgians, the Dutch, the Italians, the Spanish and the French on the one hand, and the Germans the (German) Swiss and the Austrians on the other hand. He did not believe that there could be agreement between the two groups although, he said, he would be happy to see one. 'We shall not,' he concluded 'permit ourselves to be "panmarxized" here.' Two months later he reiterated his fears of the Marxists and said that if the effect of increasing international socialist co-operation was simply a means of raising the spectre of a few *impossibilistes* (i.e. Guesde and Lafargue) then the possibilists would have no part in it:

> Il y a en France une organisation, le parti ouvrier, qui veut vivre en conformant son évolution à son milieu, et il y a en Europe une faction marxiste qui a envoyé à Paris le gendre du maître, M. Paul Lafargue et un acheté M. Jules Guesde. Je ne comprends pas qu'un homme qui a vécu comme toi l'Internationale tu puisses encore être le dupe des mêmes intrigants et des mêmes intrigues.[44]

It will be seen later that Brousse was not alone in interpreting developments in terms of the conflict which had split the First International. It is sufficient to note at this stage that this was a dominant element in his thinking about the form of a future international socialist organization, and that the possibilists duly publicized any activities they could attribute to the *coterie marxiste*.[45]

A second International Congress took place in Paris in 1886. Its organizing committee was composed of French trade-unionists, and was not amenable to the degree of possibilist control that Brousse would have wished – with the result that, according to Brousse, several delegates 'who represented nothing but the Marxist clique' were admitted.[46] On the agenda of the Conference was international labour legislation, professional and polytechnic education, trades unions, the political and economic situation of the working class, and arrangements for the 1889 international workingmen's Congress which would celebrate the centenary of the French Revolution. Attending it was an overwhelming number of French delegates, a delegation of seven from the United Kingdom, one from the German Social Democratic Party (a man called Grimpe who lived in Paris) and three Belgian delegates – Louis Bertrand, César de Paepe and Edouard Anseele.

The Congress was an uneasy mixture of socialists and trade unionists. The English trades unions had a weak political consciousness, and in so far as they were political their leadership was tied to the Liberal Party. They were not yet socialist.[47] On the other hand the French, Belgian and German delegates were committed to (various brands of) socialism, and inevitably profound differences of opinion emerged in the course of the proceedings. In a leading article in *Le Prolétariat* on the eve of the Congress, Brousse specifically came out against the English trade-union rejection of political action and the need for labour legislation, arguing that it was a result of their peculiar strength *qua* trades unions and of their isolation from the international labour market. Their policy was, he said, suitable for England; but not for France or other countries where trades unions were weak and the need was for State intervention in labour affairs. The latter was the most important question to be discussed by the Congress.[48]

Discuss it the Congress duly did, and at the end of its debate passed resolutions calling for legislation to establish: (a) the eight-hour working day, (b) protection for women and children, (c) a legal minimum wage, (d) the civil and criminal responsibility of employers, (e) factory inspection by inspectors appointed by the working class and paid by the State, (f) the abolition of night work, (g) the abolition of certain kinds of labour harmful to the workers' health, (h) hygienic conditions in all places of work, (i) the regulation and control of prison labour, (j) the abolition of work for those under fourteen years of age. The Congress also passed a resolution calling for education of all children up to the age of sixteen and the provision of State grants; a resolution calling for the abolition of the laws against the International, and the need to create national and international trade-union groupings; and a final resolution entrusting the organization of an international congress in 1889 to the Possibilist Party.[49] The demands for the eight-hour working day and for an international Congress in 1889 were both of particular significance in that it was from these resolutions that the movement for the international celebration of 1 May by the labour movement was to spring.

More significant perhaps than these resolutions was a violent

attack by Grimpe, the delegate of the German Social Democrats, on
the English trades unions and their leaders. He accused them of being
reactionaries, because they were not socialists, and traitors, because
of their association with the Gladstonian Liberals. Although Grimpe
was condemned by the majority of fellow socialists for the intem-
perance of his attack, and on the grounds that it was not the business
of the Congress to pronounce on such matters, the non-socialist and
non-political content of English trade-unionism was a problem which
Brousse faced frankly in a letter he wrote at the time to Costa. In this,
he said that while the trades unions represented a real force, their
reactionary reputation could do the possibilists little good. (The
English delegates did, in fact, abstain from voting on most of the
resolutions.) None the less, he concluded, it was better for the possibilists to form the Left wing of a working-class Congress than the
Right wing of a 'political' (i.e. Marxist) Congress.[50] This admission
deserves emphasis, because it reveals once again Brousse's central
concern with *working-class* as opposed to essentially *socialist* issues,
and as foreshadowing or laying down the main line of possibilist
efforts in the succeeding three years. A year later, after the Swansea
TUC Congress at which resolutions in favour of land collectivization
and independent Parliamentary representation were passed, Brousse
took a more positive view, and described the possibilists and trades
unions as providing 'les deux plus formidables instruments de
l'émancipation ouvrière universelle'.[51]

Grimpe's attack had indeed high-lighted the uncomfortable fact of
the presence of the trade-union element in the reviving international
movement. This was a fact with which the various socialist elements
had eventually to come to terms, culminating logically in the specific
inclusion of trades unions by a resolution passed at the London
Conference of the International in 1896.[52]

It was an ominous sign that the *Sozial Demokrat*, the organ of the
German Social Democratic Party, had rejected the resolution calling
for a Congress in 1889 and that the German delegate had so strongly
attacked the trades unions. This presaged a division which was to
assume increasing proportions as time passed. The tendency for the
German Social Democrats to hold back from the reviving international movement under the leadership of the French possibilists
was enhanced by the holding of a further international Congress in
London in 1888 from which they were effectively excluded through
the procedural rules laid down by the Parliamentary Committee of

the TUC, which had voted for such a Congress (against the wishes of the Parliamentary Committee) at its Annual Congress at Hull in 1886.[53] The Parliamentary Committee insisted that the Congress should be restricted to delegates of trades unions, and despite attempts by Liebknecht, who sent Bebel and Bernstein to London to discuss the matter with the trade-union leaders (apparently on the basis of a recommendation that negotiations could be fruitful from H. M. Hyndman, the leader of the Social Democratic Federation),[54] no agreement could be reached on this point. Following the break-down of the talks the German Social Democratic Party issued an appeal to all socialist parties urging them not to take part in the London Congress. *Le Prolétariat*, along with the Social Democratic Federation, strongly attacked this initiative by the Germans.[55]

At this stage a new and highly significant factor was introduced into the situation. When they visited London, Bebel and Bernstein had consulted Engels who, it appears, did not believe that agreement with the joint TUC–possibilist Congress was either possible or desirable. Hyndman believed that Engels and the group associated with him in London were largely responsible for the breakdown of the negotia-tions. The issue further aggravated the quarrels in London between Hyndman's Social Democratic Federation and the Engels–Eleanor Marx–Edward Aveling group. This quarrel was comparable to that between the possibilists and the Guesdists – or Marxists – in Paris, although it was primarily an affair of personality and not of doctrine. In both cases a small group with close connections with and strong allegiance to the Marx family group were accused of attempting to dictate to the indigenous socialist movement.[56] It was quite logical therefore that Hyndman should have found a natural ally in Brousse. This alliance had existed in embryo for some time previously, but the Congress of 1888 saw it crystallize into an explicitly anti-Marxist front. The non-doctrinal basis of the alliance was underlined by the fact that Hyndman came nearest (however real may have been his shortcomings, for which Engels strongly criticized him) to propound-ing Marxist theories from amongst the various elements in the nascent British socialist movement.[57] Once again, as in the First International and in the formative years of the French Socialist Party, anti-Marxism as an expression of hostility to a small clique associated with Marx and/or Engels, produced strange bedfellows.

The Congress was held in November 1888. The possibilists sent two delegates (present officially as trade-union delegates), while the

Belgians were represented by Anseele and the Italians by Lazzari. Amongst the British delegates the most notable were John Burns, Tom Mann and Keir Hardie. The TUC Parliamentary Committee fought a rearguard action against the rising tide of (foreign) socialism, but could not prevent the Congress from endorsing the resolution of the 1886 Congress calling for the eight-hour working day. The Congress also passed a resolution stressing the usefulness of trade-union co-operation in the formation of political parties, the holding of regular international congresses – and, most important of all for the possibilists, it endorsed the decision to entrust them with the calling of an international Congress in Paris in the following year.

Following the London resolution the possibilists invited all the European socialist parties to an international Congress in Paris in 1889. The invitation went counter to the intentions of the TUC (although certainly not to the majority sentiment of the Congress) which had envisaged another purely trade-union congress, but Brousse by now saw the chance of establishing a new International on the 'economic plus political' basis he had outlined to Costa in 1883 and was not prepared to let the chance pass. The result of this move by Brousse and the possibilists was to provoke an immediate counter-attack by the Guesdists, who determined to hold their own Congress in Paris. In 1886 the Guesdists had won control over the French trade-union movement, the Fédération Nationale des Chambres Syndicales (FNCS), whose Bordeaux Congress in November 1888 had called for an international Congress in 1889. The Guesdists claimed they were carrying out the responsibilities entrusted to them by that Congress.[58] From this point onwards it became a prime object of the Guesdists to prevent any strengthening of the position of the possibilists through international action.

For a considerable period of time it seemed as though the Marxists might suffer a very serious setback in the establishment of their influence over the European socialist movement. The reason for this was that the German Social Democrats under Liebknecht's leadership had by no means completely ruled out the possibility of agreement with the possibilists, and their position was still sufficiently flexible (or perhaps indecisive) for Engels and Lafargue to become seriously concerned about it. The concern of these two was for two main and overriding objectives. First, that a new international should establish the position of the Parti Ouvrier Français as the sole legitimate French Socialist Party:

The point for you is that *there should be a congress* – and in Paris – where you will be acknowledged by one and all as the only internationally recognized French Socialist Party. . . . To regain your position in France you need, primarily, international recognition. . . .[59]

Second, Engels was determined to prevent the possibilists from assuming the leadership of a new International. He held no particular brief for International Congresses, believing them to be either unavoidable evils – or even useless.[60] He stated his view unequivocally in a letter to Laura Lafargue:

I consider these congresses to be unavoidable evils in the movement . . . it is doubtful whether le jeu vaut la chandelle when there are serious differences. But the persistent efforts of the possibilists and Hyndmanites to sneak into the leadership of a new International, by means of their Congresses, made a struggle unavoidable for us, and here is the only point in which I agree with Brousse:

He continued:

it is the old split in the International over again, which now drives people into two opposite camps. On one side the disciples of Bakounine, with a different flag . . . on the other side the real working-class movement. And it was this, and this alone, that made me take the matter up in such good earnest.[61]

And he told Kautsky at about the same time that there was no other choice than that of 'Beugung unter die Allianz Brousse-Hyndman, oder aber Kampf mit ihr.'[62] (His views were thus a mirror image of those of Brousse.)

With these two objectives in mind, Engels and the leaders of the Parti Ouvrier Français set their minds on wrecking any possibility of the possibilists successfully establishing their leadership at the forthcoming Congress, and of the German Social Democrats being persuaded to support them.[63] Given the possibilists' firm stand against the Boulangists and the sympathetic attitude towards them on this issue shown by the German Social Democrats, Engels was forced to deliver some stern advice to Lafargue on how the Parti Ouvrier Français should – or rather should not – go about this task.[64]

On receiving an invitation from the Parti Ouvrier Français to attend their, rather than the possibilist, Congress, the Germans proposed a preliminary Congress to discuss the possibilities of reconciliation. The motives of Liebknecht in issuing this invitation are unclear, but it is at least evident that he hoped to 'neutralize' the Broussists by such an invitation;[65] it is possible however that his main motive was to maintain contact with Hyndman, for whom he apparently had some respect.[66] The proposal was accepted by the Guesdists, and refused by the possibilists[67] on the grounds that the invitation failed to recognize their sole right to organize the Congress.

In a situation of conflict it is often possible for one side to appear conciliatory and yet at the same time by the very procedures of conciliation deny the central demand of its opponents. In this way, and provided the conciliation procedures proposed are skilfully handled, the opponents are weakened whichever way they react. If they accept the proposals then they have conceded their position. If they reject them they appear to be acting unreasonably. This is what happened to the possibilists in the six months between the first German offer of conciliation and the holding of their Congress in June 1889.

Despite the possibilists' refusal of the German proposal, a meeting was held at the Hague in February 1889 with support from the Belgians, Dutch and Swiss parties, to draw up proposals for reconciliation. These proposals were that while the Congress should be organized under the auspices of the possibilists, the decision as to who should attend the Congress should be a decision for the Congress itself. If this condition were accepted, it would in fact mean that the inevitable German Social Democratic majority would permit the Guesdists to be present – and this conceded the possibilists' main point, that they alone were the real representatives of the French socialist movement. This was the intention of at least Engels, who regarded the conciliation proposals simply as a tactic to outmanœuvre the possibilists;[68] either way, he said, the possibilists would lose, for a refusal would alienate the smaller parties such as the Belgians and the Dutch. It is clear that Engels was instrumental at this stage in stiffening the position of the German Social Democrats.

Predictably the possibilists refused the terms offered them by the Hague Conference. In a letter sent by Lavy on behalf of the National Committee of the Party, the possibilists said first that they could not abandon the exclusive rights of organizing the Congress given to them by the 1886 and 1888 Congresses, and second, that the only acceptable validation of mandates was validation by national groupings.[69] The refusal came as a relief to Engels who, in spite of the obvious concession that would have been implied by acceptance, would undoubtedly have been seriously concerned at the probable incapacity of the Guesdists to exploit such a situation to their own advantage.[70] The fact was that it was only Engels's constant effort which prevented Lafargue from completely destroying the advantages so far gained over the possibilists.[71]

The Hague Conference called for the holding of an international Congress in September (the possibilist international conference was to be held in June). It had been agreed that if the possibilists refused the conciliation proposals, the Swiss and Belgian Socialist Parties should undertake the responsibility of convoking the September Congress which would then be organized by the Guesdists. This was vital for the Marxists because it ensured them, at last, the support of two of the most influential of the smaller parties, and vindicated Engels's belief that a possibilist refusal of terms would alienate from them precisely such elements. His concern was therefore all the greater when it appeared that Lafargue was attempting to change the Hague resolutions and to hold the Congress in June, simultaneously with that of the possibilists. He had already stressed that the Hague decision gave the Parti Ouvrier Français the first real chance to establish itself as a credible organization in the eyes of the other European socialist parties:

> It is a matter of making the Poss[ibilists'] Congress come to nothing. That is well under way if your impatience does not spoil everything. . . . The Belgians must either comply or they will put themselves in the wrong also. I beg you not to give them a plausible excuse for getting out of the difficulty. . . . So take what is offered you. In substance it is all that you are entitled to ask and, unless you on your side blunder, it will result in the international exclusion of the Poss[ibilists] and the recognition of yourselves as the only French Soc[ialists] with whom there are relations.[72]

So that when Lafargue revealed that the Guesdists were planning a Congress at a different date from that agreed at the Hague, Engels was almost beside himself with anger and placed full and entire responsibility for the possible consequences on the shoulders of the French. He went so far as to tell Lafargue that he would refuse to act as advocate of the French *vis-à-vis* the German Social Democratic Party until he had received an assurance that the Guesdists accepted the Hague resolutions;[73] for if they did not, the Belgians would seize on the excuse to withdraw their co-operation and the Guesdists would have cut their own throats:

> With the end of the *Socialiste*,[74] your Party vanished from the international scene. You had abdicated: you no longer existed for the other

Socialist parties abroad. It was entirely the fault of your workers who did not wish to read and support one of the best organs the Party ever had. But, having destroyed your medium of communication with other Socialists, they cannot avoid suffering the natural consequences of their behaviour.

The poss[ibilists], remaining in sole possession of the field, took advantage of the situation you had created for them; they had their people – in Brussels and in London – with whose help they posed to the world as the only representatives of the French socialists. They succeeded in winning over the Danes, the Dutch and the Flemings for their Congress. And you know to what trouble we went to annul the success they achieved. Now the Germans offer you the opportunity, not merely to reappear on the scene with glory, but to be recognized *by all the organized parties of Europe* as the only French Socialists with whom they wish to fraternize. You are offered the chance of wiping out at one stroke the effect of all the mistakes made, of all the defeats suffered; of rehabilitating yourselves in the position to which your theoretical knowledge entitles you, but which your incorrect tactics have jeopardized; you are offered a congress where all the genuine workers' parties, *even the Belgians*, will be present; you are offered the opportunity of *isolating the Poss[ibilists]*, so that they will have to confine themselves to a bogus congress. In short, considering the position you had created for yourselves, you are offered far more than you had any right to expect. And did you seize it with both hands? Not a bit of it. You play the spoilt child, you haggle. . . .

The point for you is that *there should be a Congress* – and in Paris – where you will be acknowledged by one and all as the only internationally recognized French Socialist Party. . . . Your Congress must meet in order to set you on your feet again, and what does it matter if in the eyes of the bourgeois public it should be a failure? To regain your position in France, you need, primarily international recognition, and international censure of the poss[ibilists]. . . .[75]

For a while it appeared as though Engels's fears would be realized. In April the Annual Congress of the Belgian Party did in fact decide to send an official delegation to the July 'possibilist' Congress – as well as deciding to be represented at the other Congress. The situation was saved when the Germans then proposed that Lafargue's original proposal – to hold the Congress to coincide with the possibilist Congress – should be taken up. Given a *fait accompli* of this sort, Liebknecht argued, the advantage given to the possibilists by the Belgian decision could be neutralized. This decisive move from the Germans significantly altered the situation once again, and preparations proceeded for the holding of the two Congresses on the same date in Paris. While the Germans still seem to have retained residual hopes of some kind of reconciliation with the possibilists, the Guesdists totally rejected any such idea in advance.

The possibilists took a similar attitude, and the importance they attached to the Congress was shown by the fact that several meetings of the National Committee were devoted entirely to the subject. In reply to a conciliatory move by the Danish socialists, Lavy replied firmly that fusion could be envisaged only on condition that verification of mandates be done in the Congress, *by nationality*; that no new subject be introduced on the agenda, and that the 'other' Congress be recognized as a dissident congress. The positions adopted by each side were mutually exclusive of each other, and no progress towards any kind of compromise was made.

On 15 July 1889 the two Congresses assembled separately in Paris; that organized by the possibilists in the rue Lancry, and that by the Guesdists in the rue Petrelle. The possibilist Congress was numerically the largest with over 600 delegates.[76] The vast majority of these were French, and the foreign delegates present were overshadowed by their far more noteworthy rivals at the other Congress. For the British there was Hyndman, and for the opening two days there was also John Burns and, for the Italians, Andreas Costa. There were also delegates from Austria–Hungary, Denmark, Spain, Portugal, Switzerland, the United States, Belgium, the Netherlands and Poland, but none from Germany. The Marxist Congress caught the big names, however. As well as the inevitably imposing German contingent which included Liebknecht, Legien and Bernstein, there was de Paepe and Anseele for Belgium, Adler from Austria-Hungary, Keir Hardie, William Morris and Eleanor Marx from the UK, and Guesde, Lafargue, Vaillant and Sebastian Faure (of the anarchists) from France. Engels's lobbying from London had been effective.

During the opening sessions of the two Congresses an attempt at unity was made by certain delegates, notably the Belgians, Italians and Danes. In the possibilist Congress conciliation proposals were rejected by Lavy, the main spokesman of the National Committee of the Fédération who had opened the proceedings of the Congress with a detailed justificatory analysis of the events leading up to the holding of the two Congresses: 'si les dissidents veulent venir avec nous, ils doivent en soumettant leurs mandats à la validation, accepter la règle commune.'[77] Although the Congress as a whole took a more conciliatory line and voted in principle for a fusion of the two Congresses, the conditions laid down for the validation of the credentials of the rival delegates was sufficient to prejudge the issue and make it impossible for them to attend, despite the efforts of Costa who acted as a go-between.

Having disposed of this troublesome problem the Congress then got down to discussing the substantive issues on the agenda: international labour legislation, the establishment of international relations within the labour movement, and industrial monopolies. The need for legislation was widely accepted, and Dumay spoke for the majority of the delegates when he said that in this task 'on doit se servir des armes fournies par la bourgeoisie'. Thus, without difficulty, a resolution was passed calling for the eight-hour working day (a demand which, as has been seen, had inspired many of the preceding Congresses), the abolition of night work, the abolition of under-fourteen child labour, and effective factory inspection. On the question of the establishment of international organizations the Congress was more specific than its rival, which debated a similar motion. There was agreement that an international organization should be set up, but Hyndman, with the lesson of the General Council of the First International and his experience of the *côterie marxiste* to enforce his case, argued strongly that it should have no power to interfere in the internal affairs of its constituent members and that its control body should simply be a 'bureau de correspondence'. The resolution as passed by the Congress stated that:

... des relations permanentes doivent être établis entre les organisations des différents pays, mais ... ces relations ne pourront porter atteinte à l'autonomie des groupements nationaux, ceux-ci étant les seuls et meilleures juges de la tactique à employer dans leurs propres pays.[78]

The Congress also passed resolutions calling for the national and international federation of trades unions, put forward a proposal for the establishment of an international journal, and suggested that in each country there should be established a central committee with the sole function of dealing with international correspondence. The usual saving clause was passed stating that all the demands called for in the resolutions passed by the Congress were simply transitory, preparing the way for the eventual appropriation and control by the working class of the means of production. The Congress then dealt briefly with rings and trusts, and urged that pressure should be put on public authorities to oppose them. It was decided that the next Congress should be held in Brussels in 1891 and be organized by the Belgians (on the same basis, i.e. with verification by national groupings). Finally, following a speech by Lavy on the dangers to the Republic presented by Boulanger, the Congress passed a resolution noting that economic reforms could only be the result of 'une complète liberté politique et le droit de vote pour tous les travailleurs', and reaffirmed the need for universal suffrage in all countries.

The Marxist Congress passed similar resolutions,[79] although predictably it was more specific in its insistence on the need for political action by the working-class parties to put pressure on their Governments for the implementation of legislation. One of its resolutions however did not find a parallel at the possibilist Congress. This was a resolution calling for a day of international demonstrations on 1 May 1890 to call for the establishment of the eight-hour working day. This resolution marked the beginning of May Day as the central date in the international socialist calendar.[80] Although opposed at first by the possibilists in France, on the grounds that it would simply turn out to be a fiasco and act as a pretext for repressive measures and/or Boulangist provocations, by 1891 they had thrown their weight behind it.[81] (At least, one should qualify, the limited weight they still enjoyed, for by that time they were no more than a minor group amidst the several groups which made up the French socialist movement. This disintegration of the possibilists after 1890 is dealt with more fully in the following section.)

In conclusion, let us summarize simply the main points arising from this examination of the international activities of the Fédération. First, the possibilists, as the strongest of the socialist groups in France, had been able to maintain strong and effective contacts with other European socialist parties throughout the 1880s, not excluding the German Social Democrats. Although their relations with the latter had never been realized in institutional links, the support amongst the German Social Democrats for their anti-Boulangist position, for example, had given rise to considerable anxieties on the part of the international overseer of Marxist orthodoxy, Engels. These international links had originated with a genuine wish to re-establish the internationalism within the socialist movement which had disappeared with the collapse of the First International, but on condition only that any new International should not repeat the faults of the old. The new International which eventually emerged was structured very carefully to avoid repetition of the evils of the First, and it was only in 1900 that the Bureau Socialiste International, with very limited functions, was set up. This was mainly due to the realities of the situation. In contrast to the situation in 1864, there were now strong national socialist parties in existence, and a central directory like the old General Council was no longer feasible. But it was also due to a quite conscious and deliberate intention to avoid a repetition of the disastrous rift which had opposed the national federations to the General Council after 1870 and split the International socialist movement. Common usage has labelled the Second International 'Marxist', which, if taken as a reflection of the predominance within it of the German Social Democrats and as a consequence, of their ideological concepts, is fair enough. But this does not mean that in some way or another the possibilist and non-Marxist Congress of 1889 was of no consequence. Simply in organizational terms it is worth remembering that the Brussels International Congress of 1891 was organized by the Belgian Parti Ouvrier which had been mandated to the task in 1889 by the possibilist, not the Marxist Congress; and that it was a result of Engels's insistence that the Zurich Committee, which had been mandated by the Marxist Congress, abandoned its own plans and that the Belgians agreed to the merger of the two Congresses, which in numerical terms alone ensured the victory of the Marxists (i.e. the German Social Democrats).[82] The strength of the opposition to Engels and the policy he wished to pursue acted as a severe limiting force on his freedom of action and helped to ensure that the Second International should not fall into the pitfalls of its predecessor.

Second, in many ways the movement to re-establish a formal socialist International was the end and not the beginning of a process. One has the constant impression that in this decade the old conflicts of the First International were simply being continued under a new guise. This can be seen both in the rivalry of Brousse and Hyndman on the one hand and Engels on the other, where perceptions were distorted to a greater or lesser extent by the rivalries of the 1870s, and in the agreement of both to exclude the anarchists from the International. (Brousse, ironically, voted against them at the 1896 London Congress.) It was not really until the mid-1890s that these issues gave way to new and different ones. The year 1889 is therefore as much the end of a process which began in 1870 as the beginning of a movement which ended in 1914. And within *that* perspective, Brousse's contribution and that of the possibilists was more important than has in the past been appreciated.

Third, the possibilists failed in their basic aim, which was to ensure international recognition of their position as the sole legitimate socialist party in France. The holding of two separate Congresses in Paris in July 1889 was more of a defeat for them than for the Parti Ouvrier Français of Guesde and Lafargue. The reason for their failure lay very largely in circumstances beyond their control, i.e. in the decisions of other national socialist parties, where the prestige enjoyed by Engels undoubtedly did a great deal to offset the possibilist cause; but it seems also true that their own intransigent self-righteousness did not help them. By any objective criterion there is no doubt that the possibilists in July 1889 came nearest to representing the majority voice of the French socialist movement, and their behaviour during the Boulanger crisis had recommended them even to the German Social Democrats. But there were stronger factors than the recognition of such objective facts to be taken account of.

5. Events leading to the split at the Chatellerault Congress, 1890

This section falls into two main parts: (a) an examination of the elements of dissent within the Fédération which manifested themselves prior to 1890; (b) a chronological account of the events in 1890 leading up to the Chatellerault Congress, with an assessment of the relative weight in this process of the various elements described in (a).

(a) *Elements of dissent*

It is useful at the start to distinguish between elements of dissent and elements of *weakness* within the Party. While the latter threw light on the nature of possibilism and became propaganda issues which were used in the split between the two factions of the Party in 1890, they do not contribute towards an explanation of why that split occurred and cannot be considered as causes of it. They were weaknesses which were showed to a greater or lesser extent by other socialist groups in France at that time. They lay in two main directions. First, the neglect by the party leadership of the provinces; and second, the failure to maintain a strong trade-union basis. The first weakness became apparent as early as 1885, when the national Congress planned for that year in Lille was cancelled because the socialists there had come under the control of the POF; the pattern was repeated in 1887, when the Party's Annual Congress was held at short notice at Charleville instead of at Troyes. There was ample evidence of concern over the position of the Party in the provinces at this time, and the National Committee took steps to arrange speaking tours by leading Party *militants*. Allemane was particularly active in this field, and openly criticized the lack of organization in the Midi which, he said, compared unfavourably with that in Algeria (which he visited). (The answer to this from some provincial delegates was, as has been seen, that action in the provinces was useless so long as the Party maintained its opposition to electoral alliances.) The evidence is however that the Party never overcame its provincial weakness, unlike its rival, the POF, and this was to become one of the main complaints of the dissidents in 1890.

The second main area of weakness was the failure of the Party to maintain its links with the trades unions. Although the 1883 Congress of the Party had made it a rule that all members should belong to a trade-union or labour association, and although the regional Congress of the Union fédérative in 1886 had, following its resolution of 1884, called for the creation of a Bourse du Travail in Paris, the attempt to provide the Party with a strong, organized trade-union basis was unsuccessful. The Fédération Nationale des Chambres Syndicales, the national organization of trades unions which was founded at the Lyon Congress of 1886, was from the outset under Guesdist control, and although the POF was soon to lose the initiative as the unions asserted their independence of all political groupings, the advantage did not accrue to the possibilists. To some extent this failure to establish a firm relationship with the organizations of the working class (as distinct from individual members of the working class itself) reflected Brousse's own long-standing coolness towards trade-union forms of action, which he had displayed as early as 1872 in Spain. He did not see trades unions as instruments of *political* struggle, and it was more important for him that the working class should be mobilized through traditional political machinery – the parties and the electoral process. He was to become a bitter opponent of the General Strike, and it was for this reason that the possibilists were to withdraw from the organizing committee for the First of May demonstrations in Paris in 1895, by which time the General Strike had become an accepted weapon of the organized and radical working class. The failure was also one of the negative results of the Party's concentration on electoral campaigns and its constant refusal to engage in militant labour agitation (as in Paris in the summer of 1888). These two main areas of weakness were not however serious causes of dissent within the Party.

On one or two occasions prior to the open declaration of war between the two factions in 1890 significant dissent from the policies or tactics of the Party had been expressed. The first such occasion was in March 1887 when the Union Fédérative, the Party's main base, rejected a plan put forward by the National Committee of the Party for the creation of a Central Electoral Committee to co-ordinate and direct the Paris municipal electoral campaign that year.[83] Although the vote was later reversed, it represented the first of a series of conflicts between the National Committee of the Party and the groups within the Union fédérative over their respective functions and powers. The conflict was magnified after the municipal elections of 1887, when nine party members were elected to the municipal council. This was because, first, most of the elected councillors were also members of the National Committee, and there were fears that power within the Party might become over-centralized; and second, because councillors increasingly sacrificed their local party work in order to concentrate on municipal affairs. This was a novel situation and it caused strains within the Party. In December 1887 the Union Fédérative passed a resolution calling for the exclusion of municipal councillors from the National Committee of the Party (a resolution 'deplored' by the latter and later reversed by the Union fédérative), and in February 1888 it passed a resolution suggesting that municipal councillors should resign their Party functions in order to devote themselves to helping electoral campaigns in the suburbs of the city.[84] It was no doubt not without significance too that in 1888 candidates for the National Committee who were also municipal councillors received significantly fewer votes than those who were not, contrary to previous voting patterns.[85]

It has been seen already how the decision of the party leadership to enter the Société des Droits de l'Homme gave rise to opposition within the Party, which eventually compelled it to leave the Society in August 1888. This was followed by specific complaints within the Union fédérative at the isolation of the National Committee from the party rank and file, and resulted in an unprecedented appeal for Party unity by Allemane in *Le Prolétariat*.[86] This was the first occasion on which the leadership had acknowledged that serious dissensions existed. The appeal was followed by a period of apparent calm, which was interrupted early in 1889 when a sizeable minority of groups within the Union fédérative voted against the decision of the National Committee to support the Jacques candidature in the January 1889 by-election, and voted instead for a separate socialist candidature (Boulé was put forward by the Guesdists as a socialist candidate). At the same time allegations were made against certain municipal councillors of having broken party discipline, and in February Lavy, a member of the National Committee, complained of the disruptive manœuvres of a handful of persons who were seeking to force a change of direction on the Party.[87]

The 'handful of persons' to which Lavy referred were a group within the Union fédérative who now increasingly registered their opposition to the Party leadership. It was undoubtedly this group which was responsible at the time for putting forward a list of candidates for the 1889 National Committee which excluded most of the Party's municipal councillors, but included Allemane and Prudent Dervillers (who dissociated themselves from it). The group's recurrent grievance was the relationship of the Union fédérative, the National Committee and the municipal councillors, although more substantive questions of Party tactics were also involved, and the very basic issue of the Party's orientation in the post-Boulanger period provided the context within which these divisions were to become irreparable. To this extent, the Party's support for the Jacques candidature marked a turning point. Immediately after the January 1889 by-election the Union fédérative voted (a) to put forward at the next election *only* class candidates and to fight all other political parties, and (b) to dissociate itself from the February demonstrations mentioned above. The debate on the issue of electoral alliances continued throughout the following weeks, usually disguised in the form of a debate over the class nature of the Party. In March 1889 the Union agreed to a proposition from Allemane that a brochure be published re-emphasizing the class nature and aims of the Party, while Prudent Dervillers, speaking for the National Committee, said that the real question to be faced was how effective action could be achieved. In May, Allemane wrote a strong article in *Le Prolétariat* attacking indiscipline in the Party and stressing the need for the building-up of its organization and respect for Party decisions.[88]

The approach of the general elections in September 1889 led to further difficulties. In July the Union fédérative succeeded in abolishing the central electoral committee (which had been a target during the 1887 municipal elections), and replaced it by a committee of the Union. Following the return to the National Assembly of the possibilist members, J.-B. Dumay[89] and Jules Joffrin, in September, the National Committee came under attack for its decision to nominate a committee to deal with Parliamentary questions of interest to the Party, on the grounds that it would further diminish the powers of the local groups. A similar dispute arose over the obligations of municipal councillors to contribute 20 francs per month to the Party for the financing of *Le Prolétariat*. Two councillors, Faillet and Rétiès, refused to be bound by the obligation, and increasingly provided the leadership of the dissident groups which stepped up their attacks on the powers of the National Committee.[90]

(b) *1890*

The election of a large number of Party members to the Paris Municipal Council in 1887 and of two members to the National Assembly in September 1889 had raised questions of mandatory responsibility and power relationships within the Party, which, as disagreements over fundamental questions of Party policy increased, assumed a serious character. Who was responsible for sponsoring Party candidates: the National Committee, the local federation, or the local groups? To whom were the elected responsible? Who should decide what policies they should argue? And underlying this, what should the Party's policy be in the post-Boulanger period? Up to the beginning of 1890 disagreements had largely been confined to levels below that of the Party leadership (i.e. the National Committee), and only towards the end of 1889 did Faillet and Rétiès, two municipal councillors, gradually emerge as leaders of the dissident groups. In 1890 however disagreements were to break out within the National Committee itself, and Allemane emerged as the leader of the Party's dissident faction.

Allemane's plea for a more militant party line and his warning of the danger of 'moderatism' in October 1889 have already been mentioned. It is very possible that the seeds of his dispute with Brousse were sown at about this time, and it is most likely that they were of a personal kind (which only later assumed political importance) revolving around the issue of control over the Party's press. Allemane had founded *Le Parti Ouvrier* in April 1888 with the apparent support of Brousse and the other possibilist leaders, who had contributed to it quite regularly, just as Allemane continued to contribute to *Le Prolétariat*, which was the Party's official organ. However in June 1889 Allemane became the principal writer in *Le Prolétariat*, and in the following month he set up his own printing works. Brousse, on the contrary, ceased to contribute to the newspaper at this time and so, at a time when Allemane controlled both *Le Prolétariat* and *Le Parti Ouvrier*, he was deprived of any outlet for the expression of his views. He began to write for the newspaper again in January 1890, at which time Allemane became its manager and *Le Parti Ouvrier* ceased publication. By March 1890 there was considerable discontent within the Union fédérative at the way the affairs of *Le Prolétariat* were being handled and at the quality of its articles (by this time the majority of municipal councillors had, for some reason, ceased to contribute to it), and in May the editorial board was back in Brousse's hands. Almost simultaneously Allemane restarted the daily *Le Parti Ouvrier*.

The meaning of these various changes is not altogether clear. However it does seem apparent that a personal rivalry between Brousse and Allemane was developing over control of the Party's propaganda outlets. This may have been conducted behind the scenes for some time, but the appearance of the second series of *Le Parti Ouvrier* in May 1890 marked a new stage, although it was some time before the opposition crystallized.

By this time quarrelling within the Party had broken into the open. On 1 April 1890 a general Party meeting took place at which Allemane proposed that during periods when they were not occupied with official business, elected members should be at the disposition of the National Committee which would organize propaganda campaigns for them in the provinces. He also proposed that a National Congress of the Party should be held as soon as possible to deal with the complex questions of the responsibilities of Party councillors and deputies. This was accompanied by a call for Party discipline and loyalty. Against this it was pointed out by one of the *militants* present that indiscipline was only to be expected so long as the Party did not return to its 'pre-1885 attitude'. Allemane, consistent with his demand for the need to fight elections on a class basis, endorsed this viewpoint. But on the more specific question of whether Party candidates should stand down in the second ballot in favour of republican candidates, the meeting voted with only one opposing vote (and two abstentions) for standing down. It was also voted that resignations should be submitted to the Union fédérative (i.e. it should be in the power of the Union fédérative to decide when an elected Party member had broken his mandate). This was by clear implication a vote of protest against the National Committee. Criticisms were also voiced against Brousse who, as the sole candidate in the forthcoming municipal elections in the Epinettes quarter, had also been adopted as a candidate by the radicals. This latter grievance was made more of at a later meeting of the Union fédérative in June, when a National Congress of the Party was again demanded.[91]

From this point onward relations within the rival groupings in the Party rapidly deteriorated – the main conflict being between the National Committee and the majority of the municipal councillors on the one hand, and *militants* within the Union fédérative on the other. By the summer of 1890 the Union fédérative had fallen under the control of the dissidents.

The personal position of Brousse came under attack once again in July 1890. He was at this time Vice-President of the municipal council, and in July his signature appeared on an invitation to an official reception to two battalions of infantry who had just completed their tour of duty in Paris. The two battalions had, it was immediately revealed, been involved in the repression of the Commune, and the occasion was immediately seized upon to mount a campaign against Brousse (at this time Brousse, in addition to his official position on the municipal council, was editor of *Le Prolétariat* and one of the 'triumvirate' on the National Committee). Called upon by the Union fédérative to justify himself, Brousse immediately dissociated himself from the invitation and pleaded guilty to an oversight. Although he withdrew his signature, a vote of censure on him at a meeting of the Union fédérative on 31 July was defeated by only one vote.[92]

Two weeks previously the National Committee had finally agreed to summon a national Party Congress at Chatellerault. Between the decision and the actual holding of the Congress in October 1890 relations deteriorated much further, and Allemane emerged as a challenger to the *de facto* leadership of Brousse within the Party.

Brousse's 'leadership' was weakened by the coincidence of the deaths of Chabert and Joffrin, two of his strongest allies, in July and September 1890 respectively. Their deaths created electoral vacancies and Allemane put forward his candidature in the 14th arrondissement to replace Chabert, against the official Party candidature of

Gély. Although the candidature was later withdrawn its meaning was clear. It was at this point that arguments over Party policies began to appear in *Le Prolétariat* and *Le Parti Ouvrier*,[93] and that the first complaints against pretensions of the latter to be the official organ of the Party were made.[94] Allemane and *Le Parti Ouvrier* had now assumed the leadership of the dissidents. On 9 September the National Committee condemned both Allemane for his candidature in the 14th arrondissement and *Le Parti Ouvrier* for giving it support.[95]

The main content of the dissidents' grievances was the power of the elected members of the Party. Consequently their main demand was for the Union fédérative to have greater control over them through the 'mandat impératif' – the lodging of a pre-signed resignation by the elected member in the hands of the local party federation. The Party statutes, on the other hand, while accepting the principle of mandatory responsibility, left the power of decision in the hands of the local electoral committees in conjunction with the electorate (Article 9 of the Party's Municipal Programme). Brousse defended the *status quo* (i.e. the maintenance of Article 9) in a characteristic way. It was, he said, a system of liberty based on the autonomy of groups and the government of the people by the people. The system proposed by the dissidents was on the contrary, he alleged, authoritarian, for it would establish the dictatorship of central committees over delegates and the people.[96]

Notwithstanding these arguments, the Union fédérative's Tenth Regional Congress, convoked hurriedly in order to precede the National Congress of the Party, voted for the repeal of Article 9 and for its replacement by a rule that a prior condition of all candidatures should be the submission of signed resignations to the sponsoring federations. The Congress also called for a reform in the composition of the National Committee. The resolutions[97] were clearly aimed at strengthening the control of the Party organization over its elected representatives, and more specifically against Brousse and the National Committee. The Congress also condemned Brousse and other municipal councillors for having circulated without official Party approval a leaflet condemning these demands. It also called for adoption of *Le Parti Ouvrier* as the Party's official organ.

These decisions by the Union fédérative were a direct challenge to Brousse, who counter-attacked at the National Congress held immediately afterwards at Chatellerault.[98] The Chatellerault

Congress was organized by, and heavily weighted in favour of, the National Committee. As in the case of the St Etienne Congress eight years previously, a split was clearly foreshadowed and prepared for on both sides. The verification of credentials provided the cause, and when the Congress refused to accept the mandates of the delegates from the Ardennes led by J.-B. Clément, a supporter of Allemane, the Allemanists withdrew *en bloc* from the Congress and went on to form a new and separate Party of their own, the Parti Ouvrier Socialiste Revolutionnaire.[99] The Congress then formally expelled Allemane and his supporters from the Party and rejected the changes in procedure which they had proposed.

Unlike the St Etienne precedent however the expulsion of the dissident minority proved to be a Pyrrhic victory. Unlike the Guesdists in 1882 the Allemanists shared, and continued to act on the basis of, many of the possibilist demands, such as the need for and possibility of immediate social reform on the municipal level. Whereas the St Etienne split had represented a logical incompatability between two differing conceptions of socialism, the Chatellerault split represented a widespread dissatisfaction with the leadership of the Possibilist Party and a wish to return to the original revolutionary spirit which had inspired many of its *militants*, especially in Paris, where the memory of the Commune nurtured a recurrent revolutionary rhetoric. The Allemanists took with them some of the most active *militants* of the Party, which had already been weakened by the deaths of Joffrin and Chabert in 1890. As a pragmatic and reformist party led by working men (and only Allemane and Malon amongst the first rank of the French socialist movement at this time qualified for this distinction), but none the less with a re-emphasized caution and mistrust towards the compromises and limits of parliamentary action, and what could be described as a strong *ouvrièriste* consciousness,[100] the POSR was to carry an appeal for intellectuals attracted to socialism – such as Lucien Herr and Charles Andler – which the possibilists never did. By striking less at the basic doctrine than at the post-1882 development and leadership of the Party, the Allemanists seriously weakened it. It is very possible that this factor alone would have been sufficient to render it politically impotent.[101] But a further blow, or rather series of blows, was struck by the change in position of the Guesdist Parti Ouvrier Français over the following three years. This was to affect the relative position of the Fédération within the wider socialist movement.

The relative passivity and indifference of the leadership of the POF during the Boulangist crisis had contrasted unfavourably with the action of other socialist groups and had led to strong criticisms from quarters which could not be totally disregarded, such as Engels, and the leadership of the German Social Democratic Party.[102] After 1889 it is likely that the leadership of the POF became more responsive to such pressures with the need to maintain international support for its claim to be the true representative of French socialism; and the leadership might well have modified its intransigent non-participatory stand in response to such letters as that of Liebknecht to Guesde in 1892, stressing the double importance for the POF to have parliamentary representation for propaganda purposes in view of the Party's weak press outlets.[103] Whatever the reason, the POF began at this time to take a new interest in gaining electoral support.

At the Party's Lyons Congress in 1891 a Municipal Programme had been drawn up and was followed by considerable successes for the Party in the municipal elections of May 1892. These successes led the Party seriously to consider a successful strategy for the 1893 general legislative elections, and at the Marseilles Congress of that year an agrarian Programme was drawn up which was a transparent attempt to gain the support of the rural voters. This Programme, and its extension at the Nantes Congress of the Party in 1894, offended Marxist orthodoxy by defending the small farmer, presented a logical challenge to strict Marxist dialectics and carried important reformist implications. It heralded the important phase in the mid-1890s when the POF abandoned its extreme revolutionary ideology, endorsed Millerand's 1896 St Mandé programme – a classic statement of reformist socialism – and enabled the various French socialist groups increasingly to collaborate together where practical matters were concerned.[104] It was certainly a successful device so far as increasing the Party's representation in the Chamber was concerned. In the parliamentary elections of 1893 six candidates of the Party were elected (Lafargue had been elected in 1891), including Guesde at Roubaix. This heralded a period of what was patently reformist practice by the POF, and it undoubtedly helped to cut further ground from underneath the feet of the possibilists, who in any case lacked strength in the provinces. Even had they been able, which is in doubt, the possibilists could not in the 1890s have offered to the electorate anything particularly unique which was not offered by any or some of the other socialist groups; and so far as the specific and avowed reformist and non-Marxist elements of the movement were concerned, the leadership was rapidly passing to independents like Millerand and Jaurès. In May 1898 the possibilists failed even to win one seat in the Chamber of Deputies (they had won two in 1889 at the height of their success), and it was clear by the mid-1890s that with the focus of the socialist movement shifted on to the national and parliamentary stage the days of the Possibilist Party as a major force within the socialist movement were numbered.

Epilogue:
Brousse's activities, 1890–1912

Despite his eclipse on the national level, Brousse remained politically active in Paris. Although a great deal of the possibilists' support had gone over to the Allemanists after the Chatellerault split, so that by 1896 the Party had only four members on the municipal council and held no national Congresses after that at Tours in 1894, Brousse kept his own strong following in the Epinettes quarter of the city (18th arrondissement). His home at 81 Avenue de Clichy was an open house for constituents who frequently consulted Brousse on their problems, in which he had a deep and sincere interest, a fact which was conceded by an otherwise strong critic of his political evolution such as Guillaume. Brousse's political outlook at this time is summed up in what he told de Silhac in about 1896:

> Voyez-vous . . . la plupart de ces braves gens viennent me dire 'J'ai faim, je suis sans travail'. Je ne vais pas leur répondre que le régime sous lequel nous vivons est détestable et que le seul conseil que je puisse leur donner est d'aller le renverser au plus vite. Je me contente de leur répondre que sous ce régime si mauvais, mais que nous sommes obligés transitoirement de subir, je puis leur faire donner 10 ou 15 francs. Et ils partent un peu moins tristes et un peu plus résignés.[1]

Concern with the concrete and practical hardships faced by the working class led him to concentrate his interest in this period on social problems, and especially on problems of sanitation and hygiene. Social Welfare was one of the few substantive issues discussed at the Chatellerault Congress, and the 1892 Congress of the Possibilist Party had been devoted almost exclusively to the subject.

It was significant that in 1905 when he visited London as leader of the Paris Municipal Council delegation to the LCC he was struck most of all by the achievements of the municipal sanitation and hygiene services. In 1908 he took an active part in discussions within the Chamber of Deputies, to which he was elected in 1906, on the conditions of mental patients in hospitals; and after his defeat in the Assembly's elections in 1910 he was appointed director of the Ville Evrard Mental Hospital, in which capacity he died in 1912 at the age of sixty-eight.

In 1905 Brousse had become President of the Paris Municipal Council and in this capacity led a delegation of sixty councillors to London in October at the invitation of the LCC for a week's official visit, the first of its kind to the LCC by a foreign municipality. The visit took place amidst considerable publicity and was referred to in *The Times* as 'L'Entente Municipale', paralleling the wider political Entente between England and France. The delegation spent a great deal of time visiting various municipal facilities in the city and was clearly impressed by the considerable municipal achievements of the LCC. It was present at the official opening by Edward VII of Kingsway and the Aldwych, and was received at Buckingham Palace and the Mansion House.[2] It was in the same capacity that Brousse in turn provided hospitality for Alfonso XIII of Spain on his visit to Paris in the same year. This ensured that Brousse would be considered by the anarchists as a traitor to his past, and it led directly to the cutting of all contacts with him by Guillaume, his former co-*militant* within the Jura Federation.

Although eclipsed on the national level, Brousse never entirely disappeared. He was a member of the Comité de vigilance – composed of the leaders of each of the socialist groups formed at the time of the Dreyfus crisis, in October 1898 – and of its successor body, the Comité d'entente socialiste. During the Millerand crisis, which destroyed the temporary unity of the socialist movement created by the Dreyfus crisis, Brousse supported the 'ministerialists' and contributed frequently to *La Pétite République*, Millerand's paper. Doctrinally Millerand's reformism was little more than a restatement of Brousse's. And it was from Brousse and the few remaining possibilists that the suggestion came that the Comité d'entente socialiste should arbitrate on the Millerand case between the various socialist groups. Agreement on this was reached, and the Committee was responsible for convoking the Salle Japy Congress in December 1899 which, while passing an equivocal resolution on the problem of membership of non-socialist Governments, unanimously approved a plan for unification and the creation of a new party, the Parti Socialiste français. Along with Jaurès, Allemane, Viviani, Vaillant, Lafargue and Guesde, Brousse was a member of the committee set up to implement this resolution.

Unity was short-lived, and by 1901 the Guesdists and Blanquists had set up their own party, the Parti socialiste de France. From 1901 to 1905 the French socialist movement remained divided between the two. The remnant of the possibilists merged with the Parti Socialiste Français of Jaurès. After 1905 and the creation of the united Section Française de l'Internationale Ouvrière (SFIO), which was to survive until 1969, Brousse became identified with its Right wing and reformist wing in opposition to the rising tide of militant syndicalism and anti-militarism within its ranks.[3] But by this time Brousse was really of negligible national significance. The reformist wing of French socialism was still headed by Guesde. It was no accident that when Jaurès wrote the Introduction to his *Discours Parlementaire* in 1904, entitled 'Le Socialisme et le Radicalisme en 1885' – a long critique of Clemenceau's radicalism and Guesde's revolutionary socialism – there was not a single mention of Brousse or of possibilism. This was a clear reflection of the relative unimportance into which Brousse had fallen by 1904 within the national leadership of the socialist movement.

Conclusion

The period 1870–90 was a crucial one in the history of the European socialist movement. It saw the First International reach the height of its influence and then collapse in the aftermath of the Paris Commune, the Franco-Prussian War and its own internal divisions. It saw the creation of the first national socialist parties and the growth of Marxism as an indispensable part of the socialist conceptual apparatus, in antithesis to which there developed a dissident anarchist *credo*. The formative experience of these two decades laid the foundation for a historiography of the movement which nurtured the myths which were to sustain it for the following six or seven decades.

Brousse's career embraced and influenced this experience, in which he played a significant part; and if ultimately he was to decline into relative obscurity, his activities from 1870 to 1890 placed him in the front rank of the French and international socialist movements.

The conflict within the First International, which resulted in the split at the Hague Congress of 1872, was not a simple struggle between Marxists and anarchists. It was very largely a struggle over the organization of the International itself, in which ideology played a part, but in which no necessary and simple direct relationship was apparent. The central conflict was between the General Council and Marx on the one hand and the majority of the component national federations on the other. The supporters of Marx in this struggle very soon became known as 'Marxists' and within a decade their political tactics had been christened 'Marxism'. The origin of these words was important, for the memory of these traumatic conflicts played an important part in determining later loyalties. This was very evidently so in Brousse's case.

As has been seen, Brousse resisted the attempts of the General Council of the International to control the activity of local sections in the South of France, and he was expelled from the International for doing so. After the collapse of the French socialist movement in

1872 he played an important role in keeping alive socialist sentiment through propaganda from Spain, where he first came under the intellectual influence of Bakunin. But he never became a 'disciple' of Bakunin.

In Switzerland Brousse was the most outstanding of the French exiles. He had not been involved in the Commune and was thus largely unaffected by the internecine quarrels arising from it within the exile community, into which he never attempted to become integrated. Instead, he made an influential contribution to the activities of the Fédération Jurassienne and the International. He created a stronghold of anarchist influence in an area hitherto unreceptive to socialist ideas, and within a short while became a serious challenge to Guillaume's unofficial leadership of the Fédération. The conflict between them was on a both personal and theoretical level. Guillaume held to an essentially syndicalist interpretation of the nature of the anarchist movement and always revealed hesitation in adopting some of the more obviously ideological positions of his co-*militants*. Brousse on the other hand was deeply influenced by the communalist and romantic vision which had its roots – along with syndicalism – in Proudhon, and which was made an effective force through the myth of the Commune and the Russian populist experience.

Brousse was essentially a man of action and a pragmatist. In a decade of reaction he developed his theory of propaganda by the deed, and when this failed to produce immediate results swallowed his pride and some of his principles and turned to electoral action. The choice he made was one way out of the dilemma faced by the anarchists in that decade; for others what had often been adopted as a provisional tactic tailored to the immediate post-communal situation – that is, electoral abstention – became a dogma, the price of which was ineffectiveness. For at least one of the leaders of the movement, the Italian Cafiero, neither alternative was acceptable, and 'not knowing how to bend, he had to break'[1] (he began to go insane in 1882). But Costa, Cafiero's co-worker in the Italian socialist movement, took the same path as Brousse.

Having helped to create, in the columns of *L'Avant-Garde*, the image of the anarchist movement which was to haunt it for decades, Brousse very soon became a leading advocate of reformist socialism. His acceptance of political action represented no compromise with Marxism. It represented rather a compromise with experience, and the form which it took – Municipal Socialism – had its roots in anarchist theory. Anarchism and the reformist socialism formulated by Brousse joined hands in a common emphasis on the value of action at the local or communal level,[2] and it is clear that in Brousse's case his change of allegiance was no sudden conversion but rather a gradual modification of his anarchism to fit the circumstances of his time. From the Commune as the focal point of revolutionary activity directed towards the emancipation of the working class, to the Commune as the focal point of pragmatic reform directed towards the betterment of working-class conditions, was not the radical change which it was depicted later as having been. Of course the abandonment of a revolutionary perspective and the explicit acceptance of the possibility of meaningful reform within the structure of the bourgeois State marked a very significant break with the past. One of the questions raised by a study of Brousse's activities is whether his evolution was any more different in kind from that of many of his contemporaries. It was not very much more different in terms of consistency or lack of consistency than that of Jules Guesde or Andreas Costa, and it could be argued that it was more honest. But the point is not whether it was more or less honest but whether within a certain framework of ideas Brousse's evolution made sense, provided a picture of reasonable self-consistency, and thereby furnishes an instructive example for those who are interested in the history of the socialist movement. The answer here is positive, both from the point of view of the historian *per se* – who should be concerned with demythologizing and correcting the imbalances in received views of the past – and from the point of view of those who are less concerned with the past than with the present. Brousse's career is of particular interest at a time when many anarchists themselves are concerned with questioning some of the movement's fundamental dogmas. When a contributor writing in the monthly theoretical organ of British anarchism can argue (and provoke anguished cries from many of his fellow anarchists) that 'the argument for piecemeal "social engineering" has been stated too conservatively by Karl Popper . . . but it is probably the best we can hope for in view of the "social inertia" inherent in any society composed of organic entities',[3] then it seems apposite that Brousse's career should be treated more seriously than in the past.

Brousse became the strongest opponent of the Marxist leaders of the newly-created French Socialist Party, and a dedicated international anti-Marxist. The foundations of this position had been laid

during the conflicts within the First International which had provided
the intellectual nursery for the leaders of the new Party. Brousse
found ready support for his opposition to Guesde and Lafargue. The
Guesdists were only one of several groups who worked for the
foundation of the French Socialist Party at the Marseilles Congress
of 1879, and the Party's *militants* were far more inclined to listen to
the anarchism of *Le Révolté*, to the reformism of Benoît Malon or to
the older revolutionaries such as Blanqui. When Brousse returned to
Paris in 1880 he found little difficulty in mobilizing opinion against
the Marxist Minimum Programme which had aroused widespread
hostility – less by its content perhaps than by its provenance. By
winning the support of the Paris socialists, forming an alliance with
the leading *militants* and gaining control of the National Committee
of the Party, Brousse soon undermined Guesde's position. In 1882
Brousse and his supporters overthrew Guesde and Lafargue and the
Marxists were expelled from the Party. A reformist and pragmatic
Programme replaced the Minimum Programme.

But Brousse's effectiveness as an activist was dependent upon
conditions which militated against his successful leadership of the
Party. He was capable of producing trenchant and effective propaganda, as had been seen in *La Solidarité Révolutionnaire* and *L'Avant-
Garde*. But this lacked the strength of sustained positive argument
and depended for its effectiveness on adversity. It was no mere
coincidence that Brousse's most effective period of political life was
in the blackest decade for the fortunes of the European socialist
movement. He thrived on opposition. The strength of his opposition
to Guesde and Lafargue within the French Socialist Party was largely
due to the fact that he was fighting again a battle fought out within
the International ten years before. The framework of reference was
already there, and so long as the conflict was carried out in essentially
similar terms Brousse was an effective leader and propagandist. Once
Guesde was defeated however his opponents found it difficult to
offer a coherent alternative which would also provide a means of
keeping the Party unified, just as the St Imier International had been
unable to do within the First International.

The one way which the anti-Marxist campaign could be continued
after 1882 was on the international level, and it is significant that it
seems to have been here that Brousse directed the major (but by no
means exclusive) part of his energies. Throughout the 1880s increasingly successful attempts were made to re-establish a new inter-

national socialist organization, or at least a forum of debate. The prime moving force in this process was the English trades unions who at that stage, unlike later, were infused with strong internationalist sentiments. It soon became apparent that the socialists could either attempt to influence the movement or be by-passed by it. They could not stop it. At this point forces which had operated during the life of the First International were remobilized, and Engels determined that if there was to be a new International it should be a Marxist one. This meant that it should not be controlled by the alliance of Brousse and Hyndman, the French and English rivals to the 'Engels-sponsored' socialist parties in these two countries.

Brousse was in his element in this conflict, which on both sides came to be seen as a continuation with only insignificant differences of that which had divided the First International (it made no difference to Engels that his rivals were reformists and not anarchists). The perceptions and judgements of both sides were clouded and distorted by the peculiar prism through which each observed the other and it is probably true to say that as far as these two extremes were concerned the actual formulation of an International became a secondary consideration. The conflict can be seen very largely in terms of a conflict within the French socialist movement itself, in which each side used the issue of the establishment of a new International as a weapon in its main preoccupation to gain recognition as the sole French socialist party. In this rivalry to establish the possibilists' influence on the new International, Brousse spent a great deal of his time and energy acting as the Party's organizing secretary for relations with foreign parties and consolidating the links with the English trades unions.

Within the French socialist movement itself Brousse's individual contribution was somewhat eclipsed by the collective leadership which emerged after the split with the Guesdists in 1882. While division existed within the Party it tended to be polarized into a personal conflict between Guesde and Brousse. Once Guesde and his followers had been expelled, personalities assumed less importance, and at the same time the tasks facing the Party changed. The qualities which had brought Brousse to the forefront of the movement in the years of exile were not necessarily those required by a Party operating within a legal context on French soil whose main aim was the building-up of a strong and effective organizational framework for the creation of a mass Party. This was a major failure of the possibilists in the

1880s – and although the blame was not Brousse's alone, his influence had its effect on those who might have done otherwise had they been subjected to, for example, the organizing drive of Jules Guesde.

It would be a mistake to blame Brousse for the organizational failure of the possibilists, if only because in the 1880s he shared the leadership of the Party with long-established Party *militants* who were in closer contact with and to an extent wielded more power or influence over the mass of the Party supporters. Men such as Jean Allemane and Jules Joffrin with a *militant* working-class background carried considerable weight within the Party, and it is clear that in Paris even they did not always have their own way. Brousse's particular *forte* was in journalism and propaganda and, after his election to the Municipal Council, in municipal affairs also.

It has been seen how the emphasis in anarchism on action outside the State and within the communal framework led Brousse to the formulation of a pragmatic programme of specific social reform once the revolutionary perspective had been abandoned. This indeed reflected his central concern with the concrete problem of working-class conditions and aspirations. Even his adoption of the most intransigent and extremist anarchist standpoint in the years 1873–8, when he became a leading exponent of propaganda by the deed, was justified in terms of the mobilizing effect this tactic would have on the average working man ignorant of revolutionary theory. (See Appendix 3.) The point of reference remained the 'average working man', and it was when he realized that this average working man was not interested in – or was unable to launch – Revolution that Brousse ceased to be an anarchist and allied himself with the working-class movement in Paris which was interested in specific and immediate social reforms. (In particular see his letter to Gross, Appendix 2.) In this connection it was certainly more than simple political expediency which led him to oppose the attempt of Allemane in 1890 to give the Party organization the right to withdraw the mandate from its elected members. This, Brousse argued, was a matter for direct settlement between the councillor and his working-class constituents.

None the less, for all his concern with the immediate problems of the working class, he and his Party lost support, and after 1890 the Party virtually ceased to exist. Several reasons can be advanced for this, primary amongst which was the failure (and whether this could have been avoided is doubtful) to overcome the bitter legacy of the Commune. It was not that the working class who supported the socialists rejected reformism in favour of Guesdism or orthodox Marxism. It was rather that they were not prepared to accept the implications of their reformism. There is little doubt that the Boulanger crisis and the entry of a sizeable number of socialist councillors into the Paris municipal council together raised issues which became a microcosm of those which later divided the French socialist movement so disastrously at the time of Millerand's entry into the Waldeck Rousseau cabinet. If one entered bourgeois institutions or was prepared to defend them then one's hands became dirty and compromise became necessary. This was a disagreeable discovery to many of those socialists who had, none the less, believed in the need for and possibility of social reform. Some were less concerned about this than others and adopted a thoroughgoing reformist position, such as Brousse himself. But the majority recoiled from the prospect, not surprisingly in view of the hatred of the *Versaillais* which existed in the popular consciousness of the Parisian working class. The memory of the repression of the Commune only twenty years previously had resulted in a very deep distrust by the working class of the institutions of the Third Republic, and a consequent reluctance to accept a strategy which advocated their manipulation.

However, once the Communard generation passed, reconciliation with the Third Republic became easier. The reformist strategy became a more viable one and was strengthened by the vital conversion of members of the intelligentsia such as Jaurès and Millerand. By this time of course the Possibilist Party was non-existent, and Brousse had ceased to enjoy any national significance. But the St Mandé Programme was virtually a restatement of arguments put forward by Brousse fifteen years earlier.[4] The political strategy propounded by Millerand and Jaurès was in its turn rejected in the name of orthodox Marxist doctrine, but not before Jaurès had infused the French movement with a democratic and reformist spirit which, however overlaid it became later, was not to be lost.

This non-Marxist component of the socialist tradition is one which has been neglected in the past. This account of Brousse's career should, it is hoped, have thrown further light on one aspect of this component and also have provided information about Brousse and the origins of the French socialist movement which was not available before. It is hoped also that it will have thrown light on certain aspects of the First International and on the early years of the European anarchist movement.

APPENDIX 1

Letter of Paul Brousse to Garcia Vinas, 17 February 1880
Nettlau Archives IISG*

Londres 17/2/1880

Mon cher ami,

Ce n'est pas inutilement que j'ai couru après ton adresse. C'était pour te mettre au courant de ce qui se passe parmi nous, et connaître à ce sujet ton sentiment. Je m'étonne que Pierre [Kropotkin], dont c'était la fonction, en qualité de secrétaire de notre intimité internationale ne l'ait pas fait déjà.

Tu sais peut-être cependant qu'Andréas [Costa] a rompu avec nous tous toute relation *politique* intime. Il a écrit à ce sujet des lettres en Suisse dont je n'ai pas pu (cela soit dit entre parenthèses) obtenir la communication. Tu peux, si tu le veux, l'intérroger à ce sujet, il te répondra. Voici son adresse: poste restante, Lugano, (Ticino), à son nom. Ce que je veux t'apprendre, c'est ma sortie de l'intimité jurassienne, et ce que je veux te soumettre, c'est ma sortie du groupe internationale intime créé à la Ch. d.f. [see my p. 303].

Tandis que nos amis suisses restent d'une fidelité absolue à notre ancienne tactique, mes idées, sur ce point, ont subi une large évolution. En conséquence, nous sommes divisés; trop pour notre coexistence dans l'intimité jurassienne; la question est de savoir si nous le sommes trop aussi pour faire partie d'une même intimité internationale? C'est sur ce dernier point que je veux prendre ton opinion.

Pour que tu puisses décider en connaissance de cause, je vais t'exposer l'état actuel de mes idées. Je ne défendrai pas celles-ci, ce serait trop long: je le fais d'ailleurs dans une série de lettres aux amis de Jura dont tu pourras demander au besoin la communication.

J'étais jadis un de ceux, tu t'en souviens, qui repoussaient avec le plus d'acharnement toute entente avec les partis socialistes voisins. Passe moi le mot: j'étais sectaire. Sur ce point ma façon de comprendre les choses s'est grandement modifié. [Cf. his letter to Gross in Appendix 2.]

Il me semble que le temps d'élaborer les programmes, de les sculpter, de les distinguer les uns des autres, est à peu près passé. Ce travail est accompli. Nous sommes à mon sens parvenus à l'époque des réalisations, et si j'en crois les signes avant-courreurs demain le grand combat va s'engager.

* Published in German by Nettlau in *Anarchisten und Sozialrevolutionäre* (Berlin, 1931), pp. 51–5. Nettlau's translation is not quite complete, omitting the first two paragraphs. I should like to thank the International Institute of Social History for their permission to reproduce this letter in its entirety.

En cette occurrence, je jette un coup d'oeil sur notre situation et que vois-je? En face de nous, une masse bourgeoise qui sait vite se rendre compacte quand le socialisme surgit. De notre côté, une foule de sectes impuissantes qui oublient l'ennemi commun pour se tirer dessus. Comment grouper *pour le combat immédiat et inévitable* un masse ouvrière capable d'entrer en lutte avec les partis bourgeois?

L'expérience me démontre qu'aucun groupe socialiste ne peut parvenir à l'hégémonie, et commander ou annuller les autres. Avant 1873 les Marxistes ont essayé de nous vaincre sans le pouvoir; depuis cette date les anarchistes victorieux ont écarté quelques uns de leurs amis anti-autoritaires; ils ont eu toute la peine du monde à vivre, et ils sont demeurés quoi qu'ils fissent impuissants.

Eh bien, voici ce que se fait en France. Nous prenons Guesde, Malon, de Ricard, et moi – je ne cite que les noms que tu connais – un point commun à tous nos programmes, pour en faire notre *revendication* immédiate, le drapeau qui *momentanément* doit rallier tous les social-istes en marche contre la bourgeoisie. Ce point me semblait etre l'auto-nomie communale; le collectivisme révolutionnaire a été préféré-Soit. Tu vois quelle est ma tactique:

Rester ce que je suis, anarchiste communiste, révolutionnaire; mais prendre une pièce importante de ce programme l'appropriation collective du sol et de l'intrument de travail et en faire une revendication immédiate en m'unissant pour l'obtenir à tous les socialistes qui la revendiquent comme moi. Ceci obtenu, je demanderai autre chose.

Cette tactique – l'entente même transitoire – avec les partis socialistes voisins, est taxée de compromis, *d'opportunisme*, de *possibilisme,** par mes amis. Moi j'appelle ça: *opportunité, possibilité*, et sans me pre-occuper autrement des mots je passe outre.

Ce n'est pas tout, cependant, et nous sommes divisés sur un point encore, sur le vote.

Nos amis restent abstentionnistes presque absolus. A mes yeux le vote n'est pas un principe mais un instrument. Je le considère comme *un coup numérique* moins puissant qu'*un coup de force*, mais qu'il peut être utile d'employer quelquefois, comme aussi il peut être utile de s'en abstenir. Sur ce point, je crois cependant que l'entente avec nos amis serait facile. Relis le Congrès jurassien de Fribourg.

Dois-je maintenant rester dans l'intimité international? Voilà la question. Nos amis le désirent [? disaient], mais ils ne font rien pour cela. J'ai tenté plusieures choses depuis que j'ai quitté la Suisse. Ils m'ont toujours refusé leur appui.

Voici le dilemme, sur lequel doit se poser toute notre attention.

Nous nous sommes prononces à la Ch. d.f. – tu t'en souviens – pour

---

* The first apparent use of the term.

l'autonomie des intimités régionales; pour l'etablissement d'un bureau en
Suisse, dont P. serait le secrétaire correspondant; pour la publication d'un
journal (Avant-Garde, ou Révolte) qui serait non pas jurassien, mais
international.

DONC:

Ou mes nouvelles idées sont trop en dehors du programme anarchiste –
ne sont plus anarchistes – selon l'Espagne, l'Italie, la Suisse, et je dois
sortir de toute intimité (*politique* s'entende) avec vous. Je suis prêt.

Ou mon programme n'est qu'une nuance du programme anarchiste
générale, et peut conduire à la constitution d'une branche spéciale du
parti anarchiste international, et dans ce cas je consens à demeurer
membre de l'intimité internationale. Mais alors je demande l'aide
mutuelle entre les intimités, ton appui, celui de P . . . etc. . . . pour ce que
j'entreprendrai, et la réouverture des colonnes de notre journal *inter-*
nationale le Révolté.

J'aime les situations nettes, et je te prie de me répondre au plus tôt sur
ce sujet. Reste-je lié avec vous, ou, suis-je libre?

Mille amitiés de nous,

Paul Brousse

APPENDIX 2

*Extract of a letter from Paul Brousse to Jacques Gross, 3 April 1883
Archief Gross-Fulpius, IISG**

... Après mille expériences nous nous sommes aperçus que les principes seuls ne sauraient grouper les masses; ils amènent les érudits et quelque dévoués. Or, dès que la petite armée qui en résulte *entre en lutte sérieux* contre la bourgeoisie elle est décimée en un rien de temps. J'ai vu cela en Espagne, en Italie, à Berne, partout. Il faut donc pénétrer plus avant dans la masse et pour cela lui parler non plus *principes* mais *intérêts immédiats, matérials.* Demandez au manœuvre qui passe s'il est collectiviste, anarchiste ...; il vous répondrait, s'il savait répondre, qu'il n'a pas eu le loisir de faire de suffisantes études économiques et politiques pour choisir un système. Mais si vous lui demandez s'il se sent l'ennemi de classe de son maître il vous comprend aussitôt et prend place dans le rang. Mais il n'y reste que si vous consentez à l'aider dans la protection de ses instincts quotidiens.

Donc, la politique réaliste exige la formation d'un large parti de classe, agissant par tous les moyens, arme et vote; groupant tous les ouvriers autour de leurs intérêts de classe, de leurs petits instincts quotidiens, et les conduisant le plus rapidement *possible* à l'idéal qui est le communisme-anarchiste, c'est-à-dire une sociéte dans laquelle le *service public* sera généralisé et le gouvernment aboli.

En un mot, nous avons le même but. Mais tandis que *vous pensez* encore qu'on l'atteindra d'un tour de main, *nous savons* qu'il est au terme d'une longue évolution dont les étapes exigent pour être rapidement franchis l'emploi de tous les moyens, même la possession momentanée transitoire du pouvoir.

* I should like to thank the IISG for permission to quote from this document.

APPENDIX 3

Article by Brousse in L'Avant-Garde, *17 June 1878*

'Hoedel, Nobiling, et la propagande par le fait'

L'Avant-Garde étant le seul journal au monde qui n'ait pas insulté Hoedel et Nobiling, le seul qui n'ait pas éprouvé le besoin de protester en principe contre le régicide, nous croyons utile de dire à nos lecteurs toute notre pensée sur les deux dernières tentatives de l'avenue des Tilleuls, et de les classer dans le mode de tactique auquel elles appartiennent.

Mais pour cela, il nous faut prendre les choses d'un peu haut. On nous le pardonnera.

Du onzième siècle au temps où nous sommes, la bourgeoisie libérale a lutté pour instaurer dans le monde un nouveau système politique et social. Le côté économique de son programme (remplacement de l'antique propriété fédérale par la propriété individuelle moderne) est un fait accompli; appuyée sur le peuple, elle lutte encore dans les trois-quarts de l'Europe pour en réaliser le côté politique, qui consiste dans la substitution complète du système électif au systéme du droit divin, ou s'il faut nous exprimer en langage plus simple, dans la destruction de la monarchie et dans l'établissement de la république.

Un homme qui a feuilleté quelque peu d'histoire, une histoire seulement, celle de France par exemple, ne soutiendra pas que la diffusion de l'idée républicaine ait été toute pacifique. Il saura qu'à côté des *démonstrations théoriques* ont surgi un bon nombre de *démonstrations pratiques*. Nier ce fait de pure observation, ce serait ignorer le caractère républicain de nos heroïques petites communes du moyen-âge, dénaturer la portée politique de cette série de mouvements insurrectionnels qui se sont développés dans la capitale depuis Etienne Marcel jusqu'à Hébert; ce serait nier l'heroïsme de Barbier, refuser du dévouement à Blanqui, et à Flourens du courage; ce serait enfin prétendre que jamais Fieschi n'a dirigé de machine infernale contre la poitrine de Louis-Philippe, et qu'Orsini n'a pas jeté de bombes fulminantes sous les pas du dernier des Napoléon.

Son tour venu, le prolétariat entre aussi dans la lice. Il apporte avec lui sa conception économique: la propriété collective, et le système politique qui découle tout naturellement de ce mode nouveau d'appropriation: la fédération libre des groupes et des individus. Maintenant il faut répandre ces principes. Nous ne nierons certainement pas la propagande faite par nos journaux, par nos brochures, par la parole ardente et convaincue de nos orateurs, mais nous demandons qu'on tienne compte de l'immense retentissement qu'a produit dans le monde la dernière Commune de Paris.

Oui, nous surprenons dans l'histoire ce fait incontestable: l'idée marche en si'appuyant sur deux forces qui se complètent: le rayonnement de *l'acte*, la puissance de la *théorie*.

Et si l'une de ces forces fait plus que l'autre, c'est l'*Acte* et non pas la *Théorie*.

Il est d'ailleurs facile de le comprendre.

Que l'on réfléchisse aux obstacles que l'on rencontre pour pénétrer les masses d'une pensée nouvellei même, si l'on a à sa disposition – ce qui n'est pas le cas pour l'ouvrier – des orateurs nombreux, des écrivains en assez grand nombre, des brochures fréquentes et des journaux quotidiens!

Voilà un homme qui pendant 12 heures a senti au niveau de son épaule la main de son contre-maître, voilà un homme qui pendant douze heurs a risqué ses membres en les sentant froler par les rouages de la machine, un homme dont l'attention a du sans cesse être en éveil, et les muscles sans cesse en mouvement; il rentre chez lui, que pensez-vous, qu'il désire? des brochures, des journaux, de gros livres? Oh, que non pas! ce qu'il veut, ce sont quelques instants de joie en famille, quelques heures de repos au foyer. Beaucoup même n'aspirent qu'à deux choses, la soupe et le lit, nourriture et sommeil.

Et qu'on ne dise pas que pour avoir raison, nous broyons à dessein, du noir sur le tableau. Les résultats de cet état de choses sent là palpables; ouvrez les yeux et regardez:

Comptez les abonnés ouvriers de toutes les feuilles, comptez les ouvriers acheteurs de brochures, comptez les ouvriers qui fréquentent les assemblées, et faites le total. Comptez maintenant la foule des travailleurs et comparez. Vous ne trouverez pas un ouvrier sur mille qui puisse se développer serieusement, et s'instruire théoriquement.

Eh bien! Fieschi tire sur un roi sa machine infernale; Orsini sème de bombes la route d'un empéreur; Hoedel tire et manque, Nobiling tire et blesse. Un point d'intérrogation se dresse immédiatement partout, sur la place publique, dans la rue, au foyer, sous le chaume et dans la mansarde. Nul ne peut rester froid, demeurer indifférent. Pour ou contre, tout le monde s'agite. Que veulent donc ces assassins dit l'ouvrier qui va à la fabrique comme le paysan qui va à sa charrue? ils ne voulent plus de rois, plus d'empéreurs? que mettrent-ils donc à la place. La république, parbleu! dit un passant.

On arrête le passant, mais le coup est donné, l'ébranlement est produit.

Que maintenant Orsini meure sur l'échafaud; que Fieschi, comme une bête blessée, soit retrouvé aux traces que laisse son sang qui coule; que Nobiling mourant gémisse sous le sabre d'un lâcho, et sous la main d'un juge à la Torquemada tripotant ses linges ensanglantes, qu'importe!

partout on discute la république, et quand on discute la république, la république s'établit.

Mais voici un fait plus puissant encore parce qu'il est plus compréhensible. Une commune proclame son indépendance en face du pouvoir central, et des hommes républicains comme en 1792, socialistes déjà comme en 1871, installent, organisent, font fonctionner le système social et politique de leur choix. Là aussi, un ébranlement puissant sera produit. Mais tout à l'heure on pouvait prétendre que les 'assassins' étaient payés par le prêtre, par la police ou l'étranger; qu'ils étaient des ambitieux ou des fous; on pouvait dénaturer leurs actes? Que répondre maintenant au fonctionnement devant tous d'un système politique social nouveau? Le juger, oui, le combattre, aussi, mais le calomnier avec succès, cela devient presque impossible. Les noms d'Orsini, de Fieschi, de Nobiling, resteront toujours un peu obscurcis dans l'histoire; on peut trop aisément les confondre avec les Jacques Clément et les Ravaillac, tandis que dans les reflets sanglants de ces mots 'Commune de Paris' tout enfant qui sait lire, lira son avenir.

Tels sont les faits que l'histoire enseigne. Voyons maintenant de leur appliquer la méthode que doivent employer les socialistes de l'école scientifique. Cette méthode consiste à observer scrupuleusement les phénomènes sociaux, à entraver la marche de ceux qui nuisent à la propagande socialiste, à aider la production de ceux qui favorisent cette propagande, et, si possible – *à reproduire ces derniers.*

Nous voyons la propagande théorique insuffisante, nous voyons la propagande pratique, puissante même quand elle n'est pas voulue, nous cherchons à inaugurer une propagande *par le fait* non plus inconsciente, mais voulue.

C'est tout simple, seulement nous choisissons.

Nous choisissons les meilleurs parmi les moyens de propagande théorique? il est évident que nous montrons la même circonspection, et beaucoup plus de prudence, dans le choix de l'acte à accomplir pour faire de la propagande pratique. Nous n'avons pas armé le pistolet de Hoedel, ni glissé des chevrotines dans la carabine de Nobiling, parce que nous savions d'abord que le régicide est une propagande purement républicaine, ensuite qu'il est trop facile de dénaturer les intentions des exécuteurs. Si nous avions voulu faire une propagande purement républicaine, nous n'eussions pas tué un roi, nous eussions fait une commune républicaine. Anarchistes, nous avons fait un 18 Mars à Berne pour prouver aux ouvriers suisses qu'ils n'ont pas la liberté de manifestation; les ouvriers suisses ont compris. Anarchistes, nos amis italiens ont promené la destruction de l'Etat à Letino, à San Lupo, à San Lupo, à Gallo; les paysans de ces contrées ont compris. Si Hoedel et Nobiling avaient été des anarchistes conscients, ils eussent attendu quelque temps encore et ils auraient fait plus et mieux.

On nous objectera que Hoedel, que Nobiling, sont non pas de-
républicains purs, mais des démocrates-socialistes. Malgré toutes les
dénégations des officiels du parti, nous reconnaissons que telle est la
vérité. Mais, Nous ferons observer une fois encore qu'en Allemagne les
deux partis républicaine-radicaux et socialistes sont confondus dans un
seul et vaste ensemble. Ces deux partis ne se scinderent comme ils l'ont
fait on Suisse, en France, et ailleurs que lorsque une République bourgeoise allemande aura des chances de s'etablir. Voilà pourquoi le parti
allemand s'appelle inconsciemment ou non: démocrate-socialiste, et non
pas comme nous: socialiste tout court, socialisme supposant démocratie
réalisée au moins dans les idées.

Nobiling donc est démocrate-socialiste. Mais au lieu d'être *démocrate-
socialiste* il est *démocrate-socialiste*. Et, il n'est pas seul dans son parti
qui soit dans ce cas. Ce qui est sorti de son fusil, c'est une *propagande
républicaine*; toute *propagande purement socialiste* est resté au fond.

APPENDIX 4

Brousse's Municipal Programme: L'Emancipation, *20 November 1880*

Le Socialisme Devant Les Elections Municipales

Les socialistes parisiens se préoccupent déjà vivement de l'action électorale. Ils ont compris que la résolution de la presque unanimité des socialistes-révolutionnaires de prendre part à l'action politique, notamment à la lutte électorale, impose le devoir d'agir immediatement. Un groupe de Montmarte, sur l'invitation de notre ami et collaborateur Paul Brousse, a proposé aux groupes socialistes un programme remarquable que nous reproduisons ci-dessus. Le programme est déjà en discussion dans une douzaine de groupes, tout fait prévoir qu'avec de légères modifications il sera accepté par tous les socialistes-révolutionnaires parisiens.

Bien qu'ayant un caractère communaliste et fédéraliste plus prononcé, le programme socialiste municipal est donné-comme étant le développement, en ce qui touche la commune, du programme électoral minimum du parti ouvrier français.

Voici ce projet:

Programme électoral municipal socialiste, accepté par les délégués réunis des trois groupes suivants; 'union des menuisiers', 'Groupe ouvrier révolutionnaire socialiste', 'Cercle d'études sociales du 18e arrondissement' et accepté comme base de discussion par 'l'Union fédérative de Paris' et les groupes dont les noms suivent: 'Le Droit des femmes'. 'l'Union des femmes socialistes'. 'le groupe ouvrier du 18 mars'. 'les Cercles du 3e arrondissement'. 'le Comité central d'initiative'. 'la Societé Egalite', 'le Groupe des 1er et 2e arrondissements'. 'l'Union de la Fédérations des menuisiers', etc., etc.

Considérant

Que la développement de la production moderne substitue progressivement dans chaque branche d'industrie la machine à l'outil, l'automatisme à la capacité technique, et l'effort collectif à l'individuel;

Que, par suite, l'appropriation des moyens de travail et des produits *doit* suivre une marche parallèle, et de presque entièrement privée qu'elle est aujourd'hui, devenir de plus en plus collective:

Considérant

Qu'actuellement les différentes industries sont inégalement développées;

Que si quelques-unes, comme les chemins de fer, sont à point pour être transformées en services publics nationaux, voire même internationaux le plus grand nombre d'entre elles, comme l'industrie du gaz par exemple, ne faisant pas encore sentir leur action hors des limites de la commune, il y a lieu d'établir, au moins transitoirement, une propriété publique communale:

Considérant

Que parmi les communes, s'il en est, où la grande industrie domine, il en est d'autres où règne presque exlusivement encore la petite culture, la petite ou moyenne industrie:

Que par suite, les mêmes mesures économiques ne pouvant être uniformement appliquées dans toutes les communes, la forme politique qui correspond et qui est le reflet de cette organisation économique, doit être une fédération communale respectant l'unité de la République;

Considérant enfin

Qu'une transformation sociale aussi complète exige de la part du prolétariat en lutte l'emploi de tous les moyens;

Les groupes du 18e arrondissement, dont les noms suivent,
Décident:

1. Qu'il ya lieu pour le prolétariat constitué comme classe et en parti politique distinct.

De poursuivre l'établissement de la propriété collective nationale ou communale, selon les cas;

De marcher à la conquête des municipalités;

De faire usage, pour atteindre ce double but de tous les moyens d'action, y compris le vote.

2. Qu'il y a lieu de faire un premier pas dans cette voie en entrant dans les élections municipales prochaines avec le programme de revendications suivant:

A. PARTI POLITIQUE

La commune rendue maîtresse de son administration, de sa police, de sa justice et de son armée;

1. Suppression des maires et adjoints choisis par le gouvernement et leur replacement par une administration élue par la commune.

2. Rémuneration des fonctions de conseiller communal et de tous délégués nommé par la commune.

3. Ratifications des délibérations prises en conseil, non plus par les agents du pouvoir, mais, dans les cas importants comme est le cas du budget par exemple, par le vote populaire.

4. Droit de vote et droit d'éligibilité rendus aux femmes dans la commune.

5. Publicité des séances.

6. Remplacement des tribunaux dans la commune par l'arbitrage et le jury;

7. Réarmement de la garde nationale communale; déarmement et licenciement des troupes de la police.

8. Droit permanent de révocabilité mandataire communal confié au comité qui a patroné son élection.

9. Liberté d'entente entre différentes communes.

B. PARTIE ECONOMIQUE

La commune maîtresse de créer tous services publics municipaux qui lui conviendra.

1. Transformation en services publics communaux des enterprises de grandes compagnies, gaz, caux, omnibus, tramways . . . etc. . . . Tous ces services devant fonctionner désormais, sinon gratuitement, au moins à prix de revient;

2. Etablissement par la commune d'industries municipales, pour donner de l'occupation aux travailleurs mis à pied par les crises, grèves, transformations d'outillage, etc., et pour acheminer la commune du régime de la propriété privée au régime de la propriété collective;

3. Enseignement intégral, gratuit de tous les enfants mis pour leur entretien à la charge de la commune, depuis leur naissance jusqu'à la charge de la commune, depuis leur naissance jusqu'à l'âge de 21 ans.

4. Création de greniers, minoteries, boulangeries, boücheries, etc., ouverture de bazars, construction de maisons salubres, le tout à titre municipal, pour combattre les speculateurs et accapareurs, au profit des travailleurs, dont le coût d'entretien baisserait par la vente et la location à prix de revient.

La commune maîtresse d'intervenir dans la question de travail:

1. Par des lois communales de garantie;

2. Par la commandité facultative donnée aux associations ouvrières;

3. Par le secours donné en cas de grève aux ouvriers contre leurs patrons; La commune maîtresse de son budget:

1. Suppression du budget des cultes;

2. Suppression des octrois et remplacement de tous impôts (directs et

indirects) par un impôt unique payé collectivement à la nation par la commune et perçu par celle-ci sous forme d'un impôt fortement progressif sur les revenus au-dessus de 3,000 fr.;

3. Cessation des alienations des biens communaux et retour à la collectivité communale de ceux déjà alienés;

4. La commune héritière dans toutes les successions, dans une mesure à déterminer.

Pour notre part, nous nous ferons un devoir d'appuyer ce programme si les groupes ouvriers et socialistes, après les discussions et les modifications qu'ils jugerent necessaires, le font leur. Et nous souhaitons que sous un pareil drapeau combattent non-seulement les socialistes parisiens, mais les socialistes-collectivistes de toute la France.

[Signed]

B. Malon

APPENDIX 5

Notes on socialism in the Midi

A. Connections with Barcelona 1873

At the end of June 1873 Gillet of the St Etienne International group, received a crate of wine from Sète, inside of which were hidden copies of *La Solidarité Révolutionnaire,** and in July the police intercepted more Manifestos destined for Lyons.† It is probable that Sète (situated at the mouth of the Canal du Midi, and at that time France's fourth most important port) was the main channel for the smuggling of illegal propaganda from Spain, and it is likely too that it was carried out by such individuals as Jean Claris, whose activities attracted the attention of the police in 1873. Claris, a wine merchant, was the son-in-law of Eugene Pradal who had been involved in and condemned to death following the insurrection at Béziers in 1851 which followed Napoleon's *coup*. Pradal fled to Barcelona, returned to the Hérault in 1870, was compromised again in the political events of 1870–1, and fled back to Barcelona.‡ He was evidently on familiar terms with both Guesde and Montels, and it was through Pradal that Montels kept in touch with Guesde.§ For a short time, and unknown to the police, Pradel visited the Hérault,‖ but had returned by August 1873 to Barcelona where he was visited by his daughter and her husband. On their return to Sète Claris was searched thoroughly and although nothing was found the police remained convinced that he was the main link between the Hérault and Barcelona.¶ It is very possible that it was Claris who arranged the smuggling of copies of *La Solidarité Révolutionaire* into France.

A clearer case was that of Pascal Verdale, another refugee of 1851, who similarly established himself in Barcelona where he ran a small café in the Montjuich quarter of the city. When Alerini presented the Congress of Geneva with a mandate from the Béziers Internationalist group it was suggested by the police that he had obtained it through either Pradal or Verdale.** If any doubt existed in their minds as to Verdale's loyalty it was removed in 1874 when he returned to the Hérault. One of his first actions was to make contact with Louis Salvan, the

* Maitron op. cit., p. 87.

† Police report of 23 July 1873, *P.Po. BA/985 (Dossier Brousse)*.

‡ c.c. Sète to Prefect, 6 August 1873; c.c. Mont. to Prefect, 10 August 1873, in *AD Hérault, 39M.254.*

§ At one time it seemed as though Guesde planned to leave Rome for Barcelona, and Pradal forwarded him money for it; Pradal to Guesde, 16 April 1873. *Fonds Guesde.*

‖ Montels to Guesde, 21 July 1873; *Fonds Guesde.*

¶ *AD Hérault,* loc. cit.

** S.-P. Béziers to Prefect, 24 September 1873, loc. cit.

founder of the Béziers Internationalist group and fellow exile of 1851,* and he emerged at the end of the decade as the leading organizer of the anarchist movement in the Department.

B. Socialist Newspapers in the Midi, 1880–2

Following the Marseilles Congress its general executive committee published a monthly bulletin, with Lombard as its chief editor, entitled *La Fédération*. As well as providing details on the national organization of the Party, largely culled from *L'Egalité* (Testut report of 26 March 1880, P.Po.Ba/1477), and providing bibliographies of socialist literature (including *La Philosophie de l'Avenir* and *Le Révolté*), it published the Manifesto and statutes of the Federation Marseillaise, adopted on 29 February 1880, to which Malon referred in his letter to Lombard and Boyer of 11 April 1880 (Chapter 5, p. 160). This described the working-class Programme as 'communiste-anarchiste' and accepted electoral action as 'un moyen de lutte transitoire' (No. 3, 7 February 1880). Its sixth number (10 June 1880) published the results of the municipal elections of April 18 in Marseilles, when the Parti Ouvrier candidates received 2,700 votes. Significantly the same issue also carried news of disruption within the Fédération between the *syndicats* and socialist groups. No further copies of the paper appear in the Bibliothèque Nationale.

In 1881 Lombard edited a Marseilles paper *Le Peuple Libre* (5 June 1881–22 January 1882). The overwhelming tone was reformist, 'idealist' and federalist, and placed great emphasis on the *republican* and *democratic* character of socialism, its continuity with the tradition of 1789. Much of it resembled a kind of Jaurèsism, as for example the following long extract from an article by Lombard entitled 'Ce que nous sommes' (No. 3, 19 June 1881):

Or, le parti socialiste, de consanguinité révolutionnaire, est républicain par essence. Sa génération ascendante appartient à cette collectivité d'hommes généreux qui, de 1789 jusqu'à nos jours, en France comme en Europe, ont combattu tous les gouvernements, toutes les oppressions, toutes les tyrannies.

Les Carbonaris, les Montagnards, les Blanquistes, suprêmes conspirateurs luttant et mourant pour un droit supérieur, *nouveau* et mal défini encore en eux, ont été les cousins germains, si je puis dire, des socialistes actuels. Ces derniers procèdent donc familialement d'eux.

Comme les socialistes, ils ont eu un idéal de justice, des principes d'égalité sociale, des vues humanitaires. Synthétisant leurs aspirations, ils ont résumé dans ce mot, *République*, tout ce pour quoi ils combattaient et mouraient. *République*, mot magique exprimant les rêves des siècles oppresses, des sociétés martyrisées, des vaincus des classes pauvres et serves! En entendant ce mot,

*For Salvan see p. 30. See also c.c. Béziers to S.-P. Béziers, 21 August 1874, *39M.258*, for contact with Verdale. Verdale went on to become a leading anarchist in the region and was largely responsible for the anarchist resolutions passed at the Southern Regional Congress of the Socialist Party held at Sète in 1881.

comme le cheval chauvit aux claironnements des batailles, les peuples se sont
levés, les masses sont entrés en rébellion, les armes ont été aiguisées. La République a été le *Messie* social de l'humanité précédante. Et maintenant encore,
malgré le forme autoritaire qu'on lui donne, elle reste comme le palladium
sacré, l'espoir immense des générations en quôte de bien-être et d'égalité.
Le parti socialiste est donc républicain.
Mais . . . le parti socialiste ne peut s'arrêter à la République de ses devanciers.
Son idéal doit être d'autant plus élargi que les données de la science contem-
poraine sont plus sûres et plus positives.
Se surajoutant au parti republicain, le parti socialiste doit être à l'avant-
garde de l'humanité nouvelle qui, décisivement, veut constituer pour elle-même
un ordre social en accord avec la science et le progrès.

There were very good reasons for this emphasis in the interpretation
of the socialist tradition, which partially highlight the antithesis between
its meridional and northern manifestations in France. Lombard and *Le
Peuple Libre* supported electoral candidates in the 1881 Legislative elections, and the Party's relative failure (see p. 173) led him to criticize
Guesdist theory and tactics on two major counts. The first was the
attempt to create a uniform, centralized party which, he claimed, was
absurd. It was totally contrary to the diversity of 'des races françaises',
and the Midi remained as independent as it had been in the Middle Ages.
The second was the attempt to narrow the Party into a Parti Ouvrier. In
many regions of France, Lombard argued, it was not the 'pure' workers
(i.e. proletariat) who supported the Party. Where the Party had fought
the elections on the basis of the Minimum Programme alone it had lost,
but where local demands had been added it had scored successes; victory in the Midi had come only with the aid of the petit-bourgeois, if
indeed this term could be said to carry much meaning in the region. (*La
Condition Ouvrière*, Nos. 16 and 18, 18 September 1881 and 2 October
1881). He argued the point further in *L'Autonomie Communale*, a weekly
journal edited by Xavier de Ricard at Montpellier (2 April 1882–31
December 1882). For example: 'Le socialisme doit croître et s'organiser
suivant les milieux, le degré de culture des cerveaux, les allures de race,
les séparations de classes.' In industrial areas the party could be a Parti
ouvrier; in rural areas it should be an agrarian party, and in areas of the
'petit-bourgeoisie' it could ally itself with radical elements (No. 4, 23
April 1882).

For a short period this newspaper ran parallel with another paper
edited by de Ricard at Montpellier, *Le Bulletin du Vote* (1 May 1880–25
February 1883), with which a previous series of *L'Autonomie Communale*
had merged briefly in August 1881. The two papers published identical
articles and often reproduced articles from *Le Prolétaire* and *L'Egalité*
(more often the former) by Brousse, Malon, Fournière, etc. Both papers
lent general support to the possibilists against Guesde and Lafargue,
publishing, for example, Brousse's 'federalist' 'Bases Constitutives du

Parti ouvrier' from *La Bataille* (*Bulletin du Vote*, 14 May 1882), and supporting the anti-Guesdists at the Reims Congress. Lombard and de Ricard engaged in a polemic with Lafargue following a series of articles by the latter in *L'Egalité* on the subject of communal autonomy, at a time (May–June 1882) when it was a major preoccupation of the Party leaders (see, e.g., Lombard's articles 'Contradiction' in *Le Bulletin du Vote*, 14 May 1882, and 'Une Réponse' in *L'Autonomie Communale*, 4 June 1882). Communalism was the central concern of de Ricard who delivered weekly attacks on authoritarianism, i.e. Guesdism, within the Party in the columns of *L'Autonomie Communale*, combining this with a 'pan-latinism' which inevitably placed him closer to Malon than Guesde (Malon joined the *Alliance Latine*, a literary and philosophical review founded by de Ricard who was intimately involved in the 'renaissance méridionale' of this period, in April 1882).

None the less, neither paper was unconditionally possibilist. Thus Lombard, in his *Réponse* to Lafargue (loc. cit.), also criticized the possibilists for failing to build up the Party on an 'economic, historical, and ethnic' basis, and concentrating unequally on *industrial* economic development. While thankful that 'le parti ouvrier s'est échappé heureusement du marxisme' at the St Etienne Congress (*Le Bulletin du Vote*, 3 September 1882), he expressed regret at the expulsion of Guesde and Lafargue. Xavier de Ricard enlarged on the criticism in an article on the same subject in *La Bulletin de Vote*, 22 October 1882, in which he attacked all the leaders of the Party who, based on Paris, had tried to impose a dictatorship on the Party. In the past, he said, the socialists of the Midi had helped the possibilists against the Guesdists (authoritarians); but they had not done so merely to establish in the Guesdists' place 'une dictature sournoise qui procédât par insinuation ou persuasion' (this was an archetypal description of the Broussist faction). The St Etienne Congress was to be criticized not so much for the expulsion of the Guesdists *per se* (the Guesdists would have acted similarly had the situation been reversed, de Ricard said), but because its sittings had come to resemble a session of the Chamber of Deputies and the Party had fallen under the control of a clique of (Parisian) politicians.

It is impossible to state firmly, without further research, that these newspapers were typical of socialist opinion in the Midi, but taken with other incidental evidence a *prima facie* case can be established for saying that they suggest a fundamental divergence between the Parisian leaders of the Party and the socialist militants in the Midi. Not only do they suggest this for the period following the foundation of the Party, but they also reinforce the point made in Chapter 5 that from its very foundation the Party was divided, and the Guesdist group could count on little support other than that granted by Guesde's immediate entourage. The anarchist and federalist tradition predominated.

APPENDIX 6

Programme adopted by the Centre Regional Congress of the Possibilist Party, Paris, 1885

Programme Legislatif

Considérant,

Que l'émancipation des travailleurs ne peut être l'œuvre que des travailleurs eux-mêmes;

Que les efforts des travailleurs pour conquérir leur émancipation ne doivent pas tendre à constituer de nouveaux privilèges, mais à realiser pour tous l'égalité, et par elle la véritable liberté;

Que l'assujettissement des travailleurs aux détenteurs du capital est la source de toute servitude politique, morale et matérielle;

Que, pour cette raison, l'émancipation économique des travailleurs est le grand but auquel doit être subordonné tout mouvement politique;

Que l'émancipation des travailleurs n'est pas un problème simplement local ou national, qu'au contraire ce problème intéresse les travailleurs de toutes les nations *dites* civilisées; sa solution étant nécessairement subordonnée à leur concours théorique et pratique;

Pour ces raisons:

Le Parti ouvrier socialiste révolutionnaire de Paris déclare:

1º Que le but final qu'il poursuit est l'émancipation compléte de tous les êtres humains, sans distinction de sexe, de race et de nationalité;

2º Que cette émancipation ne sera en bonne voie de réalisation que lorsque, par la socialisation des moyens de produire, on s'acheminera vers une société communiste dans laquelle 'chacun donnant selon ses forces, recevra selon ses besoins';

3º Que pour marcher dans cette voie, il est nécessaire de maintenir, par le fait historique de la distinction des classes, un parti politique distinct en face des diverses nuances des partis politiques bourgeois;

4º Que cette émancipation ne peut sortir que de l'action révolution-naire, et qu'il y a lieu de poursuivre *comme moyen* la conquête des pouvoirs publics dans la Commune, le Département et l'État.

PARTIE POLITIQUE

ARTICLE PREMIER. – Suppression du Sénat et de la présidence de la République, Responsabilité effective des ministres avec sanction pénale substituée à leur responsabilité parlementaire. Législation directe du peuple, c'est-à-dire sanction et initiative populaires en matiére législative. Reconnaissance par la loi du mandat impératif et son assimilation au mandat civil.

ART. 2. – Suppression du budget des cultes et retour à la nation 'des

biens *dits* de main morte, meubles et immeubles, appartenant aux corporations religieuses' (*Décret de la Commune du 2 avril 1871*), y compris toutes les annexes industrielles et commerciales de ces corporations.

ART. 3. – Suppression de la magistrature, remplacée par des jurys élus et des conseils d'arbitrage. En attendant, justice gratuite et révision dans un sens égalitaire des articles du Code qui établissent l'infériorité politique ou civile des travailleurs, des femmes et des enfants naturels.

peuple; organisation des milices nationales par région.

ART. 5. – Abrogation de toutes les lois sur la presse, les réunions, les associations, notamment de la loi contre l'Internationale.

ART. 6. – Amnestie de tous les condamnés pour faits politiques et faits connexes.

ART. 7. – Les communes maîtresses de leur administration, de leur budget, de leur police, de leur force militaire et de leurs services publics.

ART. 8. – Liberté entière de coalition pour les communes.

PARTIE ECONOMIQUE

ART. 9. – Instruction intégrale et professionnelle de tous les enfants mis pour leur entretien à la charge de la société, représentée par la Commune et par l'État.

ART. 10. – Repos d'un jour par semaine ou interdiction, pour les employeurs, de faire travailler plus de six jours sur sept.

Au-dessous de 18 ans, fixation de la durée de la journée à 6 heures.

Interdiction absolue du travail de nuit pour les enfants. Pour les adultes, durée de ce travail à 6 heures, les heures en sus devant être payées double.

ART. 11. – Réduction de la journée de travail à huit heures au maximum, avec fixation, par chaque corporation, d'un minimum de salaire. En cas de force majeure, laissée à l'appréciation des travailleurs, les heures supplémentaires seront payées double.

Application du décret de 1848 qui interdit le marchandage sous peine d'amende et de prison.

ART. 12. – Commission élue par les ouvriers pour imposer dans les ateliers et administrations les conditions nécessaires d'hygiéne, de dignité, de sécurité.

ART. 13. – Responsabilité des patrons en matière d'accident, réalisée par une indemnité, conformément aux articles 1382 et 1383 du Code civil, et par une pénalité, conformément aux articles 319 et 320 du Code pénal.

ART. 14. – A travail égal, égalité de salaire pour les travailleurs des deux sexes.

ART. 15. – interdiction pour les employeurs d'occuper des ouvriers étrangers à des conditions autres que les ouvriers français.

ART. 16. – Interdiction du travail dans les prisons au-dessous des tarifs élaborés par les Syndicats ouvriers et Groupes ouvriers corporatifs. Suppression absolue du travail dans les couvents, ouvroirs et établissements religieux.

ART. 17. – Suppression de toute immixtion des employeurs dans l'administration des caisses ouvrières de secours mutuels, de prévoyance d'assurance, etc., et leur gestion restituée aux ouvriers.

ART. 18. – Intervention des ouvriers dans les Règlements des ateliers; suppression du droit pour les employeurs de frapper d'une amende ou d'une retenue de salaire les ouvriers. (*Décret de la Commune du 27 mai 1871.*) Nul ouvrier ne pourra être puni ou chassé d'un atelier particulier ou d'État, hors un jugement rendu par ses camarades de travail.

ART. 19. – Intervention résolue de l'État dans les branches diverses du travail privé, ateliers, compagnies, banques, entreprises agricoles, industrielles, commerciales – d'*abord* pour imposer aux employeurs des cahiers des charges garantissant les intérêts des travailleurs et les intérêts collectifs, *ensuite* pour transformer progressivement toutes les industries bourgeoises en services publics socialistes, dans lesquels les conditions seront réglées par les travailleurs eux-mêmes.

ART. 20. – Annulation de tous les contrats ayant aliéné la propriété publique.

ART. 21. – La surveillance des ateliers, fabriques, usines, mines, services publics, sera exercée par des inspecteurs élus par les Chambre syndicates et Groupes corporatifs, et les infractions aux cahiers des charges, aux lois et aux règlements seront jugées sans appel par les tribunaux réorganisés de conseillers prud'hommes.

ART. 22. – Mise à la charge de la Société des vieillards et des invalides.

ART. 23. – Abolition de tous les impôts indirects et transformation de tous les impôts directs en impôt progressif sur les revenus dépassant 3,000 francs. Retour aux communes des héritages en ligne collatérale et en ligne directe de tous héritages dépassant 20,000 francs.

Programme Municipal

PARTIE POLITIQUE

*La Commune rendue maîtresse de son administration,
de sa police, de son armée.*

ARTICLE PREMIER. – Droit de nomination des maires et adjoints enlevé au gouvernement et élection d'une administration municipale par la Commune.

ART. 2. – Rémunération des fonctions de conseiller municipal et de toutes celles établies par le Commune.

ART. 3. – Ratification des délibérations prises en Conseil non plus par les agents du pouvoir, mais dans les cas importants, comme celui du budget par exemple, par le vote populaire.

ART. 4. – Droit d'initiative législatif donné en matière communale aux citoyens et obligation par le Conseil municipal de discuter, dans un délai déterminé, les projets qui lui seront soumis avec la signature d'au moins 5,000 citoyens.

ART. 5. – Les séances rendues publiques. Affichage des décisions prises au Conseil municipal. Mise à la disposition des électeurs, des Sociétés ouvriéres et des Groupes socialistes des locaux appartenant à la Commune.

Exonération du droit de timbre en matiére de publicité n'ayant pas un caractère commercial ou financier.

ART. 6. – Égalité civile et politique de la femme.

ART. 7. – Introduction en matière judiciaire du principe de l'arbitrage et des jurys élus par les électeurs de la Commune.

ART. 8. – Armement général du peuple. Licenciement des troupes de police.

ART. 9. – Droit de révocabilité du mandataire confié au comité qui a soutenu sa candidature après consultation des électeurs en réunion publique.

ART. 10. – Liberté d'entente et de coalition entre les différentes Communes.

ART. 11. – Mandat donné à chaque conseiller municipal de voter contre toute candidature de délégué sénatorial.

PARTIE ECONOMIQUE
La Commune maîtresse de ses Services publics.

ARTICLE PREMIER. – Transformation en services publics communaux ou départementaux des monopoles des grandes compagnies (Omnibus, Tramways, Bateaux, Eaux, Gaz, etc.), tous ces services devant fonctionner désormais, sinon gratuitement, au moins à prix de revient.

ART. 2. – Etablissement d'industries municipales, par la Commune pour qu'en vertu de leur droit à l'existence les travailleurs, mis à pied par les crises, les grèves et les transformations de l'outillage, reçoivent du travail, et que la Commune s'achemine ainsi du régime de la propriété privée au régime de la propriété publique.

ART. 3. – Création de greniers, minoteries, boulangeries, boucheries; ouverture de bazars, construction de maisons salubres, le tout à titre municipal, pour combattre les spéculateurs au profit des travailleurs.

Cahier des charges imposé aux propriétaires et contenant les conditions de prix, d'aménagements, etc., ainsi que l'obligation de louer aux travailleurs sans condition de métier, de nombre d'enfants ou de paiement anticipé.

Impôt de 20 p. 100 sur les locaux non loués et impôt sur les terrains non bâtis.

ART. 4. – Enseignement intégral, c'est-à-dire scientifique, professionnel et militaire de tous les enfants mis gratuitement, pour leur éducation et leur entretien, à la charge de la Commune, jusqu'au jour où la Nation prendra dans ces dépenses la part qui lui revient.

ART. 5. – Généralisation du service de statistique communale.

ART. 6. – Organisation d'un service public gratuit de médecine et de pharmacie à prix de revient.

ART. 7. – Organisation, par la Commune, de son assistance et des différents services de la sécurité publique. Mise à la charge de la Commune des vieillards et des invalides du travail.

ART. 8. – Suppression des bureaux de placement et création d'un service public de renseignements professionnels.

La Commune maîtresse d'intervenir dans les questions de travail.

1º Par des mesures de garantie;

2º Par des mesures tendant à ce que le travail des prisons et des couvents ne fasse plus concurrence au travail libre;

3º Par des secours donnés en cas de grèves aux ouvriers grévistes pour aider ces derniers à soutenir la lutte contre leurs patrons;

4º Par des règlements interdisant au nom de la sécurité publique, le travail des ouvriers étrangers à la Ville au-dessous des tarifs fixés pour les ouvriers parisiens par les Chambres syndicales et Sociétés corporatives ouvrières.

La Commune maîtresse absolue de son budget.

ARTICLE PREMIER. – Suppression du budget des cultes.

ART. 2. – Cessation des aliénations des biens communaux et retour à la collectivité de ceux déjà aliénés.

ART. 3. – Suppression des octrois et de toute taxe de consommation et leur remplacement par un impôt fortement progressif sur tous les revenus dépassant 3,000 francs et sur les héritages au-dessus de 10,000 francs.

Paiement fait directement à l'État par la Commune du montant des impôts nationaux.

APPENDIX 7

The Minimum Programme, 1880*

Programme électoral des Travailleurs socialistes

Considérant,

Que l'emancipation de la classe productive est celle de tous les êtres humains sans distinction de sexe ni de race:

Que les producteurs ne sauraient être libres qu'autant qu'ils seront en possession des moyens de production;

Qu'il n'y a que deux formes sous lesquelles les moyens de production peuvent leur appartenir:

1º La forme individuelle qui n'a jamais existé à l'état de fait général, et qui est éliminée de plus en plus par le progrès industriel.

2º La forme collective dont les éléments matériels et intellectuels sont constitués par le développement même de la société capitaliste.

Considérant,

Que cette appropriation collective ne peut sortir que de l'action révolutionnaire de la classe productive – ou prolétariat – organisée en parti politique distinct:

Qu'une pareille organisation doit être poursuivie par tous les moyens dont dispose le prolétariat, y compris le suffrage universel transformé ainsi, d'instrument de duperie qu'il a été jusqu 'ici, en instrument d'emancipation;

Les travailleurs socialistes français en donnant pour but à leurs efforts, dans l'ordre économique, le retour à la collectivité de tous les moyens de production, ont decidé comme *moyen d'organisation et de lutte* d'entrer dans les élections avec le programme *minimum* suivant:

A. – PROGRAMME POLITIQUE

1º Abolition de toutes les lois sur la presse, les réunions et les associations et surtout de la loi contre l'Association Internationale des Travailleurs – Suppression du livret, cette mise en carte de la classe ouvrière, te de tous les articles du Code établissant l'infériorité de l'ouvrier vis-à-vis du patron.

2º Suppression du budget des cultes et retour à la nation, 'des biens dits de main-morte, meubles et immeubles, appartenant aux corporations religieuses' (Décret de la Commune du 2 avril 1871), y compris toutes les annexes industriélles et commerciales de ces corporations religieuses.

3º Armement général du peuple.

4º La Commune maîtresse de son administration et de sa police.

* Published in *La Revue Socialiste*, 20 July 1880.

B. – PROGRAMME ECONOMIQUE

1º Répos du lundi ou interdiction légale pour les employeurs de faire travailler le lundi – Réduction légale de la journée de travail à 8 heures pour les adultes. – Interdiction du travail des enfants dans les ateliers privés au-dessous de 14 ans; et, de 14 à 18 ans, réduction légale de la journée de travail à 6 heures.

2º Minimum légal des salaires, déterminé, chaque année, d'après le prix local des denrées.

3º Egalité de salaire pour les travailleurs des deux sexes.

4º Instruction scientifique et technologique de tous les enfants, mis pour leur entretien à la charge de la Société représentée par l'Etat et par les communes.

5º Suppression de tout immixtion des employeurs dans l'administration des caisses ouvrières de secours mutuels, de prévoyance, etc., restituées à la gestion exclusive des ouvriers.

6º Responsabilité des patrons en matière d'acci dents, garantie par un cautionnement versé par l'employeur, et proportionné au nombre des ouvriers employés et aux dangers que présente l'industrie.

7º Intervention des ouvriers dans les règlements spéciaux des divers ateliers; suppression du droit usurpé par les patons de frapper d'une pénalité quelconque leurs ouvriers sous forme d'amendes ou de retenues sur les salaires. (Décret la Commune du 27 avril 1871.)

8º Révision de tous les contrats ayant aliéné la propriété publique (banques, chemins de fer, mines, etc.), et l'exploitation de tous les ateliers de l'Etat confiée aux ouvriers qui y travaillent.

9º Abolition de tous les impôts indirects et transformation de tous les impôts directs en un impôt progressif sur les revenus dépassant 3,000 francs, et sur les héritages dépassant 20,000 francs.

NOTES TO INTRODUCTION

1 The best and most recent source is the *Dictionnaire biographique du mouvement ouvrier français* (ed. J. Maitron), *Tome IV, 2me partie 1864–71, La Première Internationale et la Commune.*

2 G. Lichtheim, *Marxism, an Historical and Critical Study,* p. 224.

3 J. Joll, *The Second International,* p. 24.

4 G. Lefranc, *Le Mouvement socialist sous la Troisième République,* p. 8.

5 G. Lichtheim, *Marxism in Modern France,* p. 15 and *passim.*

6 G. Woodcock, *Anarchism;* J. Joll, *The Anarchists;* I. L. Horowitz (ed.), *The Anarchists;* H. Arvon, *L'Anarchisme;* L. Krimerman and L. Perry, *Patterns of Anarchy;* D. Guérin, *L'Anarchisme.* Guérin's book is the most stimulating of this collection. See also his *Jeunesse du Socialisme libertaire* and the anthology *Ni Dieu ni Maître.*

7 15 May 1882.

8 *L'Internationale, Documents et Souvenirs* (4 vols, Paris, 1905–10). Henceforth referred to as Guillaume.

9 Guillaume to Pindy, 29 May 1908, *La Chaux-de-Fonds,* MS 41; Pindy to Guillaume, 2 June 1908, *AEN* (Carton 3). Also J. Guillaume, 'Un Militant d'autrefois, Paul Brousse', in *La Bataille Syndicaliste,* 6 April 1912.

10 Note by Guillaume on text presented to him by Max Nettlau. Quoted in Marc Vuilleumier, Notes sur James Guillaume, Historien de la Première Internationale, *Cahiers Vilfredo Pareto* (Geneva, 1965).

11 *La Vie Ouvrière,* 20 April 1912.

12 M. Nettlau, *Michael Bakounine, Eine Biographie.*

13 *Der Vorfrühling der Anarchie; Der Anarchismus von Proudhon zu Kropotkin; Anarchisten und Sozial revolutionäre.*

14 E.g. A. Zévaès, *Le Socialisme en France depuis 1871,* which laid the outline for most of Zévaès's later histories of the movement. See also the books by Paul Louis.

15 Quoted in J. Pinset, 'Quelques problèmes du socialisme en France vers 1900', *Revue d'histoire économique et sociale,* XXXVI, 1958, No. 3.

16 C. Landauer, 'The Guesdists and the Small Farmer: the Early Erosion of French Marxism', *International Review for Social History,* 1961.

17 L. Derfler, 'Reformism and Jules Guesde', *International Review for Social History,* XII, 1967, 1.

18 The most valuable recent studies of the International Workingmen's Association are in J. Braunthal, *History of the International 1864–*

1964; J Rougerie, 'Sur l'Histoire de la Première Internationale. Bilan d'un Colloque et de quelques récents travaux', *Mouvement Social,* April–June (No. 51) 1965; H. Collins and C. Abramsky, *Karl Marx and the British Labour Movement, Years of the First International*; J. Freymond and M. Molnar, 'The Rise and Fall of the First International', in *The Revolutionary Internationals* (ed. Drachkovitch); M. Molnar, *Le Déclin de la Première Internationale, La Conférence de Londres, 1871*; J. Freymond, 'Etude sur la formation de la Première Internationale', in *Revue d'Histoire suisse*, 6.30, fasc. 1, 1950; R. Morgan, *The German Social Democrats and the First International*; extensive bibliographies are to be found in Collins and Abramsky, in the *Cahiers de l'Institut de Science Economique Appliquée* séries, 1964 (edition on the First International), G. del Bo, *La Première Internationale* (3 vols, Paris, 1958–63), C. Abramsky, 'Survey of Literature on the First International since 1945', *Bulletin of the Society for the Study of Labour History*, No. 9, Autumn 1964, and Supplement in No. 11. See also the three volumes published by the Commission Internationale d'Histoire des Mouvements Sociaux et des Structures Sociales in the *Répertoire Internationale des Sources pour l'Etude des Mouvements Sociaux aux XIX et XX siècles: La Première Internationale* (3 vols, Paris, 1958–63). Original documentary source material is now easily available through the publication of the debates of the Congresses of the International, and related documents, in *La Première Internationale, Recueil de Documents* (ed. Freymond), referred to hereafter as *Recueil.* See also *The General Council of the First International, Minutes; The First International – Minutes of the Hague Congress of 1872, with related Documents* (ed. H. Gerth, Madison, 1958); *Archives Bakounine* (ed. A. Lehning); Guillaume remains an essential source, while of continuing usefulness is Y. M. Stekloff, *History of the First International.*

19 See also Braunthal, op. cit., pp. 94 et seq., and Guillaume, Part I, p. 2: 'Dans toutes ces sections primitives la conception de l'Internationale était encore fort mal définie. Le mot d'ordre avait été jeté aux échos "ouvriers associez-vous". Et l'on s'était associé, groupant tous les ouvriers, indistinctement dans une seule et même section . . . et l'influence était à ceux qui savaient broder les plus belles phrases sur ce thème d'une vague si complaisante: Dieu, patrie, humanité, fraternité!'

20 *Rapport du Conseil Général, Congrès de Bruxelles, 1868,* in *Recueil,* Vol. 1, p. 260.

21 This theme is fully developed by H. Collins in his *Report to the Colloque Internationale sur l'Histoire de la Première Internationale* (CNRS, Paris, November 1964).

22 J. Rougerie, op. cit. As in England, membership of the International

was virtually restricted to traditional and artisan, not 'proletarian', sectors.

23 ... à chaque intervention de la troupe, les réformistes perdent du terrain au profit des partisans de la rupture révolutionnaire' (J. Freymond, Introduction to *Recueil*).

24 The intellectual debt of these resolutions was primarily to Colinsian, not Marxist, collectivism; the terminology of the debates was pre-Marxist. Thus there was a majority at Basle for a federalist structure of society. See the *Compte-rendu* for the Basle Congress in *Recueil*, Vol. 11. It is true that Marx asked de Paepe, the leading exponent of collectivism, to draw up a resolution on property 'eu égard aux mémoires préparés par les proudhoniens français et belges en cette matière' – cited in M. Rubel, 'Marx, une Chronologie, ler Partie', in *Cahiers de l'Institut de Science Economique Appliquée*, série S, No. 9, August 1965 – and found in de Paepe a useful ally. But it was de Paepe who at the Brussels Congress forced the issue on private property. The concepts and terminology of de Paepe's *mémoire* on property presented to the Basle Congress are certainly not Marxist; if anything, syndicalism can be said to be predominant. The contrast in spirit between the Brussels and Basle Congresses was enormous. Compare for example the Report on machinery and its social effects, which referred to 'La révolution, dans ses démolitions continues' (*Report of Brussels Congress, 1868 Recueil*, Vol. 1, p. 291) with the *Report* of the same section at Basle which said: 'Il est donc de la plus haute probabilité que la transformation de la propriété fera, non par le cours aveugle et fatal des choses mais par l'intervention intelligente et réfléchie des hommes; non par évolution, mais par révolution', a revolution conceived of as a 'secousse brusque et violente' (*Recueil*, Vol. 2, p. 80).

25 For the role of the 1848 radicals in the International see J. Dhondt, *Rapport de Synthèse, Colloque sur l'Internationale,* op. cit., p. 10: 'L'A.I.T. n'a pas été un mouvement de jeunes; ses membres sont très souvent d'anciens quarante-huitards. ... Ils constitueront l'épine dorsale du mouvement ouvrier jusqu'aux alentours de 1880.' See also J. Humbert-Droz, 'Les débuts de l'Association Internationale des Travailleurs dans le Jura', in *Etudes et Documents sur la Première Internationale en Suisse* (ed. Freymond). This was certainly true of the Hérault – see my Chapter 2. As for the Proudhonists, much can be said. The diatribes of Marx against them have been often taken too much at face value. The conflict between 'Proudhonism' and 'collectivism' was far from absolute. *Militants* could hardly be expected to show the intellectual rigour historians have often seemed to expect. De Paepe, for instance, fitted his collectivism into a mutualist framework: '... j'appartiens, comme les

citoyens Tolain et Chemalé, au socialisme mutuelliste qui veut réaliser le principe de réciprocité; mais je ne considère pas l'idée de l'entrée du sol à la propriété sociale comme ne pouvant pas s'accorder avec le mutuellisme . . .' (*Recueil*, Vol. 2, pp. 125 et seq.). There may have been some politicking here, but not much as can be seen by reading other speeches, e.g. compare the speech of Hins, a Belgian delegate, at the Brussels Congress, where he opposed de Paepe over collectivism (*Recueil*, Vol. 1, p. 396) with that he made at Basle, which is virtually syndicalist (*Recueil*, Vol. 2, p. 111). Most of the French *militants* owed their first debt to Proudhon but then accepted collectivism, although diehards such as Tolain and Chemalé often obscured this fact. Again, compare the report on mutual credit read by Albert Richard to the Brussels Congress, in which the works of Proudhon are referred to as 'l'œuvre même de la démocratie ouvrière' (*Recueil*, Vol. 1, p. 352), with his speech at Basle supporting the resolution on land (ibid., Vol. 2, p. 64). It was still the age of doctrine, not dogma, and doctrine still not articulated at a high level amongst *militants*. An illuminating example of the reaction to the Brussels resolution on land at the local level is given in Guillaume (Part I, p. 87), which provides an insight into the 'reconciliation' of mutualism and collectivism. Malon, an autodidact *militant* of the International, described the organization as 'une immense laboratoire intellectual' (*L'Internationale, son Histoire et ses Principes*). A valuable study revealing the dangers of overconceptualization of 'Proudhonism', 'Bakuninism', etc., is to be found in J. Rougerie, 'La Première Internationale à Lyon (1865–70): problèmes d'histoire du mouvement ouvrier français', in *Annali* (Milan, 1961). See also R. Hostetter, in *Annali* (1958); M. Vuilleumier, 'Quelques Proscrits de la Commune', in *Mouvement Social*, No. 44, 1962; and Rougerie, 'Les Sections françaises de l'Association Internationale des Travailleurs', *Rapport au Colloque Internationale sur l'histoire de la Première Internationale* (Paris, 1964).

26 For the Brussels debate see *Recueil*, Vol. 1, pp. 365 et seq. See also Cole, op. cit., p. 126.

27 The effect of the Europe-wide strike movement of 1869 was to lead the International to take a greater interest in trades unions which the Report of the General Council of 1866 had seen as the 'foyers organisateurs' of the working class. Already at Brussels the report of the Brussels section had said that 'nous voyons dans ces sociétés de résistance les embryons de ces grandes compagnies ouvrières, qui remplaceront un jour les compagnies de capitalistes' (*Recueil*, Vol. 1, p. 271). The Report of the Committee on Trade Unions to the Basle Congress, read by Pindy, stated pure syndicalism: '. . . le gouvernement est remplacé par les conseils de corps de métier réunis, et par un

comité de leurs délégues, réglant les rapports du travail qui remplaceront la politique' (ibid., Vol. 2, p. 109). In the debate which followed Hins (who had opposed the Brussels resolution on collectivism on Proudhonist grounds) spoke of trades unions as completely replacing the political structure in the future, while de Paepe said: '... celles-ci [i.e. trades unions], par leur fédération et leur groupement, organisent le prolétariat et finissent par constituer un Etat dans l'Etat, un Etat économique, ouvrier, au milieu de l'Etat politique, bourgeois' (ibid., Vol. 2, p. 87).

28 *Archives Bakounine*, II, pp. 255–6.

29 For a similar statement by Bakunin, see his article 'L'Organisation de l'Internationale', in *Almanach du Peuple pour 1872*.

30 See note 27, above. Hins's statement during the Basle debate included the following: 'L'Internationale est et doit être un Etat dans les Etats: qu'elle laisse ceux-ci marcher à leur guise jusqu'à ce que notre Etat soit le plus fort. Alors, sur les ruines de ceux-la, nous mettrons le nôtre tout préparé, tout fait, tel qu'elle existe dans chaque section . . .' (*Recueil*, Vol. 2, p. 111). De Paepe's article was widely reported in the Internationalist press (*Archives Bakounine*, II, p. 80). The reformist implications of the idea that working-class organizations would gradually provide a substitute for the State are vital for an understanding of Brousse's evolution to reformist socialism. This essential element in anarchist theory has never been fully explored. But see C. Rihs, *The Paris Commune*, pp. 260–1.

31 *Recueil*, Vol. 2, p. 261

32 *Archives Bakounine,* II, pp. 343–4. The post-war situation also destroyed the balance of power within the International. By creating a united Germany the war had removed much of the usefulness of the International for Liebknecht and Bebel (see Morgan, op. cit., p. 215 and *passim*). The Commune and Mazzini's reaction to it greatly strengthened the Association in Italy, where Bakuninism quickly took root (see e.g. Costa's report to the Geneva Congress 1873, in *Compte-rendu du 6ème Congrès de l'Association*, etc., p. 32). It is interesting to note however that the letter of the General Council in reply to the request of the Genevan section of the Alliance for entry, as early as 9 March 1869, had hinted at Marx's aim: '. . . cependant, la communauté d'action établie par l'Association . . . ne manqueront pas d'engendrer graduellement un programme théorique commun' (in *Les Prétendues Scissions de l'Internationale,* in *Recueil*, Vol. 2, p. 271). For a critical evaluation of the pressures which led Marx to the crucial decisions at the London Conference, see Freymond and Molnar, op. cit.

33 The *New York World*, 15 November 1871; quoted in Abramsky and Collins, p. 233.

34 The theory of a Bakuninist conspiracy within the International was developed in Marx's *Communication confidentielle* (sent to Kugelmann in Hanover), of 28 March 1870, and the *Circulaire Privée* of the General Council of 1 January 1870 (*Archives Bakounine*, II, pp. 416–17, n. 146; and ibid., I, Vol. 2, pp. 337 et seq.).

35 *Résolutions des délégues de la Conférence de l'Association Internationale*, etc., Londres, 1871, in *Recueil*, Vol. 2, pp. 233–9.

36 *Circulaire privée du Conseil Général de l'Association Internationale des Travailleurs* (Geneva, 1872).

37 Collins and Abramsky, p. 259.

38 Hostetter, *The Italian Socialist Movement, Vol. 1: Origins 1860–1882*, p. 58.

39 *Archives Bakounine*, II, pp. 137–43.

40 When Hales, secretary of the British Federation, wrote in support of the Jura Federation over its opposition to the General Council he specifically dissociated himself from anarchism (Collins and Abramsky, p. 227). That the decisive issue was the organization of the International, see M. Préaudeau, *Michel Bakounine, Le Collectivisme dans l'Internationale*, p. 315; Stekloff, p. 265; R. Hostetter in *Annali* (1958). Guillaume's speech to the Hague Congress is also significant in this respect: '. . . il y a, dans le mouvement, deux grandes idées qui sont comme juxtaposées; celle de la centralisation du pouvoir dans les mains de quelques-uns, et celle de la libre fédération de ceux que l'égalité de conditions économiques dans chaque pays a réunis autour d'une conception des intérêts communs dans tous les pays. Le mouvement ne peut être l'affaire d'un seul cerveau. La direction du mouvement n'a pas besoin d'un Conseil général revêtu d'autorité. Nous ne voulons pas d'autorité, et, dans la fédération jurassienne, nous n'en avons point. Nous nous fondons sur des expériences. Dans la lutte [grève, etc.] économique avons-nous besoin du Conseil général?' (*Recueil*, Vol. 2, p. 351).

41 E.g. the speech by de Paepe: 'Le débat entre l'Etat ouvrier et l'anarchie reste ouvert . . . Aucune [question] n'est aussi sérieuse que celle qui, sous la dénomination "par qui et comment seront faits les services publics dans la société future" agite en ce moment notre Association. Cette question embrasse toute la question sociale' (*Compte-rendu du 7ème Congrès de l'Association*, etc., p. 223).

42 '. . . the conflict between the factions led respectively by Marx and Bakunin . . . is often represented as a struggle between Social-Democracy and Anarchism; it is more accurately described as the occasion for the formation of these two rival movements' (Lichtheim, op. cit., p. 117).

43 As late as 1876 the *Bulletin de la Fédération Jurassienne* (*BFJ*) rejected the use of the term (Guillaume, Part 4, p. 14), but it became

more frequent during the dialogue with de Paepe over the public service theory (see my pp. 58–61 et seq.) and at the time of the formation of the Swiss Social Democratic Party. According to Guillaume the term was only first consciously adopted in the *BFJ* in April 1877 (Part 4, p. 178). This is borne out by its appearance in a letter from Brousse to Kropotkin of April 1877 (ibid., p. 180).

44 *Recueil*, Vol 2, pp. 281, 295.

45 'An-archie' in its Proudhonian sense was used infrequently. More common was its use in the sense of 'disorder', 'chaos', etc.; this tendency was probably strengthened by its association with nihilism. See J. Dubois, *Le Vocabulaire Politique et Social en France de 1869 à 1872*, pp. 68–9 and 208–10. At one stage Schweitzer's party in Germany was characterized as 'Bakouniniste' (*Recueil*, Vol. 2, p. 359). The verb 'anarchiser' was specifically used *vis-à-vis* action obstructing the Council (ibid., p. 389). On the other hand Bakunin referred to 'nous, les anarchistes' in a letter of 5 October 1872 (*Archives Bakounine*, II, pp. 147–8).

46 *Archives Bakounine*, II, xix.

47 Guillaume, Part 2, pp. 270–7, and *Engelsem–Lafargue Correspondence*, Vol. 1 (1868–6), pp. 24–6. It is significant that the *Bulletin* referred to 'le socialisme autoritaire', and not 'le socialisme marxiste', in discussion of the Spanish conflicts (see e.g. *BJF*, 10 May 1872).

48 Cf. Brousse in *Le Marxisme dans l'Internationale* (see my p. 182).

49 *Mémoire de la Fédération Jurassienne*, 'la côterie marxiste', pp. 204, 208; 'l'intrigue marxiste', p. 246 and *passim*. Bakunin himself rarely used the epithet *marxist*. In his *L'Allemagne et le Communisme d'Etat* (1872) he referred invariably to 'les marxiens' (*Archives Bakounine*, II, pp. 105–19). In his own *Réponse* he referred to 'la politique marxienne' (ibid., p. 123). See also his *Ecrit contre Marx* (ibid., pp. 176 et seq.).

50 C. Rihs, *La Commune de Paris, Sa Structure et ses doctrines*, p. 218.

51 Rougerie, *Rapport,* pp. 12–13.

52 For this section see E. Dolléans, *Histoire du Mouvement Ouvrier*, Vol. 1. 1830–71, pp. 278 et seq.; E. Weill, *Histoire du Mouvement Social en France*.

53 E.g. A. Richard one of the Lyons *militants*, wrote an article in the *Revue Politique et Parlementaire*, 1897, t. XI, on 'les Débuts du Parti Socialist français', which dealt with the period 1866–71 (First International). See also his 'Les Propagateurs de l'Internationale en France', *Revue Socialiste*, June 1896, No. 138.

54 Quoted in Dolléans, p. 347.

55 Ibid. p. 319. Pindy, the delegate of the Parisian Cabinet makers at the Basle Congress of the International, put forward a resolution on property which was frankly syndicalist. (See my p. 278 n. 27, and Dolléans,

p. 337.) For a very useful account of this syndicalist element, brought about by a fusion of Proudhonism with the collectivism of the First International, within the Paris Commune, see Rihs, pp. 223 et seq.

56 Although Proudhon's influence is transparent in the Commune's *Declaration to the French People* of 19 April 1871; Rougerie, op. cit., p. 155, Rihs, p. 219.

57 Rougerie, *Procès des Communards*, p. 160.

58 Dolléans, pp. 377–9; Rougerie, pp. 217 et seq.

59 K. Marx, 'The Civil War in France', in *Marx/Engels Selected Works* (Moscow, 1958), Vol. 1, p. 522.

60 V. Lenin, *Lessons of the Commune* (Moscow, 1954).

61 Marx, loc. cit., p. 542.

62 M. Bakunin, *La Commune de Paris et la notion de l'Etat* (Paris, 1899), p. 8.

63 Rougerie, p. 14.

64 Circular of the Fédération Jurassienne, *BFJ*, 15 February 1873.

65 The Paris Commune itself resulted in the presentation by various individuals of quite often detailed plans for the communal organization of France. See Rihs, pp. 229 et seq.

66 'Report of the Federal Committee to the Anarchist Congress of the Jura Federation, May 1872', *BFJ*, 8 June 1872.

67 Ibid p. 237. Malon, 'Les Collectivistes français', *Revue Socialiste*, 27 March 1887.

68 Rougerie, *Procès*, p. 243.

69 Braunthal, pp. 156–64.

NOTES TO CHAPTER 1

1 c.c. (commissaire central) Montpellier/Proc. général, Montpellier, 1 August 1879, *Brousse dossier, AR Bruxelles, 320.346.*

2 *Archives Municipales*, Montpellier (details in Bibliography). I am grateful also to Mrs Scott-James, the granddaughter of Brousse, for much useful and illuminating information.

3 J. Guillaume, 'Paul Brousse, un militant d'autrefois', in *La Bataille syndicaliste*, 6 April 1912.

4 G. Duveau, *La Vie ouvrière en France sous le Second Empire*, pp. 384, 398.

5 *Brousse Papers*; c.c. Montpellier to Prefect, 22 March 1876, *A D Hérault, 39M.261.*

6 *La Liberté*, 11 and 15 November 1869. In the latter edition Brousse's name appears on a list of subscribers for victims of the Aubin strike.

7 A. Compère-Morel, *Jules Guesde, le Socialisme fait homme*, pp. 1–76, has useful background material on *Les Droits de l'Homme* and *La Liberté*. C. Willard, *Jules Guesde, Textes Choisis*, has perceptive comments on Guesde's political evolution in this period.

8 Dumares (?) to Brousse, 25 May 1870, *Fonds Guesde*.

9 Guesde to Brousse, 14 May 1872, *Fonds Guesde*.

10 Guillaume, Vol. 3, p. 91; and see my pp. 35 et seq.

11 A small correspondence (eight letters from Brousse to Guesde) was found in Guesde's possession in 1878 by the police, *P.Po.BA29*. The letters have not been traced.

12 Emile Digeon, b. 1822, d. 1894. A victim of the 1851 *coup* he returned to his native Aude under Ollivier, and with Marcou, who proclaimed the Republic there in 1870, worked on *La Fraternité* of Carcassonne. He was a delegate with Marcou at Tours of the League of the South West. On 24 March 1871 he declared the Commune in Narbonne and he and his supporters resisted a week before being arrested on 1 April. 'Il reste mêlé à la vie politique de sa province et demeura fidèle à son idéal socialiste-révolutionnaire.' He had worked closely with Guesde in 1870 and became correspondent for Spain of Guesde's newspaper, *L'Egalité*, in 1877. He became a figure of some importance in the early years of the Parisian anarchist movement of the 1880s.

13 *A. D. Hérault, 39M.245.*

14 O. Testut, *L'Internationale et le Jacobinisme au ban de l'Empire*, Vol. 1, pp. 118–19 (letter of 28 March 1870); and c.c. to Prefect, 13 July 1871, *AD Hérault, 39M.245.*

15 G. Duveau, p. 92.

16 Testut, Vol. 2, p. 108. Also *Procés-Verbaux de la Commune* (ed. Bourgin), 1924, Vol. I, pp. 431–4.

17 Testut report in *P.Po.BA/37*. For Testut's activities as a police spy (Agent No. 47) see G. del Bo: 'Lo spinaggio intorne alla Internazionale. Oscar Testut, agente segreto Numero 47', in *Movimento Operaio* (Milan) November–December 1952; also Collins and Abramsky, pp. 310–13.

18 He left some of his papers to Lucien Descaves and they are to be found in the Descaves Collection at the IISG.

19 See Montels to Guesde, 13 December 1872; 30 January 1873; 21 July 1873, in the *Fonds Guesde*, Paris. See also the letter of Montels to Guesde of 1880, loc. cit., see my p. 166. According to Descaves (*Philémon, Vieux de la Veille*, p. 181) Montels was joint author of Guesde's pamphlet *Le Livre rouge et la Justice rurale.*

20 Testut report of 16 August 1879. *P.Po.BA/37*. See also the address book of the Jura Federation (*AFJ*) of 1873 (?) which under the entry 'Section de Béziers' – the only French group named – gives Montels's address in Lausanne where he lived for a short time.

21 Note also *Rapport présenté à la Section de Propagande de Genève, sur l'étude faite par elle depuis le 22 Novembre 1873, jusqu'au Juin 1875,* J. Montels, rapporteur, '*Qu'est-ce que la Commune?*', *AFJ* (22), 2. He was at one time editor of *Tunis Journal* (1885); see his letter in the *Revue Socialiste*, Vol. I, 1885, p. 59. In 1912 he published *Les Pieds dans le plat, Documents pouvant servir à l'histoire future du parti socialiste unifié en Tunisie* (Tunis, 1912). There is some correspondence with Pindy in the *IFHS*.

22 M. Préaudeau, *Michael Bakounine: Le Collectivisme dans l'Internationale*, p. 308.

23 For the French sections of the International, see J. Rougerie, *Les Sections françaises de l'Association Internationale des Travailleurs*, a *Report to the Colloque Internationale sur l'Histoire de la Première Internationale*, held in Paris, November 1964.

24 *Compte-rendu de la Conférence de Londres,* in *Recueil*, Vol. 2, pp. 218–21; also M. Molnar, *Le Déclin de la Première Internationale; La Conférence de Londres*, p. 27.

25 Auguste Seraillier, a shoemaker from Draguignan (Var) 1840–? He was sent by Marx or the General Council to Paris in September 1870 from London to put pressure on the French Internationalists – '... cela est autant plus nécessaire qu'aujourd'hui toute la branche française se rend à Paris pour y faire des bêtises au nom de l'Internationale. "Eux" renverseront le gouvernment provisoire, établiront la Commune, nommeront Pyat ambassadeur à Londres', etc. (Marx to Engels, 6 September 1870). Quoted in M. Rubel, 'Marx et la Première Internationale, Chronologie, 2me partie (1870–1876)', in

Cahiers de l'Institut de Sciences Economiques Appliqués, série S, No. 9. Seraillier read a long report to the General Council on French affairs on 28 February 1871, was elected to the Commune and provided Marx with much of his information on events in Paris. See M. Molnar, op. cit., pp. 65–6; J. Rocher (ed.), *Lettres de Communards et de Militants de la Première Internationale*, pp. 15, 17, 18, 27, 29; and Abramsky, p. 189 et seq.

26 Testut report loc. cit. For Calas, see *Les Droits de l'Homme* (Montpellier), 7 July. 'E.G.' is probably a reference to Eugene Garcin, a former editor of *L'Emancipation*, a radical newspaper at Toulouse (*Gazette des Tribunaux*, 16 March 1873).

27 Engels to Lafargue, 19 January 1872, *Engels–Lafargue Correspondence* Vol. 1, p. 39.

28 Cf. Bruhat, *La Commune de 1871*, p. 302: 'Dans la France entière, par exemple, la cause parisienne a trouvé chez les travailleurs du rail les agents de liaison les plus fidèles: les cheminots ont répandu partout les proclamations et affiches de la Commune.' For Masson's role see *Gazette des Tribunaux*, 16 March 1873.

29 Seraillier to Sorge, 31 December 1872, *Jung Archives, IISG, 981 a/1–3*. The claim for 130 members seems to be exaggerated.

30 London, 1873. The basis of this account appears to be an article by Engels in the *Volkstaat* of 10 May 1873.

31 This circular is mentioned by Guillaume, Part 5, Chapter 2, p. 39. It is probably the circular catalogued in the *Répertoire Internationale des Sources pour l'étude des Mouvements Sociaux aux XIX et XX siècles: La Première Internationale*, Vol. III, p. 191, which is in the Marx-Lenin Institute, Moscow. It has not been possible to consult this.

32 ? to 'Cher Citoyen', Toulouse, 17 October 1872, *Jung Archives. IISG, 951; ibid.* of 27 October 1872; Maitron, p. 84, note 4.

33 Willard, *Jules Guesde*, pp. 13–14; I. D. Belkine, *Jules Guesde et la lutte pour un parti ouvrier en France* (Moscow, 1962), quoted in Willard; Zévaès, *Jules Guesde*, p. 26; Guillaume, Part 5, p. 63; P. Brousse, *Le Marxisme dans l'Internationale*, pp. 27–30.

34 The text of the letter (parts of which are illegible), dated 'Pezenas, 12 mars 1872' is as follows: 'Monsieur le Prefet, Je vous denonce le sieur Calas ouvrier tapissier comme le correspondant direct du Geneve sur l'Internationale il affilie tout le Midi ... compte six cents ... cinq milles Montpellier et Cette jusqu'a St. Pons il est tres energique et une rude adversaire debarrassez nous de ce p ... de la famille et de la societe ou l'ordre est compromis dans nos contrees. Il recoit etrangers la nuit, il est seul, toujours seul, mais il affilie ... debarrassez nous de cet homme' [*sic*.] *AD Hérault 39M.245.* See also report of the Sub-Prefect, Béziers, to Prefect, 19 March 1872, *ibid.*

Mail was intercepted, although there is no mention of Calas's correspondence. See e.g. c.c. Sète Prefect, 11 April 1872, *AD Hérault 39M.251*; also *Gazette des Tribunaux*, 16 March 1873.

35 Seraillier to Sorge, 31 December 1872, *Jung Archives, IISG*. See also Engels to Sorge, 7 December 1872: 'Un plein pouvoir à Seraillier pour la France est *absolument* necessaire si vous ne voulez pas que tout recommence à se disloquer. Seraillier continue sa correspondance avec zèle et nous lui expédions l'argent pour cela, mais il n'est qu'un particulier tant qu'il n'a pas de plein pouvoir et les gens de France veulent décidément, avec toute leur automanie, être dirigés par un fondé de pouvoir du Conseil général. Sorge, *Correspondance*, pp. 118–19. Sorge, *Briefwechsel*, p. 84, quoted in Lehning, *Archives Bakounine, Les Conflits de l'Internationale*, Vol. II, p. 408, note 126.

36 *AD Hérault Tribunal Correctionnel (Béziers), 2U 7d.45; Procès de l'Internationale* (Toulouse, 1873).

37 Quoted in Maitron, p. 84.

38 *AD Hérault, Tribunal Correctionnel (Montpellier), 24 6d.94.* There is slight evidence to suggest that students at the University of Montpellier were active in the International; a police report of 19 February 1872 (*39M.257*) to the Prefect of the Hérault alleged that students at Montpellier had attempted to persuade students at Besancon to affiliate, but this report is marked 'sans suite'. It is, however, worth noting that Michel Sažine (Armand Ross), the founder of the Russian anarchist colony in Zurich and leading member of the Young Bakuninists, went to Montpellier for a period of a few months in 1872, remaining in contact with Guillaume in the Jura who sent him issues of the *Bulletin*. When Gustave Jeanneret was in Lyon in 1872 Guillaume recommended him to contact Sažine in Montpellier. It is possible that Sažine had contact with Russian students at the University. M. Vuilleumier, 'La correspondance du peintre Jeanneret', *Mouvement social*, April–June 1965.

39 Address book of the Jura Federation *AFJ IISG*, also in *Archives Bakounine* (ed. Lehning): *Bakounine et l'Italie 1871–2, 2me partie* (Leiden, 1963), pp. 442–3, note 3. *Le Prolétaire* (Paris), 14 January 1882, letter by Brousse ('mis en relation par le citoyen Guesde avec la Fédération Jurassienne', etc.).

40 *Bulletin de la Fédération Jurassienne (BFJ)*, 15 March 1873.

41 Maitron, p. 88.

42 Cyrille to Castelar, February 1873, in M. Vuilleumier, 'La Correspondance d'un Internationaliste, Victor Cyrille', *Movimento Operaio e Socialista*, anno XII, 3/4, 1966.

43 G. Brenan, *The Spanish Labyrinth*, p. 153, note 1. For the International in Spain see M. Nettlau, *Bakunin und die Internationale in Spanien, 1868–73*.

44 M. Nettlau, *L'Internationale en Espagne 1868–1889* (MSS in *IISG*), pp. 95–6, and *Bakunin, eine Biographie*, p. 746.

45 Camille Camet, a silk worker from Lyons and close acquaintance of Bakunin whom he met in Zurich. He was a French delegate to the St Imier Congress of 1872. He played a central role in the organization of the anarchist movement in the Lyons area and at the 'Complot de Lyon' trial of April 1874 was sentenced to five years' imprisonment. He later became an ardent Guesdist. Charles Alerini, a Corsican; apparently went with Bastelica, on Bakunin's behalf, to Spain in 1868 and was one of Bakunin's most important disciples in France. He was at one time a mathematics teacher at Aix (Provence), and editor of *Le Rappel de Provence*. He founded sections of the International in the South of France and was arrested during Napoleon's sweep against leading Internationalists in April 1870. He took part in the Marseilles Commune and kept Bakunin informed about it. He joined Bakunin's Alliance in December 1871, attended the Hague Congress and was a signatory of the minority protest of 9 September 1872. He was later imprisoned in Spain. When the Zurich colony was broken up in 1873 the Bakuninist fund was sent to Camet and Alerini in Spain (J. M. Meijer, *Knowledge and Revolution*, p. 153).

46 Guillaume, Part V, Chapter 4, p. 90. Full text in Nettlau, op. cit., 3708. For a comparison with Bakunin's disavowal of (utopian) Communism see Guillaume, Part I, p. 75.

47 At one time, Bakunin intended to go to Spain himself ('la révolution espagnole semblait prendre un développement tout à fait victorieux': Nettlau, *Bakunin und die Internationale*, p. 302).

48 *La Solidarité Révolutionnaire*, No. 1. 10 June 1873. Guesde was the paper's correspondent for Italy, through his contact with Brousse (Compère-Morel, op. cit., p. 150).

49 Nettlau MSS, p. 96.

50 *La Solidarité Révolutionnaire*, No. 1, 10 June 1873. The articles were not signed and it is not therefore possible to attribute individual authorship. It is reasonable to assume on the basis of his other known writings in this period that they were an accurate reflection of Brousse's own views.

51 Collins and Abramsky, Chapters XI–XII; G. Lichtheim, *Marxism in Modern France*, p. 14.

52 *La Solidarité Révolutionnaire*, No. 4, 1 July 1873.

53 Although Bakunin *did* see the Commune as almost certain to fail, this was because the provinces failed to support it, not because of the merits or demerits of the working-class movement. For the connection of 1848 and 1871 in anarchist propaganda see e.g. J. Guesde, *Le Suffrage Universel*, in *L'Almanach du Peuple* (St Imier, 1873).

54 *Mémoire Justificatif* (1874), quoted in Nettlau, *L'Internationale en Espagne*, p. 101, note 42.

55 *Le Bulletin de la Fédération Jurassienne* (*BFJ*), 12 October 1873; also cited in Guillaume, Part V, Chapter V, pp. 146–7.

56 It was reflected in the Russian revolutionary movement, for instance. Of the Russian nihilists Venturi says: 'It was only when the theories and psychology of anarchism had been consolidated that this tacit confession of immaturity (the assassination phase) was countered with the declared intention of not wanting a substitute for the State. In other words the anarchists welcomed as an asset what was in fact a symptom of temporary weakness in a developing revolutionary movement' (*Roots of Revolution*, p. 335).

57 Brenan, p. 168 n; J. Joll, *The Anarchists*, pp. 120–1; Hostetter, pp. 321 et seq.

58 *La Solidarité Révolutionnaire*, No. 5, 8 July 1873 (my italics). Articles in the paper were not signed, but in view of Brousse's known later views it is likely that this one (La Propagande révolutionnaire') was by him.

59 See e.g. an article ('Le Socialisme Pratique') in *La Solidarité Révolutionnaire*, No. 6, 16 July 1873, in which it was stated that the way to Revolution would only be opened when the workers realized that 'L'émancipation des travailleurs . . .' etc. See also letter by Guesde (ibid., No. 4, 1 July 1873), 'c'est en se constituant sur son propre terrain etne comptant que sur elle-même que la classe ouvrière arrivera à son émancipation'.

60 *La Solidarité Révolutionnaire*, No. 2, 17 June 1873; No. 6, 16 July 1873.

61 Ibid., No. 7, 31 July 1873: '. . . non, la corporation est un organisme du corps social, mais nous ne pensons pas qu'elle puisse être une arme suffisament organisé pour nous assurer la victoire.'

62 *AEN, Carton 4*.

63 Rihs, pp. 260–1.

64 *Le Révolté*, 1 November 1879.

65 Montels to Guesde, 21 July 1873, *Fonds Guesde; La Solidarité Révolutionnaire*, No. 8, 14 August 1873; Maitron, p. 87.

NOTES TO CHAPTER 2

1 See my p. 18.
2 M. Vuilleumier, 'Les Proscrits de la Commune en Suisse' *Revue suisse d'Histoire*, 1962, t. 2, fasc. 4; J. Joughin, *The Paris Commune in French Politics*, 2 vols, Vol. 1, pp. 83 et seq.
3 Papiers Montels, *Collection Descaves, IISG*.
4 M. Vuilleumier, 'L'Internationale à Genève et la Commune de Paris', in *Mélanges offerts à M. Paul Martin*.
5 Guesde fled from Montpellier in June 1871 and published the first exile pamphlet, his *Le livre rouge de la Justice rurale* in instalments in October 1871. According to Malon (*Histoire du Socialisme*, 1879, p. 378) the French exiles published over 100 pamphlets and books between 1871 and 1878.
6 Malon and Lefrançais were at first members of the central Geneva branch, but were expelled from this when requested – and when they refused – to choose between it and the Section de Propagande. Malon, despite the allegations of the General Council in *L'Alliance de la Démocratie socialiste et l'Association internationale des Travailleurs* (1873), acted as a moderating influence. He dissuaded, for instance, Montels (who was for a period secretary of the Section) from breaking completely with the GC following the London Conference (*Réponse de Quelques Internationaux, Bulletin de la Fédération*, 15 June 1873).
7 *AFJ, IISG*: '... nous, proscrits de la cause républicaine – socialiste ... nous centraliserons les renseignements que vous voudrez bien nous envoyer ... nous serons votre bureau central de correspondance jusqu'au moment où l'établissement des relations regulières entre vos différents groupes rendra notre concours inutile', A. Claris, *La Proscription française en Suisse*, p. 65. For Claris, see M. Vuilleumier, 'Quelques Proscrits de la Commune', in *Mouvement Social*, No. 44, July–September 1963.
8 *Le Réveil International*, 7 October 1971.
9 Vuilleumier, loc. cit.
10 *BFJ*, Nos. 15–16, August–September 1872. In December 1871 Guillaume wrote to Jeanneret: '... la réorganisation de l'Internationale en France et dans nos Montagnes neuchâteloises marche grand train. En France, nous avons déjà 12 départements couverts de sections, naturellement sections clandestins,' Guillaume to Jeanneret, 14 December 1871 in Vuilleumier, *Correspondance de Jeanneret*, op. cit. Vuilleumier is sceptical, but caution is needed in dismissing such talk as rhetoric, as the Hérault example indicates. See also Malon to Roederer, 24 May 1872: 'En France jamais l'Internationale ne fut moralement si forte...', etc. (Guillaume, Part IV, Chapter V, p. 331).

11 *BFJ*, Nos. 17–18 and 20–1, 10 November 1872.

12 *BM, the Chaux-de-Fonds*, MS 41.

13 *L'Association Internationale des Travailleurs, Congrès de Genève 1873, Compte-Rendu officiel* (Le Locle, 1874), p. 52. For other accounts of this, and subsequent Congresses of the anti-authoritarian International, see Y. M. Stekloff, *History of the First International*, and J. Braunthal, pp. 191 et seq.

14 At the Verviers Congress of the Belgian Federation in April 1873 it had been put forward as *the* means to social Revolution and was accepted by the Belgian Federation in August 1873. The *BFJ* revealed a lukewarm response to the idea. For fear of adverse publicity the debate on the Strike did not appear in the *Compte-rendu*; a résumé is to be found in Guillaume, Part V, Chapter 5, pp. 116–19, 121.

15 Ibid., pp. 116–17.

16 Guillaume, loc. cit., p. 121.

17 Ibid. In taking this attitude he was supported by Garcia Vinas and, as Guillaume noted, was almost certainly hostile to the idea as a result of the failure of the General Strike in Barcelona. Similarly, he opposed the suggestion to put the question of the General Strike on the agenda of the 1874 (Brussels) Congress of the Association.

18 *Compte-rendu*, p. 91.

19 Brousse to Kropotkin, 30 April 1877, *AEN*.

20 Op. cit., p. 6

21 E.g.: '. . . la sociologie avec la certitude inséparable de toute science pouvait nous faire prévoir les conclusions qui viennent d'être déduites de la théorie et de l'histoire.'

22 In fact he was quoting from Malon's résumé of Bakunin in his *Exposé des Écoles socialistes français*, pp. 237–8. The *Exposé* was virtually a textbook for socialist *militants* of the International. Malon's diffusion of socialism was exceptionally influential, and Malon himself a far more important figure than is often realized. Like Brousse he became a victim of misrepresentation later. He joined the Bakuninist Alliance in 1869 and became anathema to the supporters of the General Council. He repudiated the anarchists in 1876–7 and then played a leading role in the foundation of the French Socialist Party, aligning himself with the anti-Marxists. Guillaume tended to minimize his role in the Jura Federation – see Vuilleumier, *Correspondance de Jeanneret*.

23 *L'Etat à Versailles*, p. 22.

24 A. Compère-Morel, *Grand Dictionnaire Socialiste*, p. 294.

25 Guillaume, Part V, Chapter X, pp. 235–9. For this section see M. Vuilleumier, 'Les Archives de James Guillaume', in *Mouvement Social*, July–September 1964.

26 Quoted in Vuilleumier, op. cit.

27 Nettlau, *L'Internationale en Espagne*, p. 136. It was certainly not before. Bakunin made no mention of Brousse in his letter to Pindy of January 1873 (see my Chapter 2, note 12), nor was Brousse mentioned in an account of a meeting of the group during the Geneva Congress, recalled to Pindy by Guillaume in a letter of 5 January 1908 (*BM La Chaux-de-Fonds*, MS 41).

28 Guillaume, Part V, Chapter V, p. 141.

29 *Procés de l'Avant-Garde*, p. 15.

30 Guillaume to Brupbacher, 3 January 1912, *Brupbacher Archives, IISG*.

31 *De l'introduction du Marxisme en France*, pp. 122–3.

32 de Wyzewa *Le Mouvement Socialiste en Europe*, p. 69.

33 Letter of 30 January 1888 to Natalie Landsberg from her brother, and correspondence with his mother, *Brousse papers*.

34 Guillaume, *Un Militant d'autrefois*.

35 E. Drumont, *La fin d'un monde*, p. 151.

36 L. Mermeix, *La France Socialiste*. See also A. Zévaès, *Histoire du Socialisme et du Communisme en France de 1871 a 1914*, p. 122: 'Intrigant, subtil, se tenant prudemment dans la coulisse, collectionneur habile de petits papiers, pourvue d'une assez jolie fortune qui lui permet, à l'occasion, d'obliger quelques militants et par là de s'assurer leur reconnaissance. . . .'

37 Marx–Engels, *Selected Correspondence* (Moscow, 1953); Engels to Bernstein, 20 October 1882.

38 J. M. Meijer, *Knowledge and Revolution: the Russian colony in Zurich 1870–1873*; a detailed study of the conflict between Lavrov and the young Bakuninists and of the role of the colony in the history of Russian Populism.

39 R. Feller, *Die Universität Bern 1834–1934*, pp. 292–3. *Verzeichniss der Behorden, Lehrer und Studieren in der Hochschule Bern, 1873–4*, pp. 19, et seq.

40 F. Venturi, *Roots of Revolution*, p. 474. I am grateful to Brousse's granddaughter, Mrs Scott-James, for much of the information about Natalie Landsberg.

41 Natalie died in Paris on 10 July 1910. She left Brousse in 1894 on discovering his liaison with a working-class girl, Julie Josephine Aveline. She refused Brousse a divorce, although this did not prevent them from continuing to see each other frequently. Brousse married Aveline as soon as Natalie died in August 1910.

42 Rihs, op cit., pp. 227 et seq.

43 *Compte-rendu officiel du VII Congrès général de l'Association Internationale des Travailleurs, Bruxelles 1874* (Verviers, 1875). De Paepe's Report entitled 'De l'organisation des Services Publics dans la Société future; Mémoire présenté au Congrès de Bruxelles au nom de la section bruxellois', ibid., pp. 74–163.

44 Ibid., pp. 104–5, and report on de Paepe's speech in the *Bulletin de la Fédération Jurassienne* (*BFJ*), 20 September 1874. See also Woodcock, *Anarchism*, pp. 234–5.

45 Mandate of the Sonvillier section for the Congress, *BFJ*, 20 September, 1874.

46 *Compte-rendu*, pp. 164–78.

47 *BFJ*, 23 August 1874. The report of the Berne section was drawn up by Brousse, who later said that it formed the basis of his later 'public service' theory. S. Humbert, *Les Possibilistes* p. 87, quoting from the second edition of Brousse's *Les services publics et la propriété collective*.

48 A. Schwitzguébel, 'La Question des Services Publics devant l'Internationale', in *Quelques Ecrits*, pp. 117–30. See also for previous statements by Schwitzguébel of this idea, the article in the *Almanach de Peuple* 1874 (op. cit.), and also 'Le Collectivisme', in *Almanach*, 1873.

49 A classic statement of the anarchist vision of post-revolutionary society is to be found in Schwitzguébel, *Le Radicalisme et le Socialisme, Conférence publique*, pp. 24 et seq. See also his *Programme Socialiste: Mémoire présenté au Congrès Jurassien de 1880 par la fédération ouvrière du district de Courtelary;* and J. Guillaume, *Idées sur l'organisation sociale*.

50 Schwitzguébel, 'Gouvernement et Administration', in *Almanach du Peuple, 1874* (Le Locle, 1874).

51 *BJF*, 18 June 1876. Report of speech at Lausanne, 13 May 1876.

52 Geneva, 1874.

53 *Le Suffrage Universal*, p. 12. Some time later he described the transition from capitalist to anarchist society as a transition from 'l'autorité du nombre à celle de la science et de la raison pure' (*L'Avant-Garde*, 9 September 1878). In the 1890s he told Huret, author of *Enquête sur la Question sociale en Europe:* 'Tout ma vie j'ai été saisi de cette fatalité de faits sociaux auxquels il faut appliquer les mêmes principes d'analyse que Claude Bernard invente pour l'étude des diathèses et les phénomènes physiologiques. Je suis médecin, et je pense que le corps social doit s'étudier après les mêmes méthodes que le corps humain' (p.223).

54 J. Guesde, *Le Suffrage Universel*.

55 *Le Suffrage Universel*, p. 44. The Blanquist group in London published its Manifesto in July 1874. See the *BFJ*, 12 July 1874.

56 Ibid., p. 48.

57 See e.g. Brousse's article 'L'Intelligence du Parlementarisme', in *BFJ*, 7 June 1874.

58 *L'Action politique de la classe ouvrière*, *BFJ*, 23 August 1874; 30 August 1874; 6 September 1874.

59 Malon, *L'Internationale*. For Bakunin's analysis of the conflicts within the International see the *Archives Bakounine* (ed. Lehning), Vol. II, *Bakounine et les Conflits dans l'Internationale*, especially 'L'Allemagne et le Communisme d'Etat' (1872), his letter to *La Liberté* of Brussels, and his *Ecrit contre Marx*. But most of this was not published until much later.

60 Kropotkin, *The Conquest of Bread*, p. 188.

61 Kropotkin, *The Place of Anarchism in Socialistic Evolution*.

62 M. Nettlau, *Bibliographie de l'Anarchie*, pp. 56–8.

63 Kropotkin to Nettlau, 13 May 1895, *Nettlau Archives*.

64 L. Valiani, 'Dalla prima alla secunda Internazionale', *Movimento Operaio*, 1954, No. 2.

65 Nettlau, 'Algunos documentos sobre les origines del anarquismo communista' (1876–80). *La Protesta* (Buenos Aires), suplemento quincenal, 6 May 1929. Also Nettlau, *Anarchisten*, pp. 7–9. The original manuscript notes on which this article is based are in the *procès-verbaux* of the Verviers Congress, pp. 15–16, *Nettlau Archives*.

66 Brousse to Federal Committee, 14 May 1874, *AFJ*. See also *BFJ*, 3 May 1874.

67 See the file of correspondence with the Berne section, *AFJ*.

68 *Statuts de la section de propagande de Berne* (1876), *IISG*.

69 Brousse to Federal Committee, November 1874, *AFJ*. In a letter of 14 May he referred to 'le principe autonomist [qui] est la base principale et en même temps la gloire historique de notre fédération'.

70 Paul Brousse to Federal Committee, 19 June 1875, *AFJ*; for rough draft see *AJF II (Divers)*; for the Congress of 1876 see *BFJ*, 20 August 1876.

71 *BFJ*, 18 October 1874; 14 March 1875.

72 Paul Brousse to Federal Committee, 6 December 1874; 14 December 1874, 14 April 1876, *AFJ*. See also, for Brousse's 'dynamism', C. Thomann, *Le Mouvement anarchist dans les Montagnes Neuchâteloises et le Jura bernois*, p. 85.

73 For these events, see Ducrocq to Federal Committee, 27 August 1875; Küpfer to Federal Committee, 28 August 1875; Brousse to Federal Committee, 14 September 1875. An amusing sidelight is a letter from Durcocq (a Brousse supporter) to the Federal Committee of 28 August 1875 in which he says Jarretout, one of the minority, could hardly complain of his exclusion. On 26 August he had not come to the meeting, preferring to stay at home and eat 'un lapin exquis assaissonné avec des champignons succulents'. In short he had preferred 'le lapin à l'Internationale'. Jarretout's life of luxury ended a week later when he was charged with his wife's debts – see Brousse to Federal Committee, 2 September 1875, *AFJ*.

74 *BFJ*, 7 November 1875; 28 November 1875; 12 December 1875; 6 January 1875.

75 *BFJ*, 19 March 1876.

76 Brousse to Federal Committee, ? May 1874, *AFJ*. For its impact in Germany see R. Rocker, *Johann Most, das Leben eines Rebellen*, p. 98.

77 Guillaume, Part VI, Chapter 1, pp. 7 et seq. *BFJ*, 26 March 1876; 9 April 1876.

78 *BFJ*, 17 October 1875; 24 October 1875. According to a police report of 29 September 1875, Brousse had been threatened shortly before-hand with expulsion from the Canton by its Prefect if he did not pro-duce a passport. Brousse refused to produce one – he did not have one – and threatened to make the affair a public issue. The demand was dropped (*P. po. BA/985 Brousse dossier*).

79 *BFJ*, 30 March 1876.

80 *AFJ, Section de Bern* (*Socialdemokratischer Verein*); the statutes are in German with a French translation. There is no date given. Guil-laume, Part VI, Chapter 12, p. 207, says that some rules (referring to the anarchist-Communist group at Berne) were drawn up with the co-operation of Kropotkin, who sent them to Brousse. Nettlau, *Anarchismus*, p. 260, says they disappeared, so that the statutes in the *AFJ* are from a different source – as indeed the position on electoral tactics adopted by them suggests.

81 *Mitglieder Verzeichnis*, loc. cit. Guillaume said that there were also Russian students in the French-speaking section.

82 Nettlau, *Anarchisten*, p. 44.

83 Op. cit., p. 100. Werner translated Brousse's articles from French to German, and Kropotkin also contributed. Reinsdorf, from Leipzig, was executed in Germany in 1884 following the successful organiza-tion of a series of anarchist outrages in 1883.

84 *Arbeiter-Zeitung* (Berne), 15 July 1876.

85 *Arbeiter-Zeitung*, 16 October 1876, quoted in Rocker, p. 102.

86 L. Valiani, 'Dalla 1 alla 2 Internazionale', in *Questioni di Storia del Socialismo*, pp. 180–1.

87 Brousse to Kropotkin, 23 May 1877, *AEN*.

88 Kropotkin to Robin, 29 April 1877, *Nettlau Archives*.

89 Guillaume, *passim*, M Vuilleumier, *La Première Internationale en Suisse*, paper to the Colloque sur l'Internationale, Paris, November 1964, p. 14.

90 Guillaume, Part VI, pp. 31 et seq.

91 *Compte-rendu officiel du XVIII Congrès général de l'Association Internationale des Travailleurs* (Berne), 1876. Stekloff, p. 329.

92 *Compte-rendu*, pp. 65, 77–8.

93 Ibid., p. 62.

94 Stekloff described it as a *memento mori*, p. 331.
95 Paul Brousse to Jacques Gross, 3 December 1876, *Archives Gross, IISG*. See also his letters to the Federal Committee, 10 June 1876; 16 December 1876; 30 March 1877. Brousse wrote no articles for the *Bulletin* between 10 September 1876 and 3 June 1877.
96 Guillaume to Brupbacher, 11 July 1909, *Brupbacher Archives, IISG*. See also Valiani, op. cit., p. 185. See also *BFJ*, 5 November 1876.

NOTES TO CHAPTER 3

1 Joughin, *passim.*

2 The anniversaries of the declaration of the Commune in 1874 and 1875 passed without any special mention in the *BFJ*, while in 1873 Guillaume had called it a pre-ordained failure (*BFJ*, 18 March 1873, and Joughin, p. 88). In 1872 the *BFJ* had published an extremely critical article on the Commune which said that it had set back the cause of the Revolution by several years: '... au point de vue pratique, le 18 Mars a gravement compromis la cause de la révolution, dont l'avènement se trouve, par le défaite de la Commune de Paris, ajourné de bien des années peut-être' (*BFJ*, 20 March 1872).

3 Guillaume to Kropotkin, 30 April 1877, *AEN*. This letter is almost identical to an article he published in 1871 in *La Solidarité* of 23 March 1871 (Guillaume, op. cit., Part II, p. 137), and the sentiment closely echoes Bakunin's views on the superiority of the Latins and, conversely, the reactionary nature of the Germans. The francophile attitude of the Jura anarchists is discussed in Nettlau, *Anarchismus*, pp. 256–7.

4 *BFJ*, 10 May 1874; 25 October 1874; 8 August 1875.

5 See e.g. article by Spichiger, *BFJ*, 15 August 1875: also Vuilleumier, 'La Première Internationale en Suisse', in *Revue syndicale suisse*, No. 9, September 1964.

6 *AFJ*, II (Divers).

7 *Fonds Pindy (IFHS)*, *14AS 130* (224).

8 *BFJ*, 19 March 1876.

9 *Compte-rendu*, Berne (1876), pp. 10 and 97.

10 Quoted in Hostetter, p. 368.

11 Quoted in Rocker, op. cit., p. 102.

12 Guillaume, Part VI, Chapter XI, p. 162.

13 *AEN*, quoted in Vuilleumier, 'Notes sur James Guillaume ... et ses rapports avec Max Nettlau et Jean Jaurès', *Cahiers Vilfredo Pareto* (Geneva 1965). (My italics.)

14 *BFJ*, 26 March 1876.

15 Guillaume, Part VI, Chapter X, pp. 160–1; Kropotkin to Robin, 16 February 1877.

16 Kropotkin to Robin, 27 February 1877.

17 *AFJ, II* (*Divers*) 12. The Manifesto appears to have been drawn up by Landsberg.

18 Guillaume, Part VI, Chapter XI. M. Dommanget, *Histoire du drapeau rouge des origines à la guerre de 1939*, pp. 182–3.

19 This was a workers' demonstration, at which Plekhanov was present, held outside the Church of Notre Dame de Kazan in St Petersburg:

it was broken up savagely by the police and was followed by severe repressive measures. Thirty-two participitants – and one or two non-participants – were sentenced to periods of imprisonment heavy even by the standards of the time. It provided Plekhanov's political baptism, and in Axelrod's views was 'la première manifestation révolutionnaire des masses ouvrières'. See *BFJ*, 14 January 1877 and 25 February 1877 (with cutting from *L'Humanité*, 1906, containing Axelrod's statement – copy in *IISG*). Also Venturi, pp. 544–6.

20 *BFJ*, 25 March 1877.

21 Guillaume, Part VI, Chapter XI, p. 173.

22 Guillaume to Kropotkin, 27 March 1877. *AEN*, Guillaume, Part VI, Chapter XI, p. 173.

23 See for this shift in support the Report of the Federation to the Berne Congress, *Compte-rendu, Berne* (1876), p. 31; it led the Federation to consider – but reject – changing its title.

24 Robin to Kropotkin, 27 March 1877; Guillaume, Part VI, Chapter XI, p. 173.

25 Brousse to Kropotkin, 6 April 1877, *AEN*. Brousse to Guillaume, 8 April 1877. Guillaume called Brousse's expressions of enthusiasm *rodomontades*; ibid, p. 174. The *BFJ*, 15 April 1877, announced the forthcoming publication of a pamphlet, 'Le 18 Mars', with articles by Brousse, Arnould, Vallès, Reclus, etc., but it has not been possible to trace this.

26 The excitement appears to have proved too much even for Brousse's fiery southern temperament. After having given a series of speeches in the Jura on the subject of the 18 March demonstration early in April, he suffered a serious nose-bleed at Guillaume's home in Neuchâtel, and when his normal cure for these apparently frequent attacks failed – the cure consisted of wrapping himself in a wet blanket – he had to be tended by Guillaume and Kropotkin who took upon themselves the unpopular task of keeping him awake for twelve hours until the bleeding stopped. He spent a few days convalescing at Neuchâtel and was then accompanied back to Berne by Kropotkin on 21 April (Guillaume, Part VI, Chapter XII, p. 183). Brousse's enforced absence from Berne occasioned the one known letter between Landsberg and Brousse which has been traced. In it Landsberg wished him a quick recovery and went on to describe a meeting of the Socialdemokratischer Verein which the section had attended on 18 April. She noted the presence of a convert from the Schweizerische Arbeiterbund and said that later in the week a member of the section would be talking on the differences between the various parties in Switzerland, for which she had recommended the reading of Schwitzguébel's pamphlet *Radicalisme et Socialisme*. She ended on the following note: 'Blanche et tranquille je leur ai affirmé que vous

êtes bien soigné, mieux qu'autre part, car à Neuchâtel vous avez autour de vous des personnes à qui vous ne pourriez résister' (letter of 19 April 1877, *AEN*).

27 Brousse to Kropotkin, 1 May 1877; 10 May 1877; 12 May 1877. *AEN*, Guillaume, Part VI, Chapter XII, p. 190. L. Lipparini, 'Chronologia della vita di A. Costa', in *Movimento Operaio* (Milano) 1952, No. 2, p. 188. Guillaume's attitude was very ambiguous. Guesde in *Le Radical* (Paris) had attacked the Italians – for further details see his letter to Marx of April–May 1878, quoted in Zévaès, *De l'Introduction du Marxisme* pp. 92–5 – an attitude which Guillaume attacked as inconsistent with Guesde's support for the Russians in the Kazan affair (cf. Guesde to Marx, March 1880; see my Chapter 5). But at the same time Benevento was the subject of no editorial in the *Bulletin* and remained in the foreign news section; while privately Guillaume called it 'cette invraisemblable expédition coup de tête juvenile d'une poignée d'intrépides' (op. cit., p. 182). The Russian impact on the Western European formulation of the tactic of propaganda by the deed should not be underestimated: 'En réalité, elle (Propagande par le fait) n'était rien moins que la traduction en langue européen de la tactique "populiste-émeutiste" des annees 1875–1877' (B. Nicolaevsky, 'Deux billets . . . de Marx et Engels', in *IRSH*, Vol. III (1938), p. 414). This is exaggerated, but it is worth noting the role played by Kravtshinsky (Stepniak) at Benevento and by Kropotkin and Clemens in the Jura.

28 Guillaume, Part VI, Chapter XII, p. 206.

29 *BFJ*, 5 August 1877; Guillaume, Part VI, Chapter XIII, p. 224; Nettlau, *Anarchismus*, pp. 263 et seq. (on authorship).

30 *Association Internationale des Travailleurs, Fedération Française. Circulaire aux Sections,* 'Compagnons, les événements dont la province de Bénévant. . . .' (*IISG*).

31 Hostetter, pp. 377 et seq. Kropotkin sensed the difference in a note he wrote on one of Nettlau's manuscripts, in which Nettlau had described certain anarchist terrorist activities as essentially propaganda acts; Kropotkin noted that this was essentially Brousse's formula, whereas the acts to which Nettlau referred were acts of *revolt* against oppressive force (Kropotkin to Nettlau, 5 April 1898, *Nettlau Archives IISG*).

32 For the disparity of anarchist rhetoric and action see Guérin, p. 43.

33 Huret, p. 227.

34 P. Brousse, *Le Marxisme dans l'Internationale*, p. 15.

35 P. Kropotkin, *Memoirs of a Revolutionist*, Vol. 1, pp. 197, 200.

36 'Ce fut à partir de 1876 . . . que le virus chimérique et aventurist s'introduisait dans l'anarchisme' (Guérin, *L'Anarchisme*, p. 86). Guerin sees 'L'autogestion ouvrière' as an essential part of

Proudhonist and Bakuninist anarchism, abandoned by Kropotkin, Malatesta, etc., who laid stress instead on the revolutionary Commune.

37 Guillaume's standpoint was reflected in his reluctance or refusal to talk of *anarchie*. In his letter to Jeanneret of 17 January 1872 he said: 'Il y a fort longtemps que, pour ma part, je demande qu'au lieu de dire *abstentionniste*, on dise politique du prolétariat . . .' quant au mot anarchie, je ne l'ai jamais aimé et j'ai toujours demandé qu'on le remplaçat par la *fédération des communes autonomes*.' In a letter to Victor Cyrille of 22 September 1873 he wrote: 'Tu t'étonnes que j'ai proposé aux Espagnols de ne plus se souhaîter *anarchie* et *liquidation sociale*. L'explication en est bien simple. Ce sont deux expressions proudhonniennes et comme telles entâchés d'équivoques de mauvais goût et de rhétorique . . .' (in Vuilleumier, *Correspondence de Cyrille*, op. cit.). For Guillaume's opposition to the Italians in 1872 see M. Nettlau, 'Les origines de l'Internationale anti-autoritaire', *Le Réveil* (Paris), 16 September 1922: also Bakunin's letters to Ceretti and Gambuzzi, July–August 1872, in *Archives Bakounine* (ed. Lehning), Vol. II, pp. 133–5 and 402, Note 112.

38 See J. Joll, *The Anarchists*, pp. 203–5.

39 Guillaume to Brupbacher, 17 January 1912.

40 Guillaume to Brupbacher, 27 July 1907.

41 Woodcock and Avacumovic, p. 157.

42 Although Zhukovsky was a leading member of this community and was the leading exponent of the 'Guillaume tendency' (i.e. reconciliatory) in 1876, publishing a Manifesto to this effect in the autumn of 1876 (Valiani, op. cit., p. 181), the Jurassians regarded the Geneva exiles (French and Russian) with mistrust. Trouble came to a head in 1877 with the publication in Geneva of *Le Travailleur*, a review seen as a rival to the *Bulletin*, and described by Brousse as 'une machine dirigé en Suisse contre le Bulletin et en France contre nos amis' (Brousse to Guillaume, 8 April 1877). It was largely through Brousse and Landsberg that Kropotkin was dissuaded from co-operation on the review (Guillaume, Part VI, Chapter XII, p. 181); Guillaume to Kropotkin, 14 April 1877, *AEN*; Kropotkin to Robin, 24 April 1877.

43 This *may* have led to the meeting mentioned in the Brousse-Vinas letter of February 1880 (Appendix 1), a meeting of which Nettlau says that it probably reflected as much Brousse's and Kropotkin's need for action, and questions raised by the foundation of the French Federation, as any desire to co-ordinate action for the Ghent Congress (Nettlau, Spain MSS, p. 136 n). See however my note 72.

44 Brousse had founded three new sections in Berne immediately prior

to the Congress: the section de Plâtriers-peintres, the section de charpentiers-menuisiers, and the section de langue italienne. These sent a total of eight delegates (out of twenty-one) to the St Imier Congress. There were also sections represented in the revived French Federation. Cf. de Paepe's sarcastic reference to 'quelques sections françaises formées à Berne' in a letter to Malon of 11 October 1877, *Revue Socialiste*, 1913, I, p. 399.

45 '... pour la première fois, le programme anarchiste et collectiviste a été développé devant le public sur tous ses points et dans toute son étendue' (*BFJ*, 12 August 1877).

46 *L'Avant-Garde*, 11 August 1877.

47 The report is in Montels' writing (*AFJ*, 22.4).

48 'Considérant que si la révolution sociale est, par sa nature même internationale, et s'il est nécessaire pour son triomphe qu'elle s'étende à tous les pays, il y a néanmoins certains pays qui, par leurs conditions économiques et sociales se trouvent plus que les autres à même de faire un mouvement révolutionnaire, le Congrès déclare qu'il est du devoir de chaque révolutionnaire, de soutenir moralement et matériellement chaque pays en révolution, comme il est du devoir de l'étendre, car par ces moyens seulement il est possible de faire triompher la Révolution dans les pays où elle éclate' (*BFJ*, 23 September 1877). For Guillaume's comment see Guillaume, Part VI, Chapter XIV, p. 261. See also Stekloff, pp. 338–9.

49 *Procès-verbal* (2me séance) Verviers–Ghent Congress file, *Nettlau Archives*.

50 Guillaume, Part VI, Chapter XIV, p. 260.

51 Text: 'Le Congrès, tout en reconnaissant l'importance des corps de métier et en recommandant la formation sur le terrain international, déclare que le corps de métier, s'il n'a d'autre but que l'amélioration de la situation de l'ouvrier, soit par la diminution des heures de travail, soit par l'augmentation du taux de salaire, n'amènera jamais l'émancipation du prolétariat: et que le corps de métier doit se proposer, comme but principal, l'abolition du salariat, c'est-à-dire l'abolition du patronat, et la prise de possession des instruments de travail par l'expropriation de leurs détenteurs' (*BFJ*, 23 September 1877).

52 De Paepe to Malon, 11 October 1877, *Revue Socialiste*, 1913, I, pp. 394 et seq. For accounts of the Ghent Congress see Guillaume, Part VI, pp. 265–80. Stekloff, pp. 340–8. Valiani, op. cit., pp. 188 et seq. According to some sources the account in Guillaume is inaccurate – see the Bibliography in G. Haupt, 'Notes sur les archives de la Première Internationale réunis par le B.S.I.', in *Mouvement Social*, No. 44, 1963.

53 *La Revue Socialiste*, loc. cit.

54 Maitron, *Le Mouvement anarchiste*, p. 88; Nettlan, *Anarchisten*, p.
  42. The whole question of the survival of the socialist movement in
  France after 1873 is one which has never been dealt with thoroughly.
  It is an area which could profitably be more deeply studied. The few
  indications given here suggest that in many places the *militants* of the
  late 1870s were old members of the International from the period
  1868–70, who kept in some kind of contact with socialist ideas;
  many trades unions had been affiliated to the IWMA. There is a
  Testut report in *P. Po. BA/1476 (Le Socialisme à Marseille)*, dated 18
  August 1875, entitled *Situation actuelle de L'Internationale dans les
  Bouches-du-Rhonè*, which reveals that the Marseille socialists corresponded with the International Bureau of the International and had
  plans to send a delegate to the 1876 Congress at Berne.
55 Brousse to Federal Committee, 8 May 1874, *AFJ*, II.13.
56 Charles Chabert, b. 1818, d. 1890, a metal engraver. He was active in
  the 1848 Revolution and was deported after the 1851 *coup*. He
  returned to Paris and joined the First International towards the end
  of the Second Empire, and was a member of the Comité central
  républicain des vingt arrondissements. Although involved in the
  Commune he avoided deportation, and in 1872 was one of the
  organizers of the Cercle de l'union syndicale ouvrière. He was active
  within the co-operative movement and as well as being one of the
  leading members of the working-class delegation to the Vienna
  Congress. He presided over the first working-class Congress held in
  Paris in 1876, and was a delegate of the Paris Union des Travailleurs
  to the second Congress at Lyons in 1878, at which for the first time
  he came out in support of collectivism. He became an ardent propagandist for the collectivist cause and was one of the first candidates
  of the Socialist Party. In 1882 he followed Brousse, and attended the
  international congresses of 1883, 1886 and 1889. He was elected a
  municipal councillor in 1884.
57 *BFJ*, 16 July 1876.
58 *Les Droits de l'Homme*, 12 June 1876. Quoted in police report,
  signed Ludovic, 17 June 1876, in *P. Po. BA/985 (Brousse dossier)*.
59 *P. Po.BA/25: P.Po. BA/29* (in the series *Congrès*), *Analyse des scelle
  Massard*, 89. Unfortunately there is no trace of the originals of these
  letters. There is one letter in the *Fonds Guesde* which suggests that at
  this time Brousse and Guesde were in contact; Marx to Guesde,
  3 January 1877, in which Marx asked Guesde to ascertain Digeon's
  address *via* Brousse.
60 Kropotkin to Robin, 3 July 1877.
61 Police report of 21 December 1876 in *P. Po BA/25 (Surveillance
  générale des étudiants)*.
62 Rudolph Kahn (a leading member of the Jura Federation based at

Lausanne) to 'Citoyen Langier', 19 December 1876, announcing its publication, asking for help in distribution, and requesting all letters be addressed to Landsberg at Berne. This letter has mistakenly been placed in the file on Malon in *P. Po.BA/1170.* A copy of the pamphlet is in the *IISG* (*Descaves Collection*).

63 The *Almanach* had ten contributors, including Brousse (La Liberté), Elisée Reclus, Arthur Arnould, Oelsnitz, Schwitzguebel, Gambon, Clémence and Zemfiry Ralli. Reclus (two articles) discussed the bourgeois stranglehold on education and law, while Oelsnitz presented the populist legend of Stenka Razin. Ralli's contribution was the most interesting, for he drew a direct parallel between the 'natural' socialism of Russia (in the *Obhschina*) and that of the West in the Paris Commune, defining the Commune as the point of departure – in emphasizing that 'the people must emancipate themselves – for Russian socialism. For further discussion of this see Venturi, pp. 441–2.

64 Jules Montels to Kropotkin, 24 July 1877, *AEN* (3). For the *Nabat*, see Venturi, pp. 417 et seq.

65 Brousse crossed the border into France following a meeting at Porrentruy on 7 January. He was aided by the local Prefect who provided him with a gendarme escort to help him avoid the French frontier police (Guillaume, Part VI, Chapter X, p. 142). In Paris not only was he in contact with Massard, etc., but also with Guesde who was working on *Le Radical*, amongst whose editors it appears that he had 'many friends' (Guillaume to Kropotkin, 2 March 1877, *AEN* (3)); see also Kropotkin to Robin, 11 February 1877.

66 Kropotkin to Robin, 4 February 1877 and 11 January 1877. Guillaume, Part VI, Chapter X, p. 134; Nettlau, *Anarchismus*, pp. 254–5.

67 Report signed '47', Lyon, 8 June 1877 (*P. Po./BA/985*).

68 *Le Travailleur*, Geneva, May 1877–March 1878. Contributors included the Reclus brothers, Ralli, Oelsnitz, Arnould, Lefrançais, Klemens and Axelrod; the participation of the last two was of great significance for the development of Russian populism (Venturi, op. cit., pp. 604 et seq.), while the review itself did much to create the myth of the Commune – see Joughin, Vol. 1, *passim*. The most interesting articles are those of Axelrod attacking the bureaucratic tendencies of the German Social Democratic Party and anticipating Michel's critique by several years ('. . . il s'est constitué une sorte d'aristocratie bureaucratique qui . . . devient une sérieuse entrave au dévelopement révolutionnaire des ouvriers allemands', etc. (No. 1, May 1877 et seq.).

69 It was *à propos* of collaboration on *Le Travailleur* that Brousse and Guillaume dissuaded Kropotkin from association with the group.

70 Jean-Louis Pindy, 1840–1912. A leading Communard from Brest.

He lived at La Chaux-de-Fonds after 1874 and played an important part in administering the permanent fund for deportees of the Commune (Guillaume, Part III, p. 191). He attended the Brussels and Berne Congresses, was secretary of the Bureau federal international 1876–7, was corresponding secretary of the French Federation and was responsible for the administration of *L'Avant-Garde*. His name was useful as a Communard, but he played an essentially secondary role. See also C. Thomann, J.-L. Pindy.

71 *Compte-rendu, Berne* (1876), p. 43.

72 Brousse to Kropotkin, 12 July 1877, *AEN*; also Guillaume, Part VI, Chapter XII, p. 220. He wrote to Kropotkin asking him to instruct Pindy to write to Hubertine Auclert in Paris (later a leading figure of the Société des Droits de la Femme) telling her to found a secret Internationalist group; also, Pindy should write to Jeallot (also of Paris), Ballivet (Lyons), and George (?), as well as the Besançon contacts. According to Nettlau (MSS *L'Internationale en Espagne*, p. 136) the Congress was simultaneous with, or immediately successive to, that of the *intimité* mentioned in the Brousse –Vinas letter of February 1880 (see my Appendix 1). See also Woodcock and Avacumovic, p. 161. Brousse's remarks about the newspapers (see letter) make it, however, difficult to place the meeting of the *intimité* in August – *L'Avant-Garde* had been published since June 1877. For Ballivet's participation, see J. Guillaume, 'A propos du discours de Ballivet', in *La Vie Ouvrière*, 5 July 1910. Early in July 1877 Kropotkin began to make plans to visit Paris in order to arrange for the distribution of *L'Avant-Garde*, and to arrange for the sending of delegates to the La Chaux-de-Fonds Congress. Immediately prior to leaving however Kropotkin received a warning from Ralli in Geneva that the French police had been warned about the journey and that he would be liable to arrest as soon as he stepped inside France (Testut, it is worth noting, had well-informed agents working within the International in Switzerland). Brousse suspected Ralli's warning as a device of the Geneva community aimed against the Jura anarchists, but agreed that the visit should be postponed until after the August Congress, saying that by then the French elections would have been held, followed possibly by a revolutionary situation and a *coup*, in which case 'un homme sur à Paris' would be indispensable. In fact Kropotkin did not go to Paris until after the Ghent Congress. See Guillaume, Part VI, Chapter XII, pp. 219–20. Kropotkin to Robin, 3 July 1877; Brousse to Kropotkin, letters of 12 July and 15 July 1877. The crisis of 16 May and the revolutionary atmosphere it engendered were central motives for the revival of revolutionary socialism, especially in the exile communities.

73 See my p. 31. See also Montels to Pindy, 17 July 1877 (in *Anarchisten,*

45) on the importance of railway workers. The F⁷ series on anarchists in the *Archives Nationales*, Paris, reveals this very clearly.

74 Brousse to Kropotkin, 30 April 1877 and 5 May 1877.

75 Kropotkin to Emile Darnaud, 5 June 1890, quoted in Darnaud to Gross, 20 January 1890, *Gross Archives, IISG*.

76 Kropotkin to Darnaud, loc. cit.

77 *L'Avant-Garde*, 2 June 1877. The State was described as 'le contre-poid' used by the minority against the majority – the same expression as used in *L'Etat à Versailles* (see my pp. 53 et seq.), extracts of which appeared in *L'Avant-Garde*, 15 June 1877.

78 Ibid., 1 July 1877–10 March 1878.

79 Willard, *Les Guesdistes*, p. 14. See also Costa's statement at his trial in 1878 for Internationalist activities in France: 'J'avais formulé avec quelques amis le programme que devait soutenir M. Dupire au Congrès de Lyon,' Bosio and Della Peruta, 'La "svolta" di Andrea Costa' (*Movimento operaio*, 1952, I).

80 Guillaume, 'A propos du Discours de Ballivet', *La Vie Ouvrière*; Max Nettlau to Jacques Gross, 12 September 1912, *Archives Gross-Fulpius*, University Library, Geneva.

81 *L'Egalité*, 10 February 1878; *Le Travailleur*, February–March 1878.

82 *L'Avant-Garde*, 8 and 23 February 1878.

83 Pindy to Guillaume, 2 June 1908, *AEN*. Pindy's recollections were vague and cannot be taken as completely accurate; e.g. the Internationalists had been tried for *droit commun* offences and thus could not expect preferential treatment. Moreover, Pindy says Brousse returned to Berne after a second intervention by Schwarzenbach with the authorities. This is highly unlikely, and Brousse himself said at his 1879 trial that he went to live in Zurich. Pindy seems on this point to have confused 1875 and 1877.

84 Blum, p. 22.

85 Guillaume, Part VI, p. 305.

86 Nettlau, *Anarchismus*, p. 273. Brousse was delegate of the Zurich section at the 1878 Fribourg Congress of the Federation; and Guillaume, Part VI, p. 289, Note 1.

87 Although the Berne authorities, acting on rumour, brought in troops to deal with an expected influx of 2,000 Communard refugees and sympathizers. Amidst great excitement they arrested a man at the railway station thought to be carrying the red flag wrapped in a cloth. The bundle turned out to contain nothing more subversive than dirty underwear, *BFJ*, 25 May 1878; *L'Avant-Garde*, 24 March 1878.

88 *Procès-verbaux de la Fédération Jurassienne*, Séance 23 May 1878, *AEN*.

89 Kropotkin to Robin, 1 November 1879.

90 *Procès-verbaux*, loc. cit., 12 June 1878; *L'Avant-Garde*, 29 July 1878.

91 *L'Avant-Garde*, 12 August 1878, 9 September 1878.

92 In an article published in the Zurich review *Die Neue Gesellschaft*, February 1878, Brousse had reviewed Arthur Arnould's *L'Etat et la Révolution*. While fully endorsing Arnould's arguments against the State, and the entire political aspect of Arnould's critique, he criticized it for its lack of economic arguments in favour of an anarchist society, refuting the argument often made that anarchism was incompatible with industrial production processes: 'l'autonomie du groupe doit obéir aux lois scientifiques de la production . . . la loi de la division du travail qui a pour suite la spécialisation des industries et les bornes posées à la puissance des machines offre un champ immense à la réalisation des principes d'autonomie' (*BFJ*, 18 February 1878).

93 In the *Mémoire de district de Courtelary* (Geneva, 1880) Schwitzguébel was to argue that if the anarchists could not enter into the sphere of governmental action without denying their anarchist principles, at least 'nous pourrons et devons être parti de l'introduction des revendications économiques des classes travailleuses dans la Commune' because 'ce n'est qu'autour d'intérêts immediats, locaux et regionaux, que se grouperont les masses' (pp. 18–19). This *mémoire* is also significant in showing the increased emphasis on the Commune as the unit of social reorganization and regeneration, the result largely of Kropotkin's Report noted above. Guérin, *L'Anarchisme*, p. 70, points out that the report fails to resolve the contradiction within the anarchist movement between syndicalism and communalism.

94 *Le Révolté*, 1 November 1879 ('Idée anarchiste au point de vue de sa réalisation pratique'). A translation of this appeared in *Freedom*, 1967.

95 A series of articles entitled 'L'Attitude politique du parti Démocrate socialiste de l'Allemagne' appeared in *L'Avant-Garde*, Nos. 34–7, 9 September–21 October 1878. It criticized the absorption of socialist by bourgeois republican demands in the Programme of the Party at the 1878 elections, and contrasted the weakness of Bebel and Liebknecht in the face of Government repression with the attitude of Guesde at the suppression of the Paris International Socialist Congress. The articles placed the German Empire at a stage of historical development equivalent to that of France in 1848, with Liebknecht playing the role of Louis Blanc. In *L'Avant-Garde*, 6 May 1878, there was a forthright condemnation of the electoral tactics of the Social Democrats on the grounds that it caused demoralization. The Fribourg Congress condemned the tactics of the German Party in its resolution on the question (the attitude of the anarchists towards State socialism).

96 Hostetter, pp. 412–45.
97 From about 1876–7 the *sections de métier* had broken away from the central (political) sections of the Jura Federation. This was accompanied by a 'refroidissement idéologique'; A Sergent and C. Harmel, *Histoire de l'Anarchie*, p. 446; see also C. Thomann, *Le Mouvement anarchiste*, Chapter IX, pp. 224–6.
98 Kropotkin to Robin, 4 August 1878; 1 November 1878.
99 B. Malon, *Histoire du Socialisme*, Vol. V (1883), p. 140: 'L'Avant-Garde fut surtout régicide; elle marque une recrudescence des intrigues et la décadence rapide du parti anarchiste.'
100 *L'Avant-Garde*, 3 June 1878 (Correspondance d'Allemagne).
101 Ibid., 18 November 1878.
102 *Le Citoyen*, 22 March 1881.
103 Kropotkin to Robin, 17 January 1879.
104 Report of Morel, Procureur-général, to the Conseil Fédéral. Archives fédérales suisse (Bundesarchiv), *Polizeidienst, Dossier Avant-Garde/Brousse. Pièce 170*, 38 pp. p. 25: *Polizeidienst 1889–1920, Bd.80 (Berne)*.
105 Nettlau, *Anarchismus*, p. 273.
106 *Polizeidienst, Pièce 5*. The action in going over the heads of the Neuchâtel authorities caused a subsidiary conflict between the Canton and the Federal Government. It was widely believed that the suppression of the paper was the result of diplomatic pressure and *The Times*, for example, reported that it followed representations from four foreign powers (*The Times*, 13 December 1878). This the Government denied – it had little alternative – but reaction abroad was clearly a main motive in their action; on 11 December the Department of Police and Justice circulated details to Swiss Embassies in Berlin, Vienna, Paris and Rome. The Swiss Government were extremely embarrassed by the influx of German socialist refugees following Imperial oppression in 1878, and at the beginning of December the Department of Police and Justice circulated the police in nine Cantons asking their co-operation in the supervision of the activities of exiles. The *l'Avant-Garde* affair marked the beginning of the departure from the traditional Swiss tolerance of political refugees, and from the beginning of 1879 the Swiss Government began to expel anarchists and socialists who were liable to cause friction with foreign powers. The Swiss were particularly sensitive to the reactions of Bismarckian Germany. This led Schwitzguébel to publish a short trenchant attack on the Federal Government in his *La Police politique fédérale* (Geneva, 1879). In 1885 the Government ordered an inquiry into anarchist activities; carried out by the Procureur général it was remarkably liberal-minded in its conclusion that 'le moyen le plus efficace de combattre l'anarchisme est de faire

droit d'une manière aussi large que possible à celles des reclamations de la classe laborieuse qui sont marqués au coin de la justice. L'Anarchisme n'est pas un pur effet d'hasard ...' (*Rapport du Procureur général ... sur les menées anarchistes en Suisse,* mai–juin 1885, in *Feuille fédérale suisse* (extrait), année XXXVII, Vol. III, pp. 487–665).

107 *The Times,* 20 December 1878.
108 J. Langhard, *Die Anarchistische Bewegung in der französischer Schweiz,* Chapter XV, pp. 126–30. Also *Polizeidienst, passim.*
109 *Polizeidienst, Pièce 15.*
110 Kropotkin to Robin, 17 January 1879, *Nettlau Archives.*
111 *Polizeidienst, Pièce 170,* p. 6.
112 For an account of the trial see *Procès de l'Avant-Garde,* 1879.
113 Ibid., p. 45. Brousse intended to develop the argument in favour of anarcho-Communism.
114 See Note 106 above.
115 17 March 1879, quoted in Langhard, p. 135.
116 The costs amounted to 1665 francs (*Polizeidienst, Pièce 93*). The sentence was reported in *The Times,* 19 April 1879. Following Brousse's imprisonment the paper carried reports of several demands from Russia for the extradition of nihilists. On 24 March 1879 for instance its Geneva correspondent reported that the *Journal de St Petersburg* had alleged Switzerland was a hive of criminals and regicides.
117 *The Times,* 28 April 1879.
118 *Journal de Genève,* 27 February 1886.
119 Kropotkin to Robin, 3 January 1879; 10 April 1879; 17 January 1879; 29 January 1879.
120 P. Kropotkin, 'Comment fut fondé Le Révolté', in *Les Temps Nouveaux,* 20 and 26 February 1904.
121 *Le Révolté,* 22 February 1879.
122 *Polizeidienst, Pièces 131, 132;* and Brousse to Robin, 15 June 1879.

NOTES TO CHAPTER 4

1 The letters were first brought to light by Marc Vuilleumier in his article 'Paul Brousse et son passage de l'anarchisme au socialisme', in *Cahiers Vilfredo Pareto* (Geneva), Vols. 7–8, 1965. This article gives extensive quotations from the correspondence with Jeannerret, leaving out nothing of any great significance. I am grateful however to M. Blaise Jeanneret, the son of Gustave Jeanneret, for allowing me to look at the letters which include one or two notes from Landsberg to Jeanneret's parents. For the full (or almost full) texts of letters, see Vuilleumier, op. cit.

2 Brousse to Jeanneret, 27 June 1879 (note by Landsberg).

3 A. Breton to G. Jeanneret, 11 June 1879; Brousse to Robin, 15 June 1879.

4 Brousse to Jeanneret, 4 July 1879; 16 July 1879.

5 Brousse to Jeanneret, 10 August 1879.

6 Brousse to Jeanneret, 4 July 1879.

7 Report of comm. de police, Verviers, 25 July 1879, *Archives générales du Roxaume, Bruxelles, Police des Etrangers, 320.346.*

8 The Brussels section of the International published a Manifesto (*Protestation contre l'expulsion des citoyens Johann Most . . . et Paul Brousse*) against the expulsions. See also *Le Prolétaire*, 23 August 1879.

9 Brousse to Jeanneret, 18 November 1878.

10 He lived for a short while at 52 Kenton Street, Brunswick Square, then moved to 41 Bayham Street, Camden Town.

11 See *Le Révolté*, 18 October 1879; and Brousse to Jeanneret, 18 November 1879.

12 Hostetter, p. 376.

13 Quoted in Bosio and Della Peruta, 'La "svolta" di Andreas Costa, con documenti sul soggiorno in Francia', in *Movimento Operaio*, 1952, 1, pp. 298–307.

14 Hostetter, pp. 414–17.

15 Costa's activities in Paris and his differences with the anarchist group there were reported back to Pindy in Switzerland as secretary of the French Federation. Precisely what the difference was about is not clear. Hostetter (p. 413) suggests it was because of Costa's contact with Guesde, etc., but it may well have been over Costa's notorious indiscretion (leading eventually to his arrest) which led Guillaume to write and threaten him with expulsion from the *intimité* (Nettlau, *Anarchismus*, p. 271, note 290), Guillaume (Part VI, p. 321). In any case it led Brousse to write to Chopart, one of the Paris anarchists, suggesting that if many had complaints about Costa they should

form a new group (Bosio and Della Peruta, op. cit.). See my Appendix 1 for Brousse's letter to Vinas.

16 Hostetter, p. 410.

17 Guillaume to Brupbacher, 12 February 1912.

18 Hostetter, p. 408.

19 Bernstein (op. cit. pp. 98–9) says for example that: 'In 1879 he went to London where he met Marx, and the change in his ideology commenced. He eventually abandoned anarchism for socialism.'

20 Nettlau, *Anarchismus*, p. 288.

21 Karl Marx, *Oeuvres* (ed. Rubel), *Economie I* (Paris, 1963), p. clxviii.

22 *La Crise, sa Cause, son Remède* (Geneva, 1879). Following an expression used by Brousse in the first of the series in *Le Révolté*, 'nos petits juifs de l'époque', there was an outburst of anti-semitic opinion in the columns of the paper (see e.g. 6 September, 4 October 1879) to which Brousse referred in a letter to Jeanneret of 7 April 1879. In an article published in *Le Travail* entitled 'L'Industrie horlogère et les horloges pneumatiques' (op. cit., No. 2) he referred at one point to 'la baudeville des juifs agioteurs'. The crisis in the Jura engendered an amount of anti-semitism, which was not rare in the socialist movement, but Brousse's attitude at this time should be compared with his Introduction to Lombroso's *L'Antisémitisme* (Paris, 1899), published at the height of the Dreyfus affair. Brousse also wrote a pamphlet, anonymously, on *Libre Echange et Protectionisme* (Geneva, 1879), in which both free trade and protectionism were attacked as bourgeois panaceas. The pamphlet may well have been published in view of the dissension on free trade and protectionism at the Marseilles Congress. See *Compte-rendu* (Marseilles), Séance, pp. 671 et seq.

23 See e.g. I. L. Horowitz (ed.), *The Anarchists*: 'If anything, nineteenth and twentieth century forms of anarchism are a self-conscious "minority" report on the progress of man in contrast to the "majority" report filed by the Marxists' (pp. 22–3).

24 *Le Travail*, No. 1, April 1880.

25 *Le Marxisme dans l'Internationale*, pp. 13–14.

26 'La conception matérialiste de l'histoire', *La Bataille* (Paris), 28 May 1882; and *Le Prolétaire*, 14 April 1883.

27 Cf. N. McInnes, 'Les debuts du marxisme théorique en France et en Italie', in *Cahiers de l'Institut de Sciences Economiques Appliquées*, loc. cit.

28 Leo Hartmann, a suspected would-be assassin of Alexander II and a leading member of the Russian socialist movement, who contributed to Brousse's *Le Travail*. In February 1880 when he was in Paris the Russian Government requested his extradition, and he was arrested, but following protests he was released, expelled and went to London. For Brocher, see Nettlau, *Anarchisten*, pp. 181–3. Little is yet known

about the London exile community; Valiani, op. cit. is the best
source. Details can occasionally be found in foreign publications
where appeals were made for Communard exiles. Soho was the main
residential centre. For the Circolo see its manifesto dated 3 June
1878; also a prospectus ('Biblioteca di Studi Sociali') in *Jung Archives,
IISG*. Some of the thirty-nine tried in Paris in 1878 were found in
possession of its Programme (*Le Congrès ouvrier socialiste internationale devant le 10 Chambre*, p. 67).

29 *La Guerre Sociale*, Nos. 1–4, 2 October 1878–2 November 1878.

30 Nettlau, *Anarchismus*, p. 288, note 2. See letter Brousse to Brocher of
4 June 1880 – just prior to his departure for Paris – asking Brocher to
show him round the British Museum 'au moins une fois avant mon
départ' (Dossier Congrès Verviers–Ghent 1877 in *Nettlau Archives,
IISG*) It was probably through Brocher that he met Herman Jung to
whom he wrote in April 1880 announcing the publication of *Le
Travail* and offering him the use of its columns (Brousse to Jung, 12
April 1880, *Jung Archives, IISG*).

31 Brousse to Jeanneret, 28 December 1879: Brousse to Guesde, 28
December 1879; Brousse to Jeanneret, 16 January 1880. (In this
letter Brousse did mention that Zanardelli's 'certain and continued
presence' in London would be of great value.) The Brousse–Vaughan
correspondence at the *IISG* is also relevant to the setting up of *Le
Travail*.

32 *Gross Archives, IISG*.

33 Brousse to Jules Loetscher(?), 27 March 1880; and Brocher to
Nettlau, 22 April 1924, *Nettlau Archives*; also Nettlau, *Anarchisten*,
p. 182.

34 Brousse to Jeanneret, 7 April 1880.

35 A reference to Brousse's own articles on the watch-makers in *La
Crise*.

36 For the *Revue* see my Chapter 5. At the same time Costa brought out
a similar 'integrationist' magazine, published monthly, the *Rivista
Internazionale del Socialismo* (Milan), in May 1880. Copies Vol. 1,
Nos. 1–6 (May–October 1880) and Vol. 2, Nos. 1–2 (November–
December 1880) are in the British Museum. It had an impressive list
of collaborators who included (at least nominally) Bernstein,
Bertrand, Borde, Brousse, de Paepe, Dragomanov, Gnocchi-Viani,
Guesde, Kachelhofer, Lavrov, Lombard, Massard, Merlino, Malon,
de Ricard and Vollmar. It recommended *La Revue Socialiste* to its
readers, and said: 'Il socialismo per noi non e un sistema, ma la piu
ampia espressione della perfectibilita del'uomo'. It defined its aim as
to 'offrira . . . une libera tribuna a chiunque voglia discutere in buona
fede i problemi sociali'. Articles by Dragomanov (No. 1), Metchin-
koff (No. 4), Arnould (No. 5), Reclus (ibid.), and Lefrançais (Vol. 12,

No. 2) were taken from articles which had appeared in *Le Travailleur* (Geneva), 1877–8. Other articles included a study by Borde of Colins's contribution to socialism, de Paepe on surplus value, Pistolesi on Marx's theory of value and on Saint-Simon, and Reclus on evolution and Revolution, as well as several articles by Gnocchi-Viani, and by Costa on the Italian socialist movement. Brousse contributed one article (No. 3, July 1880) on property. For the foundation of the review, see Hostetter, p. 421.

37 Brousse to Jeanneret, 8 May 1880.

38 Vuilleumier, op. cit., p. 76, note 26.

39 Police Report, 10 June 1880, *P.Po.BA/985*; Zanardelli to Guesde, 10 June 1880, *Fonds Guesde*, Paris. There is a complicated correspondence Zanardelli–Guesde/Deville and Malatesta–Guesde/Deville over a dispute between the two Italians which apparently demanded a duel. The outcome is unclear, but on 10 June 1880 Zanardelli wrote that Malatesta had asked him to get in touch *via* Brousse 'avec lequel je suis brouillé et qui est très lié avec Malatesta'. Brocher, on the other hand (to Nettlau, loc. cit.) said that Brousse feared Malatesta getting hold of *Le Travail*, and called him a fanatic.

40 *AD Hérault, 39M.261.*

41 *Quelques Mots sur les Etudes de Fruit* (Montpellier, 1880).

42 Malon to Guesde, 23 August 1880, *Fonds Guesde*; Lafargue to Guesde, August 1880, *Guesde Archives, IISG* (550/3).

43 Police Report, 13 October 1880, *P.Po.BA/985.*

44 Brousse to Jeanneret, 3 October 1880.

NOTES TO CHAPTER 5

1 The main works are: A. Zévaès, *Le Socialisme en France depuis 1871; De la Semaine sanglante au Congrès de Marseille; Les Guesdistes; De l'Introduction du Marxisme en France:* P. Louis, *Histoire du Socialisme en France;* L. de Seilhac, *Les Congrès ouvriers en France 1876–1897;* D. Ligou, *Histoire du Socialisme en France;* A. Noland, *The Founding of the French Socialist Party;* S. Bernstein, *The Beginnings of Marxian Socialism in France;* C. Mauger, *Les Débuts du Socialisme Marxiste en France;* E. Dolléans, *Histoire du Mouvement ouvrier 1871–1920:* O. Zetkin, *Der Sozialismus in Frankreich seit der Kommune,* a German version of the Guesde–Lafargue pamphlet: R. Joucla, 'Renaissance du Mouvement ouvrier français après la Commune', *Cahiers Internationaux,* 1955. Above all in the establishment of this orthodoxy was Engels. See e.g. his letters to Bernstein of 20 and 25 October 1882 in *Die Briefe von Engels an Eduard Bernstein.*
2 E.g. 'la scission intervenue à Saint-Etienne est l'oeuvre de Paul Brousse'. A. Zévaès, *Histoire du Socialisme et du Communisme en France de 1871 à 1914,* p. 20.
3 Engels and Lafargue, *Correspondance.* C. Willard, *Jules Guesde, Textes Choisis,* and *Le Mouvement Socialiste en France: Les Guesdistes.* N. McInnes, 'Le Débuts du Marxisme théorique en France et en Italie (1880–1897)' in *Cahiers de l'Institut de Science économique appliqué,* serie S, *Cahiers de Marxologie,* No. 3, June 1960: also 'Les Partis socialistes français 1880–1885, Lettres et extraits des lettres d'Engels à Bernstein', ibid, No. 4, January 1961; G. Lichtheim, *Marxism in Modern France.*
4 Baron Hippolyte de Colins, a Belgian (1783–1859), produced a socialist system with common ownership of the land as its cornerstone; see G. D. H. Cole, *A History of Socialist Thought: Marxism and Anarchism,* pp. 57 et seq.
5 B Malon, 'Le Collectivisme en France de 1875 à 1879 (Les Collectivistes en France'), in *Revue Socialiste,* 1886, Vol. 2. Also Bernstein, The *Beginnings of Marxian Socialism* (op. cit. pp. 105–8). *Le Prolétaire* is discussed on my pp. 154–5. The Colinsian group at least provided the counterpoint against, and environment within which, *militants* articulated their own socialism. Fournière later recalled the debate on Colinsian socialism which took place in the columns of *Le Prolétaire.* In a letter to Borde, one of the leading French exponents of de Colins, he said: 'Cette discussion . . . m'est chère car c'est elle qui a attiré sur moi l'attention de celui qui devait former et diriger ma pensée. Autant qu'il m'en souvienne je soutenais l'orthodoxie marxiste d'une manière hétérodoxe et j'avais fait à Delaporte [another exponent of de Colins] de très grandes concessions, notam-

ment sur l'impossibilité de l'accumulation capitaliste dans des mains individuelles en régime d'appropriation sociale de la propriété immobilière ... c'est cette discussion qui me mit en rapport avec Benoit Malon...' (Fournière to Borde, 3 February 1904, *Fonds Fournière, IFHS, 14 AS 181*). Yet at other times Fournière described himself as a disciple of Guesde; see J. Raymond, 'E. Fournière', in *L'Actualité de l'Histoire* (Paris), No 25, 1958.

6 A. Moutet, 'Le Mouvement ouvrier à Paris du lendemain de la Commune au premier congrès syndical en 1876', *Mouvement Social*, 58, January–March 1967.

7 See e.g. Dufaure's Senate speech of 21 March 1876, quoted in Joughin, op. cit., Vol. 1, p. 104. Also my Chapter 3, p. 102.

8 M. Perrot, 'Le premier journal marxiste français: L'Egalité de Jules Guesde', in *L'Actualité de l'Histoire*, July–September 1959. Guesde's pamphlet, *La Loi des Salaires*, openly acknowledged the debt to Lassalle, and made the *loi d'airain* the conclusive proof of the need for Revolution: 'la cinquième et dernière conséquence ... est d'ordre *conclusif*... c'est la nécessité ... pour les prolétaires ... de sortir du salariat comme ils sont sorti de l'esclavage et du servage. En dehors de l'abolition du salariat dont ils connaissent desormais la loi ... susceptible d'aucune amélioration, ils n'ont devant eux que la perspective d'une misère eternelle ... (ibid. pp. 30–1). Malon gave an account of Lassalle in his *Histoire du Socialisme* and translated Lassalle's *Bastiat-Schulze Delitsch* under the title of *Capital et Travail* in 1880. This was reviewed in *Le Prolétaire* of 17 February 1880 by Prudent Dervillers, who called it 'le manuel de socialisme'. He also popularized Guesde's earlier exposition – see *Le Prolétaire*, 25 December 1878. See also A. le Roy, *Réflexions sur le Programme du Parti Ouvrier*, p. 16. In Malon's *Le Nouveau Parti* (Vol. 1, 1881) it is the cornerstone of his proof for the need to abolish the 'salariat'. The Congrès du Centre, 1880, passed a resolution on this subject, revealing the effective penetration of the theory; *Le Prolétaire*, 31 July 1880.

9 *Catéchisme* (Bruxelles, 1878), p. 83; *L'Avant-Garde*, 23 September 1878. When the Jura Federation discussed in 1878 the need for an anarchist 'textbook' it was suggested that the *Catéchisme* was sufficient. In fact the *Catéchisme* was written in 1872 in Rome when Guesde was strongly under the influence of anarchism.

10 E. J. Fournière, *La Crise Socialiste*, pp. 41–2. The anarchist influence, combined with extremist language encouraged by the amnesty campaign, led *L'Egalité* to send an address to the Gotha Congress of 1878 from which *Vorwärts* dissociated itself as too violent: Malon, *Le Collectivisme en France*. Fournière himself could be extremely violent in language as his performance at the Marseille Congress

revealed. He remained however totally within a French tradition. He defended utopianism as having communicated the will to act ('l'idée grandiose du communisme'); with necessity, the revolutionary synthesis appeared: '... c'est de cette idée imposèe par la *nécessité* économique d'accord avec la plus grande somme de *justice* ... qu'est né le *collectivisme*', series 'Le Collectivisme révolutionnaire', in *Le Prolétaire*, 3 April–12 June 1880. Kropotkin and Costa worked with Guesde founding socialist groups at this time: Kropotkin, *Memoirs*, Vol. 2, pp. 214–15.

11 *Séances du Troisième Congrès Ouvrier, Marseille 1879.* Introduction, p. IV, also see ibid., *Addresse du Commission d'organisation*, February 1879, V–VIII, and Lombard's report pp. 34 et seq.

12 J. Joughin, Vol. 2, p. 289, and *passim* for amnesty campaign. Also Zévaès, *De la Semaine sanglante*, 'la revendication de l'amnistie ... tenait une place essentielle. C'était autour d'elle que se formaient les groupements révolutionnaires et républicains-démocrats d'où allait sortir bientôt le mouvement socialiste renouvelé (p. 29). Paulard, closely associated with *Le Prolétaire*, was head of the general committee to aid the amnestied, which broke away from the Louis Blanc committee; Joughin, pp. 260–4.

13 E.g. Delory, *Aperçu historique sur la Fédération du Nord*, p. 30, says that 'collectivisme co-opératif' was defeated by the 'collectivisme révolutionnaire et scientifique' of Guesde at the Marseilles Congress.

14 Marx (*Capital*) was quoted frequently in a series of articles on *La Grève* which appeared between 27 December 1879 and 17 February 1880, articles signed 'A.T.' Extracts by J. Delaporte from the Colinsian review *Philosophie de l'Avenir* appeared under the title 'Les Collectivistes du Socialisme rationnel' between 25 December 1878 and 10 May 1879. A reply by Guesde appeared in 11 January 1879 and 15 January 1879. Under the title 'Le Collectivisme au Congrès de Marseille' Delaporte wrote another series, 21 February–27 March 1880, a review of the pamphlet of that name by F. Borde (Paris, 1880). For Lassalle see my p. 157. Malon describes its general tenure best: '... le socialisme de classe fut d'abord la reprise et l'accentuation de la politique proudhonnienne inaugurée par le Manifeste des Soixante ...', op. cit., p. 1009. For *Le Prolétaire* and *L'Egalité* see Mauger, op. cit., pp. 34–5.

15 Prudent Dervillers had apparently worked with Deynaud and A. Boyer on a previous working-class paper, *Les Cahiers du Prolétariat*, mentioned by Malon, op. cit. For articles by Dervillers see *Le Prolétaire*, 21 December 1878, 25 December 1878; also 17 May 1879 – leading article 'La République et les Grèves' calling for collectivism by *force*.

16 *Le Prolétaire*, 13 September 1879.

17 *The Programme* revealed the same 'collectivist synthesis' as the socialism of *L'Egalité*; anarchist or federalist content is revealed by the demand that education be administered by the Communes and that collective property be administered by 'des groupes producteurs'. Signed by 54 individuals and groups it received support from three main areas; the Paris region, the Centre-East, and the Mediterranean South. It was signed by, amongst others, Dervillers, Fournière, Labusquière, Paulard, Chasse (imprisoned in 1879 as director of *Le Prolétaire*) and Chabert, leading figure of 1876 Paris Congress and recent convertee to collectivism. Lefranc, op. cit., pp. 36–7; Willard, op. cit., pp. 14–15.

18 For Jean Lombard see P. Lombard, *Au Berceau de Socialisme français*, pp. 79 et seq.

19 *Le Révolté*, 17 May 1879.

20 Willard, op. cit., p. 16 based on the doubtful reference to Lombard in Compère-Morel's hagiography (op. cit., p. 152).

21 The importance of *Le Socialisme Progressif* is noted in P. Lombard, op. cit., p. 41. Also see Bernstein, op. cit., pp. 142 et seq. See also Malon's letter of 25 July 1879 to Lombard and Boyer, in which he advised them to use the opening speech to the Congress as a 'monument in the history of the working-class socialist movement', and in which he discussed the plans to persuade the delegates to give the Congress the title of 'Congrès ouvrier socialiste' (ibid., pp. 48–53).

22 *L'Autonomie Communale* (Montpellier), 4 June 1882.

23 *Le Prolétaire*, 15 March 1879, 18 October 1879. For *L'Autonomie Communale*, see my Appendix 6B.

24 *Le Révolté*, 17 May 1879. Under the rubric *Mouvement Social* it discussed articles by Guesde and de Ricard which had appeared in *La Commune libre*. Its anonymous author demanded a synthesis of collectivism as the theoretical and practical basis of the party, insisting that the realization of socialism be attempted *locally*. For the de Ricard–Guesde contact, see his letter to Guesde of 26 April 1879, *Fonds Guesde*. De Ricard was author of *Le Fédéralisme* (Paris, 1877) and *L'Esprit politique de la Réforme* (Paris, 1893), a Languedocian view of the Reformation, and he translated Pi y Margall's *Les Nationalités* (Paris, 1879). He also contributed to *Le Travail* (see my Chapter 4), and to *La Revue Socialiste*, and he was the principal founder of *L'Alliance Latine*, a literary association with which Malon became closely associated. Further details of his career in Lombard, op. cit., Chapter XV.

25 *Séances du Congrès Ouvrier socialiste de France, Marseille 1879,* p. 38.

26 Blum, p. 43.

27 In addition to the *Compte-rendu* see e.g. note 9 of Bernstein's letter to Engels of 28 November 1882 in McInnes, *Les Partis Socialistes*

français: 'Le délégué qui intervint le plus énergiquement en faveur du programme collectiviste fut, autant que je m'en souvienne, Jean Lombard, ami de Malon.'

28 *Compte-rendu*, pp. 489–93. For the debate on the *salariat*, see ibid., pp. 452 et seq.

29 Ibid., p. 510.

30 Malon, 'Le Congrès de Marseille', *Revue Socialiste*, 1886, Vol. 2.

31 'La nationalisation des capitaux, mines, chemins de fer, etc., mis directement ensuite entre les mains de ceux qui les font produire, c'est-à-dire les travailleurs eux-memês.' The resolution was proposed by Bernard of Grenoble (*Séances*, p. 812). See also Lombard's speech, ibid., pp. 493–513. Many of the *rapporteurs* were anarchists.

32 *Séances*, p. 817.

33 Malon wrote to Lombard on 25 July 1879 that rumours of an Internationalist meeting to be held in Marseilles were probably police-inspired. Guesde, he said, knew nothing of it. Should it be true, he (Malon) was in touch with Costa, who would divert his friends from the supposed plan. Malon also expressed regret at the disappearance of *La Commune Libre* (Lombard, loc. cit.). During the Congress there was a small pressure group of non-delegates amongst whom was Ferroul of Narbonne, who had been associated with *La Commune Libre*. According to Malon he worked with Fauché and Fournière in drawing up the resolution on collectivism (Malon, *Le Congrès de Marseille*). Fournière later recalled that he was subject to pressure (of what kind he did not specify) from Reclus and Kropotkin during the Congress (he does not make it clear whether or not they were actually present) (Fournière, *La Crise socialiste*, p. 41). In view of Malon's statements in his letter to Lombard and Boyer it is interesting to note that a report of the Deputy [*sic*] Prefect of the Bouches-du-Rhône to the Ministry of the Interior early in September expressed fears of anarchist infiltration of the Congress, and said that: 'depuis le mois de mai dernier j'apprenais que le docteur Brousse . . . était en relation avec les délégués du Midi,' and reported that Pindy had been raising funds to send delegates to the Congress (report of 2 September 1879 in *P.Po.BA/32*).

34 Nos. 20–1, 15–29 November 1879.

35 *Séances*, p. 539 and pp. 385–6.

36 Willard, *Les Guesdistes*, p. 17. Willard has revealing things to say on the Guesdist use of the word 'collectivist' as a means of gaining support, pp. 16–17.

37 Malon, 'Le Programme de 1880', *Revue Socialiste*, 1887 (1). The programme appeared in *Le Prolétaire*, 1 May 1880. For discussions within the Parisian movement on this and other projects, see *Le Prolétaire*, 29 May 1880 et seq.

38 Paris, 1879. It was seized by the police and Le Roy was imprisoned. A review of the pamphlet appeared in *La Revue Socialiste*, January 1880.

39 The latter, living in London, was contributing to the second series of *L'Egalité*, which appeared in January 1880, and was influencing it in the direction of a purer Marxism than that of its predecessor.

40 I am indebted to M. J.-M. Guesde, the grandson of Jules Guesde, for allowing me to consult the correspondence of his grandfather in his private archives (referred to as the *Fonds Guesde*).

41 Guesde–Marx, March 1880; in Karl Marx, *Oeuvres*, Economie I (ed. M. Rubel) (Paris, 1965), p. clxviii.

42 Malon to Guesde, 3 April 1880, *Fonds Guesde*. Malon brought out *La Revue Socialiste* on 20 January 1880. Both Guesde and Lafargue wrote for it, and extracts from Engels's *Utopian and Scientific Socialism* were published in three parts beginning on 20 March 1880.

43 Lombard, op. cit., pp. 54–8.

44 Malon to Guesde, 8 April 1880 (cf. Guesde–Marx, March 1880; see my p.160).

45 Malon to Guesde, 27 April 1880.

46 Malon to de Paepe, 2 May 1880, 'Correspondance de Benoît Malon', in *La Revue Socialiste*, 1909 (1) pp. 80–1. This series includes his correspondence with E.-J. Fournière.

47 *Le Programme de 1880*, loc. cit.

48 Brousse to de Paepe, 24 December 1883 (*IFHS*).

49 See also undated letter Lafargue–Malon, read out to the St Etienne Congress by Brousse (*Le Prolétaire*, 7 October 1882).

50 Malon later made out that he had been taken by surprise and indeed tricked by Guesde's visit to London and the drawing up of the Minimum Programme (*Le Programme de 1880*, loc. cit.). However, this is not borne out by the correspondence with Guesde (see especially, his letter of 27 April 1880) before the visit, or indeed after it. See e.g. his letter of 25 May 1880: 'La bonne impression a été mutuelle à Londres. Lafargue m'écrit de vous avec enthousiasme. Le premier peut-être vous avez contraint Marx à modifier ses vues (sur le minimum de salaires dont je vous félicite vivement). Les trois sont[?] de vous. Brousse, que est vraiment un homme charmant, m'a écrit vous avoir vu au passage. Je viens de lancer 15 copies du programme à l'appui. Je vous remercie de l'épreuve de confiance, mais il vaut mieux que le programme ait une origine collective. J'avais d'ailleurs écrit en ce sens. . . '. He continued by saying 'le programme est très bien, les considérants surtout'. In a letter of 3 June 1880 he suggested various amendments to the Programme in the light of criticisms he had received of it. While it is clear that Malon was working for a reformist Programme, it is also clear that his attitude to Guesde was ambiguous, and that in general he approved of the

Programme. Indeed, it is likely that he knew beforehand of Guesde's visit to London. Guesde wrote to someone, and all the evidence points to it having been Malon, on the eve of his visit: 'Je pars ce soir pour Londres. Il s'agit du programme à arrêter et qui ne saurait être retardé plus longtemps sans péril pour notre parti tiré â hue a dia [? *sic*] par ''l'anarchisme'' de certains groupes ... il s'agit aussi de *l'Egalité*, qui malgré son succès, aurait absolument besoin d'un billet de 1000 francs pour éteindre la dette de ses quatres premiers numéros' (this letter was quoted by Brousse in *Le Prolétaire*, 1 March 1883). The Programme was published in *L'Egalité*, 30 June 1880, *La Revue Socialiste*, 20 July 1880, and *Le Prolétaire*, 10 July 1880. It was presented to a meeting held at the Salle d'Arras on 3 June as the work of 'un des chefs proscrits du socialisme français' (*Le Prolétaire*, 12 June 1880), and in the following issue A. le Roy attributed it to Malon (ibid., 19 June 1880). Malon replied on 26 June 1880 from Zurich that he was not the sole author, and agreed with certain criticisms of it made by le Roy, such as the absence of certain immediately necessary reforms (e.g. the abolition of night labour and the need for factory hygiene laws). See also Marx to Sorge, 5 November 1880, on the Programme.

51 Engels to Bernstein, 25 October 1881, in *Die Briefe von Engels an Eduard Bernstein* (Berlin, 1925), pp. 30–6. See also his reference to Brousse in a letter to Kautsky of 27 August 1881; 'a jolly good chap, but extremely confused, who considered the first task of the whole movement to be the conversion of his former anarchist friends' (Engels–Kautsky Correspondence, Vienna 1955). Engels could only see in Brousse his anarchist opponent of the International – and vice versa.

52 Postscript to Engels's letter of 25 October 1881, ibid., p. 36. See also McInnes, *Les Partis socialistes français, passim*.

53 Paul Brousse to Herman Jung, undated letter (but 1882), in the *Archief Jung, 512/1 IISG*. Marx had expected such reactions amongst the *militants* of the French movement (Marx to Sorge, 5 November 1880) but naïvely expected that by not talking about his contacts with Guesde the reactions would not be too strong.

54 Malon, 'Programme électoral des Travailleurs socialistes', *Revue Socialiste,* 29 July 1880.

55 Although Lafargue had published in *La Revue Socialiste*, 20 February 1880 and 20 March 1880, an article 'Le Parti Ouvrier et l'Alimentation publique' which came very close to Malon's position: '. . . la ler étape du parti . . . dans sa lutte . . . sera la conquête des municipalités', in which commerce (but not property) could be transformed. He later justified the article by the tactical need in 1880 to conciliate the reformists (see my Chapter 5, note 130).

56 *Le Prolétaire*, 12 June 1880, article by le Roy; his comments on the Programme can also be found in 'Réflexions sur le Programme du Parti', in *Fusillé deux Fois*. Also, *Le Prolétaire*, 31 July 1880.

57 For Guesde's revolutionism and his Blanquist leanings see McInnes, op. cit., pp. 13–18. The Guesdist failure ever to gain much trade-union support is well known. See Willard, op. cit., pp. 350–1. And see his letter to Marx of March (my p. 160).

58 J. Maitron, *Histoire du Mouvement anarchiste en France*, pp. 94–5; D. Ligou, op. cit., pp. 40–1.

59 Ligou, pp. 40–1; Maitron, pp. 100–1. The Southern Federation went completely anarchist, while anarchist propaganda seriously disrupted the Federation of the East throughout 1880–1 (see report of Gillier to Reims Congress, *Compte-rendu* (1881), p. 65). Anarchist influence is clearly to be seen in the report of the Marseilles federation presented at the same Congress (ibid., pp. 67–70), e.g.: 'La Révolution ne se commande pas, elle se subit. Elle est un mouvement spontané d'insurrection de la classe opprimé contre la classe oppressive.' It was pointed out by A. Lavy in *Le Prolétaire*, 23 March 1881, that 'déjà le midi ouvrier de la France s'est séparé du reste de notre pays au point de vue doctrinal'. (See also Appendix 6.)

60 *Le Révolté*, 24 July 1880.

61 *Le Mouvement libertaire*, p. 14.

62 *L'Egalité*, 11 August 1880.

63 Willard, op. cit., p. 194.

64 Bernstein correctly referred to Lafargue as a 'cutting polemicist' who, as the recognized 'spokesman' of Marx, did a great deal to discredit Marxism (*Briefe an Engels*) It was against Lafargue rather than Guesde that Brousse later directed his polemics, although this was motivated rather by the role which Lafargue had played in the International as a Marxist. See e.g. Brousse, *Le Marxisme dans l'Internationale*, pp. 1 and 26. Cf. also de Paepe's criticism of Lafargue in reference to his articles 'La lutte des classes au Flandres' which appeared in *L'Egalité* (3rd series) in 1882: 'Ce ton méprisant, cet air suffisant, cette prétention à l'infaillabilité scientifique et historique, ce dédain des travaux intellectuels d'un prolétaire intelligent et studieux, m'agacent toujours, *de quelque part qu'ils viennent*' (De Paepe to Malon, 2 January 1882, *IFHS*).

65 Montels to Guesde, 12 August 1880, *Fonds Guesde*; undated letter, 1880; undated letter, between 19 August and 13 September 1880; 13 September 1880; 23 August 1880; *L'Emancipation* (Lyons, 31 October–24 November 1880) was edited by Malon. It announced its editorial policy in its first issue in the following terms: 'Au point de vue pratique l'Emancipation sera tout d'abord un organe de conciliation entre les différents fractions du parti socialiste, sans départer

néanmoins des conclusions scientifiques modernes.' It had the close co-operation of Guesde but was quickly forced out of existence by financial problems and disagreements within its editorship.

67 See e.g. Brousse's correspondence with César de Paepe between 1882 and 1884, *passim*, but especially 24 December 1883 (*IFHS*). Also McInnes, op. cit., p. 11. On this theme there is an interesting police report signed 'Gontrans' of 14 August 1880 (i.e. simultaneously with the publication of the Lafargue article) which reads: 'Paul Lafargue n'est pas un nom, c'est un pseudonym derrière lequel s'abriterait un socialiste allemand' (*P.Po.BA/1477*). Lafargue himself wrote to Guesde in August 1880: '. . . je suis dégoutté des accusations lancées contre les allemands par les phraseurs de l'anarchisme, comme si rien n'aurait pas été plus facile à Marx et Engels de faire des émeutes qui auraient sonné en Europe le tocsin de la réaction' (*Guesde Archives, IISG 550/3* – incorrectly dated 1882). These and similar allegations about Marxism and the First International reached their apogee in J. Guillaume, *Karl Marx, pangermaniste, et l'Association Internationale des Travailleurs*, e.g.: 'Dès sa constitution sous l'inspiration de Marx la Sozial-Demokratie allemands a été un parti *impérialiste . . .*' (p. 111).

68 The Union fédérative was formally established on 17 May 1880 with Fauché, a leading Guesdist *militant*, as its secretary, and Paulard, a future possibilist, as its President. The Union was from the first almost exclusively under the control of the collectivists, the Blanquists having withdrawn at an early stage; this process was aided by a judicious arrangement of regional boundaries by the Executive Committee of the Marseilles Congress (report by 'Labori' in *P.Po.BA/1477*, 22 April 1880). The Union was effectively infiltrated by police spies (see *P.PoBA/1477/1478*, 1880–1).

69 Account of meeting in the Salle d'Arras, 27 June 1880 in *Le Prolétaire*, 10 July 1880.

70 In October 1880 Clemenceau, the emerging leader of the Radicals, put forward a Programme advocating 'social justice' in which he called, *inter alia*, for the creation of co-operative societies. This was interpreted by the socialists as an attempt to undermine their own influence amongst the working class.

71 A central feature of the creation of the Socialist Party in France was the division between the majority of the old Communard exiles, fixed in the sterility of their past beliefs, and the post-Communard generation: '. . . on voit que, parmi les anciens hommes de la Commune, y compris Rochefort, il y a entre eux et les socialistes militants une grande antipathie. On peut déjà prévoir que s'il y a, aux élections prochaines, des candidats socialistes, ou collectivistes, ce seront des nouveaux venus' (report 'Hilaire', 6 August 1880, *P.Po.BA/1477*).

The Union fédérative later lent support to the idea for a meeting to be held with the former exiles to urge them to stop feuding amongst themselves ('Gontran' report, 5 November 1880, loc. cit.). The Alliance was stronger in Paris than the Parti Ouvrier – see e.g. Malon, *Le Nouveau Parti* (Vol. 2), pp. 125–6. See Engels–Bernstein, 16 December 1882, in which he says that the Alliance received almost as many votes as the Parti Ouvrier in the August 1881 elections; also A. Zévaes, *Histoire du Socialisme et du Communisme en France de 1871 à 1947*, pp. 113–14.

72 It was, for instance, defended in this sense against the anarchists by le Roy in *Le Prolétaire*. 6 November 1880.

73 A new Article 5 was added to Part B (Économique) of the Programme, calling for the 'Mise à la charge de la société des vieillards et des invalides du travail'; Article 10 (9 of the original Programme) was amended to read: '. . . dépassant 3,000 francs, suppression de l'héritage en ligne collaterale et de tout héritage en ligne directe dépassant 20,000 francs.' The amended Programme was adopted as the resolution on the first question before the Congress ('De l'attitude du prolétariat dans la lutte électorale', *Le Prolétaire*, 31 July 1880).

74 Report 'Hilaire', 6 August 1880, *P.Po.BA/1477*.

75 He joined the Cercle d'Etudes du XVIII arrondissement in October 1880; report of 13 October 1880, *P.PoBA/985*. Lafargue wrote on 24 October 1880 [? to Malon]: '. . . le programme minimum . . . est pour moi le seul possible en ce moment, en dépit de Brousse qui me parle d'une plus vaste synthèse.' Quoted in *Rapport du Comité National, Congrès de Saint-Etienne, Le Prolétaire*, 7 October 1882. This in fact makes nonsense of Engels's statement that Brousse and Malon adopted the Minimum Programme 'with the secret intention of killing it' (Engels to Bernstein, 20 October 1882, loc. cit.).

76 *L'Emancipation*, 9 November 1880. 'Vous, vous avez refusé de signer, avez même protesté contre, et suspendu votre collaboration dans *L'Emancipation* à son sujet' (Lafargue to Brousse, 25 May 1881), quoted by Brousse at St Etienne Congress in 1882 in *Le Prolétaire*, 7 October 1882.

77 Report of 22 November 1880 in *P.Po.BA/985*.

78 A report of 'Ludovic' of 22 December 1880 stated that: 'Maria [Secretary of the Electoral Committee] tient trop au programme minimum qui n'est accepté que difficilement dans les arrondissements' (*P.Po.BA/1477*). Despite this the electoral committee was often in conflict with the executive committee of the Union, and behind the frequent conflicts of personalities (especially that between Maria and Fauché) it is possible to discern a conflict on theoretical issues, with the electoral committee lending support to the reformist

demands of Brousse; it fell under his control early in 1881 and organized meetings and conferences independently of the Executive committee.

79 *Le Prolétaire*, 4 November 1880.

80 On the first resolution before the Congress, on property, an amendment was adopted stating that collective property was merely a transitory stage to 'communisme libertaire'. This was the work of Rudolf Kahn, Brousse's former co-*militant* in the Swiss anarchist movement. In 1880 he published in Paris *La Question électorale*, probably the first anarchist pamphlet published there. See M. Nettlau, 'Algunos Documentos sobre les origines del anarquismo communista 1876–1880', *La Protesta* (Buenos Aires), suplemento quincenal, 6 May 1929.

81 For the Havre resolutions see *Compte-rendu du 5ème Congrès national* (Reims, 1881), pp. 82–90.

82 The report of the Congress was 'lost' by Guesde (McInnes, *Les débuts du Marxisme,* loc. cit.). He persisted in referring to the '10-point' Programme as approved at the Centre Congress. See e.g. *Le Programme du Parti Ouvrier*: also a series of articles in *Le Citoyen* of 1881 (?) to be found in the *Guesde Archives* (600/1). Brousse pointed out this omission in *Le Prolétaire*, 24 February 1882.

83 For the group's statutes, see Malon, *Le Nouveau Parti*, Vol. 1, pp. 99–101.

84 *Le Prolétaire*, 26 February 1881; 23 April 1881; 'cette nomination met le secrétariat de l'Union fédérative entre les mains de Brousse' ('Ludovic' report, 27 April 1881, *P.Po.BA/1478*).

85 Decisions of the regional, including the Centre, federations. *Le Prolétaire*, 6 August 1881; 13 August 1881; 20 August 1881.

86 *Le Citoyen*, 10–22 August 1881. See also Lafargue to Malon, undated letter, but August 1881: 'Vous avez eu grand tort de refuser, et Guesde plus grand tort de vous conseiller de refuser. Aux élections legislatives, il FAUT que, vous et Guesde, vous soyez portés.' It seems as though Guesde, for different reasons, was also reluctant to stand. But the elections coincided with a visit to Paris by Marx, who visited Guesde, who then stood for election (Brousse at St Etienne Congress, *Le Prolétaire*, 7 October 1882). Engels told Kautsky that Brousse was revealing his anarchist past (see my Chapter 5, note 51). This betrayed a total misunderstanding of Brousse's position. Obsessed by Brousse's anarchism within the International, Engels could only present a caricature, e.g. his letter to Bernstein of 22 September 1882 (McInnes, loc. cit.): '. . . avec Brousse, pas moyen de maintenir la paix. Il est et restera anarchiste des pied à la tête, sans qu'il a admis la participation aux élections; en rejetant les autres hors de la Fédération du Centre Malon et lui ont poussé la lutte à

l'extrême, et Brousse la même avec toute la tactique bakouniste; calomnies, mensonges et toutes les infâmies possibles.' See also a letter to Bernstein, 20 October 1882 ibid.

87 Report 'Hilaire' 10 August 1881, *P.Po.BA/1478*. For an account of the Massard–Fournière dispute see *Rapport du Comité national* to the St Etienne Congress.

88 *Le Prolétaire*, 10 September 1881; 17 September 1881; 24 September 1881; 1 October 1881.

89 In September 1881 the Broussist group gained control over *Le Prolétaire*; Brousse was elected to the editorial committee on 4 October 1881 along with Prudent Dervillers, Deynaud, E.-J. Fournière, F. Harry, J. Labusquière and Benoît Malon. On 17 September 1881 the Union fédérative decided to lend its support to the paper.

90 Malon and Joffrin were chosen as delegates; Joffrin obtained 26 votes, Malon 13 and Guesde a mere 4 (*Le Prolétaire*, 8 October 1881); only Malon however seems to have attended (see my Chapter 6).

91 *Le Prolétaire*, 22 October 1881; according to a police report this was a device to kill the Guesdist plan for the reappearance of a new *L'Egalité* series (report 'Hilaire', 7 July 1881, *P.Po.BA/1478*), and in another report there is a reference to 'la lutte de Brousse et ses consorts contre l'Egalité', which seems to refer to a newspaper, not a group (report 'Gontran', 12 October 1881, ibid.).

92 *Compte-rendu du 5me Congrès National, Reims 1881* (Paris, 1882). See also *Le Prolétaire*, 12 November 1881: 'Ce programme notoirement insuffisant . . .' (Labusquière).

93 *Le Prolétaire*, 19 November 1881.

94 The Congress declared 'collectivism' as only a first stage towards Communism, with the ultimate goal being 'chacun selon ses besoins', etc. See article by Joffrin, *Le Prolétaire*, 15 July 1882.

95 *Le Prolétaire*, 10 December 1881. The Manifesto said that the diversity of conditions in France necessitated a Programme based on autonomy, but saw four points of common action: (a) strikes, (b) conquest of municipalities, (c) electoral action, (d) numerical increase of Party. (All these points in fact were discussed at the 1882 Centre Congress.)

96 *Le Citoyen*, 24 November 1881. There was also an attack on the Manifesto of the Committee in *L'Egalité*. See also *Le Citoyen*, 28 November 1881; 2 December 1881; 3 December 1881.

97 *L'Egalité*, 11 December 1881. Engels at first disapproved of the project to publish this 3rd series, Engels to Bernstein, 25 October 1881, loc. cit.

98 *Le Prolétaire*, 24 December 1881. Brousse later argued, however, that the Havre Congress had voted the Minimum Programme for the year only; it had been dictated by electoral necessities (*La Bataille*,

324   *From Anarchism to Reformism*

15 May 1882). For the Guesdist view of the International, see *L'Egalité*, 25 December 1881: 'Les considérants de *l'Internationale*, même avec les compléments y apportés, n'excluent pas la propriété individuelle, de même que *l'Internationale* n'excluait pas les individualists (mutuellists, co-operatists, etc.). Ils ne soufflent mot d'autre part de la nécessité de l'action révolutionnaire' (Guesde, 'Notre Abstention', in *L'Egalité*, loc. cit.).

99 The Guesdists withheld support from Leonie Rouzade in a municipal contest in the 12th arrondissement (*Le Prolétaire*, 10 December 1881). Rouzade was an ardent feminist and utopian. In December 1881 Benoît Malon wrote to Fournière that: 'Les attaques maladroits contre les femmes et contre l'Internationale ainsi que contre nos amis de Montmartre auront, je pense, gâté les affaires des autoritaires ... le quator bourgeois de l'*Egalité* préfère briser le parti que de voir un parti indépendant. Cultivons les cercles de femmes, qui seront outrées de voir que l'Egalité s'est prononcé contre la citoyenne Rouzade' (in *La Revue Socialiste*, 1907 (2), pp. 184–5). See also *Rapport du Comité National* (St Etienne) in *Le Prolétaire*, 7 October 1882.

100 Brousse remained firmly committed to this part of his anarchist faith. See e.g. 'Le Mouvement Communiste et les intérêts de Classe', *La Bataille*, 11 June 1882. *L'Egalité*'s reply to these arguments was that: (a) the preamble to the International's statutes made no mention of collectivism; (b) that the Montmartre Programme had also dropped the eight-hour working day demand adopted at Le Havre (and, Guesde pointed out later, adopted by the 1866 Geneva Congress): *L'Egalité*, 15 January 1882 and Lafargue, ibid, 26 February 1882, 5 March 1882, 12 March 1882; (c) and that the minimum wage and inheritance clauses had been dropped not because they were 'unmarxist' but as concessions to the bourgeois-radical elements within the Party (*L'Egalité*, 15 January 1882). Guesde in fact defended the minimum wage as a genuine expression of the demand of the Parisian workers (ibid.).

101 Lafargue's attack on autonomy was sometimes more serious than this; see, e.g. his series 'La lutte de Classes en Flandres' in *L'Egalité*, 22 and 29 January 1882. As early as October Lafargue had addressed a letter to the L'Egalité group in which he said he had sent two letters to *Le Prolétaire*, in one of which 'je dénonce les anarchistes, qui, après avoir désorganisé l'Internationale, se sont glissés parmi nous et travaillent à sêmer par leurs intrigues et leurs calmonies la division dans nos rangs. Je crois de mon devoir de dénoncer leur tactique à tous les membres du parti' (quoted in Compère-Morel, op. cit., p. 223).

102 Guesde was, in fact, quoting from a letter by Lafargue sent to *Le*

Prolétaire on 21 October 1881, which is clearly that referred to in note 101 above.

103 Malon to Fournière, December 1881, in *La Revue Socialiste*, March 1908. Lafargue, for all his accusations of 'opportunism' against the possibilists, had in fact himself proposed an alliance with the Clemenceau radicals if circumstances were favourable. See his letter to Malon (?), 2 June 1881, quoted by Deynaud in the Report of the National Committee to the St Etienne Congress (*Le Prolétaire*, 7 October 1882).

104 Brousse spoke against expulsion at the meeting of 17 January (see Malon to Fournière, 18 January 1882, loc. cit.) Following the withdrawal the group announced the 'need' to reconstitute the Centre Federation. It set up its own rival federation with Fréjac, the former secretary of the Union fédérative as its secretary, and it met in the same building as the Union. Gaining the support of about a dozen groups it proved no more than a minor embarrassment to the Union, which grouped about eighty to ninety groups and societies (*Le Prolétaire*, 11 February 1882; 4 March 1882). The dissident groups were expelled from the Union fédérative at its May Congress (*Le Prolétaire*, 20 May 1882).

105 *L'Egalité*, 5 February 1882. Lafargue was largely responsible for the polemical tone of the Guesdist attack; he began his own column in *L'Egalité* on 19 February 1882, entitled 'Proletariana', with the express object of ridiculing the reformists.

106 A. Zévaès, *Une Génération* (Paris, 1922), p. 40. It was true that the possibilist Programme showed common features with that of the radicals – for instance communal autonomy – which made the Guesdist charge seem to some extent valid. Yet it differed strongly from radicalism in its continued insistence on class antagonism. And in practice the possibilists were strongly opposed to the Radicals; in November 1881, for instance, the Union fédérative voted against participation in radical-sponsored meetings (*Le Prolétaire*, 2 December 1881); and P.L. to F.E., 6 May 1889, *Correspondence*, Vol. 2.

107 *Le Marxisme dans l'Internationale*, pp. 4, 7, 11.

108 Undated (*Jung Archives, IISG*).

109 *Dictature et Liberté*, p. II.

110 *La Bataille*, 10 May 1882.

111 The best example of this rhetoric was during the Montceau – les Mines affair, which brought from Brousse echoes of his more violent past: 'Les uns croient – je l'ai jadis cru avec eux – que le meilleur moyen de former une armée révolutionnaire est l'organisation d'émeutes, de combats d'avant-garde, pour me servir du terme d'école, *la propagande par le fait insurrectionel.*

Le parti ouvrier estime, au contraire (et, expériences faites, je me suis rangé à cette opinion) qu'il faut d'abord détromper le peuple de ses espérances réformistes: par une série de mises en demeure, *par une propagande par le fait légal* demasquer le mauvais vouloir bourgeois, et n'entrer en ligne de bataille à main armée que lorsqu'une portion assez considérable de la classe ouvrière sera enfin detrompée et aura pris place conscienment sous le drapeau de la révolution . . . Que chacun *agisse* comme il pense, et l'experience, cette naturelle leçon des choses, dira qui a raison (*Le Prolétaire*, 26 February 1882).

In an important article Carl Landauer has argued that a distinction needs to be drawn between possibilism and reformism, with the latter developing only in the second half of the 1880s with Malon and *La Revue Socialiste* ('The origin of Socialist reformism in France', *IRSH*, Vol. XII, 1967, 1). Professor Landauer holds that the reformist content of possibilism was only conditional, *attempting* peaceful change, but *preparing* for revolutionary change ('Brousse's position did not preclude the assumption that the movement could – or the postulate that it should – be speeded up by revolution'). Certainly Brousse's rhetoric suggested this, but as with propaganda by the deed there was a large 'safety-net' calculation inherent in it. This author would be inclined to be somewhat sceptical about *Brousse's* belief in Revolution, although certainly amongst many of the possibilist *militants* genuine revolutionism existed. This was why Brousse used the rhetoric.

112 Brousse, op. cit., p. 8. His reference to Guesde's statement was to a letter from Guesde published in *La Justice*, mentioned by Deynaud in the Report of the National Committee to the St Etienne Congress (*Le Prolétaire*, 7 October 1882).

113 This is an argument very similar to that found in much anarchist literature, that within capitalist society associations were developing which, as they were, would provide essential elements of anarchist society. See e.g. Kropotkin's praises for the European railway networks, the Red Cross and the English Lifeboat Association in *The Conquest of Bread*, pp. 179 et seq.

114 Brousse envisaged the competition of public enterprises gradually eliminating private industry. His theory that socialism could be achieved by the gradual capture of the public services *within* the framework of the capitalist state was bitterly attacked by Guesde in his pamphlet *Services Publics et Socialisme*. Guesde said that while he was in favour of public services (e.g. housing, welfare) the essential prerequisite was the establishment of socialism through Revolution. The strengthening of these services within capitalism merely served the ends of the bourgeoisie and strengthened the State.

115 P. Brousse, *Trois Etats* (Paris, 1883).
116 Huret, op. cit., p. 222.
117 P. Brousse, *La Commune et le Parti Ouvrier*, p. 6.
118 Brousse's programme of gradualism and municipal socialism resembled and anticipated much in English Fabianism, which was in fact partly influenced by possibilism A. M. McBriar, *Fabian Socialism and English Politics 1884–1918*, p. 21. Compare for example Brousse as quoted here with Bernard Shaw in his essay 'Transition' in *Fabian Essays* (ed. Briggs, London, 1962), p. 222 et seq. Ironically, the LCC was to become a model for Brousse. See his argument for municipalization in Brousse et Bassède, *Les Transports* (2 vols., Paris, 1912), Vol. 1, pp. 162 et seq.
119 *Le Prolétaire*, 20 and 29 May 1882.
120 *La Bataille*, 12 May 1882
121 *Le Prolétaire*, 20 May 1882; 3 June 1882. See also Malon, *Le Nouveau Parti*, Vol. 2, p. 80 for the text of the Congress resolution on municipal socialism.
122 Report of the National Committee, *Compte-rendu du Congrès de Saint Etienne* (1882), in *Le Prolétaire*, 7 October 1882.
123 Allemane, Jean, b. 1843, d. 1920; typographer. Allemane was politically active from an early age and was an influential *militant* in the 5th arrondissement during the Paris Commune. He was sentenced to imprisonment and exile in New Caledonia and was one of those amnestied in 1880. On his return he threw himself actively into the affairs of the socialist movement and enjoyed considerable respect for his activities within the Commune.
124 In July, for instance, Deynaud was sent to 'direct discussion' in the Federal Committee (*Le Prolétaire*, 28 July 1882). On 18 July the Union fédérative agreed to charge 5 cents per member for Joffrin's financial support.
125 *La Bataille*, 3 June 1882; 5 June 1882; 7 June 1882; 8 June 1882; 12 June 1882; 18 July 1882; 19 July 1882; 24 July 1882; 5 August 1882.
126 *Le Prolétaire*, 24 June 1882.
127 *L'Egalité*, 28 May 1882.
128 *Le Citoyen*, 16 May 1882.
129 *L'Egalité*, 30 April 1882. Also see 23 April 1882; 7 May 1882; 21 May 1882.
130 Lafargue was attacked by Lombard in *L'Autonomie Communale* (see Appendix 5) for discrepancy between articles published in *La Revue Socialiste* in 1880 (see my Chapter 5, note 58), and in *Le Citoyen* and *L'Egalité* in 1882. He defended what he had written in *La Revue* on the grounds of tactical necessity: 'Les anarchistes étaient dans nos rangs, prêchant la doctrine bourgeoise de laissez-faire et du laissez passer politique; ils étaient peu nombreux mais

leur braillerie grandissait leur importance, et étouffait les autres voix. Beaucoup des possibilistes du jour étaient alors des anarchistes. Pour faire accepter l'action politique de la classe ouvrière, il fallait présenter la question par le petit bout, par la conquête des municipalités. La conquête de l'Etat, la dictature transitoire du Prolétariat semblaient alors des monstruosités. Cette idée en tête j'écrivis mes trois articles sur les municipalités qui eurent la male-chance de fournir au doctissime docteur possibiliste les éléments économiques dont il avait besoin pour élaborer ses bons petits plans communalistes dans lesquels il voudrait enfermer et paralyser l'action du Parti ouvrier. . . .' (*L'Egalité*, 28 May 1882.)

131 *L'Egalité*, 18 August 1882. Only two weeks prior to this Guesde, at a public meeting on the housing question, had said that the Revolution would be hastened by the failure of the Government to solve the problem, and that it (the Revolution) was only 'l'affaire de quelques années à peine' (Compère-Morel, op. cit., pp. 244–55). See also Lafargue to Engels, 16 June 1882, *Correspondance*, 1.

132 *Le Prolétaire*, 12 and 19 August 1882. Brousse's supporters included Labusquière, Marouck and Deynaud. The first two had worked on the second series of *L'Egalité*.

133 *L'Egalité*, 29 August 1882. On 21 October 1882 he wrote to the Egalité group that he had sent two letters to *Le Prolétaire*, in the first of which he had disposed of certain charges against himself and Guesde, and in the second of which he had denounced the anarchists within the Party (Compère-Morel, op. cit., p. 223; and see my Chapter 5, notes 101 and 102). A week previously *Le Prolétaire* had announced that it had received a letter from Lafargue, the publication of which it considered unnecessary and liable to revive quarrels in the Party (*Le Prolétaire*, 15 October 1882). Brousse did in fact later produce this letter to the St Etienne Congress; it read partly as follows: 'Au contraire, j'ai trouvé que Guesde était un homme très populaire, très aimé et ayant des fanatiques, et c'est bien heureux, car je ne connais personne en France qui ait sa valeur. Il est mieux que Lassalle, *l'homme pour CRÉER le parti*: comme intelligence il lui est supérieur; s'il lui est inférieur comme érudition, comme agitateur il l'égale, et comme caractère privé et publique il n'y a pas de comparaison, Lassalle était un pourri.'

134 See e.g. two articles by Paulard making explicit comparisons between Marxist actions within the International and within the *Parti Ouvrier* in *Le Prolétaire*, 16 September 1882, and articles by Deynaud, Allemane and Gély calling for expulsion. Paulard had taken the lead in January 1882 in calling for the expulsion of the Guesdists from the Union fédérative (Malon to Fournière, 18 January 1882, *Fonds Fournière*).

135 Lafargue to Engels, 10 October 1882, *Correspondance* 1, pp. 101–5. It seems as though Guesde had been considering the move since June 1882 (Willard, *Les Guesdistes*, p. 23, note 6); on the other hand Bernstein said that the initiative lay entirely with Lafargue who had precipitated Guesde into the move only during the Congress (*Die Briefe von Engels an Bernstein*, op. cit.) Three days before the Congress opened, on 22 September, Engels wrote to Bernstein saying that it was impossible to work with Brousse 'avec Brousse, pas moyen de maintenir la paix. Il est et restera anarchiste des pieds à la tête, sauf qu'il a admis la participation aux élections . . .' (loc. cit.).

136 *Le Prolétaire*, 7 October 1882.

137 Engels to Bebel, 28 October 1882.

138 To give him some credit, Engels was fairly critical of Guesde and Lafargue. See his letter to Bernstein of 25 October 1882.

139 Fourniére and Rouanet were censured at the 1883 Party Congress for having broken Party discipline in a legislative campaign at Narbonne. They both later became associated with Malon on *La Revue Socialiste*. For Malon's split with Brousse see my ch. 6, n. 20.

NOTES TO CHAPTER 6

1 *Fédération des Travailleurs socialistes de France. Compte-rendu du 7me Congrès National, Paris, 1883.*

2 *Le Prolétaire,* 20 October 1883.

3 *Compte-Rendu, 1883,* p. 17. The Congress also passed the following resolution: 'Le Congrès pense que le système parlementaire actuel disparaîtra avec la domination politique et économique de la classe dont il est l'expression et que la forme sociale future sorti de nos sociétés ouvrières devenus les principaux rouages des services publics, l'administration nationale et internationale étant formée tout simplement par les Comités de ces sociétés chaque jour perfectionnés dans les différents Congrès du Parti' (ibid. p. 15).

4 *Fédération des Travailleurs socialistes de France. Compte-rendu du 8me Congrès National, Rennes, 1884.*

5 Noland, p. 22.

6 J. Néré, *La Crise Industrielle de 1882.* This is an invaluable study for any account of the working-class movement in Paris in this period.

7 *Le Prolétaire,* 8 December 1883.

8 See Lafargue to Engels, 10 December 1884, *Correspondance,* Vol. 1.

9 *Le Prolétaire,* 17 January 1885.

10 For Lafargue's reaction to the election results, see his letter to Engels of 11 October 1885, *Correspondance,* Vol. 1.

11 *Le Prolétariat,* 10–17 October 1885.

12 Ibid., 6–13 November 1885.

13 Ibid., 16–23 January 1886.

14 Ibid., 13–20 March 1886.

15 Ibid., 15–22 May 1886.

16 Ibid., 17 February 1887.

17 The proposal to create a Bourse du Travail in Paris had been first mooted in 1875, and had entered the Party's Programme in a resolution of the Union fédérative in January 1884. Joffrin and Chabert had fought for its establishment within the municipal council, which had finally been persuaded in 1886 to vote 1 million francs for its establishment, an example which was to be followed shortly afterwards by other cities, so that by 1892 when the Fédération des Bourses du Travail was set up there were fourteen Bourses.

18 See e.g. Laura Lafargue to Engels, 27 December 1888 and F.E. to L.L., 7 May 1889, *Correspondance,* Vol. 2.

19 Brousse to his mother, 27 January 1888, *Fonds Brousse.*

20 Landauer (*The Origin of Reformism in France,* p. 103) suggests that in the 1880s there might have operated a kind of 'division of labour' within the Party between Brousse and Malon. It is on the contrary clear that by 1884 Malon was no longer an effective member of the

Party, and from 1885 on, through *La Revue Socialiste*, was to argue the 'unionist' case which was rejected by the possibilist leadership. As early as May 1883 Brousse was warning Herman Jung, with whom he was in close contact, to beware of Malon (P.B. to H.J., 30 May 1883, *Jung Archives, IISG*). In August 1883, when Brousse resigned for a short period from the National Committee of the Party, he told Jung that this was because of accusations of dictatorship against him and also because of the abandonment of the Party's Programme by one of its groups as a result of Malon's intrigues. (P.B. to H.J., 27 October 1883, loc. cit.). It appears that within the possibilist–English trade union alliance there was a division between Smith and Brousse on the one hand and Malon and Shipton on the other (ibid., 12 September 1883). In February 1884 Lafargue told Engels that Brousse had got rid of Malon (P.L. to F.E., 15 February 1884) and on 5 September 1884 Brousse told Jung that Malon was 'zéro dans le parti'.

21 *Le Prolétaire*, 14 June 1884.

22 Néré, pp. 166–9.

23 *Le Prolétariat*, 1–21 August 1886. It was because the Blanquists and Guesdists had not imposed a clearly defined socialist Programme on Roche, the candidate they supported in a Parliamentary by-election in May 1886, that the possibilists had put forward their own separate candidate, Soubrié, one of the Decazeville *militants*. See Humbert, p. 31.

24 *Compte-rendu*, p. 31.

25 Néré, p. 216.

26 Boulanger was characterized in *Le Prolétariat* on 19 November 1887 as 'Boulanger assassin' for his role in the massacre of the Paris Communards in May 1871, and at a meeting in the Salle Levis Brousse drew the parallel with Louis Napoleon and the 1851 *coup d'état*.

27 This, characteristically, was Allemane's argument. See *Le Prolétariat*, 14 January 1888.

28 See Brousse's argument in ibid., 26 November 1887.

29 Ibid., 31 March 1888. The strength of his opposition to Boulanger has been explained in terms of Allemane's memory of the Commune. See the *Dictionnaire Biographique*.

30 *Le Parti Ouvrier*, 26 May 1888.

31 *Le Prolétariat*, 4 August 1888; 11 August 1888.

32 *Le Parti Ouvrier*, 23 August 1888.

33 Néré, p. 512. Possibilist opposition to the demonstrations was also connected with the fact that they were led in Paris by Boulé, leader of the navvies' strike the previous summer and the separate socialist candidate in the January by-election.

34 *Le Prolétariat*, 12 October 1889.

35 Braunthal, *History of the International 1864–1914*, p. 194. See also Engels to Becker, who had proposed a revival of the International, on 10 February 1882; *Marx-Engels Selected Correspondence*, p. 420.

36 Valiani, *Dalla Prima alla Secondo Internazionale*, loc. cit., pp. 211 et seq.

37 Adolphe Smith (Headingley). A member of the First International and acquaintance of many trade-unionists. It was through Smith, who was fluent in French, that the Congress of November 1882 was organized, and he acted as an interpreter at several later international Congresses. Because of his association with rivals of Marx and Engels in the First International he was strictly *persona non grata* chez Engels (see e.g. Hyndman, *Record*, pp. 252–3). He also acted as official interpreter when Brousse visited London in 1905, and for a period in the 1880s acted as the London correspondent for *Le Prolétariat*.

38 *Le Prolétaire*, 3 November 1883.

39 Ibid., 9 December 1882.

40 *Le Prolétariat*, 15 December 1883. The Germans were not invited to the 1883 Paris Congress, and no delegates from the Guesdist POF took part. According to Brousse there were three main reasons why only the English trades unions, the Italians and the Spanish were invited. They were: (a) fear of transgressing the Dufaure law; (b) public opinion in France might, if Governmental action were taken, be against the Germans; and (c) the Germans, led by Engels, were on bad terms with Brousse and supported Guesde and considered the trades unions as 'vendus' Letter to Herman Jung, 19 September 1883, IISG. See also *Le Prolétaire*, 10 November 1883.

41 Brousse to de Paepe, 11 February 1884, *IFHS*.

42 Haupt, op. cit., p. 71.

43 In a letter of 24 December 1883 (*IFHS, Fonds Fournière, 14 AS 181 (10) No. 125*, incorrectly dated as 1889.)

44 Brousse to de Paepe, 11 February 1884 (Brousse accused de Paepe of favouring the Guesdists). A year later in talking of the international movement Brousse complained bitterly to Herman Jung of 'les intrigues Engeliennes' (letter of 29 March 1885, *IISG*).

45 See e.g. the article by Adolphe Smith in *Le Prolétariat*, 10 January 1885, attributing a split within the SDF to Engels.

46 Brousse to Costa 16 September 1886. See also P.L. to F.E. 18 September 1886, *Correspondance*, Vol. 1; B. Malon, 'Les Conférences Internationales ouvrières de Paris', *Revue Socialiste*, No. 21 September 1886.

47 Broadhurst, secretary of the TUC's Parliamentary Committee, was appointed Under-Secretary of State for Home Affairs in Gladstone's third ministry in February 1886.

48 *Le Prolétariat*, 21–8 August 1886.
49 A. Smith, *Report of the International Trades Union Congress, 1886*. Brousse told Costa that despite his initial lack of control over the Congress, the resolutions voted were drawn up by his own men (letter to Costa, 16 September 1886). The *Sozial Demokrat*, organ of the German Socialists, described the last resolution (on the 1889 Congress) as premature (Valiani loc. cit.).
50 Loc. cit. See also, in this connection, his critical comments to Jung on Broadhurst and the reactionary attitudes of the trades unions following the 1883 Paris Congress (letter to Jung 9 January 1884).
51 *Le Prolétariat*, 17 September 1887.
52 G. Haupt and J. Verdes, *De la Première à la Deuxième International Mouvement Social*, No. 51, 1965. G. Haupt, *La Deuxième Internationale, étude critique des sources, essai bibliographique*.
53 A. Smith, *A Critical Essay on the International Trade Union Congress 1888*.
54 Valiani, op. cit., pp. 222–3.
55 *Le Prolétariat* published the SDF's counter-Manifesto, 7 April 1888.
56 For Hyndman and his rivalry with the Engels group in London, see two books by C. Tsuzuki, *H. M. Hyndman and British Socialism*, esp. pp. 114 et seq., and *The Life of Eleanor Marx, 1855–1898*, esp. pp. 187 et. seq.
57 Hyndman did however express his admiration for the work of the possibilists on the Paris municipal council, and was especially impressed by the establishment of *cantines scolaires* (see Hyndman, *Record of an Adventurous Life*, pp. 301–3). In 1887 Hyndman called for the creation of a Great Central Council for London which would help to solve London's social problems, *A Commune for London* (London, 1887). This may have been influenced by possibilist theories.
58 *Congrès International ouvrier socialist: Rapport de la Commission d'organisation* (Paris, 1889).
59 Engels to Lafargue 27 March 1889, *Correspondance*, Vol. 2. In 1882 Engels had told Becker that the need to recognize *publicly* one of the two French factions in a new International was one of the reasons he opposed such a course. At that time, Engels was extremely critical of the 'tactical blunders' of the Guesdists (Engels to Becker, loc. cit.).
60 F.E. to L.L., 28 June 1889, and F.E. to L.L., 11 June 1889. *Correspondance*, Vol. 2.
61 F.E. to L.L., 11 June 1889. Cf. Engels to Sorge, 8 June 1889, in Marx–Engels *Selected Correspondence*. 'The main thing is – and this was the reason I put my shoulder to the wheel – that it is again the old split in the International that comes to light here, the old battle of the Hague. The adversaries are the same, only with this difference,

that the banner of the anarchists has been replaced by the banner of the possibilists. . . . And the tactics are exactly the same. The Manifesto of the SDF, obviously written by Brousse, is a new edition of the Sonvillier Circular.'

62 F.E. to K.K., 21 May 1889 (quoted in *Wilhelm Liebknecht Briefwechsel mit Karl Marx und Friedrich Engels*, p. 313).

63 P.L. to E.E. 27 November 1888, *Correspondance*, Vol. 2. 'In my view L[iebknecht] and the rest of them are slightly too well disposed towards the possibilists, which is stupid, for Brousse and Co. do not represent the Socialist Party, but the party of the traitors inside the government. . . . The Germans must be prevented from going to the possibilist Congress; they would be ruined in the eyes of French Socialists and do us great harm.' See also P.L. to F.E., 6 December 1888, and L.L. to F.E., 21 December 1888, ibid.

64 Engels pointed out to Lafargue that the hesitancy of the German Social Democrats in coming out fully in support of the Guesdists and their Congress was due to the Guesdists' attitude towards the Boulangists. So long as the Guesdist position (and especially of Lafargue personally) remained equivocal, Engels said that he could not encourage the Germans to attend the Guesdist Congress (F.E. to L.L., 2 January 1889 *Correspondance*, Vol. 2).

65 F.E. to P.L., 14 January 1889, *Correspondance*, Vol. 2.

66 Valiani, op. cit.

67 *Le Prolétariat*, 16 February 1889. An article in the same edition also attacked the German Social Democrats for supporting the Guesdists in the Boulangist crises: 'Dans nos luttes intestines, les amis extérieures de MM. Guesde et Lafargue ont toujours agi – dans le limite de leurs moyens – au profit des ennemis du Parti Ouvrier et contre le même parti.'

68 F.E. to P.L., 10 April 1889 (loc. cit. Vol. 2).

69 *Le Prolétariat*, 23 March 1889.

70 F.E. to P.L., 12 March 1889. Engels had told Lafargue earlier that if the possibilists agreed to conciliation proposals, 'it will be your own fault if you are not capable of proving to everyone that it is you, and not they, who represent French socialism' (F.E. to P.L., 14 January 1889).

71 Following the March refusal by the possibilists, Engels wrote a pamphlet, under Bernstein's name, against the Brousse–Hyndman alliance, *The International Working Men's Congress of 1889*.

72 F.E. to P.L., 21 March 1889. See also F.E. to P.L., 23 March 1889, loc. cit., Vol. 2.

73 F.E. to P.L., 25 March 1889, ibid.

74 *Le Socialiste* had appeared irregularly between 1885 and 1888 as the Guesdist newspaper. Engels was constantly critical of the Guesdists'

failure of communication with foreign socialists, especially the
Germans. See e.g. F.E. to P.L., 13 October 189 (*Correspondence*,
Vol. 3).

75 F.E. to P.L., 27 March 1889.

76 *FTSF: Compte-rendu du Congrès Internationale ouvrier socialist tenu
à Paris du 15 au 20 Juillet 1889 (Paris, 1889). Report of the International Workingmen's Congress, Paris, 1889* (London s.d.).

77 *Compte-rendu*, p. 50. Although Brousse was present at the Congress
he kept well in the background.

78 *Compte-rendu*, p. 79.

79 See B. Malon, 'Les Congrès Socialiste internationaux de 1889',
Revue Socialiste, 56, 1889.

80 M. Dommanget, *Histoire du Premier Mai*, pp. 97–112.

81 *Le Prolétariat*, 3 May 1890. Lafargue made a great deal of the damage
supposedly done to the possibilists by their attitude towards the 1
May demonstrations (see e.g. P.L. to F.E., 4 August 1889). As the
possibilists controlled the Paris Bourse du Travail, the demonstrations in Paris did not have full support. However they did not maintain their attitude in 1891, and even succeeded in undercutting
Guesdist control of its organization. Engels was critical of the
Guesdists' handling of events (F.E. to P.L., 19 March 1891, 29 May
1891, E.E. to L.L., 4 May 1891).

82 Haupt, op. cit., pp. 115–16.

83 *Le Prolétaire*, 12 March 1887.

84 *Le Prolétariat*, 24 December 1887, 14 January 1888, 28 January
1888; 25 February 1888.

85 E.g. Allemane received 68 votes, Ribanier (secretary of the Bourse
du Travail) 56 Brousse 29, Joffrin 26 and Lavy 29 (*Le Prolétariat*, 25
February 1888).

86 *Le Prolétariat*, 6 October 1888.

87 *Le Prolétariat*, 9 February 1889.

88 *Le Prolétariat*, 23 March 1889; 30 March 1889; 11 May 1889.

89 Dumay, exiled in Switzerland for his activities at Le Creusot during
the period of the Commune, seems to have oscillated uneasily in his
loyalty to the possibilists and was excluded by the 'triumvirate' of
Brousse, Joffrin and Chabert from positions of influence. He joined
Allemane's POSR shortly after the split at Chatellerault in 1890. See
P. Ponsot, 'Un militant socialiste du XIX siècle: J.-B. Dumay', in
Revue Socialiste No. 188, 1965.

90 *Le Prolétariat*, 19 October 1889; November 1889–January 1890.

91 *Le Prolétariat*, 5 April 1890; 12 April 1890; 14 June 1890.

92 *Le Prolétariat*, 8, 9, 26–7 August 1890.

93 In *Le Prolétariat* of 13 September 1890 Brousse defended an article
he had written on the question of workers' ownership and control of

industry, against attacks by *Le Parti Ouvrier*. Brousse opposed 'La mine aux Mineurs' on the grounds that it led to corporation. This was *the first time* the newspapers indulged in polemics, coming long after the first serious divisions within the Party.

94 *Le Prolétariat*, 6 September 1890.
95 Ibid., 13 September 1890.
96 Ibid., 4 October 1890.
97 Characteristically, the resolutions were published in full by *Le Prolétariat*. Despite his personal views Brousse treated the paper's function as the Party's official organ seriously (*Le Prolétariat*, 11 October 1890). See also M. Charnay, *Les Allemanistes*, pp. 9–10.
98 *FTSF: Compte-rendu au X Congrès régional tenu à Chattellerault, 9–15 Octobre 1890* (Poitiers, 1891).
99 The Report of the POSR to the 1891 Congress of the International (Brussels) read by Allemane, defined the foundation of the Party as representing 'le retour aux principes, l'effacement des personnalités encombrantes'. Unlike the possibilists, the POSR was to hold regular National Congresses throughout the 1890s.
100 One of the charges made against the leadership of the possibilists after the rupture with Allemane was that it had struck at working-class militancy in opposing the 1 May 1890 demonstrations. It is worth noting that Allemane was one of its strongest opponents.
101 Willard, op. cit., p. 399. The Guesdists were of course delighted at the split, and did as much as they could to profit from it. See P.L. to F.E., 30 March 1891 (*Correspondance*, Vol. 3). Despite this however it is noteworthy that the Guesdists failed in this task, and in fact *lost* control of the Paris organizing committee for the 1 May demonstrations of 1891 to the Blanquists, Allemanists and possibilists. Engels took this as further evidence that the Guesdists had no strength in Paris (see F.E. to P.L., 29 May 1891, *Correspondance*, Vol. 3).
102 See my p. 223. The leadership of the German Social Democratic Party received most of its information about the French movement through contacts with the possibilists in Paris, and consequently it tended to view them more sympathetically than the Guesdists. See e.g. Bernstein's comments to Engels in their *Correspondence* (extracts translated in McInnes, op. cit.) and Engels's continued complaints to Lafargue.
103 Willard, op. cit., p. 62.
104 Landauer, 'The Guesdists and the Small Farmer: Early Erosion of French Marxism' (*IRSH*, Vol. VI, 1961). L. Derfler, 'Reformism and Jules Guesde' (*IRSH*, Vol. XII, 1967).

NOTES TO EPILOGUE

1 De Seilhac, *Le Monde Socialiste*, p. 28.
2 *The Times*, 16–18 October 1905.
3 Humbert, pp. 85–6.

NOTES TO CONCLUSION

1 Cited in Hostetter, op. cit., p. 431.
2 See also Carl Landauer's article, 'The Origin of Socialist Reformism in France' (*IRSH*, Vol. XII, 1967, 1). This useful article rightly brings out the important link between anarchism and reformism, which is an underlying theme of this study. To quote at length: 'French possibilism, which developed into reformism, has one of its historical roots in anarchism. The anarchist beginnings of Brousse and Malon . . . still exerted an influence on their thinking and on the policy of the Fédération des Travailleurs Socialistes. In the early phase, the heritage of anarchist extremism which especially Brousse brought into the new Party, helped to prevent a premature tendency toward moderation – premature in view of the sentiment of a large section of the working class. In the second phase the emphasis, inherited from anarchism, on social progress outside the state machinery, helped apply the pragmatic orientation of incipient reformism at a time when socialist influence in the national legislature was still too limited for immediate great results. Although the idea of a universal gratis supply of public services was of course unrealizable, the concentration on work in city councils proved a healthy thing for a party which could vindicate its emphasis on reform only by achieving reform . . . a tendency towards anarchism is not in all situations a clear opposite to reformism; there can be conditions in which a modified anarchist influence operates as a force promoting the evolutionary rather than the revolutionary tendency in socialism. This is one of the lessons drawn from the origin and development of French Possibilism.'
  This general statement of Landauer's should, if the present study has fulfilled at least part of its aim, be fully borne out by what is said here.
3 *Anarchy* (London), Vol. 74, 1967.
4 Compare the text of the Programme in R. C. K. Ensor, *Modern Socialism* (London, 1910), pp. 48–55, with Brousse's pamphlet of 1883, *La Propriété Collective et les Services Publics* (see my p.185).

Bibliography

List of abbreviations used in text

AD Hérault	Archives Departementales, Hérault
AEN	Archives de l'Etat, Neuchâtel
AFJ	Archives de la Fédération Jurassienne (*IISG*)
AR Bruxelles	Archives générales du Royaume, Brussels
BFJ	Bulletin de la Fédération Jurassienne
BM La Chaux-de-Fonds	Bibliothèque Municipale, Chaux-de-Fonds
IFHS	Institut Français d'Histoire Sociale
IISG	International Institut voor Social Geschiedenis, Amsterdam
IRSH	International Review for Social History
P.Po	Archives de le Préfecture de Police, Paris

I. PRIMARY SOURCES

A. *Manuscripts**

1. Internationaal Instituut voor Sociale Geschiedenis, Amsterdam (*IISG*).
   (a) Papiers Montels, *Collection Descaves* (uncatalogued).
   (b) *Guesde Archives.*
   (c) *Jung Archives*, 501–512, letters Brousse–Jung.
   (d) *Gross Archives* (uncatalogued).
   (e) *Brupbacher Archives* (uncatalogued).
   (f) *Nettlau Collection.* This vast collection remains largely un-catalogued. It includes the Archives of the Fédération Jurassienne (three boxes), Nettlau's correspondence with Guillaume, Brupbacher, and other *militants* of the socialist and anarchist movements: copies of the Kropotkin–Robin correspondence of 1876–7: and a vast miscellany of letters between *militants*, including a few by Brousse.

2. Archives Fédérales, Berne.
   (a) *Dossier Avant-Garde–Brousse: Polizeidienst 1889–1920, Bd 80.*

3. Staatsarchiv, Berne.
   (a) *Ad acta der Direktion der Justiz und Polizei, 1875.*
   (b) *Hochschule, Philos. Fak II, Chemisches Laboratorium, 1875–89.*

* Abbreviations as used in the text in parentheses.

M

4. *Brousse Papers.* Private papers in the possession of the Brousse family.

5. *Brousse–Jeanneret Correspondence, 1879–1880.* Private papers in the possession of the Jeanneret family.

6. Archives générales du Royaume, Brussels (*AR Bruxelles*).
   (a) *Dossier Brousse: Police des Etrangers 320, 346.*

7. Bibliothèque de la Ville de Chaux-de-Fonds (*BM Chaux-de-Fonds*).
   (a) Guillaume–Pindy Correspondence, *Ms 41.*

8. Dépôt du Centre International de Recherches sur l'Anarchisme, Bibliothèque Universitaire, Geneva.
   (a) *Gross-Fulpius papers.*

9. Archives Départmentementales de l'Hérault, Montpellier, Hérault (*AD Hérault*).
   (a) *Série 39M (Police générale et politique)*, côtes 210, 245, 247, 248, 250, 251, 252, 253, 254, 255, 256, 257, 258, 261, 262, 263, 265, 266, 267, 277, 278, 279, 280, 281, 283, 284, 285, 286, 287.
   (b) *Série 47M (Anarchistes)*, côtes 1–10.
   (c) *Série 58M (Cercles, Associations)*, côtes 31–3, 51, 52, 70–2.
   (d) *Tribunal Correctionel, 1873 (Béziers)*, 20, 7d 45.
   (e) ibid., *(Montpellier)*, 20, 6d 94.

10. Archives Municipales, Montpellier.
    (a) *Registre des Naissances 1815, 1822, 1844.*
    (b) *Registre de Mariages 1842.*

11. Université de Montpellier.
    (a) *Faculté de Médecine, Archives, Dossier V. Brousse.*

12. Archives Nationales, Paris.
    (a) *Série F⁷ 12504–12518 (Anarchistes).*
    Dossier Dentraygues, BB24–792, S73–3987.

13. Archives de la Préfecture de Police, Paris (*P.Po.*).
    (a) *Série BA*, côtes 28–38 *(Congrès socialistes).*
    – 73–80 *(réunions anarchistes).*
    – 387, 435, 437, 438, 441 *(Internationale).*
    – 1476–1480 *(Possibilistes).*
    (b) *Dossiers personnels:* 985 *(Brousse)*, 1170 *(Malon)* 1038 *(Deynaud).*

14. *Fonds Guesde*, Paris. Private papers, which includes Malon–Guesde correspondence, in the possession of the Guesde family.

15. Institut français d'Histoire sociale, Paris (*IFHS*).
    (a) *Fonds Fournière*, 14AS 181(2); 14AS 181(10), Correspondence Brousse–de Paepe.
    (b) *Fonds Pindy.*

16. Archives de l'État, Neuchâtel (*AEN*).
    (a) *Guillaume Archives* (uncatalogued), five boxes. An inventory by Vuilleumier can be found in *Mouvement Social*, 1964, 48.

17. Archives Communales, Imola (Italy).
    (a) Correspondance Brousse–Costa, 1882–98.

B. *Newspapers* and Periodicals*

L'Autonomie Communale (Montpellier), 1882.
L'Avant-Garde (Berne–Chaux-de-Fonds), 1877–8.
Die Arbeiter-Zeitung (Berne), 1877–8.
La Bataille (Paris), 1882.
Le Bulletin du Vote (Montpellier), 1882.
Bulletin de la Fédération Jurassienne (La Chaux-de-Fonds), 1872–8.
Le Citoyen (Paris), 1881.
La Commune, revue socialiste (Geneva), 1875.
Les Droits de l'Homme (Montpellier), 1871.
L'Emancipation (Lyons), 1880.
L'Egalité (Paris), série 1, 1877–8; série 2, 1880; série 3, 1881–2.
La Fédération (Marseilles), 1879.
La Guerre Sociale (London), 1878.
Le Peuple Libre (Marseilles), 1881–2.
Le Prolétaire (Paris), 1878–84.
Le Prolétariat (Paris), 1884–90.
Le Révolté (Geneva), 1879–82.
La Revue Socialiste, série 1, 1880, série 2, 1885.
La Solidarité Revolutionnaire (Barcelona), 1873.
Le Socialisme Progressif (Zurich), 1878.
Le Travail (London), 1880.

C. *Bibliographies, etc.*

Comité Internationale des Science historiques. Répertoire internationale des Sources pour l'Étude des Mouvements Sociaux aux XIX et XX siècles, *La Première Internationale*, 3 vols, Paris, 1958–63.
Dictionnaire biographique du Mouvement ouvrier français (ed. Maitron), Vols 4 and 5, Paris, 1967–8.
Dolléans, E. and Crozier, M., *Mouvement ouvrier et socialiste, Chronologie et Bibliographie,* Paris, 1950.
Nettlau, M., *Bibliographie de l'Anarchie,* Paris, 1898.
Rubel, M., Bibliographie de la Première Internationale, *Cahiers de l'Institut de Science économique appliquée. Série S. Cahiers de Marxologie,* 1964.
Stammhammer, J., *Bibliographie des Socialismus und Communismus,* 3 vols, Jena, 1893–1909.

D. *Printed Works*

Allemane, J., *Memoires d'un Communard*, Paris, 1880.
—— *Notre Programme développé et commenté*, Paris, 1895.
—— *Programme Municipal.*

* The dates given refer only to the dates consulted.

342 *From Anarchism to Reformism*

L'Alliance de la Démocratie Socialiste et l'Association Internationale des Travailleurs, London, 1873.
Almanach du Peuple pour 1871, St Imier.
Almanach du Peuple pour 1872, St Imier.
Almanach du Peuple pour 1873, St Imier.
Almanach du Peuple pour 1874, Le Locle.
Almanach du Peuple pour 1875, Le Locle.
Arnould, A., *L'État et la Révolution*, Geneva, 1877.
Bakunin, M., *Correspondance. Lettres à Herzen et à Ogareff* (ed. Dragomanov), Paris, 1896.
—— *Oeuvres (1868–1872)*, 6 vols, Paris, 1907–13.
—— *L'Organisation de l'Internationale*, Geneva, 1914.
—— *Revolutionary Catechism, Contrat Social*, 1957.
Baldwin, R. (ed.), *Kropotkin, Revolutionary Pamphlets*, New York, 1927.
Bernstein, E., *The International Working Men's Congress of 1889*, London, 1889.
Bourgin, G. (ed.), *Procès-Verbaux de la Commune*, Vol. 1, Paris, 1924.
Brousse, P., *L'Etat à Versailles et dans L'Association Internationale des Travailleurs*, Geneva, 1873.
—— *Le Suffrage Universel et le Problème de la Souveraineté du Peuple*, Geneva, 1874.
—— *La Crise, sa Cause, son Remède*, Geneva, 1879.
—— *Libre Echange et Protectionnisme*, Geneva, 1879.
—— *Quelques Mots sur l'Étude des Fruits*, Montpellier, 1880.
—— *Le Marxisme dans l'Internationale*, Paris, 1882.
—— *La Commune et le Parti Ouvrier*, Paris, 1882.
—— *Trois États*, Paris, 1883.
—— *La Propriété Collective et les Services Publics*, Paris, 1883.
—— *Dictature et Liberté*, Paris, 1884.
—— and Bassède, A., *Les Transports*, Paris, 1912.
—— and Turot, H., *Consulat et Empire 1799–1815* (Tome VI of Histoire Socialiste).
—— *L'Etat et l'Ecole: Monopole ou Contrôle*, Paris, 1910.
—— 'Les Dangers du Radicalisme', *L'Almanach du Peuple pour 1875*, Le Locle, 1875.
—— 'La Liberté', *La Commune, Almanach Socialiste*, Geneva, 1877.
—— 'La Proprieta', *Rivista Internationale des Socialismo*, I, 3, 1880.
Circolo di Studi Sociali, Della Utilita e della Scopo di in Circolo Italiano di Studi Sociali a Londra . . . (Zanardelli), London, 1879.
La Commune, Almanach Socialiste pour 1877, Geneva, 1877.
Compte-rendu du Sixième Congrès de l'Association Internationale des Travailleurs, Geneva, 1873.
Compte-rendu du VII Congrès générale, Bruxelles, Verviers, 1875.
Compte-rendu du VIII Congrès générale, Berne, Berne, 1876.
Compte-rendu des séances du Congrès socialiste tenu à Gand, 1877, s.d.sl.
Compte-rendu du Congrès Internationale ouvrier socialiste tenu à Paris du 15 au 20 Juillet 1889, Paris, 1891.
Congrès Ouvrier de France, Séances de la Session de 1876, Paris, 1877.

Congrès Ouvrier de France, Séances de la Deuxième session Lyon 1878, Lyon, 1878.

Congrès ouvrier socialiste de France. Séances de la Troisième session. Marseille, 1879, Marseille, 1879.

Congrès ouvrier socialiste de France, Cinquième Congrès national, Reims, 1881.

Congrès ouvrier socialiste de France, Sixième Congrès national, Saint-Etienne, 1882, St Etienne, 1882.

Descaves, L., *Philémon, vieux de la veille*, Paris, 1913.

(Engels, F.), *Die Briefe von Friedrich Engels an Eduard Bernstein*, Berlin, 1925.

—— *Briefwechsel mit Karl Kautsky*, Vienna, 1955.

—— and Paul and Laura Lafargue, *Correspondance*, 3 vols, Moscow, 1959–61.

Fédération des Travailleurs socialistes de France: Compte-rendu du VII Congrès National, tenu à Paris du 30 Septembre au 7 Octobre 1883, Paris, 1883.

(ibid.): *Compte-rendu du VIII Congrès National, tenu à Rennes du 12 au 19 Octobre 1884*, Paris, 1885.

(ibid.): *Compte-rendu du IX Congrès National tenu à Charleville*, Paris, 1888.

(ibid.): *Compte-rendu du X Congrès National tenu à Chatellerault 9–15 Octobre 1890*, Poitiers, 1891.

Fournière, E.-J., *La Crise socialiste*, Paris, 1908.

Freymond, J. (ed.), *La Première Internationale, Recueil de Documents*, 2 vols, Geneva, 1962.

Gély, A., *Paria parmi les parias*, Paris, 1879.

General Council of the First International 1864–1870 (minutes), 3 vols, London, 1963–6

Guesde, J., *Le Livre rouge de la Justice rurale*, Geneva, 1871.

—— *La loi des Salaires*, Paris, 1878.

—— *Catéchisme Socialiste*, Paris, 1878.

—— *Le Congrès ouvrier socialiste internationale devant la 10ème Chambre*, Paris, 1879.

—— *Services Publics et Socialisme*, Prison de Pélagie, 1883.

—— *Le Collectivisme*, Paris, 1893.

—— *Ca et Là*, Paris, 1914.

—— and Lafargue, P., *Le Programme du Parti*, Prison de Pélagie, 1883.

Guillaume, J., *Idées sur l'Organisation sociale*, La Chaux-de-Fonds, 1876.

—— *Le Collectivisme de l'Internationale*, Neuchâtel, 1904.

—— *L'Internationale, Documents et Souvenirs*, 4 vols, Paris, 1905–10.

—— *Karl Marx, pangermaniste, et l'Association Internationale des Travailleurs de 1864 à 1870*, Paris, 1915.

—— 'A propos du discours de Ballivet', *La Vie Ouvrière*, 5 July 1910.

—— 'Paul Brousse. Un Militant d'autrefois', *La Bataille Syndicaliste*, 6 April 1912.

Headingly, A. S. (Adolphe Smith), *A Critical Essay on the International Trade Union Congress London 1888*, London, 1889.

Hyndman, H. M., *Record of an Adventurous Life*, London, 1911.

International Socialist Congress 1899, *Rapport de la Commission d'organisation*.

Krimerman, L. and Perry, L., *Patterns of Anarchy*, New York, 1966.

Kropotkin, P., *Paroles d'un Révolté*, Paris, 1885.

—— *Aux jeunes gens*, Geneva, 1884.

—— *Law and Authority*, London, 1886.

—— *The Place of Anarchism in Socialistic Evolution*, London, 1886.

—— *The Commune of Paris*, London, 1895.

—— *The State: its historic role*, London, 1898.

—— *Memoirs of a Revolutionist*, 2 vols, London, 1899.

—— 'Comment fut fondé le Révolté'. *Les Temps Nouveaux*, 20 and 27 February 1904.

—— *The Conquest of Bread*, London, 1906.

Labusquière, J., *Le Tiers Etat et le Peuple ouvrier*, Paris, 1879.

Lavy, A., *La Représentation du Prolétariat au Parlement*, Paris, 1879.

Lecler, A., *La Quintessence du Collectivisme*, Paris, 1881.

Lehning, A. (ed.), *Archives Bakounine*. (I) *Bakounine et l'Italie 1871–2*, 2 vols, Leiden, 1961–3. (II) *Michael Bakounine et les Conflicts dans l'Internationale 1872*, Leiden, 1965.

Le Roy, A., *Les Réformes sociales urgentes*, Paris, 1879.

—— *Fusillé deux fois*, Paris, 1891.

Lettres des Communards et des Militants de la Première Internationale à Marx, Engels (etc.), Paris, 1934.

Malatesta, E., *Anarchy*, London, s.d.

—— *A Talk about Anarchist Communism*, London, s.d.

Malon, B., *Capital et Travail (Lassalle)*, Paris, 1880.

—— *Histoire du Socialisme depuis ses origines jusqu'à nos jours*, Lugano, 1879.

—— *L'Internationale*, Lyon, 1872.

—— 'Les Collectivistes français', *Revue Socialiste*, 1887 (et seq.)

—— *Exposé des Ecoles socialistes françaises*, Paris, 1872.

—— *Précis historique, théorique et pratique du Socialisme*, Paris, 1892.

—— *Le Nouveau Parti*, 2 vols, London, 1882.

—— *Histoire du Socialisme*, 5 vols, Paris, 1882–5.

—— 'Correspondance avec César de Paepe', *Revue Socialiste*, 1908 and 1913.

—— 'Correspondance avec Fournière 1881–85', *Revue Socialiste*, 1907–8.

—— 'Les Conférences internationales ouvrières de Paris', *Revue Socialiste*, 1886 (ii).

Marouck, V., *Juin 1848*, Paris, 1880.

Marx, K. and Engels, F., *Selected Correspondence*, 2 vols.

—— and Engels, F. L., *L'Alliance de la Démocratie Socialiste et l'Association Internationale des Travailleurs*, London, 1873.

—— *Selected Works*, 2 vols.

—— and Liebknecht, W., *Briefwechsel*, Amsterdam, 1963.

Mémoire de la Fédération jurassienne, Sonvilier, 1873.

Mémoire du District de Courtelary, Geneva, 1880.

Montels, J., *Lettre aux Socialistes révolutionnaires du Midi de la France*, Geneva, 1876.

—— *La Justice de l'Ordre en 1851*, Béziers, 1881.

Nettlau, M., *M. Bakunin, Eine Biographie*, 2 vols, London, 1896–8.

—— 'Les origines de l'Internationale anti-autoritaire', *Le Reveil*, 16 September 1922.

—— *Die Vorfrühling der Anarchie*, Berlin, 1925.

—— *Der Anarchismus von Proudhon zu Kropotkin*, Berlin, 1927.

—— *Anarchisten und Sozialrevolutionäre*, Berlin, 1931.

—— Algunos Documentos sobre les origines del anarquismo communista 1876–1880; *La Protesta*, suplemento quincenal, 6 May 1929.

—— *L'Histoire de l'Internationale en Espagne et la Fédération espagnole 1868–1889*, MSS in *IISG*.

—— *Bakunin und die Internationale in Spanien 1868–1873*, Leipzig, 1913.

de Paepe, C., *Les Services Publics*, Brussels, 1895.

Procès de l'Avant-Garde, La Chaux-de-Fonds, 1880.

Procès de l'Internationale, Toulouse, 1873.

Proudhon, P., *Oeuvres*, 19 vols, Paris, 1923–59.

Rapport du Procureur générale de la Confédération . . . sur les menées anarchistes en Suisse, Berne, 1885.

Reclus, E., *L'Évolution et Révolution*, Geneva, 1884.

—— *Correspondance 1850–1905*, 3 vols, Paris, 1911–25.

Report of the International Trade Union Congress, held at Paris (by A. H. Smith), London, 1886.

de Ricard, X., *Le Fédéralisme*, Paris, 1877.

—— *Les Nationalités* (Pi y Margall), 1879.

Rivista Internazionale del Socialismo, Milan, 1880.

Schwitzguébel, A., *Le Radicalisme et le Socialisme*, St Imier, 1876.

—— *La Police politique fédérale*, Geneva, 1879.

—— *Programme Socialiste: Mémoire présenté au Congrès Jurassienne de 1880 par la fédération ouvrière du district de Courtelarcy*, Geneva, 1880.

—— *Quelques Ecrits*, Paris, 1908.

Statutes de la Section de Berne, Berne, 1876.

II. SECONDARY WORKS

Abramsky, C. and Collins, H., *Karl Marx and the British Labour Movement, Years of the First International*, London, 1965.

Abramsky, C., 'Survey of Literature on the First International since 1945', *Bulletin of the Society for the Study of Labour History*, No. 9, Autumn 1964, Supplement ibid., Autumn 1965.

Arvon, H., *Michel Bakounine ou la vie contre la science*, Paris, 1966.

—— *L'Anarchisme*, Paris, 1951.

Bernstein, S., *Essays in Political and Intellectual History*, New York, 1955.
—— *Origins of Marxian Socialism in France*, New York, 1928.
—— 'The First International and the Great Powers', *Science and Society*, 1952.
—— 'Papers of the General Council of the IWMA New York, 1872–1876, *Annali*, anno IV, 1961.
Bestor, A. E., (Evolution of the Socialist Vocabulary', *Journal of the History of Ideas*, June 1948.
Blum, L., *Les Congrès Ouvrier et Socialistes français*, Paris, 1901.
Bo, G. del, *La Première Internationale, une Bibliographie*, 3 vols, Paris, 1958–63.
—— 'Lo spinaggio intorno alla Internazionale, Oscar Testut, agento numero 47', *Movimento Operaio*, November–December 1952.
Bourgin, G., *La Commune*, Paris, 1953.
—— 'La Lutte du Gouvernement français contre la 1ère Internationale', *International Review for Social History*, Vol. IV, 1939.
Braunthal, J., *History of the International 1864–1914*, London, 1966.
Brenan, G., *The Spanish Labyrinth*, Cambridge, 1962.
Bruhat, J., *La Commune de 1871*, Paris, 1960.
Brupbacher, F., *Marx und Bakunin: Ein Betrag zur Geschichte der Internationalen Arbeiterassoziation*, Berlin, 1922.
Carr, E. H., *Michael Bakunin, 1814–1876*, London, 1937.
—— *Studies in Revolution*, London, 1950.
Caute, D., *The Left in Europe since 1789*, London, 1966.
Charnay, M., *Les Allemanistes*, Paris, 1911.
Claris, A., *La Proscription française en Suisse 1871–1872*, Geneva, 1872.
Clarke, J. A., 'French Socialist Congresses 1876–1914', *Journal of Modern History*, Vol. 31, 1959.
Clère, J., *Les Hommes de la Commune, biographie complète*, Paris, 1871.
Cole, G. D. H., *History of Socialist Thought*, Vol. 2, London, 1954.
Colloque Internationale sur l'Histoire de la Première Internationale Novembre 1964 (Centre Nationale de la Recherche Scientifique).
Compère-Morel, A., *Encyclopédie Socialiste*, 12 vols, Paris, 1912–21.
—— *Grand Dictionnaire Socialiste*, Paris, 1924.
—— *Jules Guesde, Le Socialisme fait homme, 1845–1922*, Paris, 1937.
Darnaud, E., *Notes sur Bakounine*, Foix, 1890.
—— *Notes sur le Mouvement*, 3 vols, Foix, 1891.
—— *Précis du Mouvement*, Foix, 1892.
Delaporte, J., *Les Collectivistes du Socialisme rationnel*, Paris, 1878.
Delory, J., *Aperçu historique sur la Fédération du Nord*, Lille, 1921.
Derfler, L., 'Reformism and Jules Guesde', *International Review of Social History*, Vol. XII, L, 1967.
Dolléans, E., *Proudhon*, Paris, 1948.
—— *Histoire du Mouvement ouvrier*, 3 vols, Paris, 1957.
Dommanget, M., 'La Première Internationale à son declin', *Revue d'histoire économique et sociale*, Vol. XLIII, 3, 1964.
—— *Histoire du Premier Mai*, Paris, 1953.
—— *Histoire du Drapeau rouge*, Paris, 1967.

Dormoy, J., *Rapports et Résolutions des Congrés ouvriers de 1876 à 1883,* Paris, 1883.

Drachkovitch, M. (ed.), *The Revolutionary Internationals 1864–1943,* London, 1966.

—— *De Karl Marx à Leon Blum,* Geneva, 1954.

Drumont, E., *La fin d'un monde,* Paris, 1889.

Dubois, J., *Le Vocabulaire politique et sociale en France de 1869 à 1872,* Paris, 1962.

Duveau, G., *La Vie ouvrière en France sous le Second Empire,* Paris, 1946.

Eltzbacher, P., *Anarchism,* London, 1960.

Esch, P. van der, *La Deuxième Internationale 1889–1923,* Paris, 1957.

Feller, R., *Die Universität Bern 1834–1934,* Berne, 1934.

Freymond, J., *Études et Documents sur la Première Internationale en Suisse,* Geneva, 1964.

—— 'Étude sur la Formation de la Première Internationale', *Revue suisse d'Histoire,* Vol. 30, 1, 1950.

—— and Molnar, M., 'The Rise and Fall of the First International', *The Revolutionary Internationals* (ed. Drachkovitch), London, 1966.

Fribourg, E., *L'Association Internationale des Travailleurs,* Paris, 1871.

Gans, J., 'L'Origine du mot "socialiste" et ses emplois les plus ancien', *Revue d'Histoire économique et sociale,* Vol. XXV, 1, 1957.

Grave, J., *Le Mouvement libertaire sous la Troisième République,* Paris, 1931.

Gross, F., *European Ideologies,* New York, 1948.

Guérin, D., *La Jeunesse du Socialisme libertaire,* Paris, 1959.

—— *L'Anarchisme,* Paris, 1965.

—— (ed.) *Ni Dieu ni Maître,* Paris, 1967.

Guéroult, G., *Les Théories de l'Internationale,* Paris, 1872.

Halévy, E., *Histoire du Socialisme Européen,* Paris, 1948.

Hampden Jackson, J., *Marx, Proudhon, and European Socialism,* London, 1957.

Haupt, G., 'Notes sur les Archives de la Première Internationale', *Mouvement Social,* July–September 1963.

—— La Deuxième Internationale 1889–1914, Paris, 1964.

—— and Verdes, J., 'De la Première à la Seconde Internationale', *Mouvement Social,* No. 51, 1965.

Horne, A., *The Fall of Paris,* London, 1965.

Horowitz, I., *The Anarchists,* New York, 1964.

Hostetter, R., 'Review of Répertoire Internationale des Sources . . .', in *Annali,* 1, 1958.

—— *The Italian Socialist Movement, 1. Origins 1860–1882,* Princeton, 1958.

l'Huilier, F., *La Lutte ouvrière à la fin du Second Empire,* Paris, 1958.

Humbert, S., *Les Possibilistes,* Paris, 1912.

—— *Le Mouvement Syndical,* Paris, 1912.

Huret, J., *Enquête sur la Question sociale en Europe,* Paris, 1897.

Joll, J., *The Anarchists,* London, 1964.

—— *The Second International,* London, 1955.

Jolly, J. (ed.), *Dictionnaire des Parlementaires français 1889–1940,* Paris, 1960.

Joucla, R., 'Renaissance du Mouvement ouvrier français après la Commune: Congrès de Marseille', *Cahiers Internationaux,* No. 65, 1955.

Joughin, J., *The Paris Commune in French Politics, 1871–1881. The History of the Amnesty of 1880,* Baltimore, 1956.

Kriegel, A., 'Vie et Mort de la Première Internationale', *Revue Socialiste,* No. 181, March 1965.

Laidler, H., *Social-Economic Movements,* New York, 1946.

Langhard, J., *Die Anarchistische Bewegung in der Schweiz,* Berlin, 1903.

Landauer, C., *European Socialism,* 2 vols, Berkeley, 1959.

—— 'The Guesdists and the Small Farmer: Early Erosion of French Marxism', *International Review of Social History,* Vol. VI 1961.

—— 'The Origin of Socialist Reformism in France', *International Review of Social History,* Vol. XII, 1967.

Lefranc, G., *Le Mouvement socialiste sous la Troisième République, 1875–1940,* Paris, 1963. (See also 'Montreuil, J.' – pseudonym).

Lichtheim, G., *Marxism, an Historical and Critical Study,* London, 1961.

—— *Marxism in Modern France,* New York, 1966.

Ligou, D., *Histoire du Socialisme en France,* Paris, 1962.

Lipparini, L., *Chronologia della vita di A. Costa. Movimento Operaio,* 2, 1952.

Lombard, P., *Au Berceau du Socialisme français,* Paris, 1922.

Longuet, J., *La Politique Internationale du Marxisme. Karl Marx et la France,* Paris, 1918.

Louis, P., *L'Avenir du Socialisme,* Paris, 1905.

—— *Histoire du Socialisme en France,* Paris, 1901.

—— *Histoire du Mouvement Syndical en France 1789–1906,* Paris, 1907.

Maitron, J., *Le Mouvement anarchiste en France 1880–1914,* Paris, 1955.

—— 'L'Anarchisme français 1945–1965', *Mouvement Social,* January–March 1965.

—— 'La Première Internationale à Brest', *Mouvement Social,* October–December 1962.

Manévy, R. and Diole, P., *Sous les plis du Drapeau Noir,* Paris, 1949.

Mauger, C., *Les Débuts du Socialisme Marxiste en France,* Paris, 1908.

Maximoff, G., *The Political Philosophy of Bakunin,* New York, 1964.

Meijer, J., *Knowledge and Revolution,* Assen, 1955.

Mermeix, L., *La France Socialiste,* Paris, 1886.

Molnar, M., *Le Déclin de la Première Internationale: la Conférence de Londres de 1871,* Geneva, 1963.

Montreuil, J. (Lefranc, G.), *Histoire du Mouvement ouvrier en France,* Paris, 1946.

Morgan, R., *The German Social Democrats and the First International,* Cambridge, 1964.

Moutet, A., 'Le Mouvement ouvrier à Paris au lendemain de la Commune au premier Congrès syndical en 1876', *Mouvement Social,* 58, 1967.

McBriar, A., *Fabian Socialism and English Politics 1884–1914*, Cambridge, 1966.

McInnes, N., 'Les Débuts du Marxisme théorique en France et en Italie, 1880–1887', *Cahiers de l'Institut de Science économique appliquée*, série S. *Cahiers de Marxologie*, No. 3, 1960.

—— 'Les Partis socialistes français 1880–1895', ibid., No. 4, 1961.

Néré, J., *La Crise Industrielle de 1882 et le mouvement boulangiste* (thèse de Docteur es Lettres, Sorbonne, 1959).

Nicolaevsky, B., 'Deux Billets de Marx à Engels', *International Review for Social History*, III, 1938.

Noland, A., *The Founding of the French Socialist Party*, Cambridge, 1956.

Nollau, G., *International Communism and World Revolution*, London, 1961.

Nomad, M., *Apostles of Revolution*, New York, 1933.

—— *Rebels and Renegades*, New York, 1932.

—— 'Le Communisme libertaire', *Contrat Social*, Vol. III, 1959.

—— 'The Evolution of Anarchism and Syndicalism: a Critical View', *European Ideologies* (ed. Gross, F.), New York, 1948.

Olivesi, A., *La Commune à Marseille*, Paris, 1950.

Osmin, L., *Figures de Jadis*, Paris, 1934.

Pelloutier, F., *Histoire des Bourses de Travail*, Paris, 1902.

Perrot, M., 'Le premier journal marxiste français, L'Egalité', *L'Actualité d'Histoire*, July 1959.

Pinset, J., 'Quelques Problèmes du socialisme en France vers 1900', *Revue d'Histoire économique et sociale*, Vol. XXXVI, 1958.

Ponsot, P. 'Un militant socialiste du XIX siècle: J.-B. Dumay', *Revue Socialiste*, No. 188, 1965.

Préaudeau, M., *Michel Bakounine: le Collectivisme dans l'Internationale*, Paris, 1912.

Prélot, M., *L'Evolution politique du Socialisme*, Paris, 1939.

La Première Internationale, edition on, *Mouvement Social*, 51 April–June 1965.

Prolo, J., *Les Anarchistes*, Paris, 1912.

Puech, J. L., *Le Proudhonisme dans l'Association Internationale des Travailleurs*, Paris, 1907.

Richard, A., *L'Association Internationale des Travailleurs*, Lyons, 1872.

—— 'Les Propagateurs de l'Internationale en France', *Revue Socialiste*, June 1896.

—— 'Bakounine et l'Internationale à Lyon', *Revue de Paris*, September 1896.

—— 'Les Débuts du Parti Socialiste français', *Revue politique et parlementaire*, January 1897.

Richards, V. (ed.), *Enrico Malatesta, his Life and Ideas*, London, 1965.

Rihs, C., *La Commune de Paris: sa structure et ses doctrines*, Geneva, 1955.

Rocher, J. (ed.), *Lettres de Communards et de Militants de la Première Internationale*, Paris, 1934.

Rocker, R., *Johann Most, das Leben eines Rebellen*, Berlin, 1924.

—— *Anarchism and Anarcho-Syndicalism*, in Gross, op. cit.

Rougerie, J., 'Sur l'Histoire de la Première Internationale, Bilan d'un Colloque et de quelques récents travaux', *Mouvement Social*, April–June 1965.

—— 'La Première Internationale à Lyon 1865–1870', *Annali*, 1961.

—— *Procès des Communards*, Paris, 1964.

Rubel, M., 'Marx et la Première Internationale, Une Chronologie', *Cahiers de l'Institut de Science économique appliquée, série S. Cahiers de Marxologie*, No. 8, 1964. Part Two, ibid., No. 9, 1965.

—— 'La Charte de la Première Internationale', *Mouvement Social*, April–June 1965.

—— (ed.), *Karl Marx, Oeuvres*, Paris, 1963.

Salmon, A., *La Terreur noire*, Paris, 1959.

de Seilhac, L., *Les Congrès ouvriers en France de 1876 à 1897*, Paris, 1899.

—— *Le Monde Socialiste, groupes et programmes*, Paris, 1896.

Sergent et Harmel, *Histoire de l'Anarchie*, Vol. 1, Paris, 1949.

Stegmann and Hugo, *Handbuch das Socialismus*, Zurich, 1897.

Stekloff, Y., *History of the First International*, London, 1928.

Testut, O., *L'Association Internationale des Travailleurs*, Lyon, 1870.

—— *Le Livre bleu de l'Internationale*, Paris, 1871.

—— *L'Internationale – son but – son caractère*, Paris, 1871.

—— *L'Internationale et le Jacobinisme au ban de l'Empire*, 2 vols, Paris, 1872.

Thomann, C., *Le Mouvement anarchiste dans les Montagnes neuchâteloises et le Jura bernois*, La Chaux-de-Fonds, 1947.

—— *Jean Louis Pindy*, La Chaux-de-Fonds, 1951.

Tsuzuki, C., *The Life of Eleanor Marx 1855–1898*, Oxford, 1967.

—— *H. M. Hyndman and British Socialism*, London, 1961.

Valiani, L. 'Dalla prima alla secunda Internazionale', *Movimento Operaio*, 1954, 2.

—— *Questioni di Storia del Socialismo*, Turin, 1958.

Venturi, F., *Roots of Revolution*, New York, 1966.

Verdes, J., 'Les Délégués français aux Congrès de l'Internationale', *Cahiers de l'Institut de Science économique appliquée, série S*, No. 8, 1964.

Vuillemier, M., 'L'Internationale à Geneve et la Commune de Paris, 1871', *Mélanges offerts à M. Paul E. Martin*, Geneva, 1961.

—— 'Les Proscrits de la Commune en Suisse 1871', *Revue suisse d'Histoire*, t.12, 1962.

—— 'Le Gouvernement de Versailles, les Autorités suisses, et les proscrits de la Commune en 1871', *Le Mouvement Social*, January–March 1962.

—— 'Quelques Proscrits de la Commune', ibid. July–September 1963.

—— 'La Première Internationale en Suisse', *Revue syndical suisse*, 9, 1964.

—— 'Les Archives de James Guillaume', *Mouvement Social*, July–September, 1964.

—— 'Les Sources de l'Histoire sociale: Max Nettlau et ses Collections', *Cahiers Vilfredo Pareto,* No. 3, 1964.

—— 'Bakounine, l'Alliance internationale de la Démocratie socialiste et la Première Internationale à Genèva 1868–1869', ibid., No. 4, 1964.

—— 'La Première Internationale en Suisse', *Nuova Rivista Storica,* May–August 1965.

—— 'Paul Brousse et son passage de l'anarchisme au socialisme', *Cahiers Vilfredo Pareto,* 7–8, 1965.

—— 'La Correspondance du peintre Gustave Jeanneret', *Mouvement Social,* April–June 1965.

—— 'Notes sur James Guillaume, Historien de la Première Internationale et ses rapports avec Max Nettlau et Jean Jaurès, *Cahiers Vilfredo Pareto,* 7–8, 1965.

—— 'La Correspondance d'un Internationaliste, Victor Cyrille', *Movimento Operaio e socialista,* Vol. XII, 3–4, 1966.

Weill, G. *Histoire du Mouvement social en France,* Paris, 1904.

Willard, C. (ed.), *Jules Guesde, Textes Choisies 1867–1882,* Paris, 1959.

Willard, C., *Le Mouvement socialiste en France 1893–1905: Les Guesdistes,* Paris, 1965.

Wolfe, B., 'French Socialism, German Theory, and the Flaw in the Foundation of the Socialist Internationals', *Essays in Russian and Soviet History in honour of G. T. Robinson* (ed. Curtiss, J.), Leiden, 1963.

Woodcock, G., *Anarchism,* London, 1963.

—— *Proudhon,* London, 1956.

—— and Avakumovitch, L., *Kropotkin, the Anarchist Prince,* London, 1950.

de Wyzewa, T., *Le Mouvement socialiste en Europe,* Paris, 1892.

Zévaès, A., *Le Socialisme en France depuis 1871,* Paris, 1908.

—— *De la Semaine sanglante au Congrès de Marseille 1871–1879,* Paris, 1911.

—— *Les Guesdistes,* Paris, 1911.

—— *Jules Guesde 1845–1922,* Paris, 1929.

—— *Histoire du Socialisme et du Communisme en France de 1871 à 1947,* Paris, 1947.

—— *De l'Introduction de Marxisme en France,* Paris, 1947.

—— *Une Génération,* Paris, 1922.

—— *Notes et Souvenirs d'un Militant,* Paris, 1913.

Zetkin, O., *Der Socialismus in Frankreich seit der Pariserkommune,* Berlin, 1894.

Index

Index

'PB' refers throughout to Paul Brousse